"THE EVIL IS REAL, AND
THEY'RE THE ONLY ONES
WHO CAN STOP THEM.
HAVE FAITH."

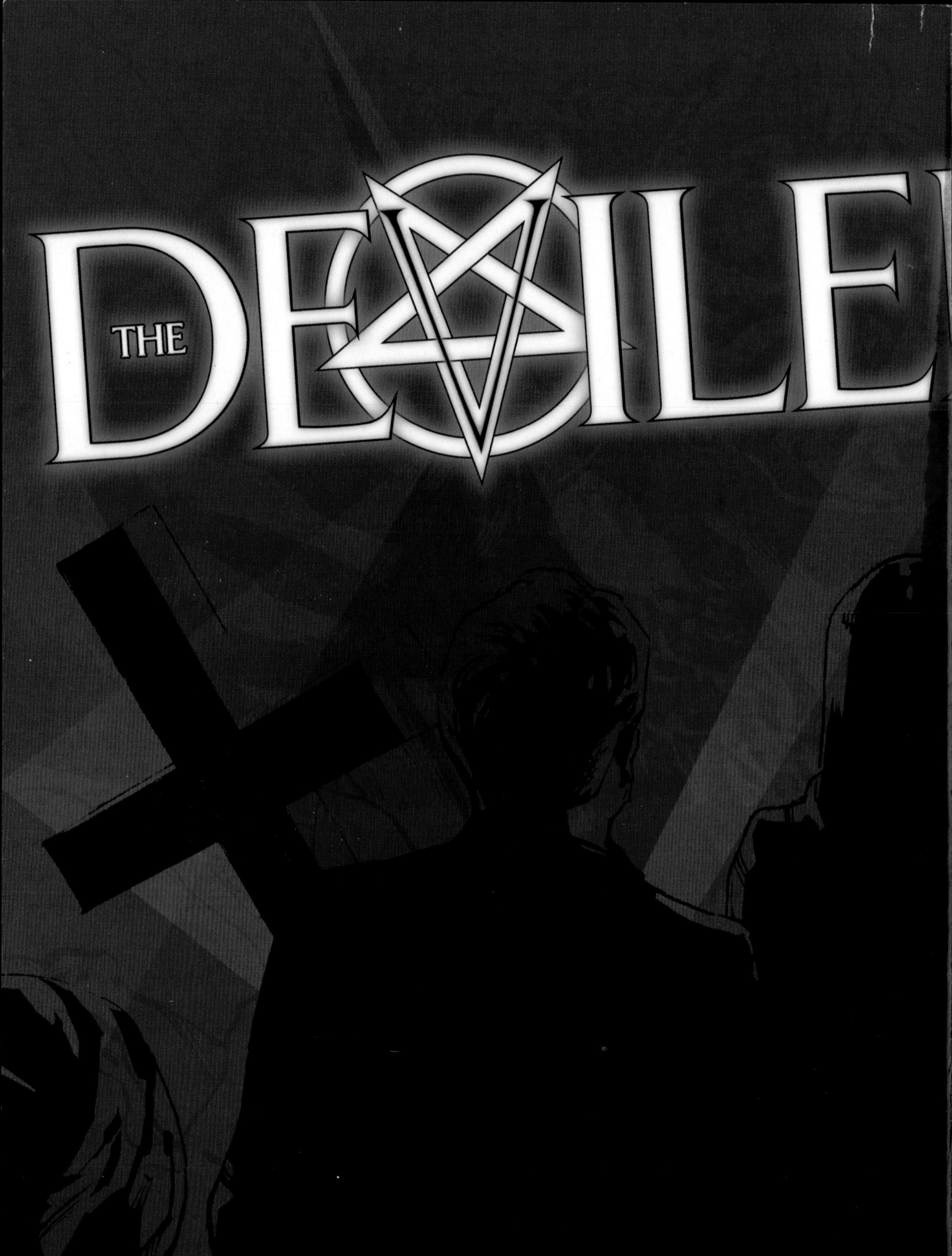
THE

RS™

written by
JOSHUA HALE FIALKOV

illustrated by
MATT TRIANO

issues #1-6 colored by
MARK ROBERTS

issue #7 colored by
INLIGHT STUDIOS

lettered by
SIMON BOWLAND

collection cover art by
JOCK

This volume collects issues one through seven of the Dynamite Entertainment series, The Devilers

collection design by
JOSH JOHNSON

DYNAMITE®

Nick Barrucci, CEO / Publisher
Juan Collado, President / COO

Joe Rybandt, Senior Editor
Rachel Pinnelas, Associate Editor
Kevin Ketner, Editorial Assistant

Jason Ullmeyer, Art Director
Geoff Harkins, Graphic Designer
Alexis Persson, Production Artist

Chris Caniano, Digital Associate
Rachel Kilbury, Digital Assistant

Brandon Dante Primavera, Director of IT/Operations
Rich Young, Director of Business Development

Keith Davidsen, Marketing Manager
Pat O'Connell, Sales Manager

Online at WWW.DYNAMITE.COM
Twitter @dynamitecomics
Facebook /Dynamitecomics
Instagram /Dynamitecomics
YouTube /Dynamitecomics
Tumblr dynamitecomics.tumblr.com

THE DEVILERS™, VOLUME ONE. Contains materials originally published in magazine form as The Devlers #1-7. Published by Dynamite Entertainment. 113 Gaither Dr., STE 205, Mt. Laurel, NJ 08054. Printed in China.

For media rights, foreign rights, promotions, licensing, and advertising: marketing@dynamite.com

ISBN-10: 1-60690-893-6
ISBN-13: 978-1-60690-893-8

First Printing
10 9 8 7 6 5 4 3 2 1

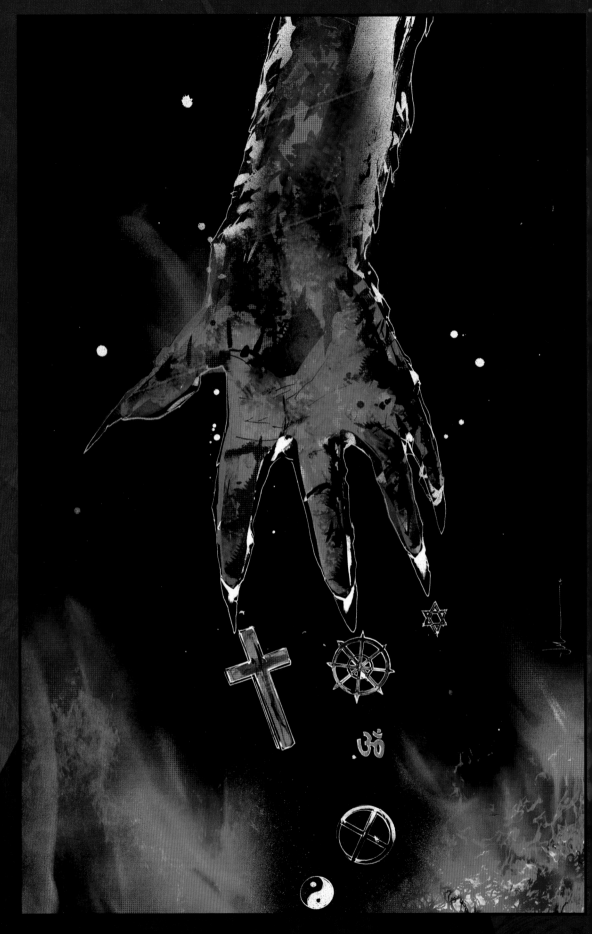

ISSUE #1 cover art by JOCK

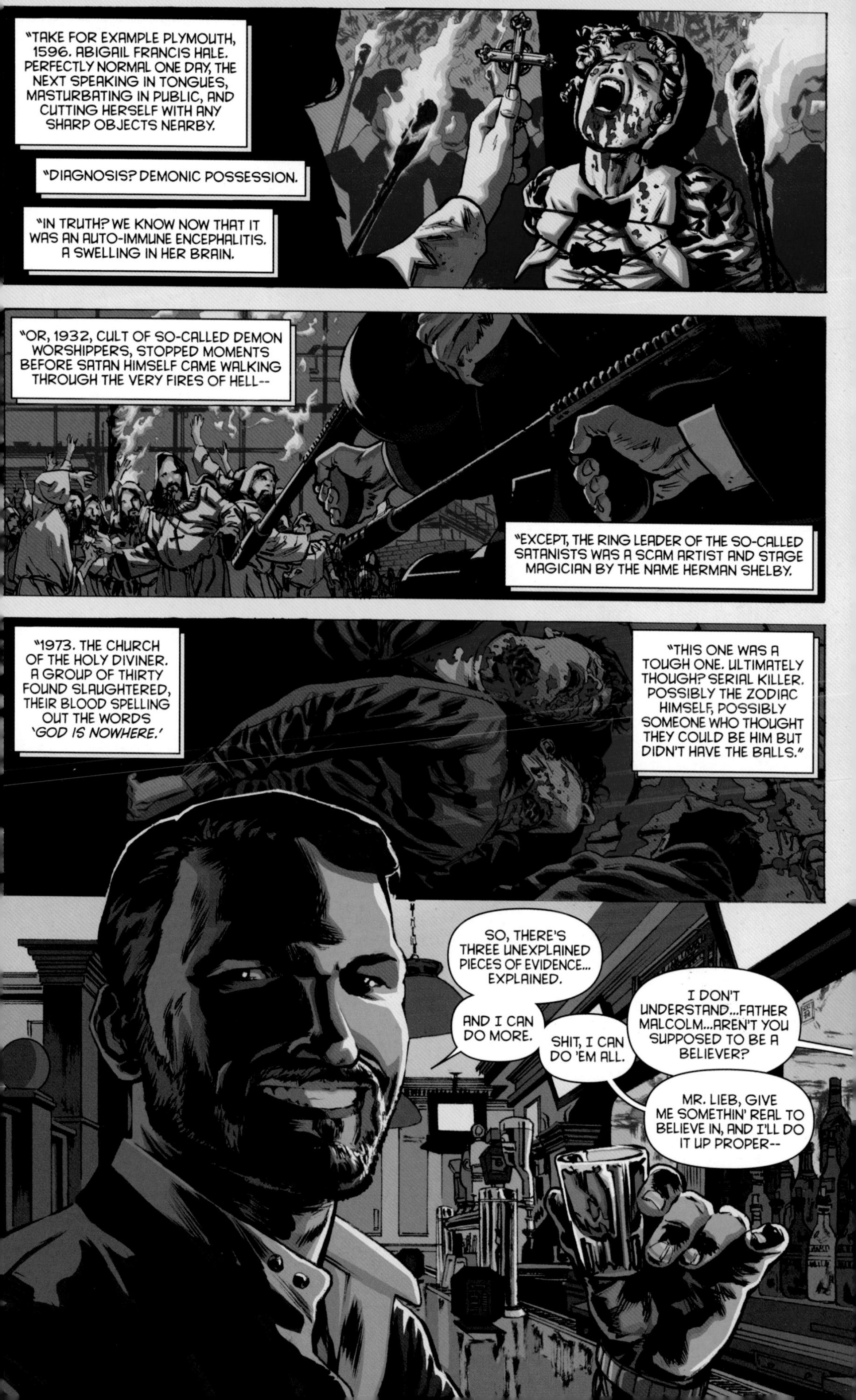
"TAKE FOR EXAMPLE PLYMOUTH, 1596. ABIGAIL FRANCIS HALE. PERFECTLY NORMAL ONE DAY, THE NEXT SPEAKING IN TONGUES, MASTURBATING IN PUBLIC, AND CUTTING HERSELF WITH ANY SHARP OBJECTS NEARBY.
"DIAGNOSIS? DEMONIC POSSESSION.
"IN TRUTH? WE KNOW NOW THAT IT WAS AN AUTO-IMMUNE ENCEPHALITIS. A SWELLING IN HER BRAIN.
"OR, 1932, CULT OF SO-CALLED DEMON WORSHIPPERS, STOPPED MOMENTS BEFORE SATAN HIMSELF CAME WALKING THROUGH THE VERY FIRES OF HELL--
"EXCEPT, THE RING LEADER OF THE SO-CALLED SATANISTS WAS A SCAM ARTIST AND STAGE MAGICIAN BY THE NAME HERMAN SHELBY.
"1973. THE CHURCH OF THE HOLY DIVINER. A GROUP OF THIRTY FOUND SLAUGHTERED, THEIR BLOOD SPELLING OUT THE WORDS *'GOD IS NOWHERE.'*
"THIS ONE WAS A TOUGH ONE. ULTIMATELY THOUGH? SERIAL KILLER. POSSIBLY THE ZODIAC HIMSELF, POSSIBLY SOMEONE WHO THOUGHT THEY COULD BE HIM BUT DIDN'T HAVE THE BALLS."
SO, THERE'S THREE UNEXPLAINED PIECES OF EVIDENCE... EXPLAINED.
AND I CAN DO MORE.
SHIT, I CAN DO 'EM ALL.
I DON'T UNDERSTAND...FATHER MALCOLM...AREN'T YOU SUPPOSED TO BE A BELIEVER?
MR. LIEB, GIVE ME SOMETHIN' REAL TO BELIEVE IN, AND I'LL DO IT UP PROPER--

"Y'SEE, THE FACT IS, I'VE SEEN EVIL AND I'VE SEEN THE CRUELTY IN MEN'S HEARTS.
"I'VE WATCHED PEOPLE BE BORN, AND I'VE WATCHED PEOPLE DIE.
"BUT I'VE NEVER SEEN NOTHIN' FROM THE OTHER WORLD. NO DEMONS WALKIN' AMONG US, NOTHING OF THE SORT--"
"HEY, MAL, TAKE A LOOK AT THIS--"
LIVE
BREAKING NEWS
NEWS ROOM
DISASTER AT

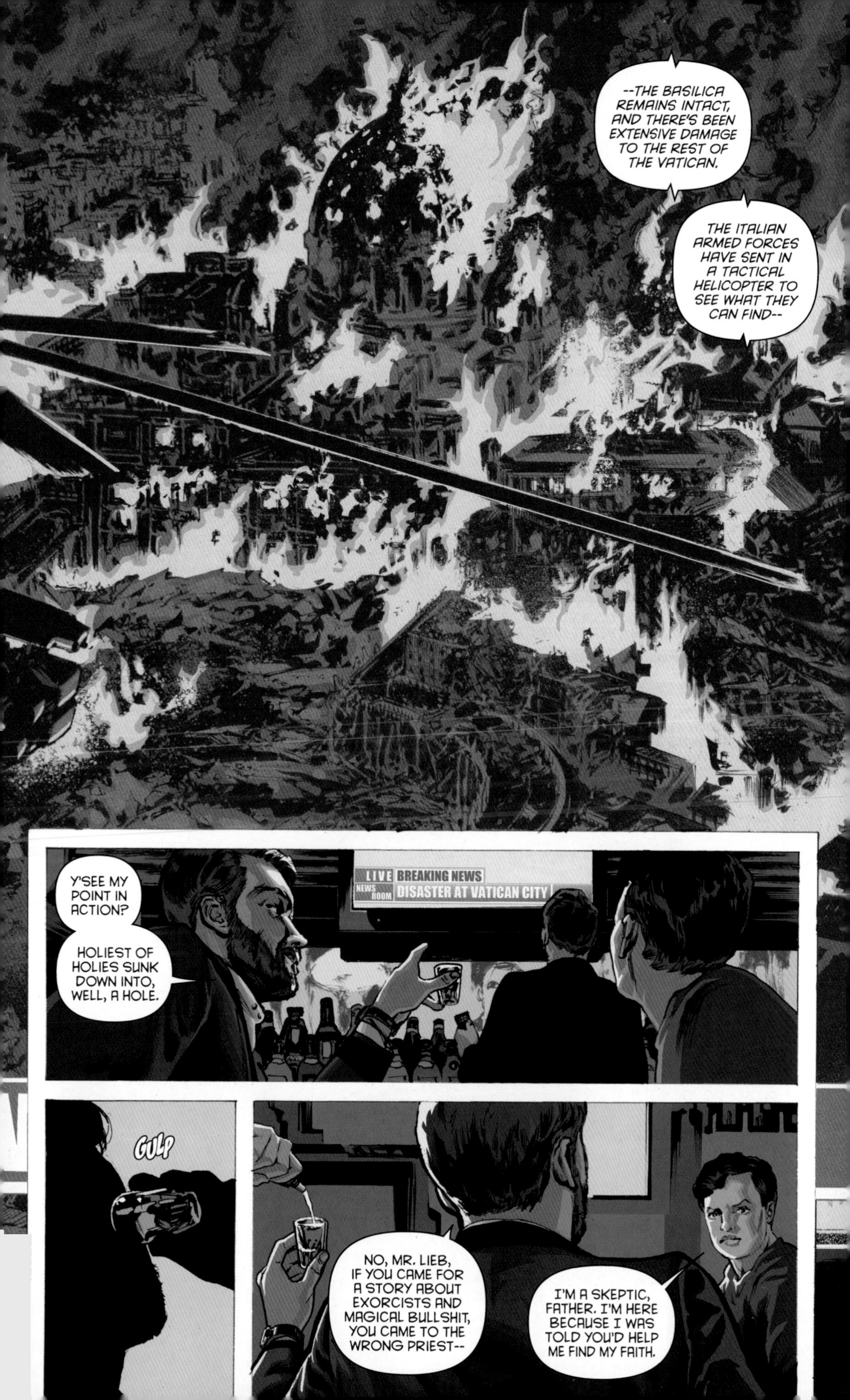
--THE BASILICA REMAINS INTACT, AND THERE'S BEEN EXTENSIVE DAMAGE TO THE REST OF THE VATICAN.
THE ITALIAN ARMED FORCES HAVE SENT IN A TACTICAL HELICOPTER TO SEE WHAT THEY CAN FIND--
LIVE
NEWS ROOM
BREAKING NEWS
DISASTER AT VATICAN CITY
Y'SEE MY POINT IN ACTION?
HOLIEST OF HOLIES SUNK DOWN INTO, WELL, A HOLE.
GULP
NO, MR. LIEB, IF YOU CAME FOR A STORY ABOUT EXORCISTS AND MAGICAL BULLSHIT, YOU CAME TO THE WRONG PRIEST--
I'M A SKEPTIC, FATHER. I'M HERE BECAUSE I WAS TOLD YOU'D HELP ME FIND MY FAITH.

Hm.

SORRY TO DISAPPOINT.

NO, IT'S JUST...YOU WERE THE GUY EVERYONE SAID COULD CONVINCE ME--

AH. SO YOU WANT *THAT* STORY.

THAT'S HOW I KNOW THERE'S NO DEMONS THE WAY MY BOSSES IN THE HOLE OVER THERE THINK THERE ARE.

"WHEN I WAS A BOY, I GOT HIT BY A CAR. SOME ENGLISH PRICK WAS DRIVING TOO FAST, DIDN'T KNOW THE COUNTRY ROADS.

"CAR SWERVED, HIT A POLE, KNOCKED ME FLAT, THE DRIVER WASN'T WEARING A BELT--

"NOBODY DID BACK THEN.

"HE WENT THROUGH THE WINDSHIELD.

"WHEN I WOKE UP, MY LEGS WERE BROKEN, MY RIGHT ARM AND LEFT WRIST, TOO.

"SO I COULDN'T MOVE. BUT, I LOOKED OVER, AND THERE HE WAS, LAYIN' THERE, WITH A BEAST STANDING ON HIM.

"IT WAS...I GUESS EATIN' HIM? I DUNNO. IT WAS SWALLOWING SOMETHING BRIGHT AND FLESHY AND...

"HIS SOUL, I SUPPOSE--

"BUT IT FELT LIKE I WAS SEEING EVERYTHING THROUGH HIS EYES.

"EXCEPT, I REMEMBER IT TURNING AND SMILING AT ME."

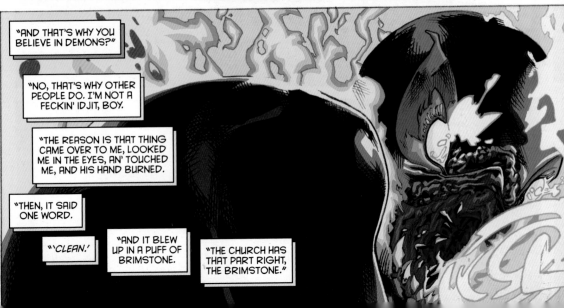

"AND THAT'S WHY YOU BELIEVE IN DEMONS?"

"NO, THAT'S WHY OTHER PEOPLE DO. I'M NOT A FECKIN' IDJIT, BOY.

"THE REASON IS THAT THING CAME OVER TO ME, LOOKED ME IN THE EYES, AN' TOUCHED ME, AND HIS HAND BURNED.

"THEN, IT SAID ONE WORD.

"'CLEAN.'

"AND IT BLEW UP IN A PUFF OF BRIMSTONE.

"THE CHURCH HAS THAT PART RIGHT, THE BRIMSTONE."

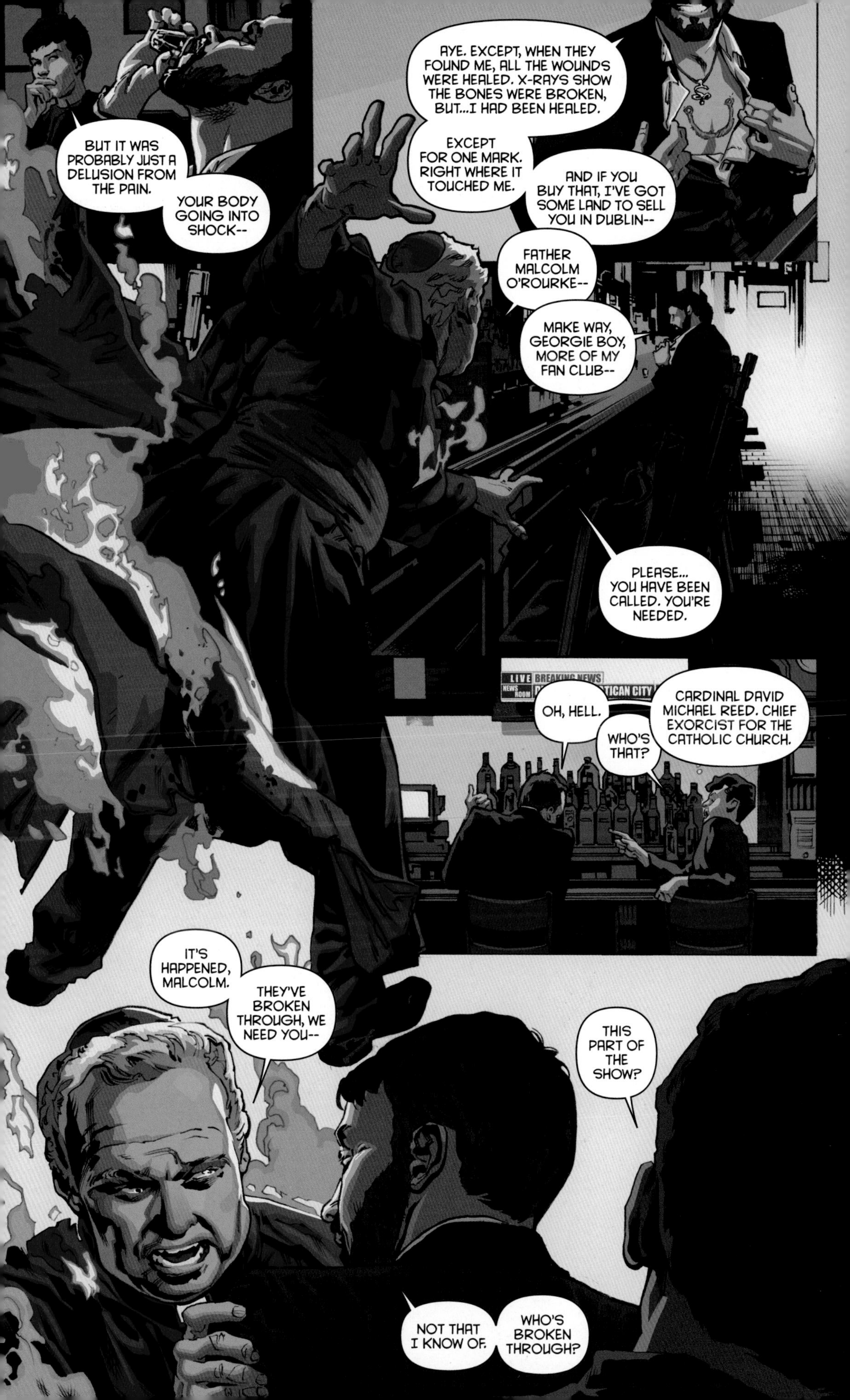

BUT IT WAS PROBABLY JUST A DELUSION FROM THE PAIN.
YOUR BODY GOING INTO SHOCK--
AYE. EXCEPT, WHEN THEY FOUND ME, ALL THE WOUNDS WERE HEALED. X-RAYS SHOW THE BONES WERE BROKEN, BUT...I HAD BEEN HEALED.
EXCEPT FOR ONE MARK. RIGHT WHERE IT TOUCHED ME.
AND IF YOU BUY THAT, I'VE GOT SOME LAND TO SELL YOU IN DUBLIN--
FATHER MALCOLM O'ROURKE--
MAKE WAY, GEORGIE BOY, MORE OF MY FAN CLUB--
PLEASE... YOU HAVE BEEN CALLED. YOU'RE NEEDED.
LIVE BREAKING NEWS
NEWS ROOM
OH, HELL.
WHO'S THAT?
CARDINAL DAVID MICHAEL REED. CHIEF EXORCIST FOR THE CATHOLIC CHURCH.
IT'S HAPPENED, MALCOLM.
THEY'VE BROKEN THROUGH, WE NEED YOU--
THIS PART OF THE SHOW?
WHO'S BROKEN THROUGH?
NOT THAT I KNOW OF.

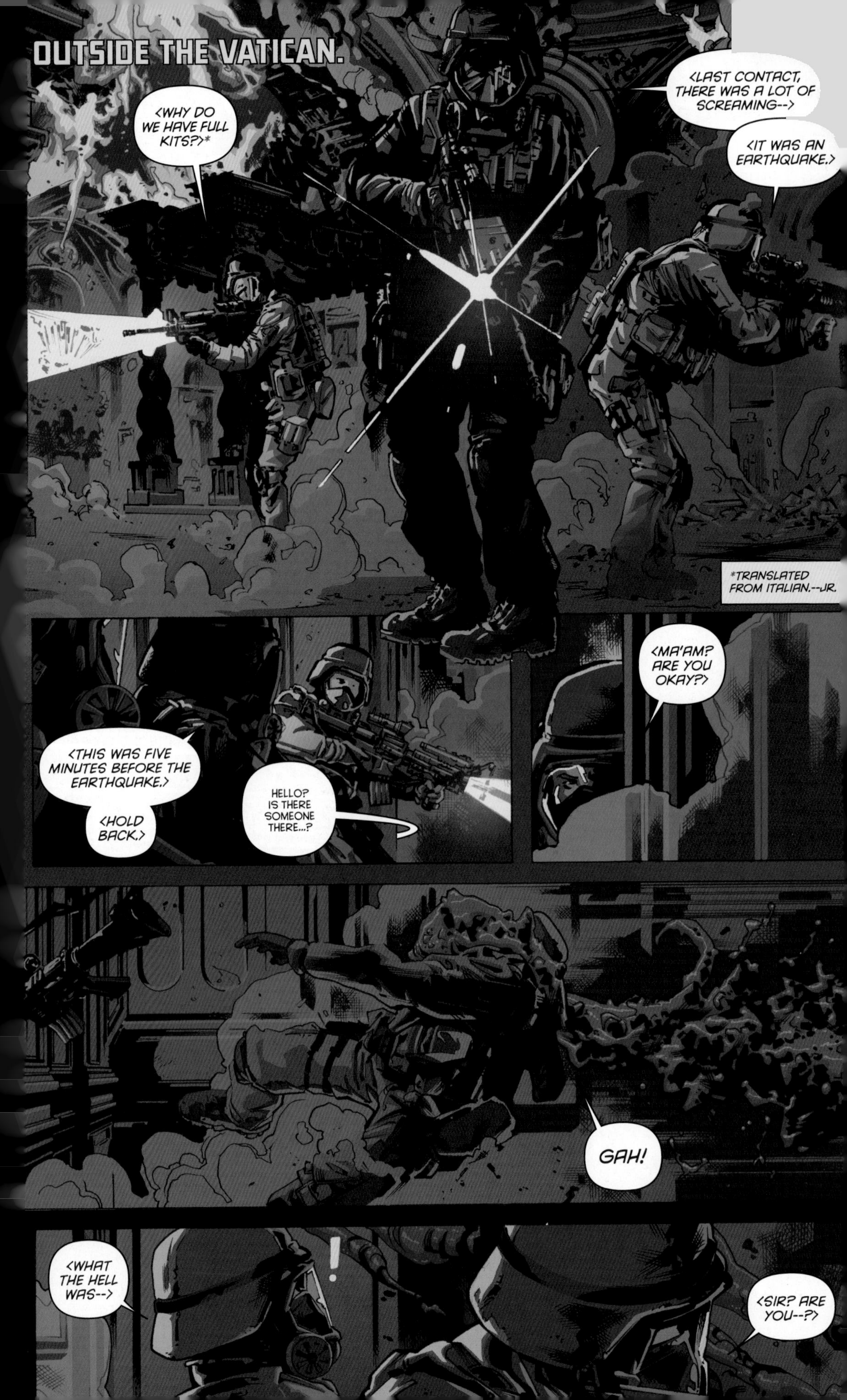
OUTSIDE THE VATICAN.
<WHY DO WE HAVE FULL KITS?>*
<LAST CONTACT, THERE WAS A LOT OF SCREAMING-->
<IT WAS AN EARTHQUAKE.>
*TRANSLATED FROM ITALIAN.--JR.
<THIS WAS FIVE MINUTES BEFORE THE EARTHQUAKE.>
<HOLD BACK.>
HELLO? IS THERE SOMEONE THERE...?
<MA'AM? ARE YOU OKAY?>
GAH!
<WHAT THE HELL WAS-->
!
<SIR? ARE YOU--?>

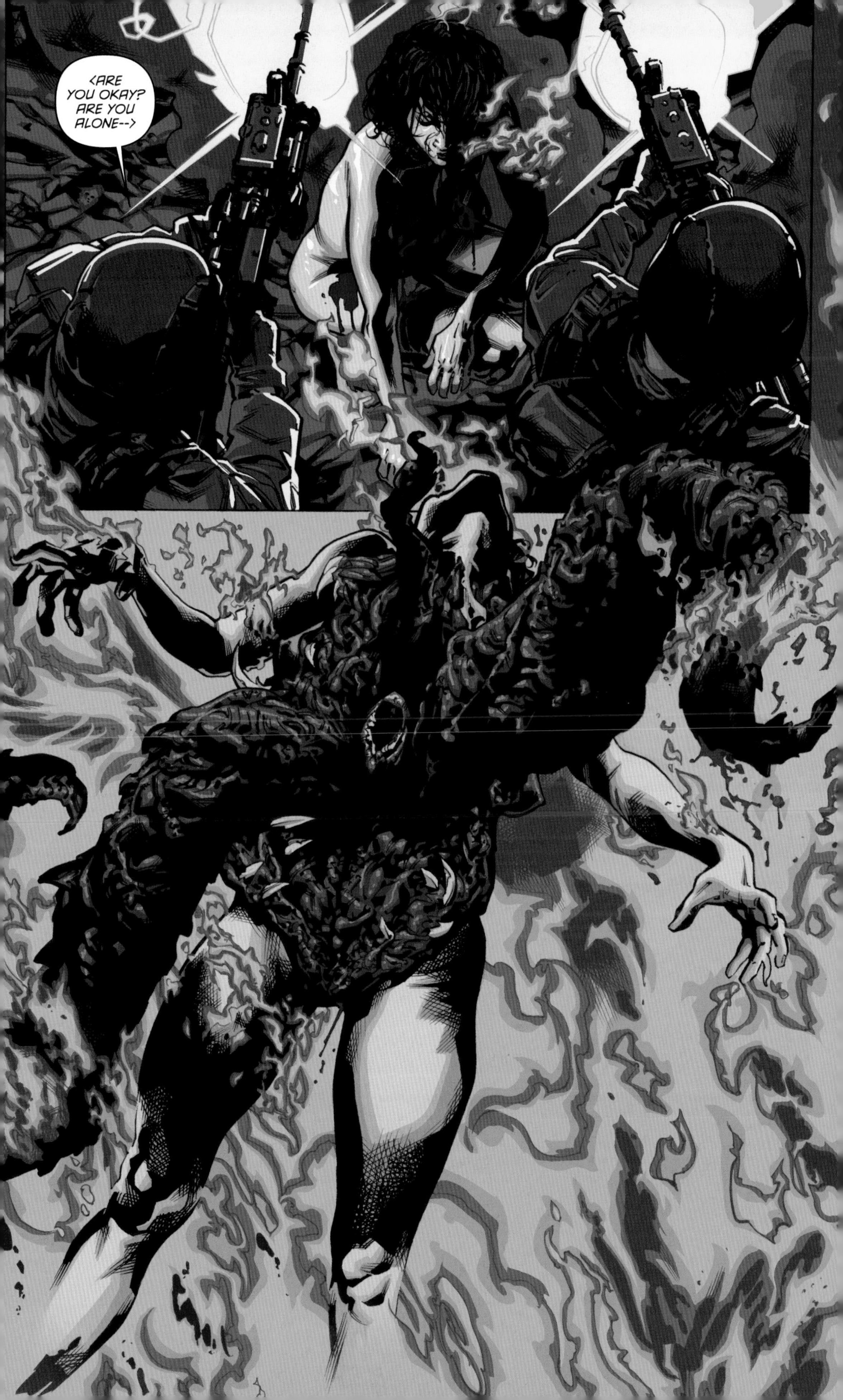
<ARE YOU OKAY? ARE YOU ALONE-->

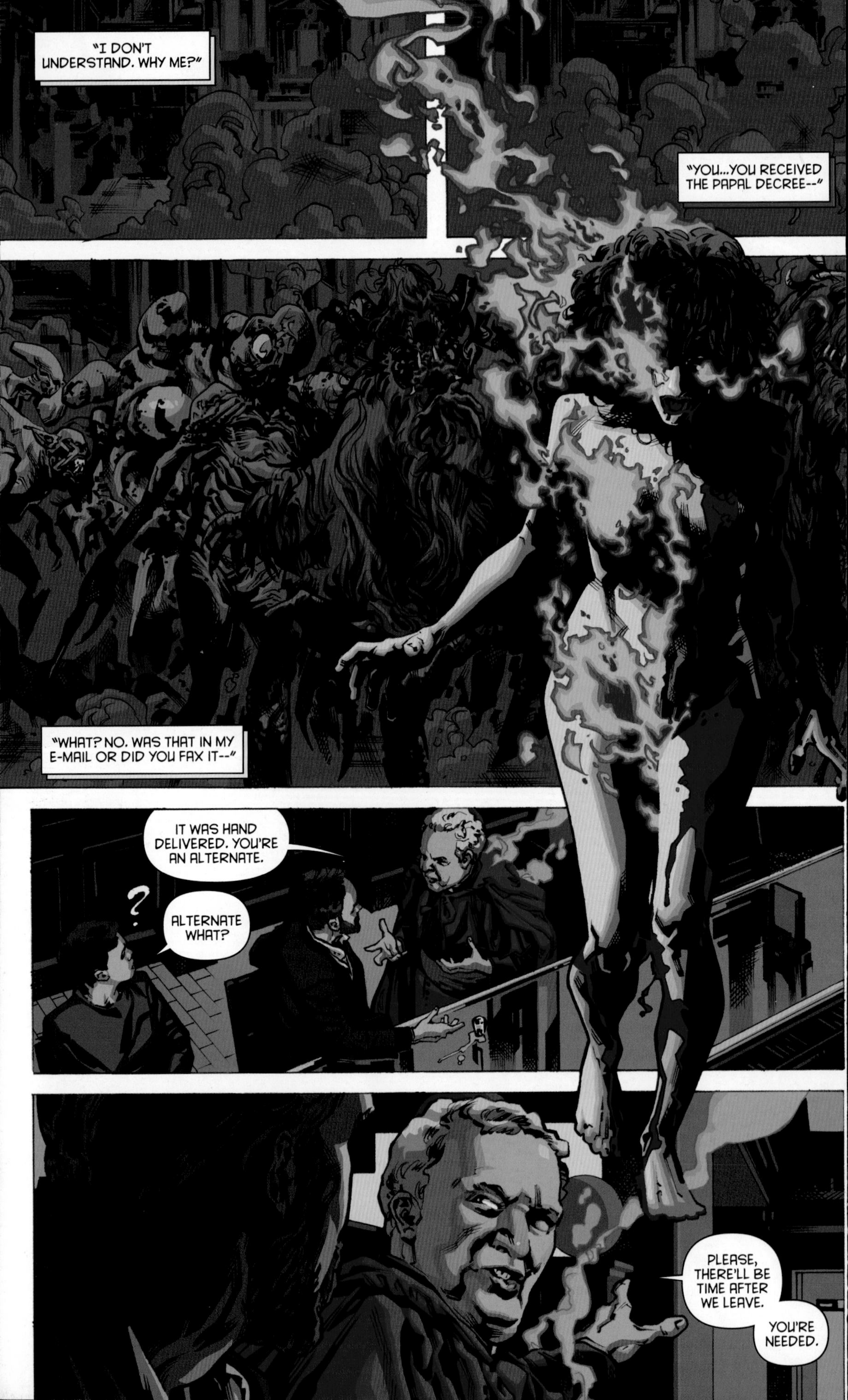
"I DON'T UNDERSTAND. WHY ME?"
"YOU...YOU RECEIVED THE PAPAL DECREE--"
"WHAT? NO. WAS THAT IN MY E-MAIL OR DID YOU FAX IT--"
IT WAS HAND DELIVERED. YOU'RE AN ALTERNATE.
?
ALTERNATE WHAT?
PLEASE, THERE'LL BE TIME AFTER WE LEAVE.
YOU'RE NEEDED.

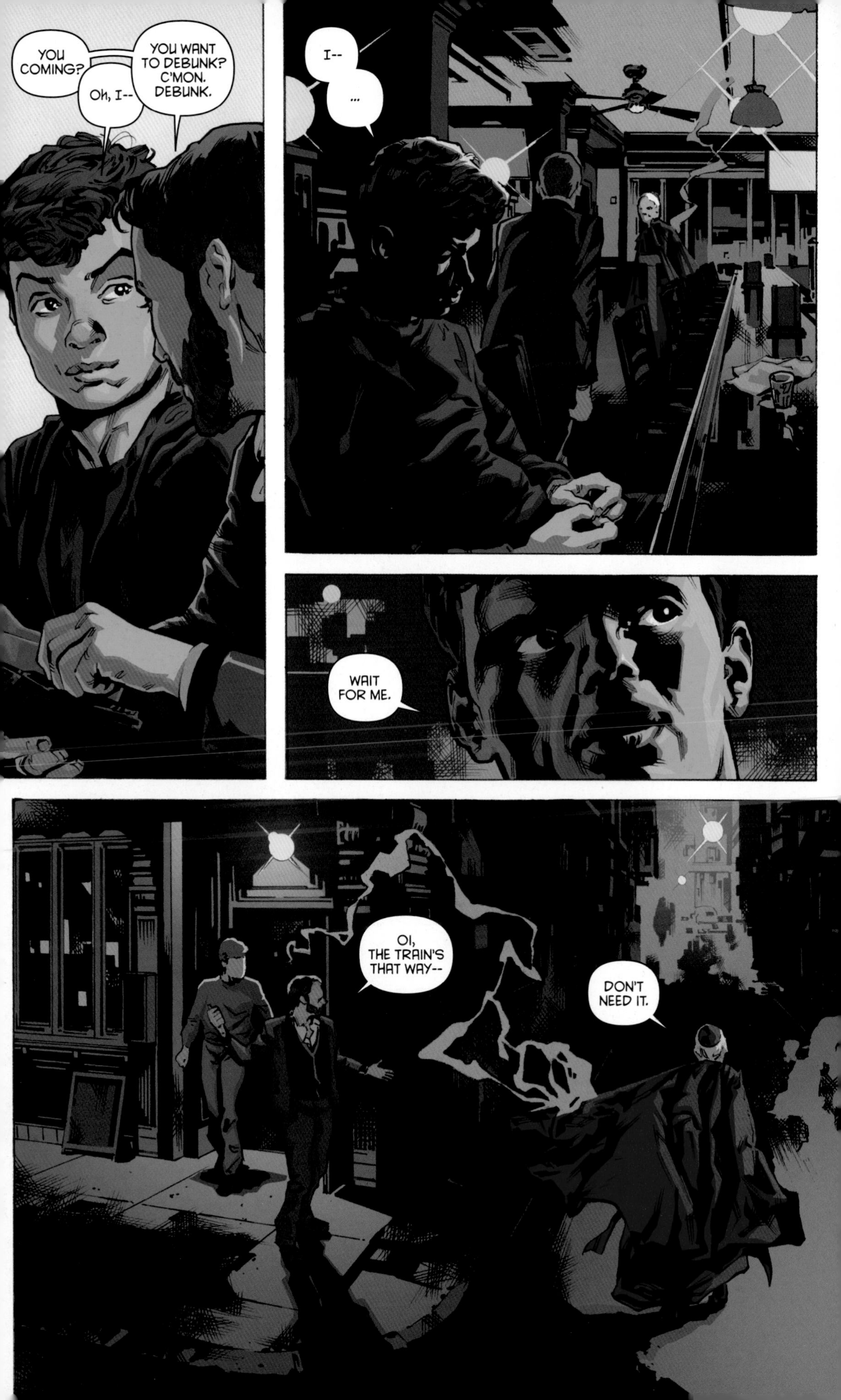
YOU COMING?
Oh, I--
YOU WANT TO DEBUNK? C'MON. DEBUNK.
I--
...
WAIT FOR ME.
OI, THE TRAIN'S THAT WAY--
DON'T NEED IT.

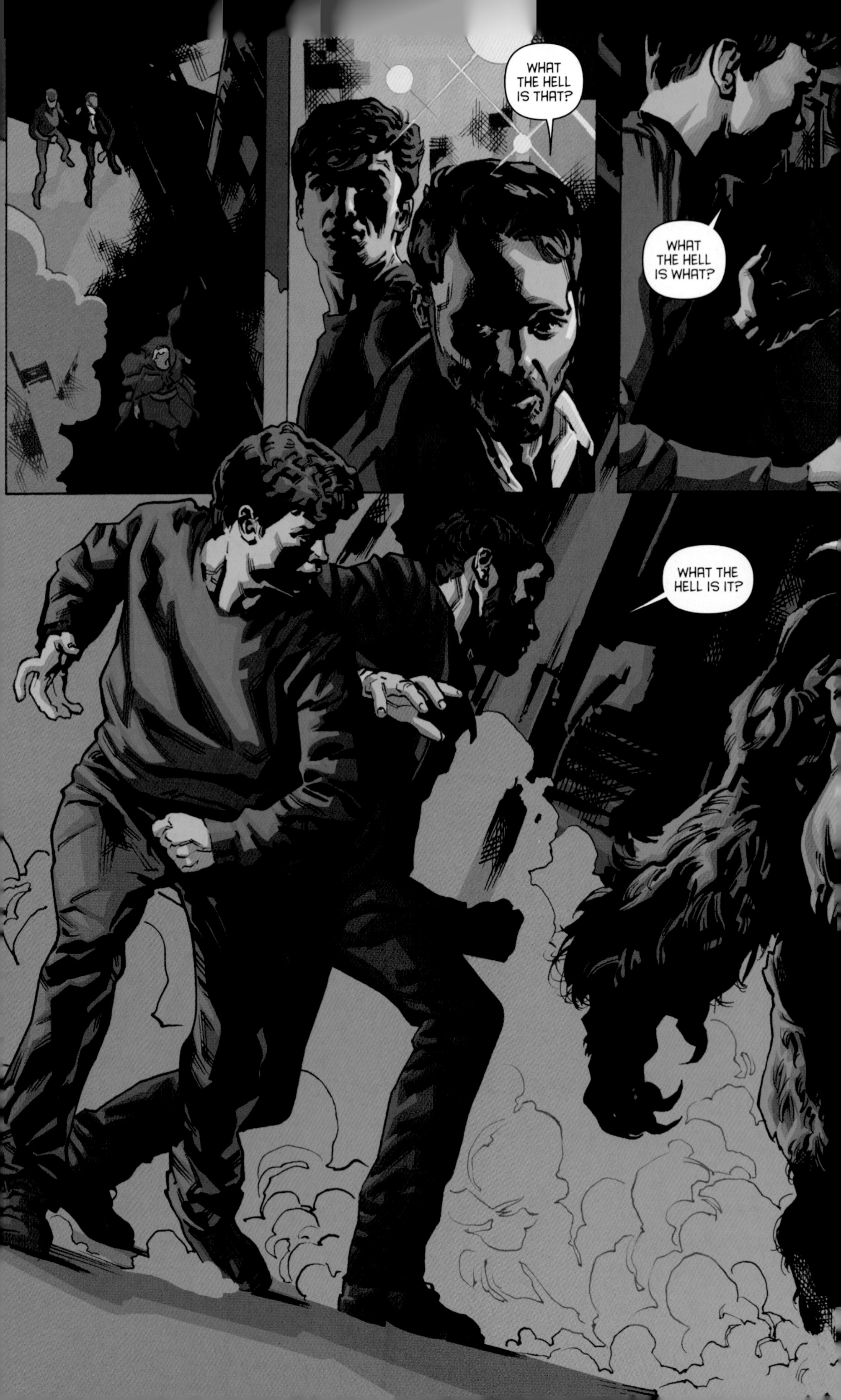
WHAT THE HELL IS THAT?
WHAT THE HELL IS WHAT?
WHAT THE HELL IS IT?

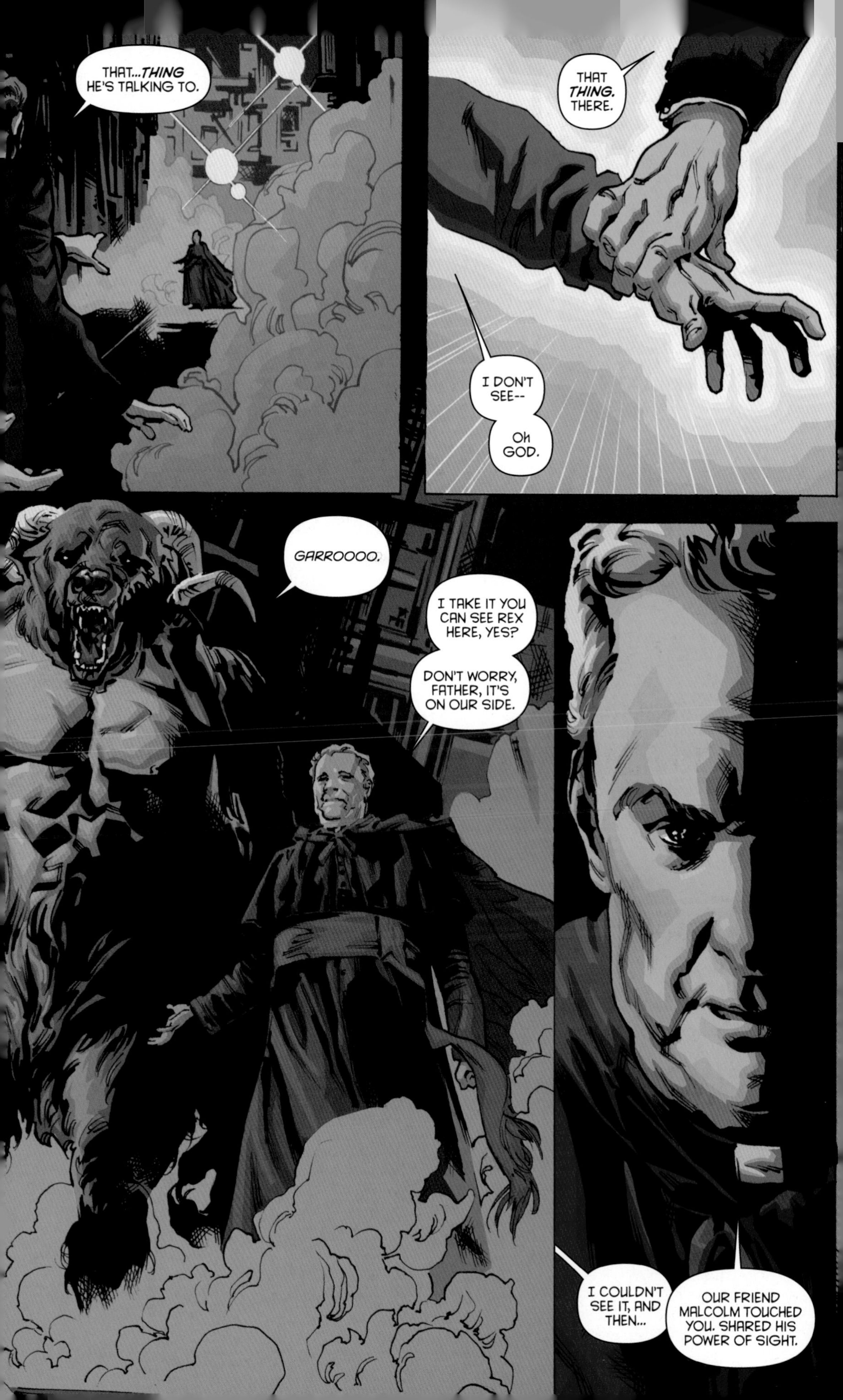
THAT...THING HE'S TALKING TO.
THAT THING. THERE.
I DON'T SEE--
Oh GOD.
GARROOOO.
I TAKE IT YOU CAN SEE REX HERE, YES?
DON'T WORRY, FATHER, IT'S ON OUR SIDE.
I COULDN'T SEE IT, AND THEN...
OUR FRIEND MALCOLM TOUCHED YOU. SHARED HIS POWER OF SIGHT.

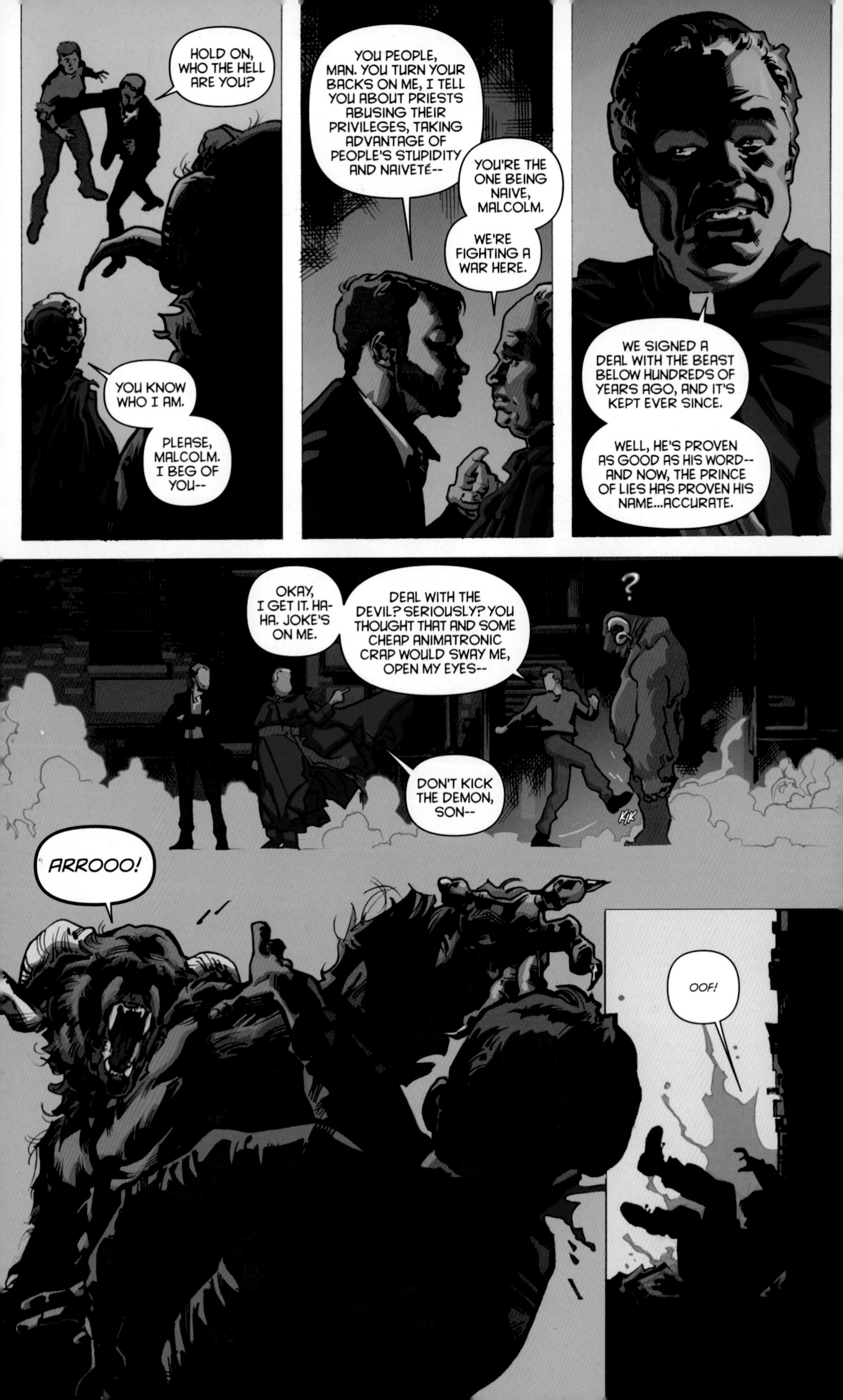
HOLD ON, WHO THE HELL ARE YOU?
YOU KNOW WHO I AM.
PLEASE, MALCOLM. I BEG OF YOU--
YOU PEOPLE, MAN. YOU TURN YOUR BACKS ON ME, I TELL YOU ABOUT PRIESTS ABUSING THEIR PRIVILEGES, TAKING ADVANTAGE OF PEOPLE'S STUPIDITY AND NAIVETÉ--
YOU'RE THE ONE BEING NAIVE, MALCOLM.
WE'RE FIGHTING A WAR HERE.
WE SIGNED A DEAL WITH THE BEAST BELOW HUNDREDS OF YEARS AGO, AND IT'S KEPT EVER SINCE.
WELL, HE'S PROVEN AS GOOD AS HIS WORD-- AND NOW, THE PRINCE OF LIES HAS PROVEN HIS NAME...ACCURATE.
OKAY, I GET IT. HA-HA. JOKE'S ON ME.
DEAL WITH THE DEVIL? SERIOUSLY? YOU THOUGHT THAT AND SOME CHEAP ANIMATRONIC CRAP WOULD SWAY ME, OPEN MY EYES--
?
DON'T KICK THE DEMON, SON--
KIK
ARROOO!
OOF!

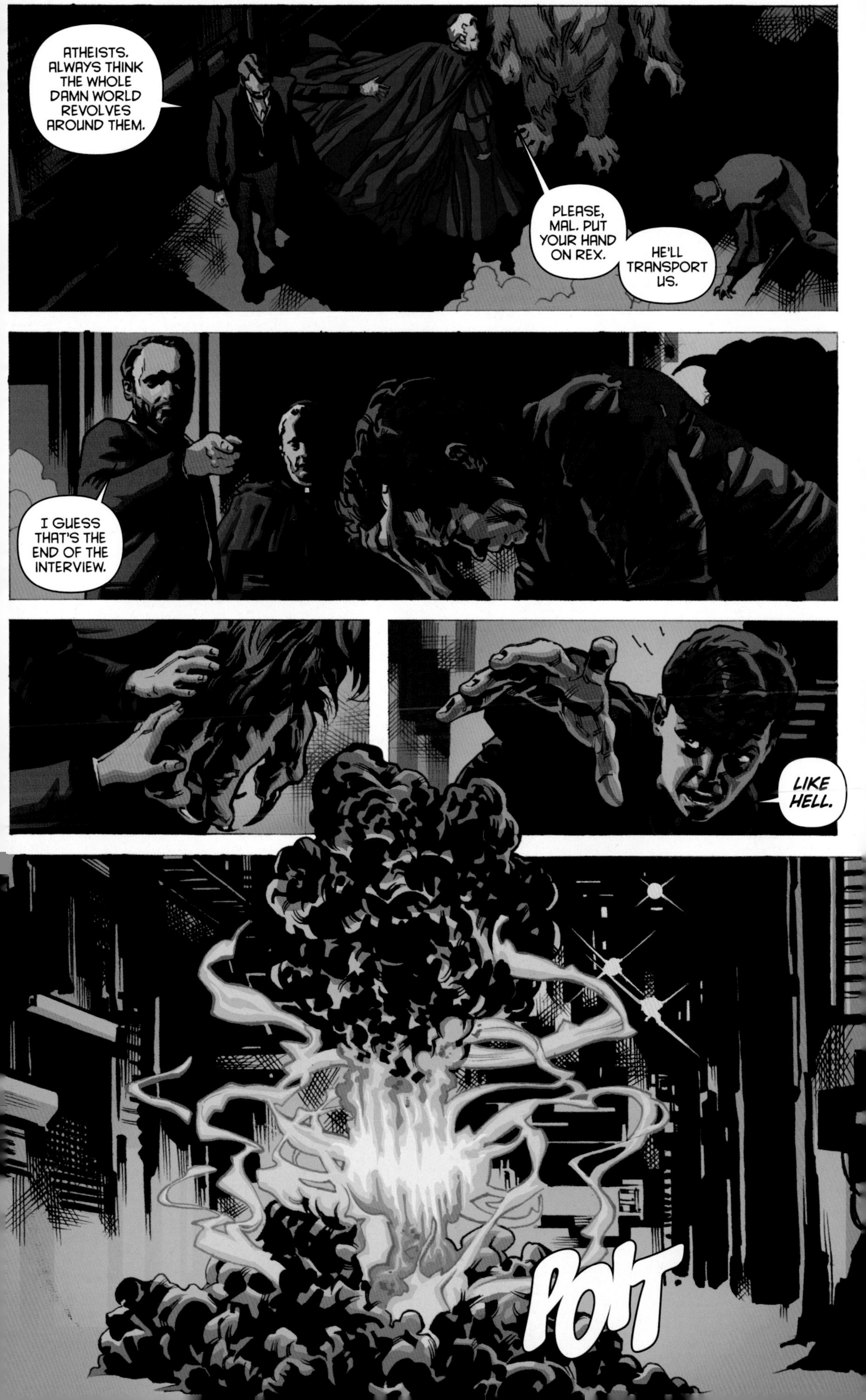
ATHEISTS. ALWAYS THINK THE WHOLE DAMN WORLD REVOLVES AROUND THEM.
PLEASE, MAL. PUT YOUR HAND ON REX.
HE'LL TRANSPORT US.
I GUESS THAT'S THE END OF THE INTERVIEW.
LIKE HELL.
POIT

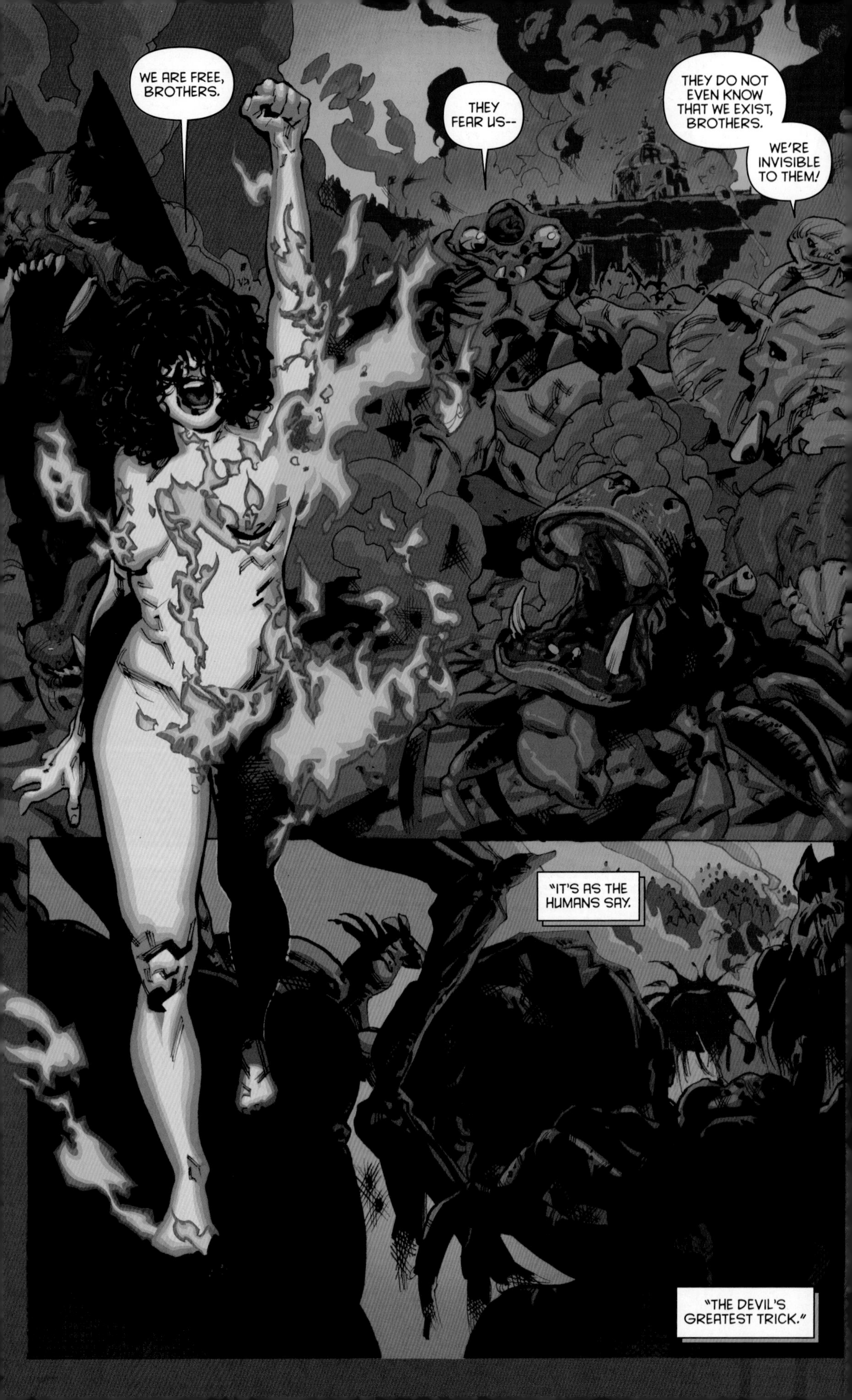

WE ARE FREE, BROTHERS.
THEY FEAR US--
THEY DO NOT EVEN KNOW THAT WE EXIST, BROTHERS.
WE'RE INVISIBLE TO THEM!
"IT'S AS THE HUMANS SAY.
"THE DEVIL'S GREATEST TRICK."

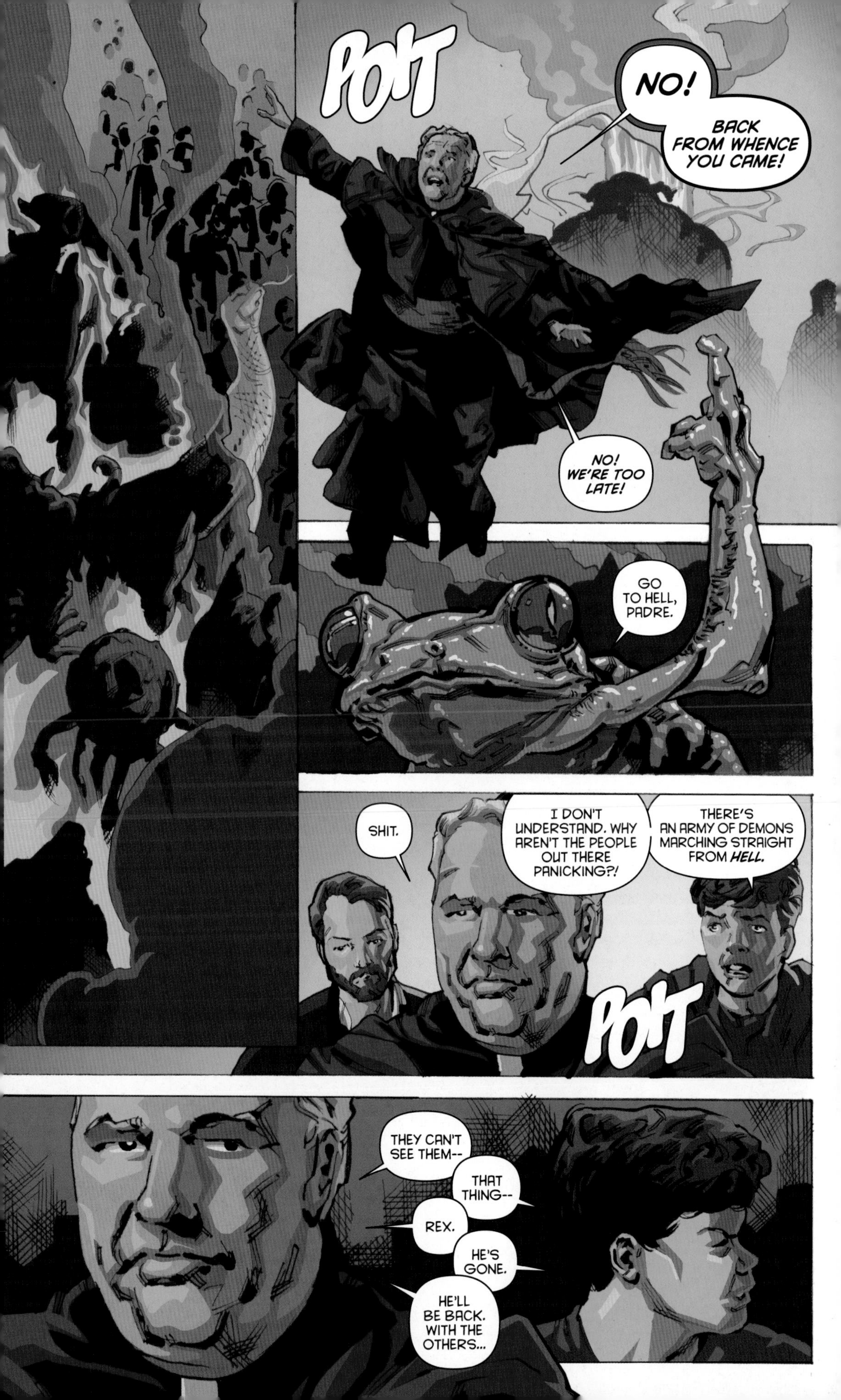
POIT
NO!
BACK FROM WHENCE YOU CAME!
NO! WE'RE TOO LATE!
GO TO HELL, PADRE.
SHIT.
I DON'T UNDERSTAND. WHY AREN'T THE PEOPLE OUT THERE PANICKING?!
THERE'S AN ARMY OF DEMONS MARCHING STRAIGHT FROM HELL.
POIT
THEY CAN'T SEE THEM--
THAT THING--
REX.
HE'S GONE.
HE'LL BE BACK. WITH THE OTHERS...

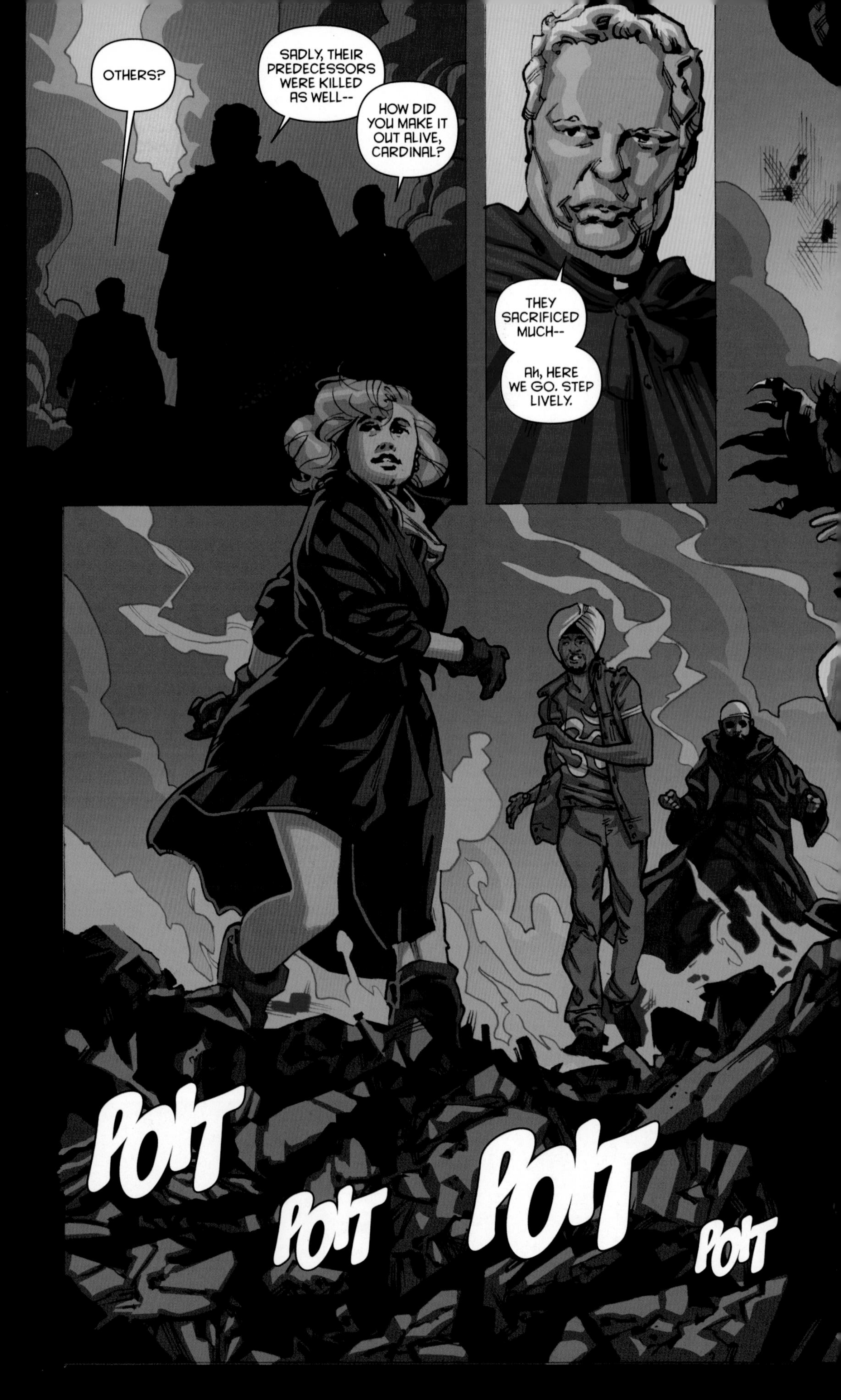
OTHERS?
SADLY, THEIR PREDECESSORS WERE KILLED AS WELL--
HOW DID YOU MAKE IT OUT ALIVE, CARDINAL?
THEY SACRIFICED MUCH--
Ah, HERE WE GO. STEP LIVELY.
POIT
POIT
POIT
POIT

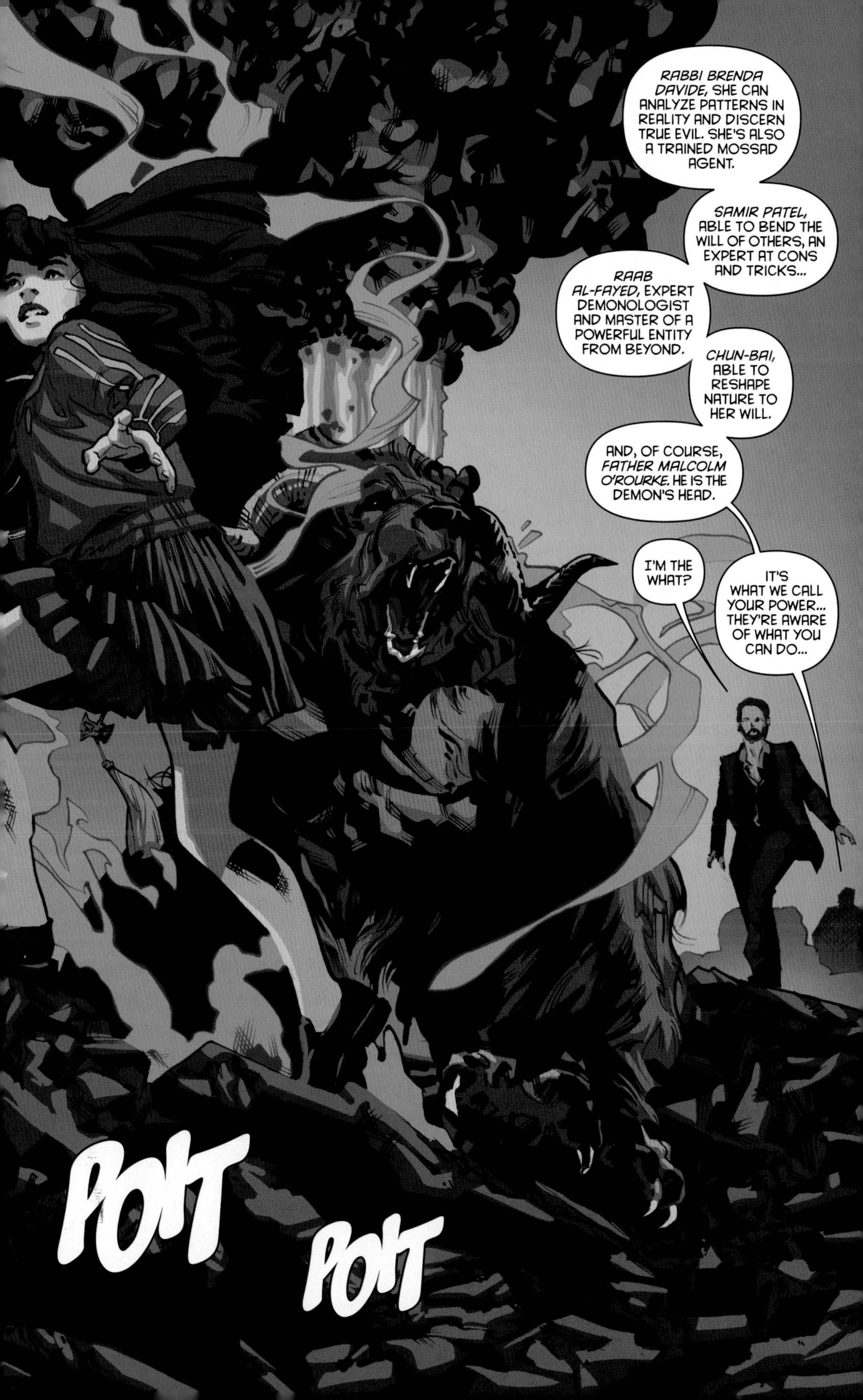
RABBI BRENDA DAVIDE, SHE CAN ANALYZE PATTERNS IN REALITY AND DISCERN TRUE EVIL. SHE'S ALSO A TRAINED MOSSAD AGENT.
SAMIR PATEL, ABLE TO BEND THE WILL OF OTHERS, AN EXPERT AT CONS AND TRICKS...
RAAB AL-FAYED, EXPERT DEMONOLOGIST AND MASTER OF A POWERFUL ENTITY FROM BEYOND.
CHUN-BAI, ABLE TO RESHAPE NATURE TO HER WILL.
AND, OF COURSE, FATHER MALCOLM O'ROURKE. HE IS THE DEMON'S HEAD.
I'M THE WHAT?
IT'S WHAT WE CALL YOUR POWER... THEY'RE AWARE OF WHAT YOU CAN DO...
POIT
POIT

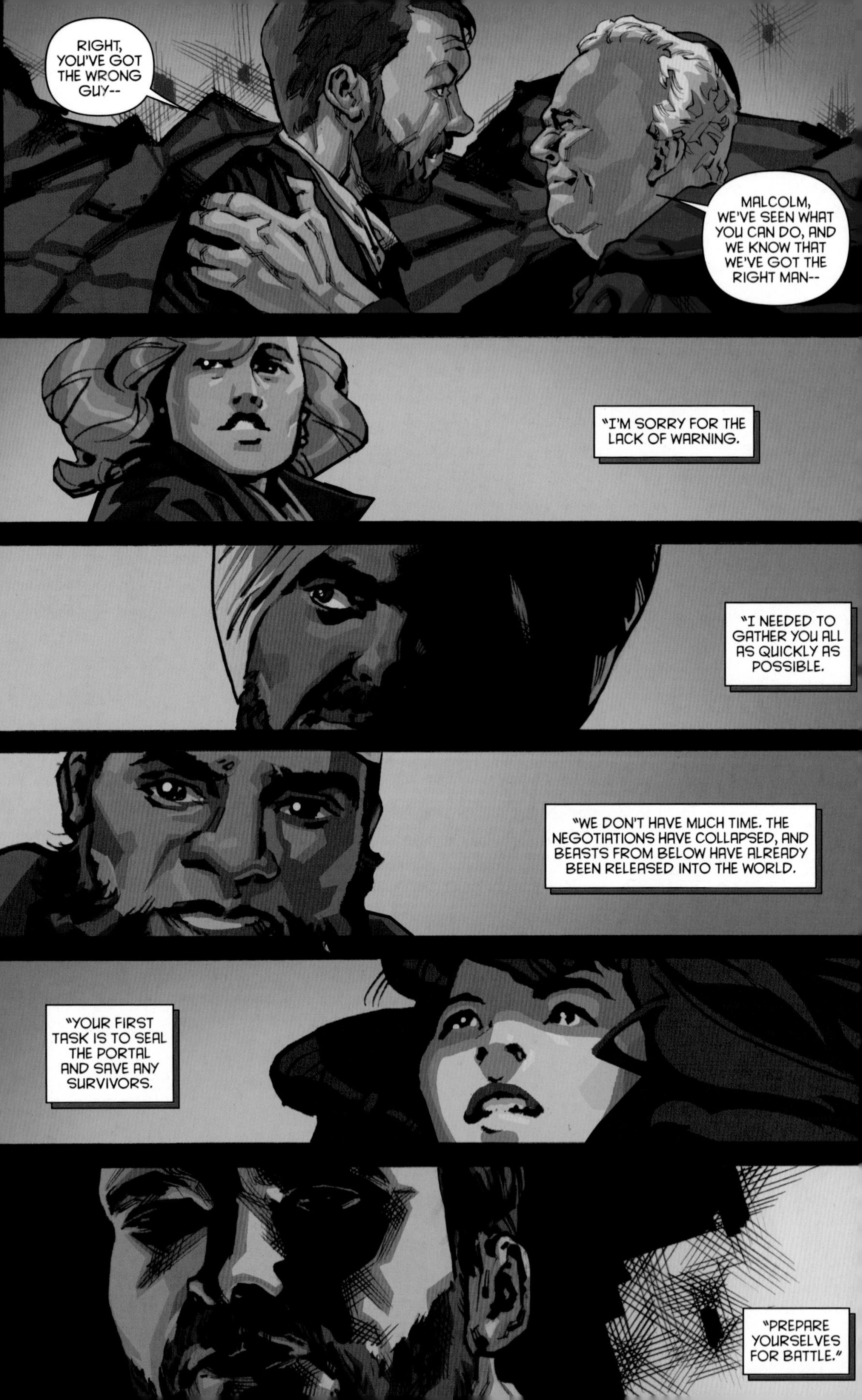
RIGHT, YOU'VE GOT THE WRONG GUY--
MALCOLM, WE'VE SEEN WHAT YOU CAN DO, AND WE KNOW THAT WE'VE GOT THE RIGHT MAN--
"I'M SORRY FOR THE LACK OF WARNING.
"I NEEDED TO GATHER YOU ALL AS QUICKLY AS POSSIBLE.
"WE DON'T HAVE MUCH TIME. THE NEGOTIATIONS HAVE COLLAPSED, AND BEASTS FROM BELOW HAVE ALREADY BEEN RELEASED INTO THE WORLD.
"YOUR FIRST TASK IS TO SEAL THE PORTAL AND SAVE ANY SURVIVORS.
"PREPARE YOURSELVES FOR BATTLE."

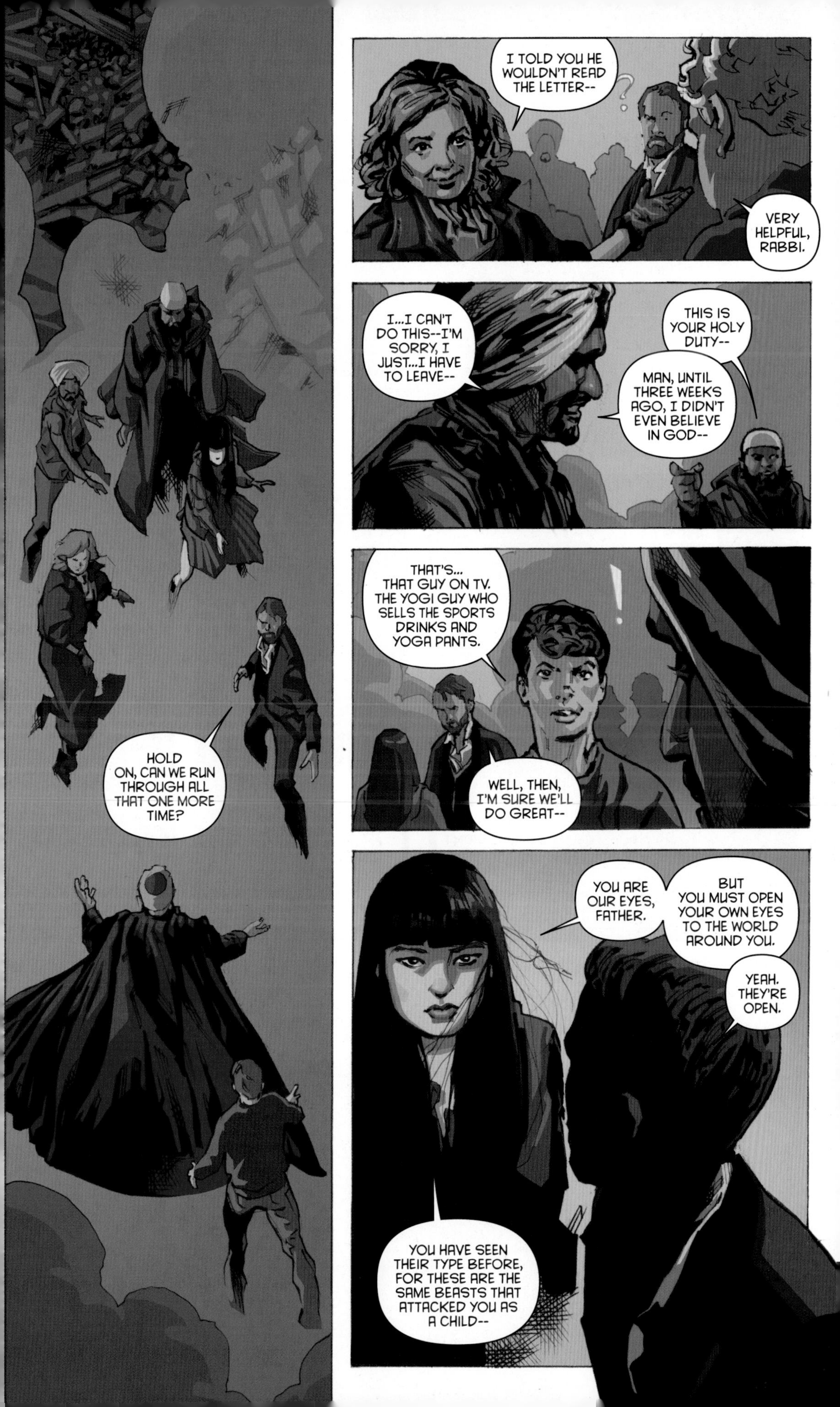
HOLD ON, CAN WE RUN THROUGH ALL THAT ONE MORE TIME?
I TOLD YOU HE WOULDN'T READ THE LETTER--
?
VERY HELPFUL, RABBI.
I...I CAN'T DO THIS--I'M SORRY, I JUST...I HAVE TO LEAVE--
THIS IS YOUR HOLY DUTY--
MAN, UNTIL THREE WEEKS AGO, I DIDN'T EVEN BELIEVE IN GOD--
THAT'S... THAT GUY ON TV. THE YOGI GUY WHO SELLS THE SPORTS DRINKS AND YOGA PANTS.
!
WELL, THEN, I'M SURE WE'LL DO GREAT--
YOU ARE OUR EYES, FATHER.
BUT YOU MUST OPEN YOUR OWN EYES TO THE WORLD AROUND YOU.
YEAH. THEY'RE OPEN.
YOU HAVE SEEN THEIR TYPE BEFORE, FOR THESE ARE THE SAME BEASTS THAT ATTACKED YOU AS A CHILD--

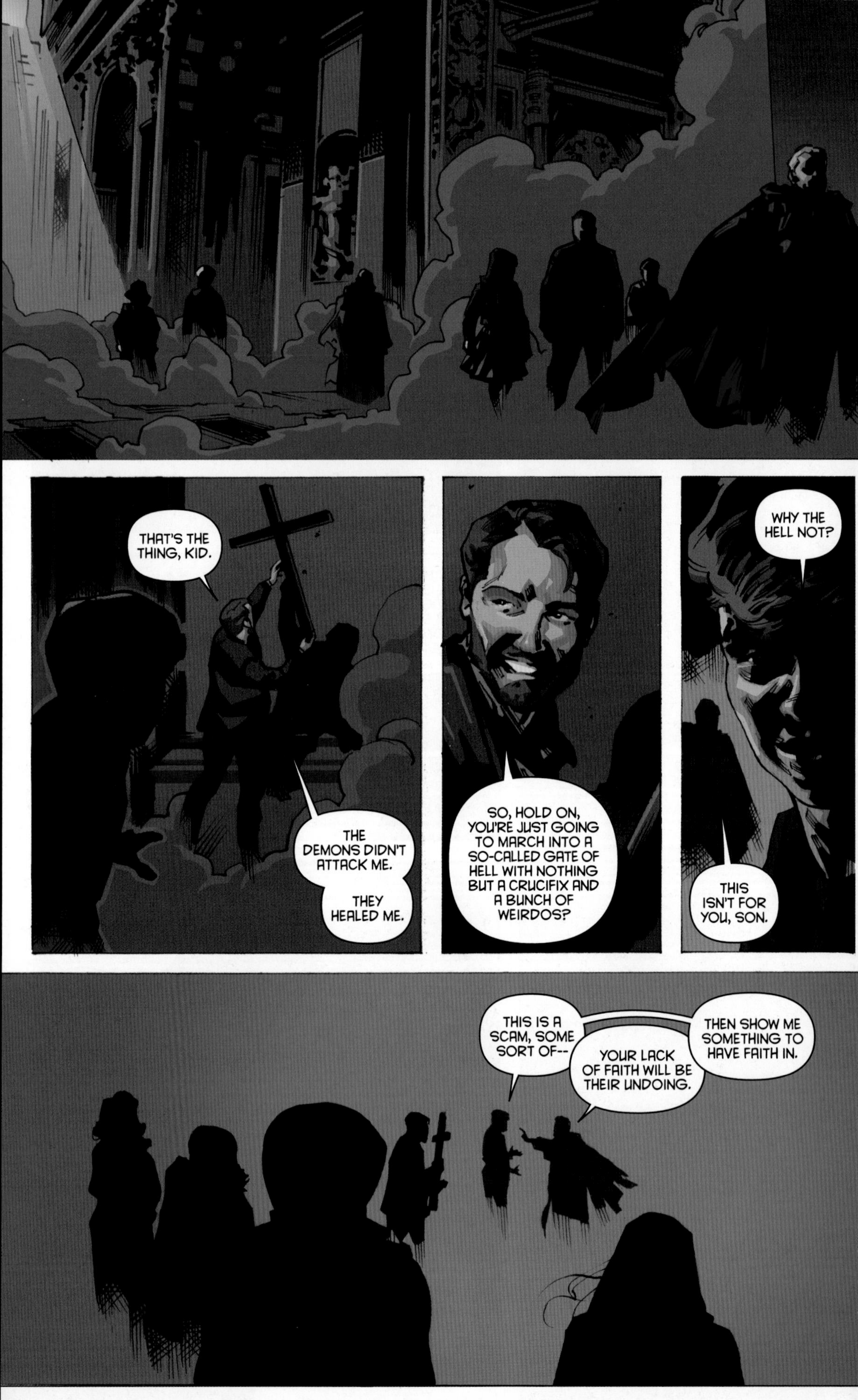
THAT'S THE THING, KID.
THE DEMONS DIDN'T ATTACK ME.
THEY HEALED ME.
SO, HOLD ON, YOU'RE JUST GOING TO MARCH INTO A SO-CALLED GATE OF HELL WITH NOTHING BUT A CRUCIFIX AND A BUNCH OF WEIRDOS?
WHY THE HELL NOT?
THIS ISN'T FOR YOU, SON.
THIS IS A SCAM, SOME SORT OF--
YOUR LACK OF FAITH WILL BE THEIR UNDOING.
THEN SHOW ME SOMETHING TO HAVE FAITH IN.

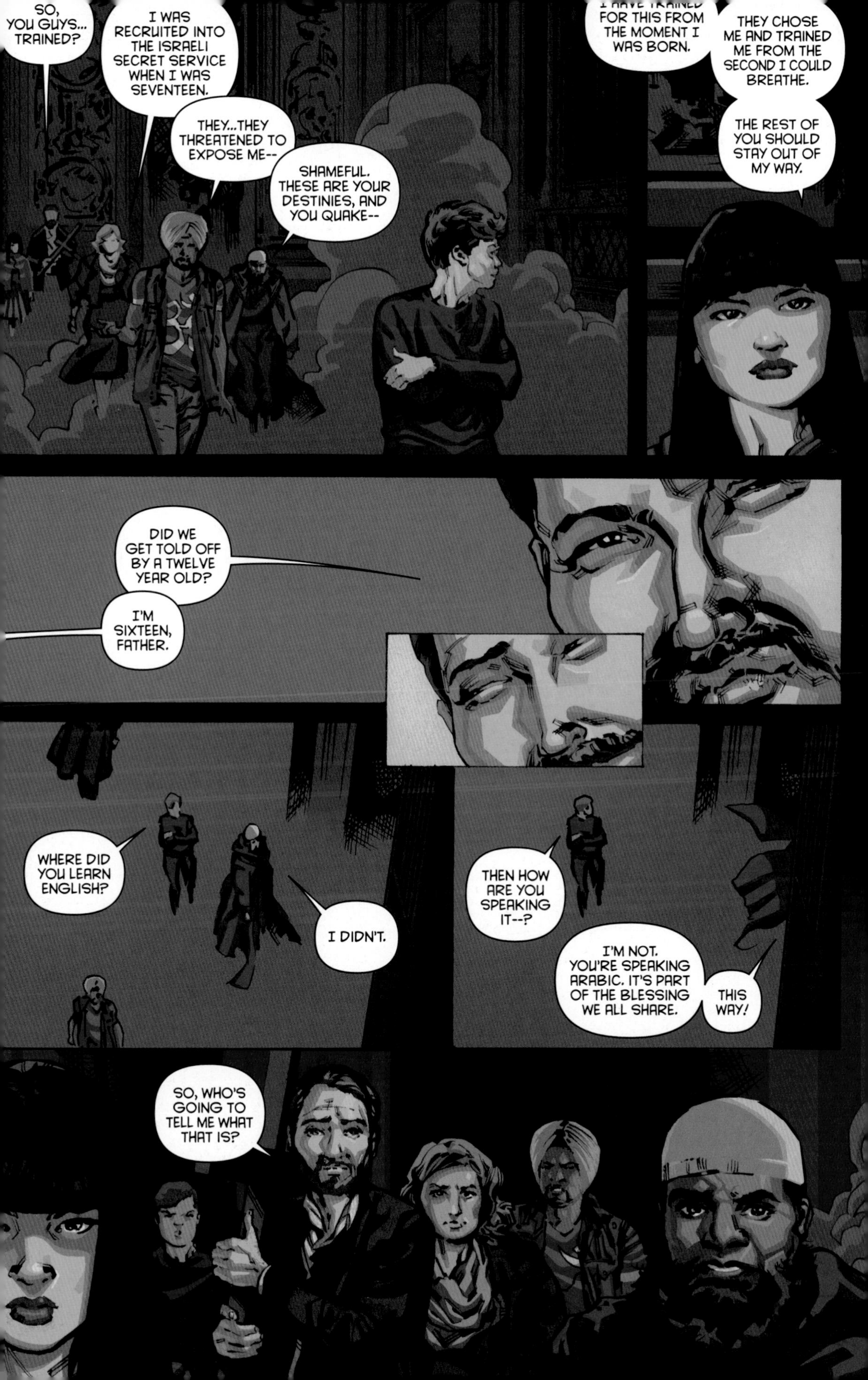
SO, YOU GUYS... TRAINED?
I WAS RECRUITED INTO THE ISRAELI SECRET SERVICE WHEN I WAS SEVENTEEN.
THEY...THEY THREATENED TO EXPOSE ME--
SHAMEFUL. THESE ARE YOUR DESTINIES, AND YOU QUAKE--
FOR THIS FROM THE MOMENT I WAS BORN.
THEY CHOSE ME AND TRAINED ME FROM THE SECOND I COULD BREATHE.
THE REST OF YOU SHOULD STAY OUT OF MY WAY.
DID WE GET TOLD OFF BY A TWELVE YEAR OLD?
I'M SIXTEEN, FATHER.
WHERE DID YOU LEARN ENGLISH?
I DIDN'T.
THEN HOW ARE YOU SPEAKING IT--?
I'M NOT. YOU'RE SPEAKING ARABIC. IT'S PART OF THE BLESSING WE ALL SHARE.
THIS WAY!
SO, WHO'S GOING TO TELL ME WHAT THAT IS?

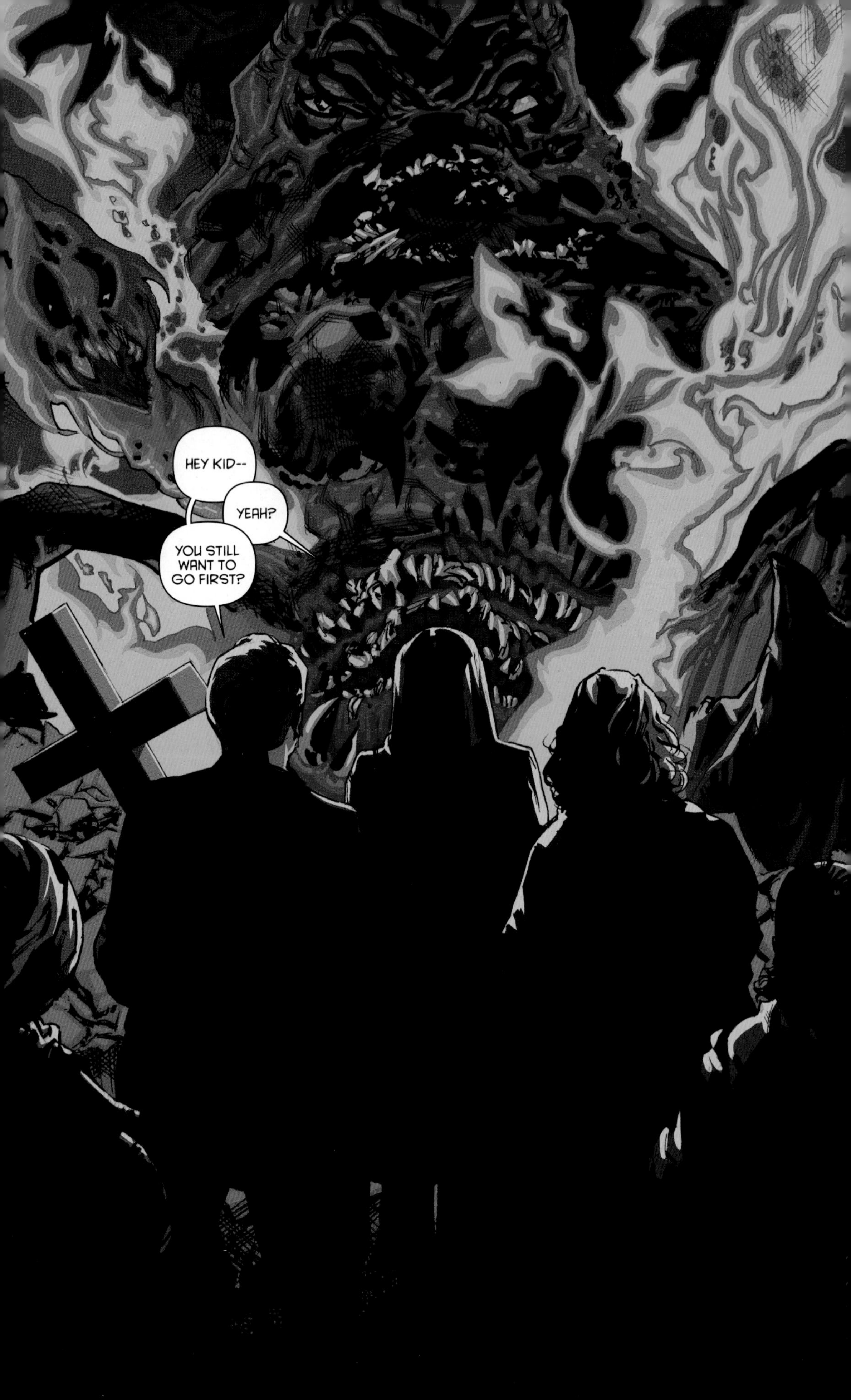
HEY KID--
YEAH?
YOU STILL WANT TO GO FIRST?

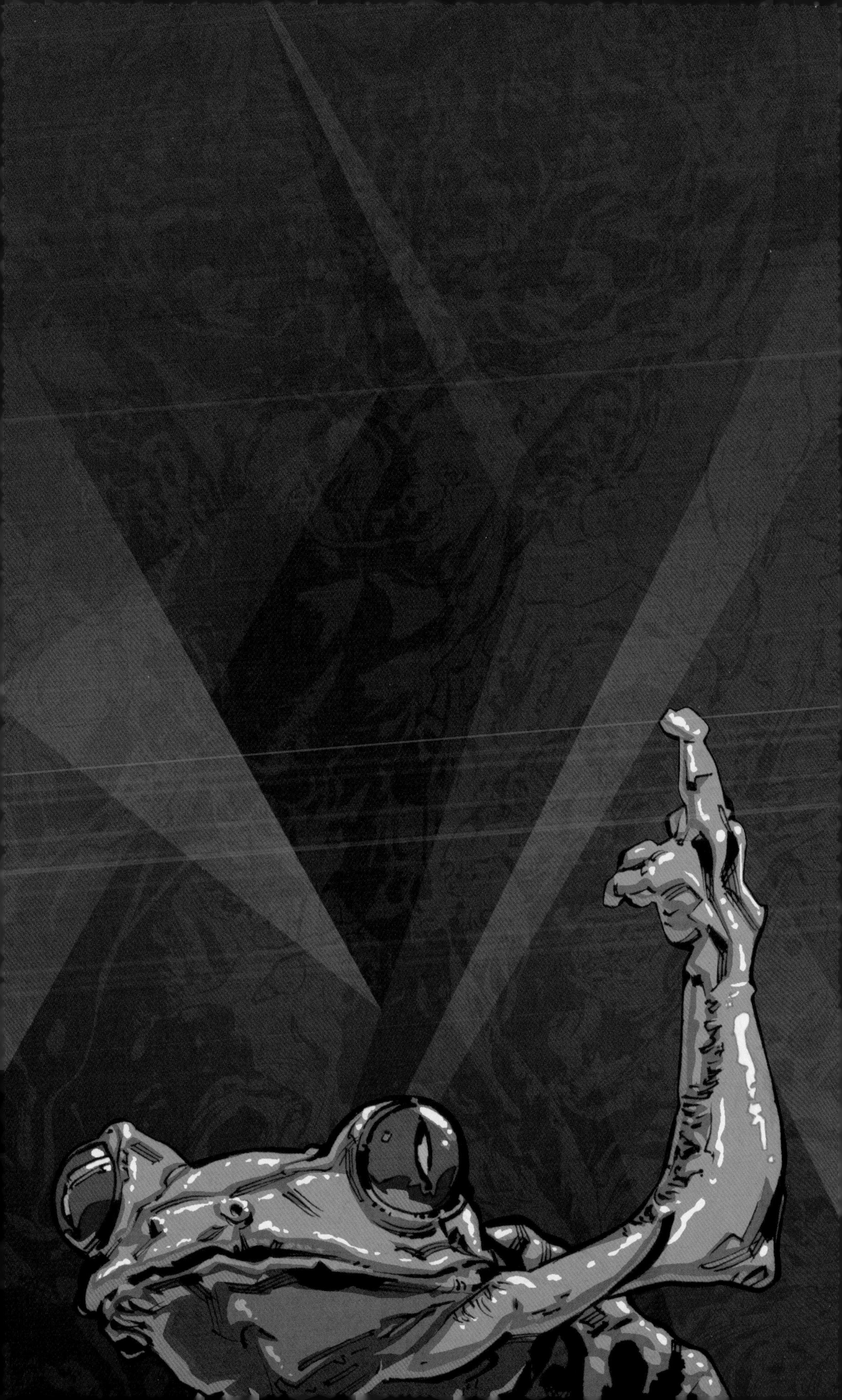

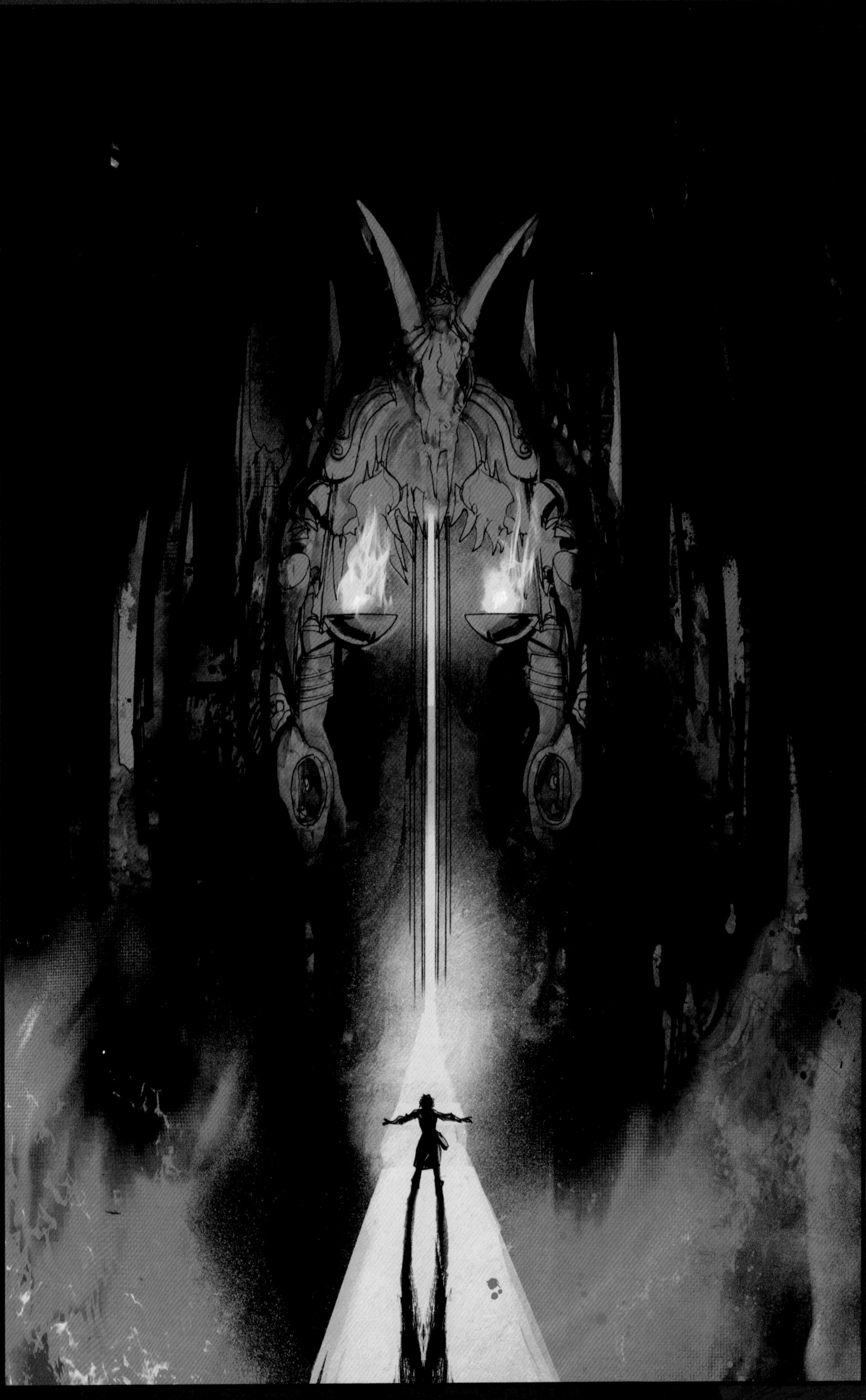

ISSUE #2 cover art by **JOCK**

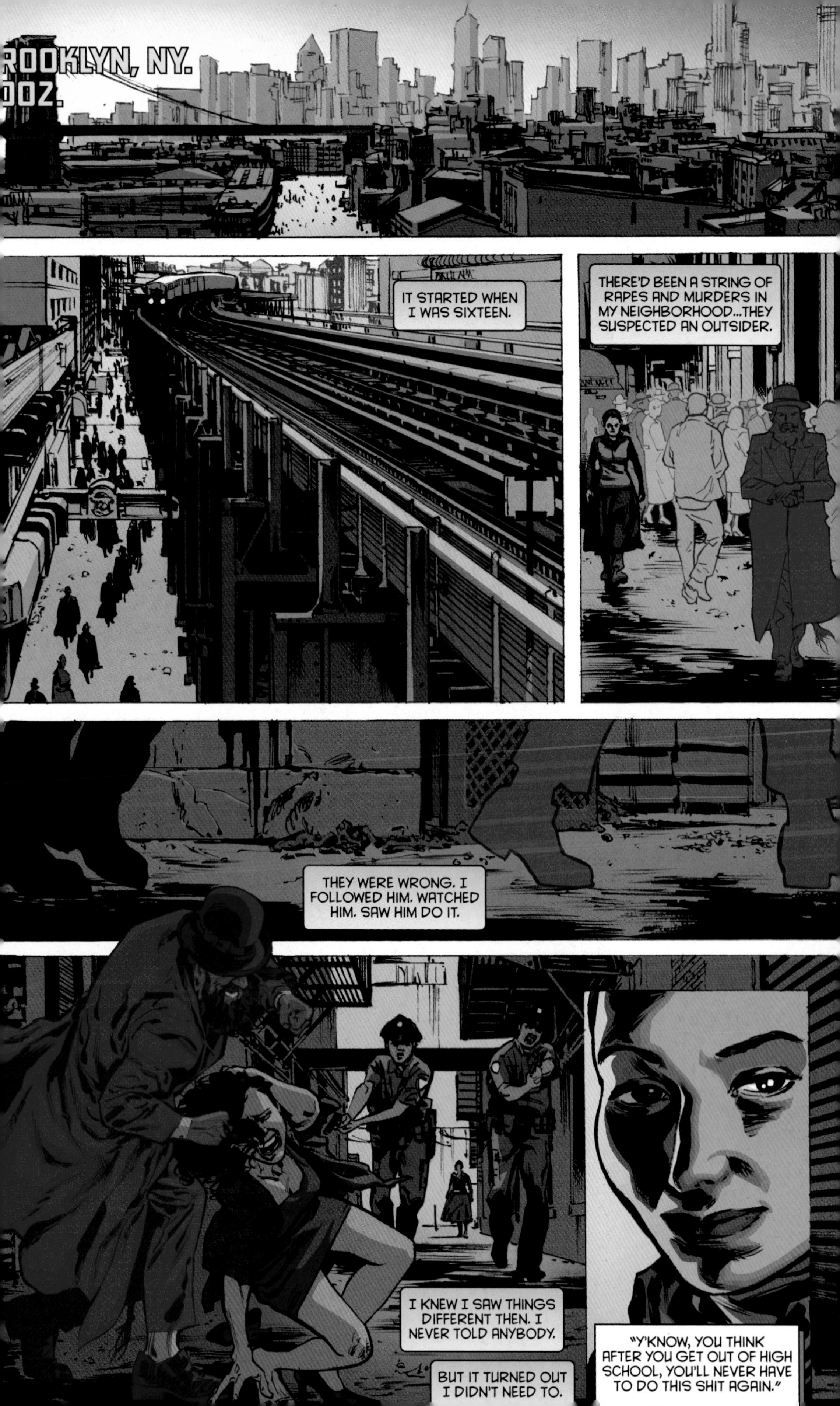
ROOKLYN, NY.
002.
IT STARTED WHEN I WAS SIXTEEN.
THERE'D BEEN A STRING OF RAPES AND MURDERS IN MY NEIGHBORHOOD...THEY SUSPECTED AN OUTSIDER.
THEY WERE WRONG. I FOLLOWED HIM. WATCHED HIM. SAW HIM DO IT.
I KNEW I SAW THINGS DIFFERENT THEN. I NEVER TOLD ANYBODY.
BUT IT TURNED OUT I DIDN'T NEED TO.
"Y'KNOW, YOU THINK AFTER YOU GET OUT OF HIGH SCHOOL, YOU'LL NEVER HAVE TO DO THIS SHIT AGAIN."

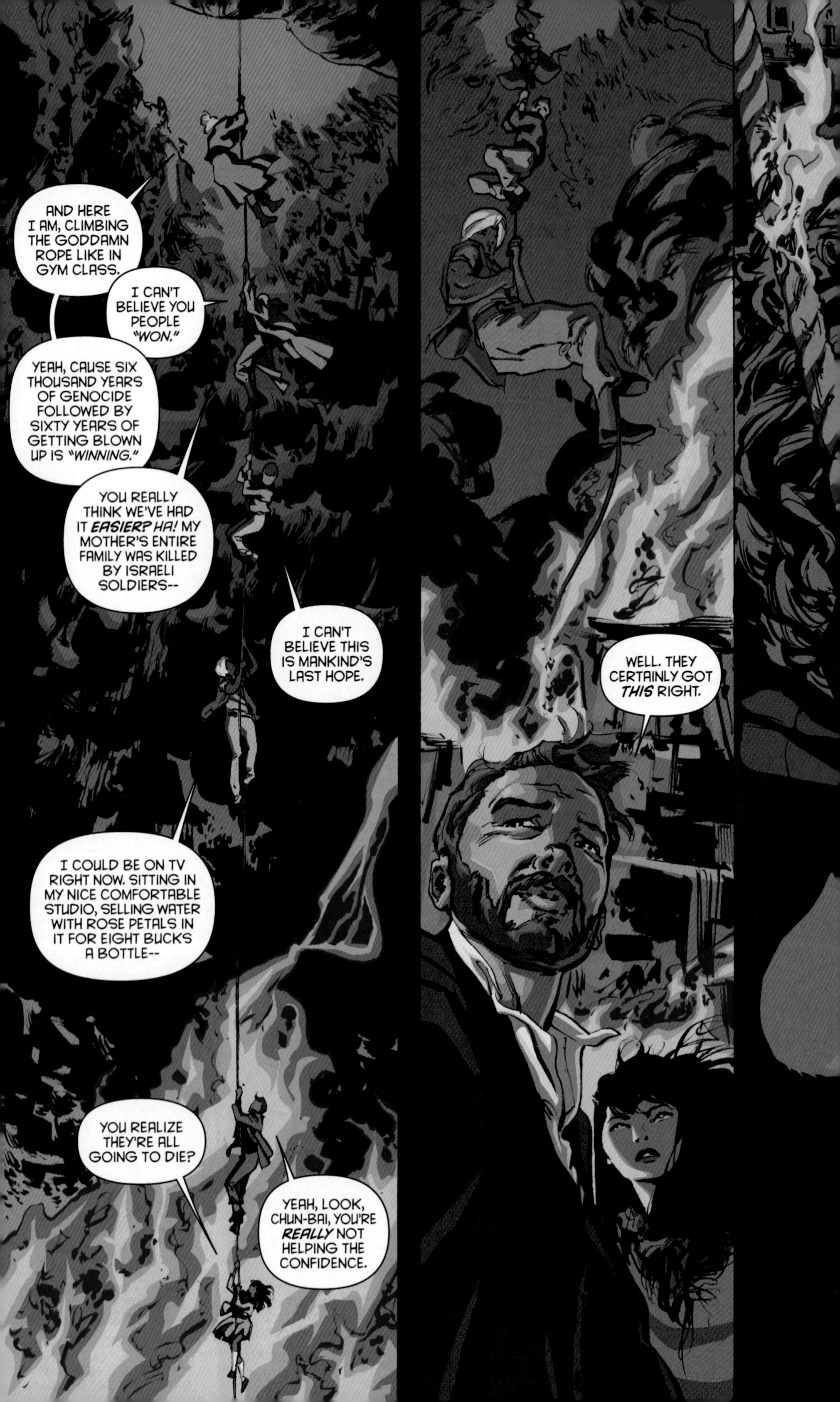
AND HERE I AM, CLIMBING THE GODDAMN ROPE LIKE IN GYM CLASS.
I CAN'T BELIEVE YOU PEOPLE "WON."
YEAH, CAUSE SIX THOUSAND YEARS OF GENOCIDE FOLLOWED BY SIXTY YEARS OF GETTING BLOWN UP IS "WINNING."
YOU REALLY THINK WE'VE HAD IT EASIER? HA! MY MOTHER'S ENTIRE FAMILY WAS KILLED BY ISRAELI SOLDIERS--
I CAN'T BELIEVE THIS IS MANKIND'S LAST HOPE.
I COULD BE ON TV RIGHT NOW. SITTING IN MY NICE COMFORTABLE STUDIO, SELLING WATER WITH ROSE PETALS IN IT FOR EIGHT BUCKS A BOTTLE--
YOU REALIZE THEY'RE ALL GOING TO DIE?
YEAH, LOOK, CHUN-BAI, YOU'RE REALLY NOT HELPING THE CONFIDENCE.
WELL. THEY CERTAINLY GOT THIS RIGHT.

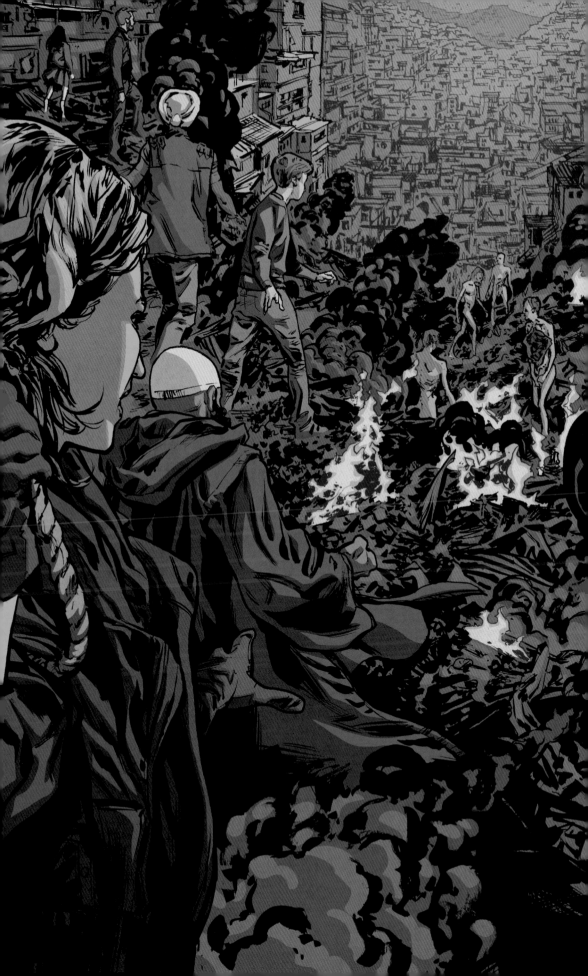

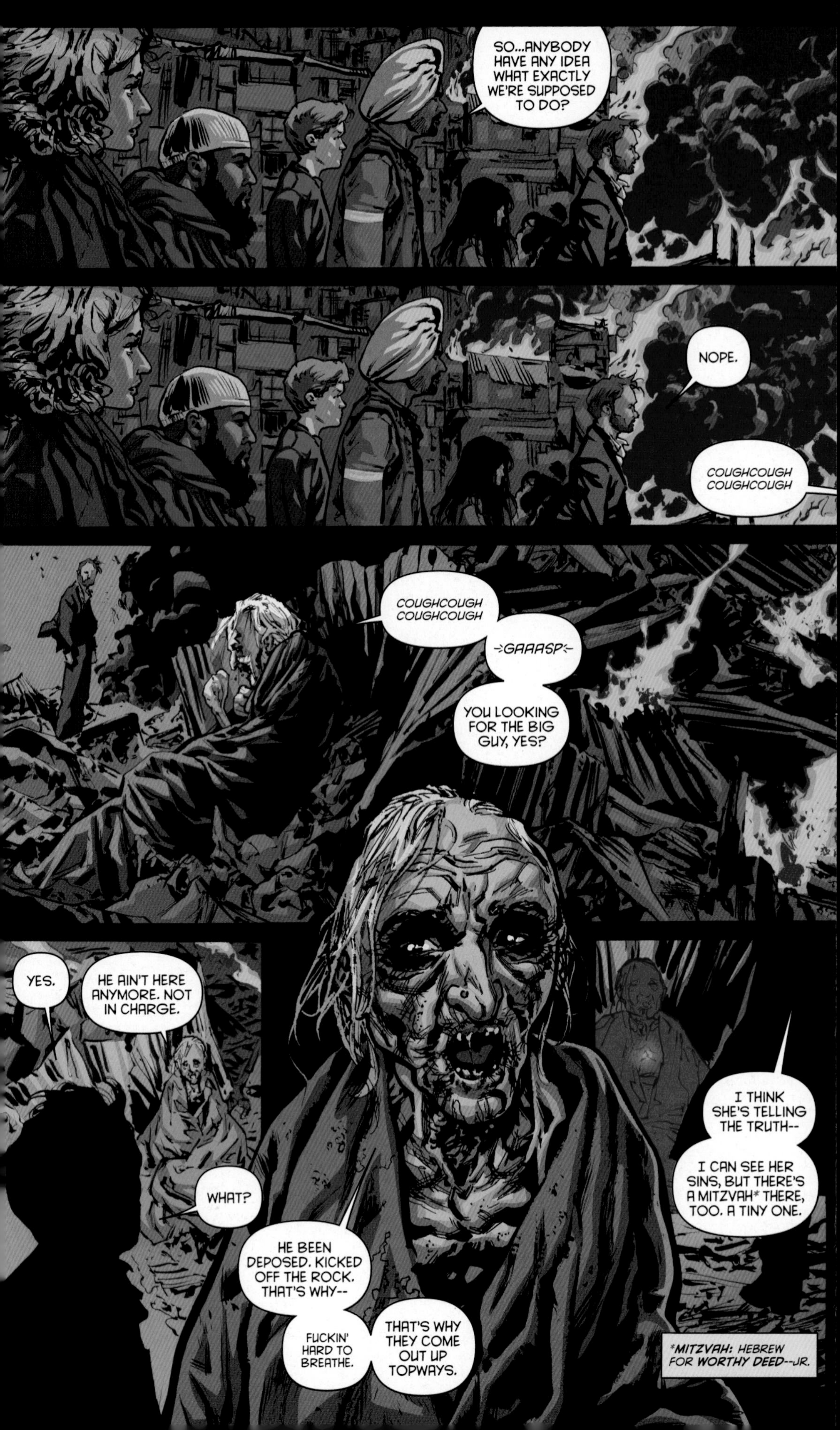
SO...ANYBODY HAVE ANY IDEA WHAT EXACTLY WE'RE SUPPOSED TO DO?
NOPE.
COUGHCOUGH COUGHCOUGH
COUGHCOUGH COUGHCOUGH
GAAASP
YOU LOOKING FOR THE BIG GUY, YES?
YES.
HE AIN'T HERE ANYMORE. NOT IN CHARGE.
WHAT?
HE BEEN DEPOSED. KICKED OFF THE ROCK. THAT'S WHY--
FUCKIN' HARD TO BREATHE.
THAT'S WHY THEY COME OUT UP TOPWAYS.
I THINK SHE'S TELLING THE TRUTH--
I CAN SEE HER SINS, BUT THERE'S A MITZVAH* THERE, TOO. A TINY ONE.
*MITZVAH: HEBREW FOR WORTHY DEED--JR.

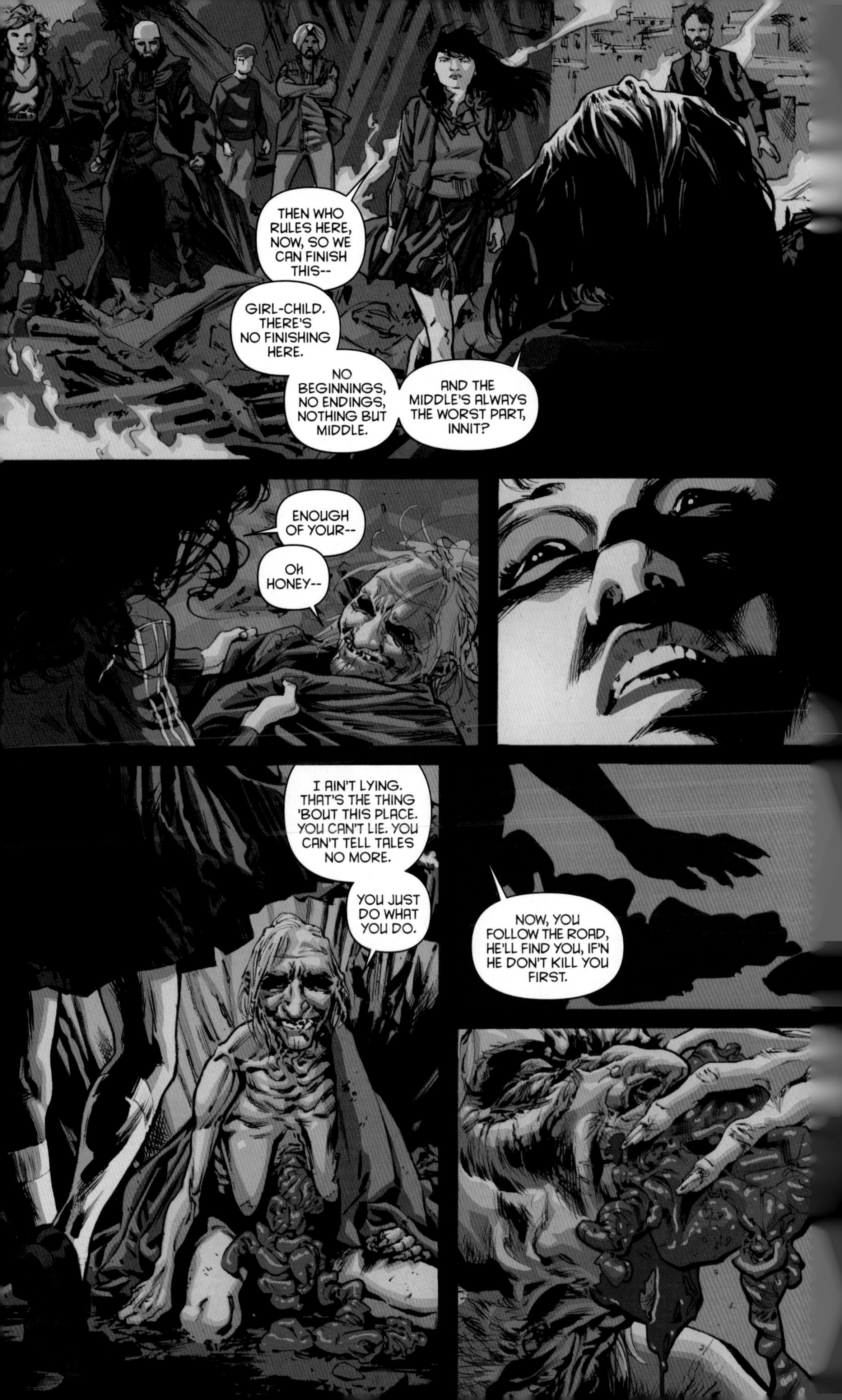
THEN WHO RULES HERE, NOW, SO WE CAN FINISH THIS--
GIRL-CHILD. THERE'S NO FINISHING HERE.
NO BEGINNINGS, NO ENDINGS, NOTHING BUT MIDDLE.
AND THE MIDDLE'S ALWAYS THE WORST PART, INNIT?
ENOUGH OF YOUR--
Oh HONEY--
I AIN'T LYING. THAT'S THE THING 'BOUT THIS PLACE. YOU CAN'T LIE. YOU CAN'T TELL TALES NO MORE.
YOU JUST DO WHAT YOU DO.
NOW, YOU FOLLOW THE ROAD, HE'LL FIND YOU, IF'N HE DON'T KILL YOU FIRST.

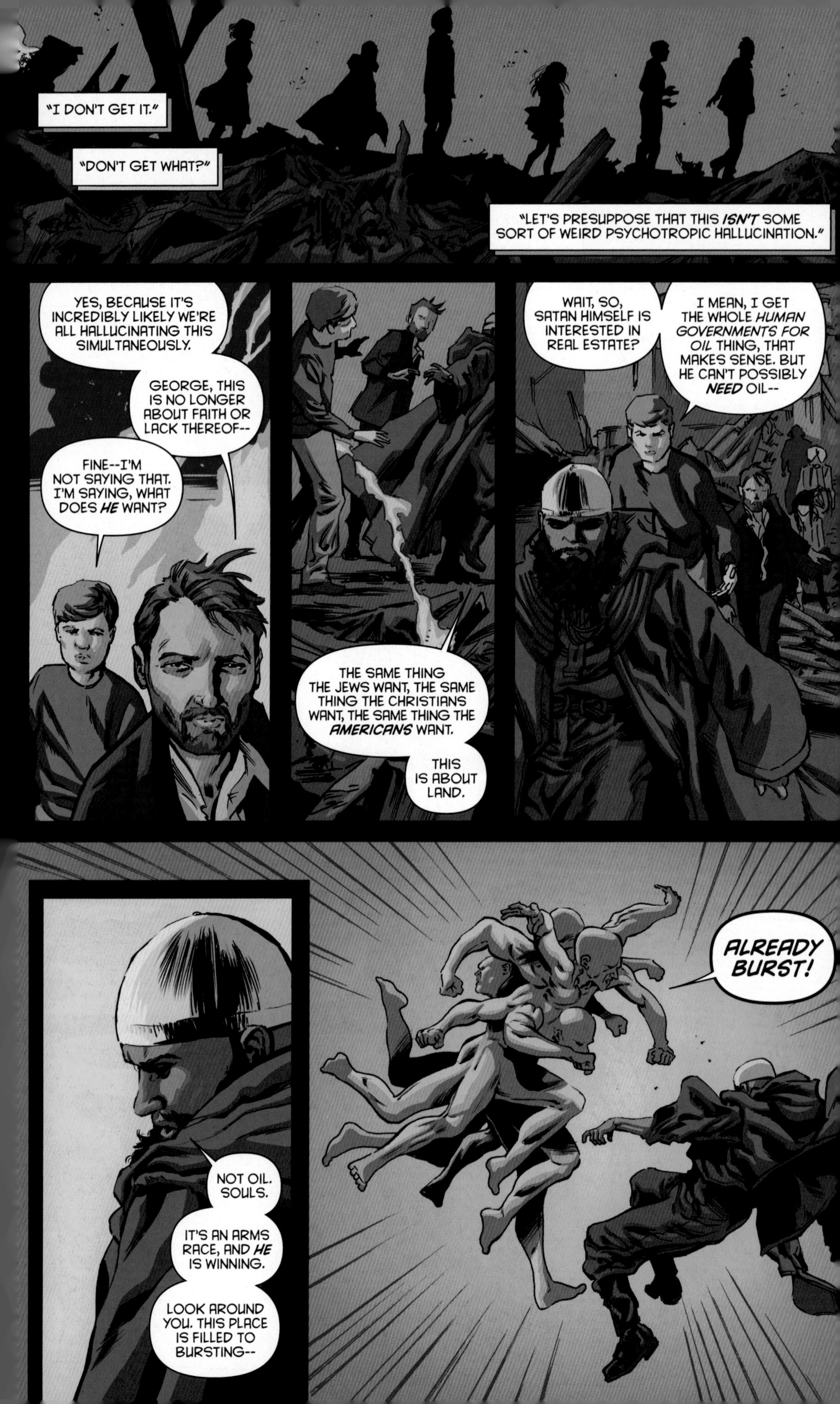
"I DON'T GET IT."
"DON'T GET WHAT?"
"LET'S PRESUPPOSE THAT THIS *ISN'T* SOME SORT OF WEIRD PSYCHOTROPIC HALLUCINATION."
YES, BECAUSE IT'S INCREDIBLY LIKELY WE'RE ALL HALLUCINATING THIS SIMULTANEOUSLY.
GEORGE, THIS IS NO LONGER ABOUT FAITH OR LACK THEREOF--
FINE--I'M NOT SAYING THAT. I'M SAYING, WHAT DOES *HE* WANT?
THE SAME THING THE JEWS WANT, THE SAME THING THE CHRISTIANS WANT, THE SAME THING THE *AMERICANS* WANT.
THIS IS ABOUT LAND.
WAIT, SO, SATAN HIMSELF IS INTERESTED IN REAL ESTATE?
I MEAN, I GET THE WHOLE *HUMAN GOVERNMENTS FOR OIL* THING, THAT MAKES SENSE. BUT HE CAN'T POSSIBLY *NEED* OIL--
NOT OIL. SOULS.
IT'S AN ARMS RACE, AND *HE* IS WINNING.
LOOK AROUND YOU. THIS PLACE IS FILLED TO BURSTING--
ALREADY BURST!

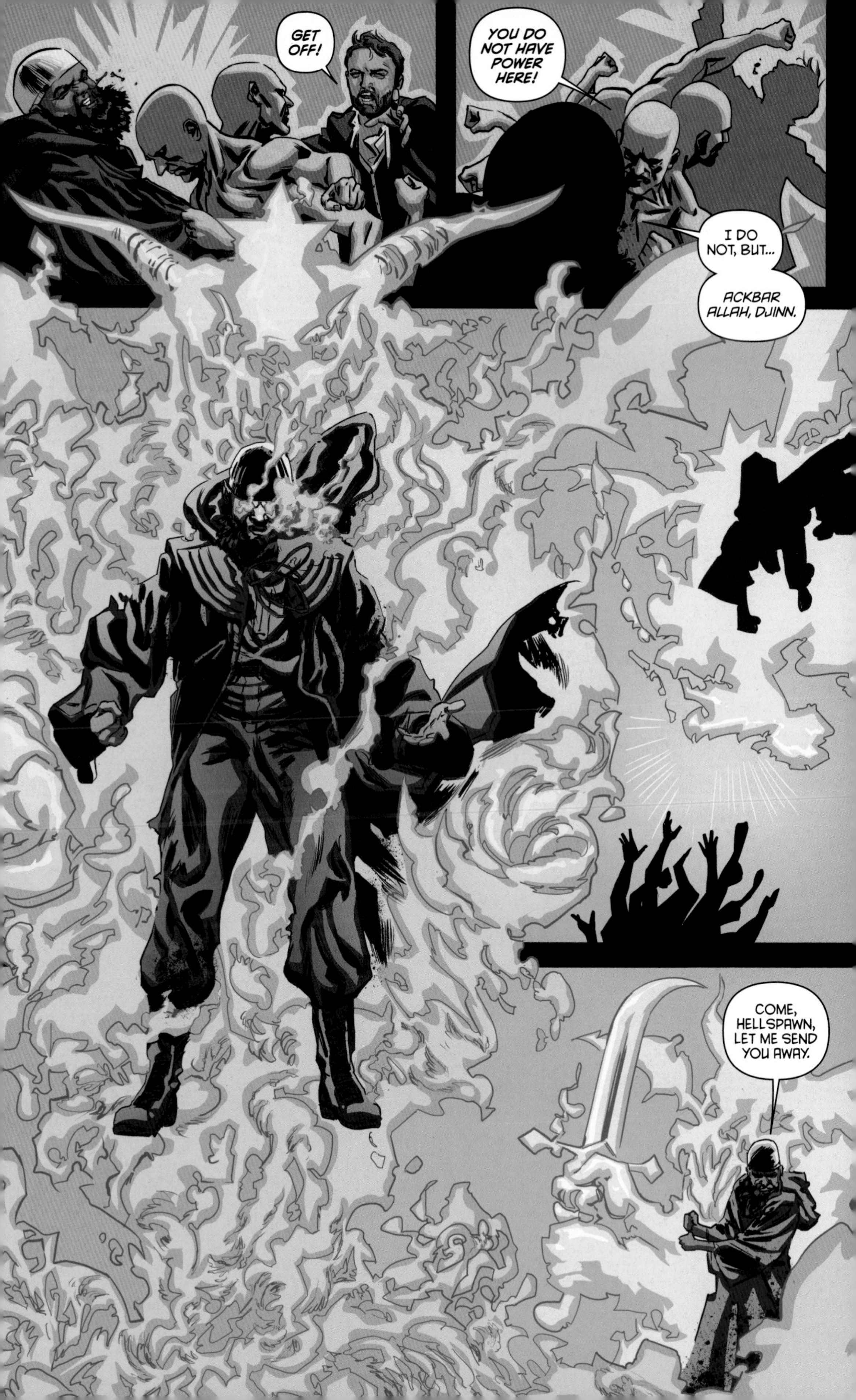
GET OFF!
YOU DO NOT HAVE POWER HERE!
I DO NOT, BUT...
ACKBAR ALLAH, DJINN.
COME, HELLSPAWN, LET ME SEND YOU AWAY.

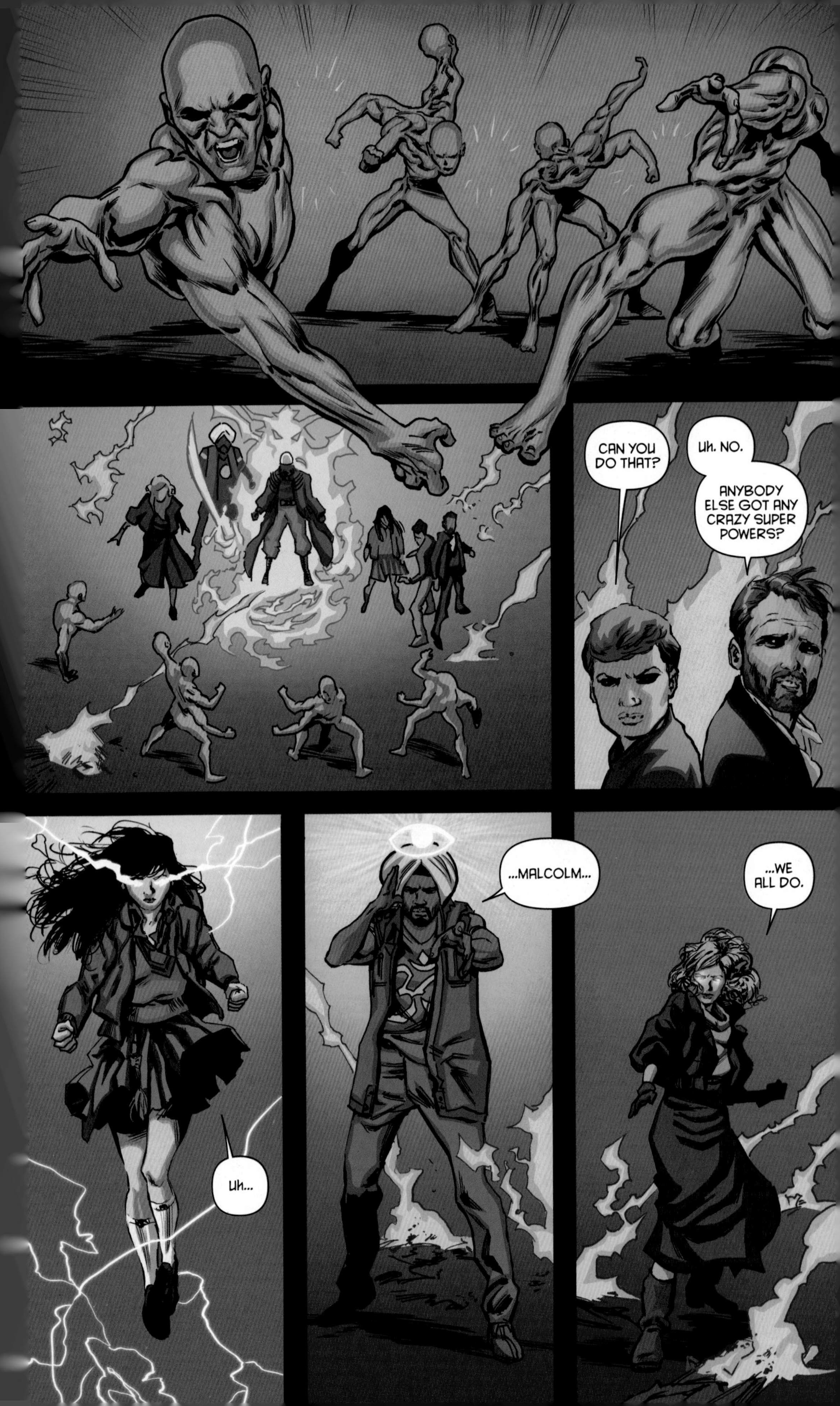
CAN YOU DO THAT?
UH. NO.
ANYBODY ELSE GOT ANY CRAZY SUPER POWERS?
UH...
...MALCOLM...
...WE ALL DO.

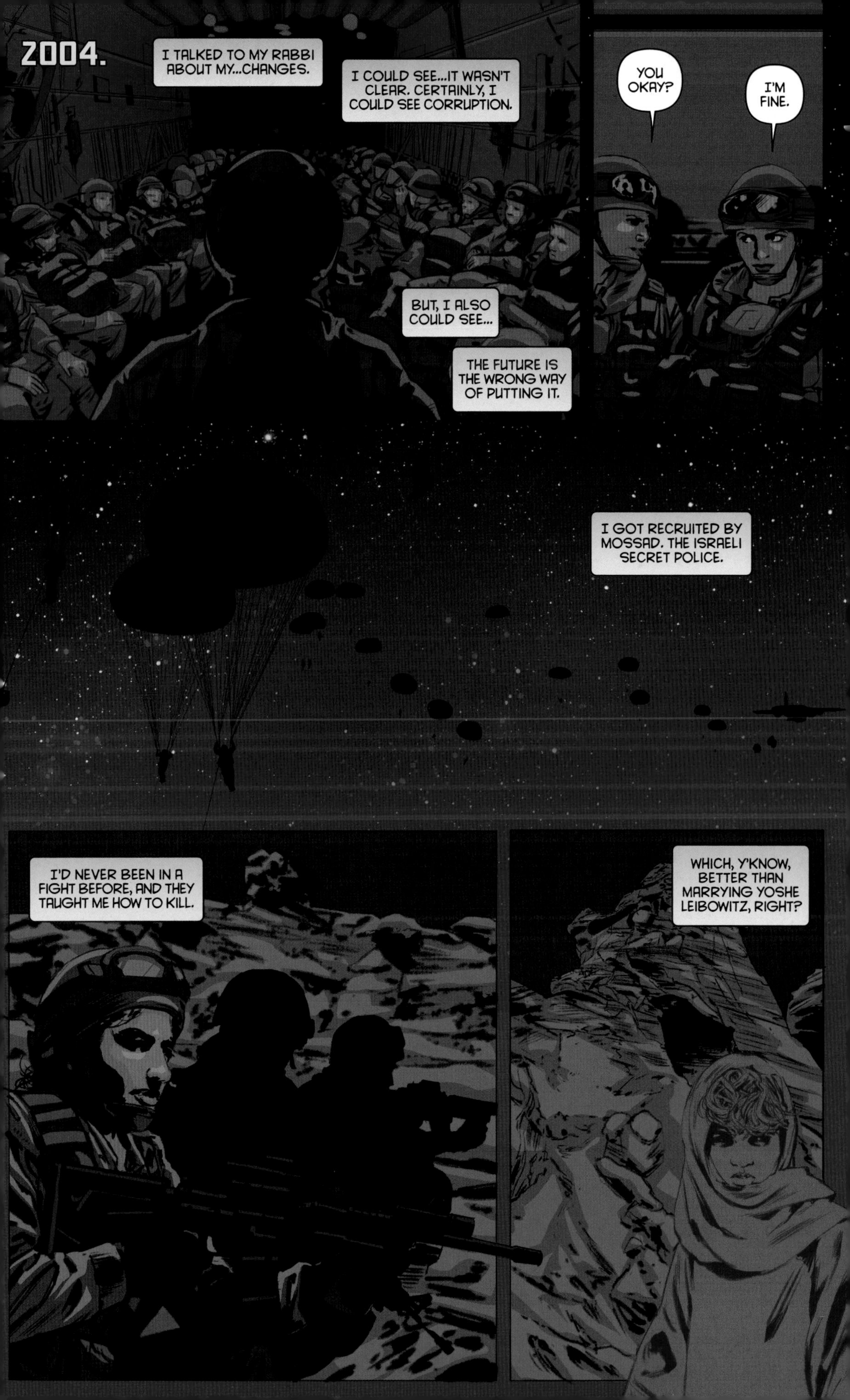
2004.
I TALKED TO MY RABBI ABOUT MY...CHANGES.
I COULD SEE...IT WASN'T CLEAR. CERTAINLY, I COULD SEE CORRUPTION.
BUT, I ALSO COULD SEE...
THE FUTURE IS THE WRONG WAY OF PUTTING IT.
YOU OKAY?
I'M FINE.
I GOT RECRUITED BY MOSSAD. THE ISRAELI SECRET POLICE.
I'D NEVER BEEN IN A FIGHT BEFORE, AND THEY TAUGHT ME HOW TO KILL.
WHICH, Y'KNOW, BETTER THAN MARRYING YOSHE LEIBOWITZ, RIGHT?

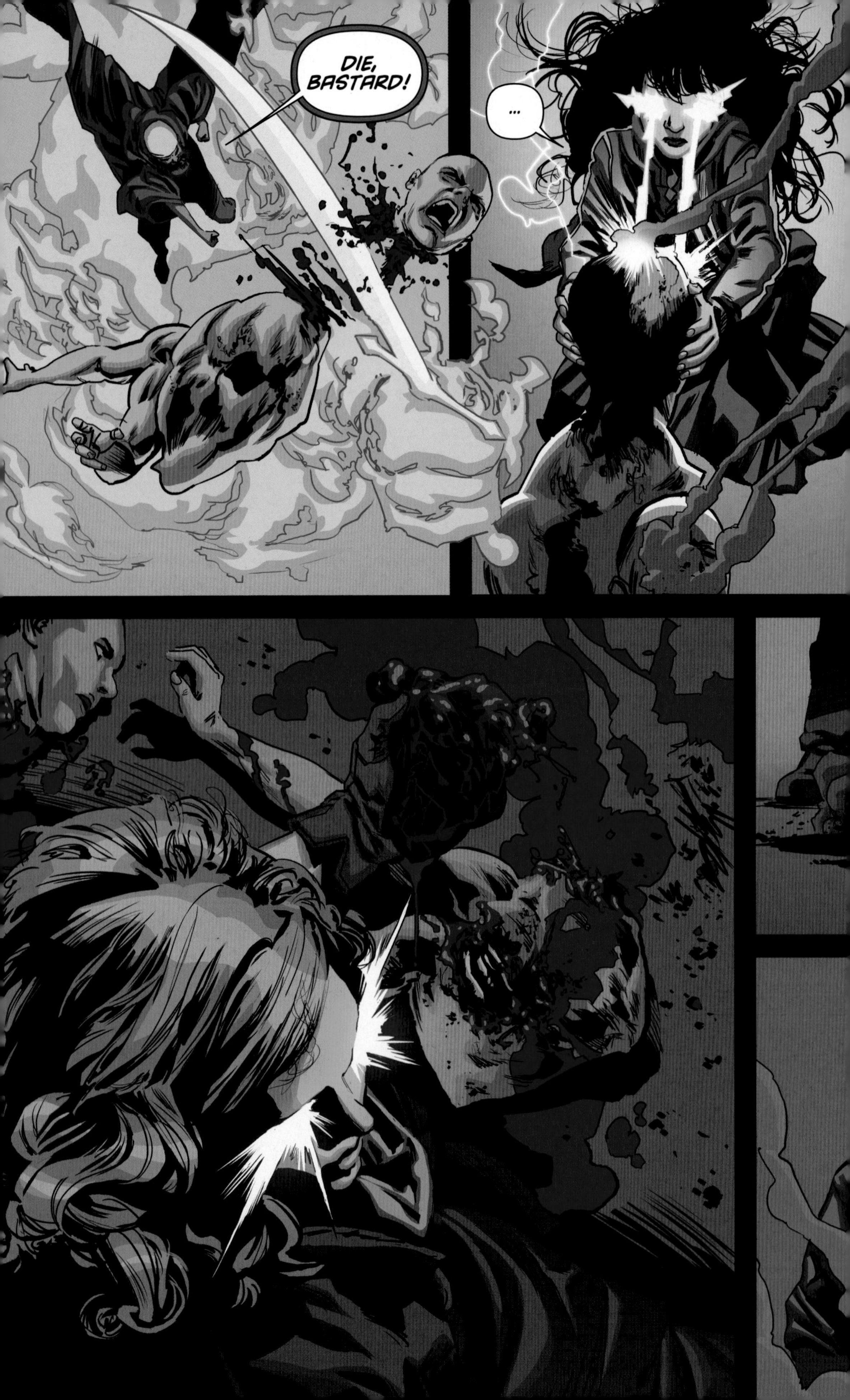
DIE, BASTARD!
...

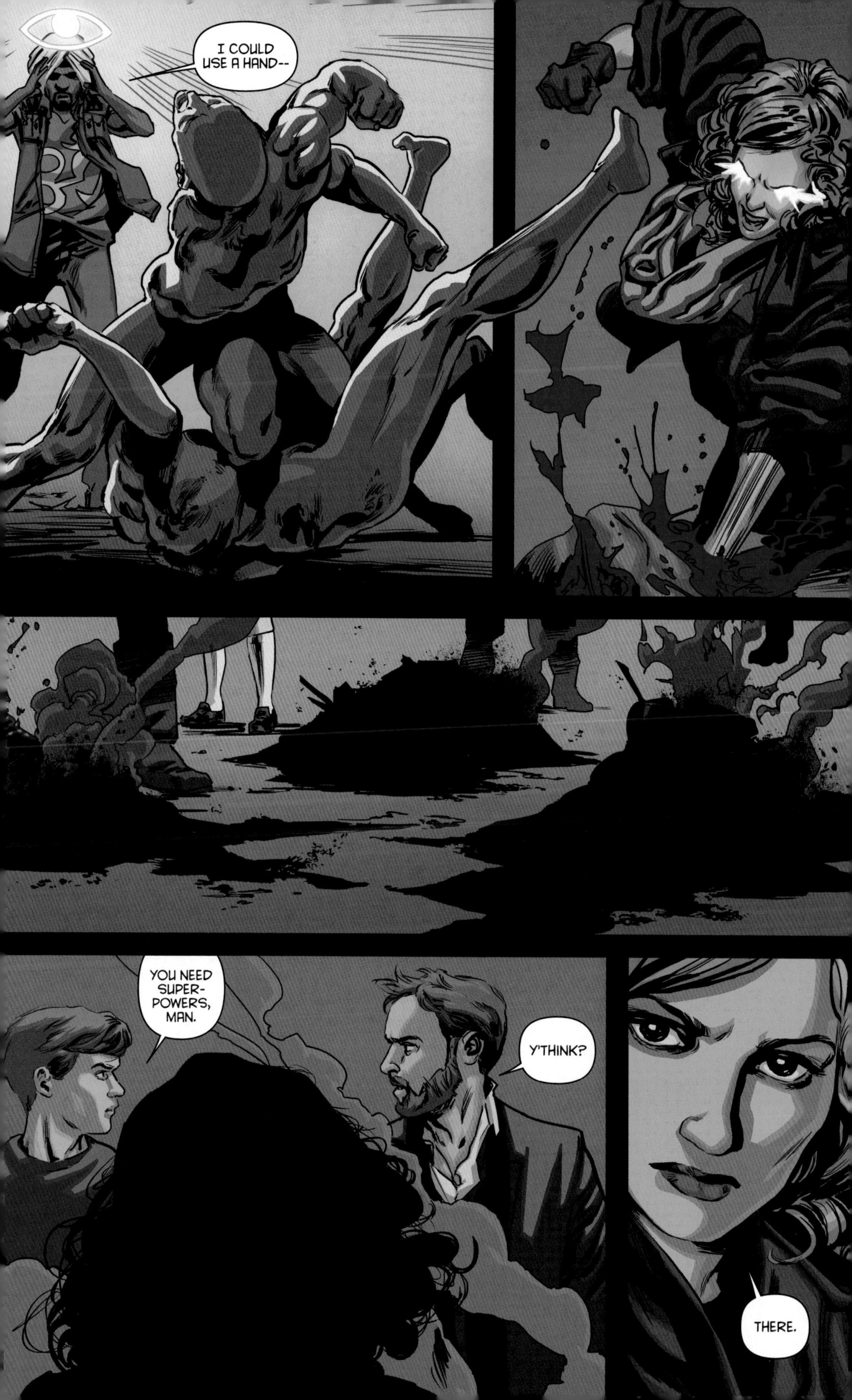
I COULD USE A HAND--
YOU NEED SUPER-POWERS, MAN.
Y'THINK?
THERE.

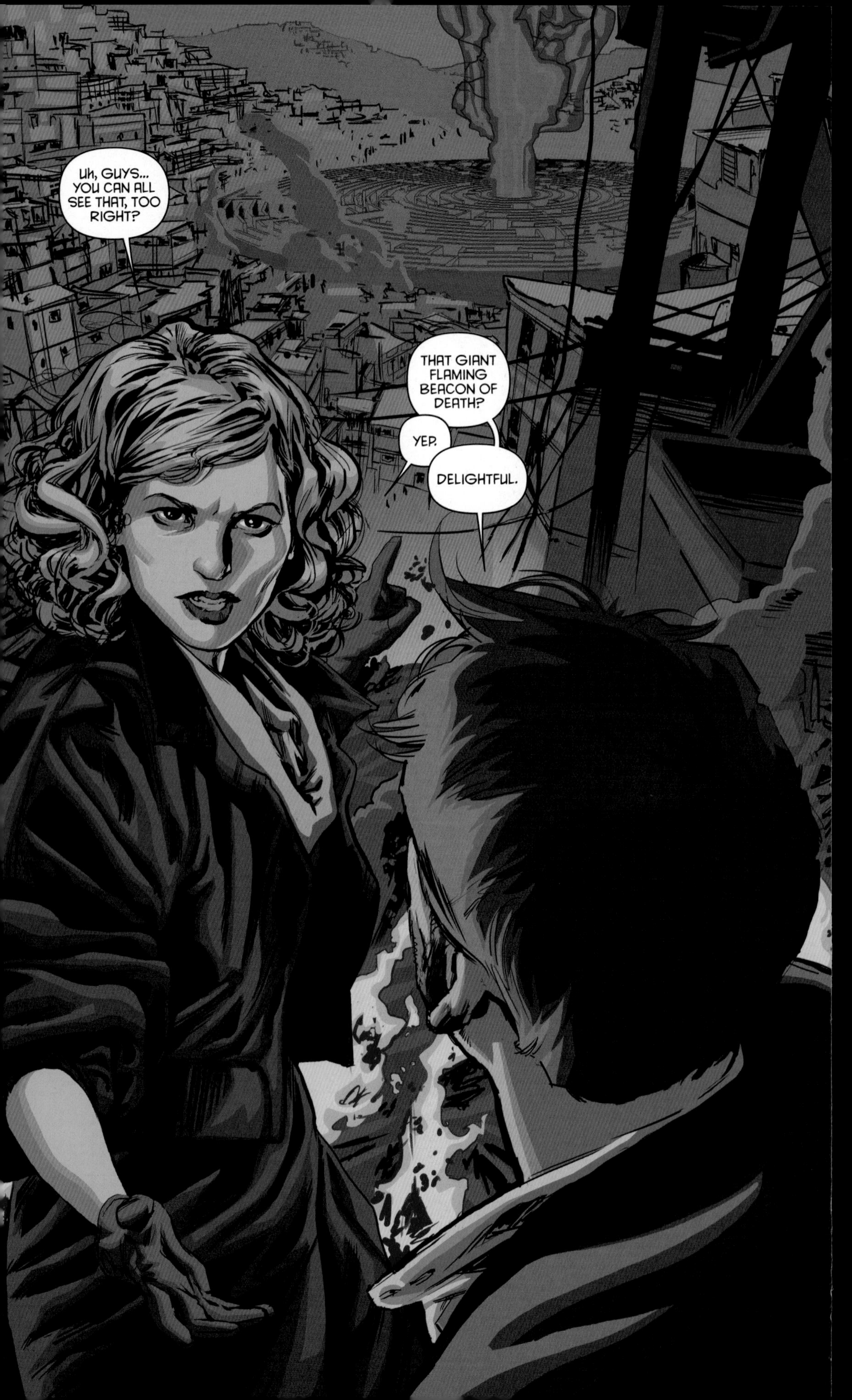
Uh, GUYS... YOU CAN ALL SEE THAT, TOO RIGHT?
THAT GIANT FLAMING BEACON OF DEATH?
YEP.
DELIGHTFUL.

2008.

I DON'T UNDERSTAND WHY YOU'RE HERE, CARDINAL--

NO. I SUPPOSE YOU WOULDN'T.

WE NEED YOU.

I'M SORRY, THE CATHOLIC CHURCH NEEDS A JEWISH SOLDIER?

YOU'RE JUST A SOLDIER LIKE I'M JUST A SUNDAY SCHOOL TEACHER.

THAT MY GOVERNMENT LET YOU IN HERE IS...ODD ENOUGH--

YES, BECAUSE I'M SOME SORT OF JEWISH SUPERHERO.

EXCEPT FOR THE PART WHERE I TORTURE A SMALL CHILD--

THE BOY IS WHY I KNOW WE NEED YOU.

BRENDA...WE KNOW ABOUT YOUR GIFT. WE KNOW MORE ABOUT IT THAN YOU DO.

AND WHEN I SAID "WE" NEED YOU, I DIDN'T MEAN THE CATHOLICS.

I MEANT HUMANITY.

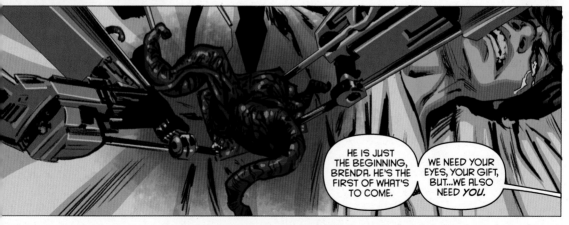

HE IS JUST THE BEGINNING, BRENDA. HE'S THE FIRST OF WHAT'S TO COME.

WE NEED YOUR EYES, YOUR GIFT, BUT...WE ALSO NEED YOU.

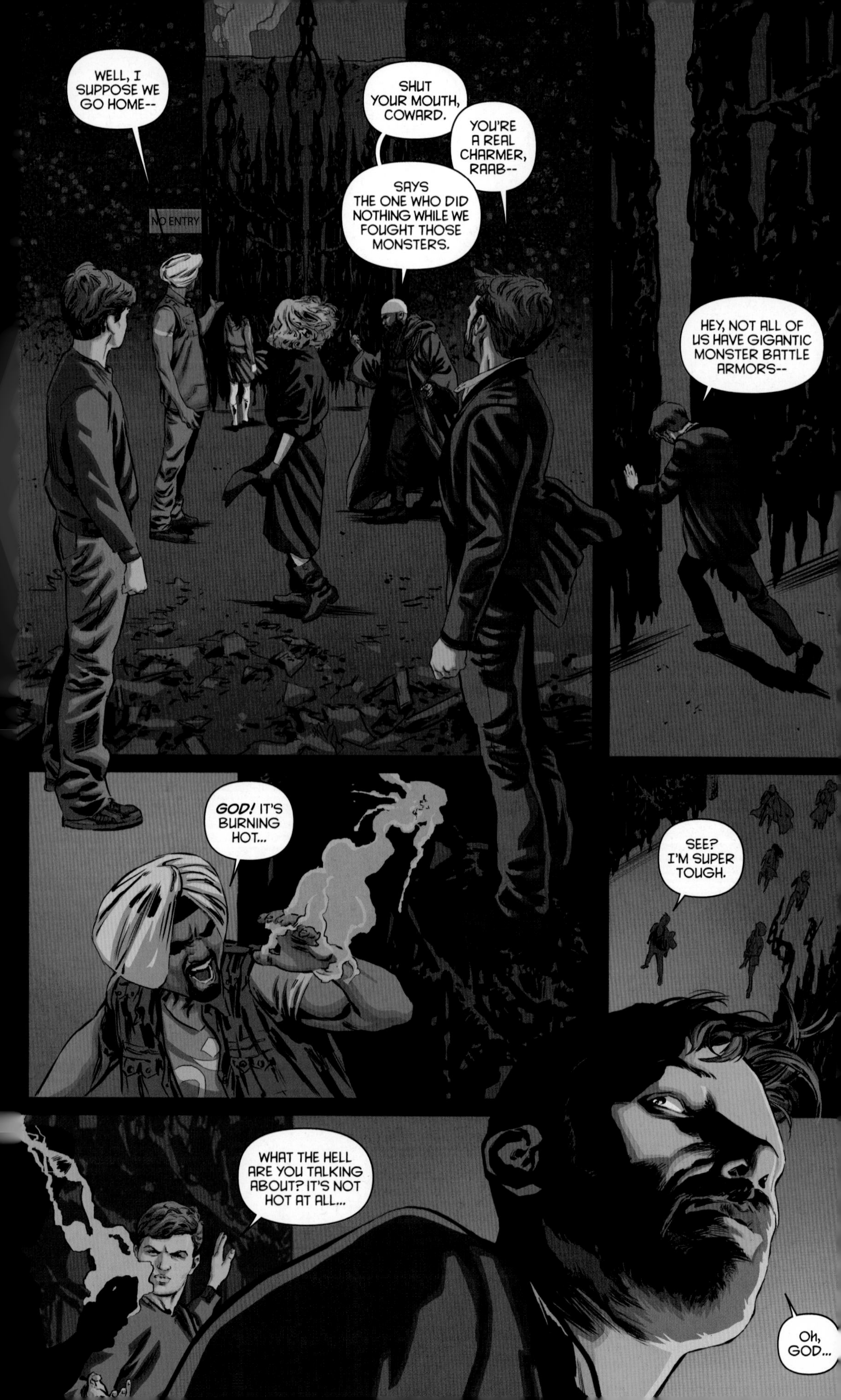
WELL, I SUPPOSE WE GO HOME--
NO ENTRY
SHUT YOUR MOUTH, COWARD.
YOU'RE A REAL CHARMER, RAAB--
SAYS THE ONE WHO DID NOTHING WHILE WE FOUGHT THOSE MONSTERS.
HEY, NOT ALL OF US HAVE GIGANTIC MONSTER BATTLE ARMORS--
GOD! IT'S BURNING HOT...
SEE? I'M SUPER TOUGH.
WHAT THE HELL ARE YOU TALKING ABOUT? IT'S NOT HOT AT ALL...
OH, GOD...

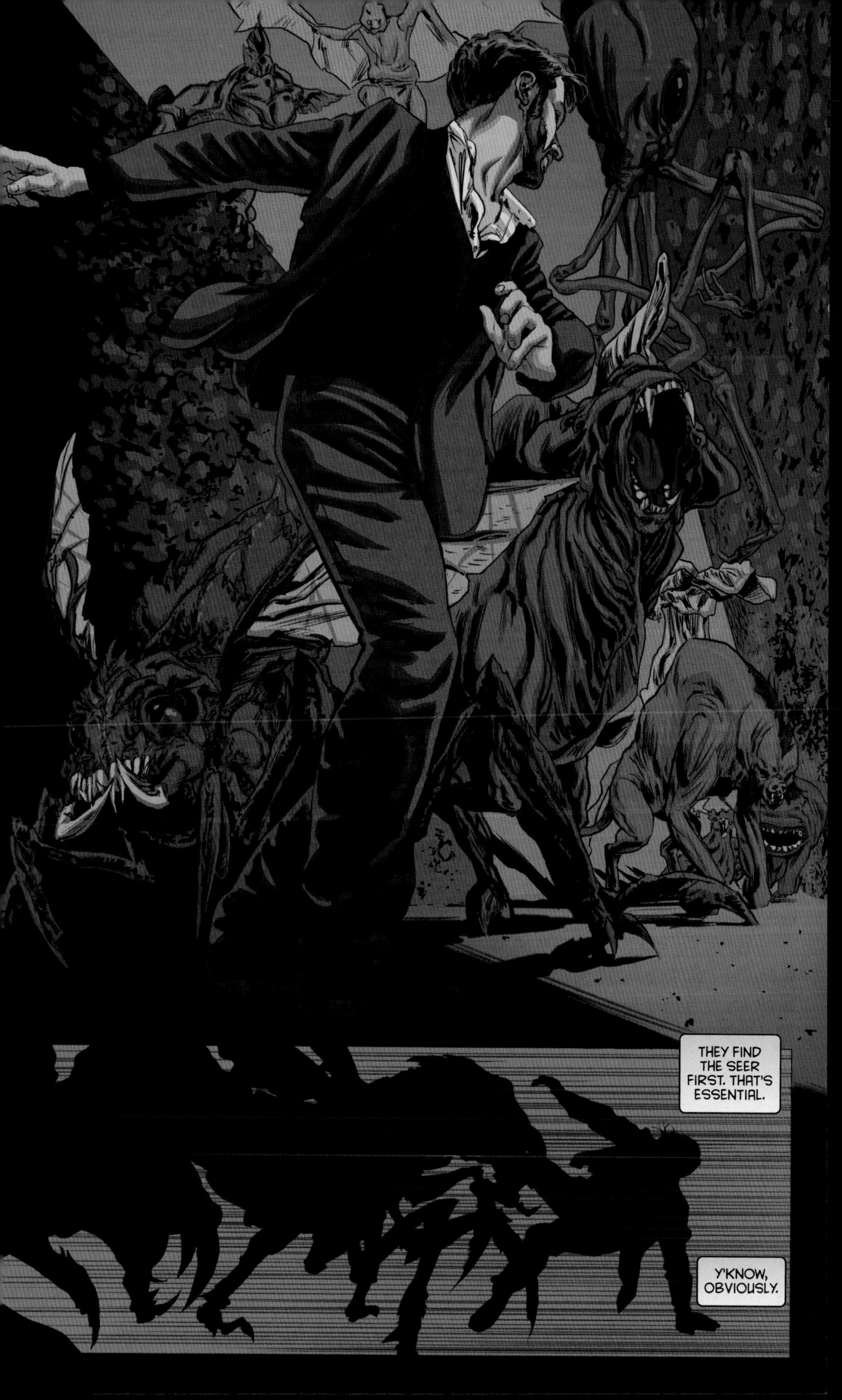
THEY FIND THE SEER FIRST. THAT'S ESSENTIAL.
Y'KNOW, OBVIOUSLY.

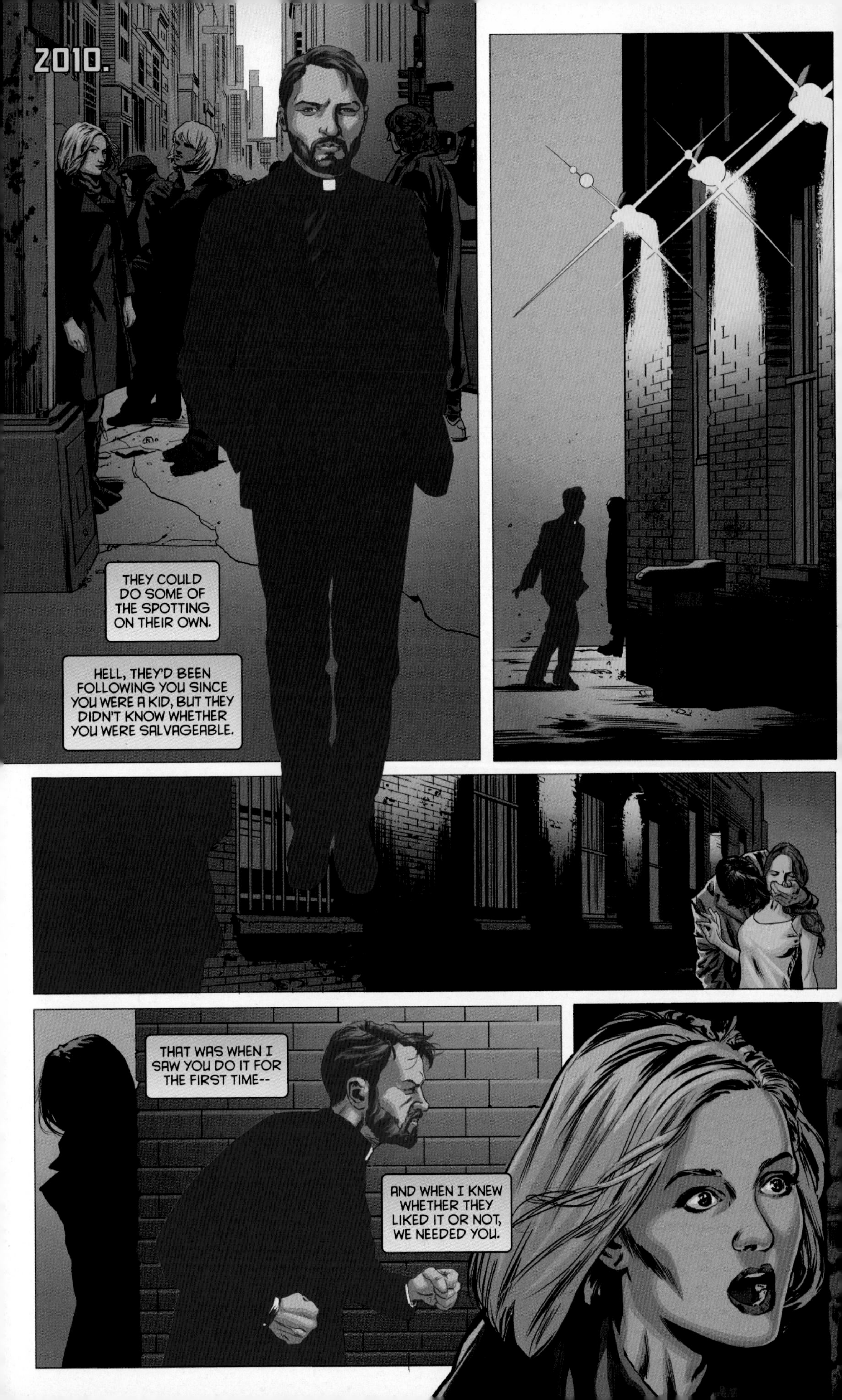
2010.
THEY COULD DO SOME OF THE SPOTTING ON THEIR OWN.
HELL, THEY'D BEEN FOLLOWING YOU SINCE YOU WERE A KID, BUT THEY DIDN'T KNOW WHETHER YOU WERE SALVAGEABLE.
THAT WAS WHEN I SAW YOU DO IT FOR THE FIRST TIME--
AND WHEN I KNEW WHETHER THEY LIKED IT OR NOT, WE NEEDED YOU.

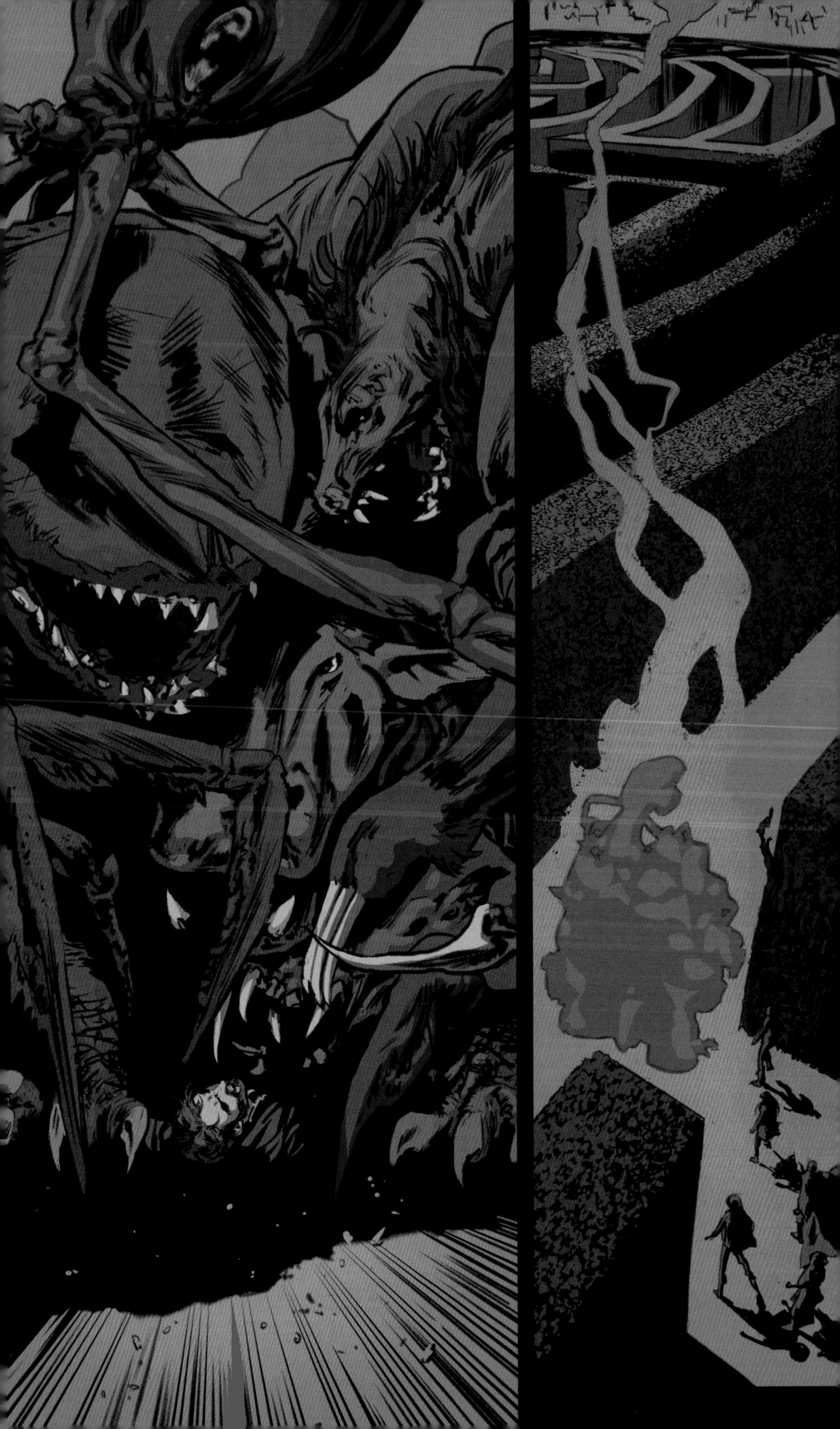

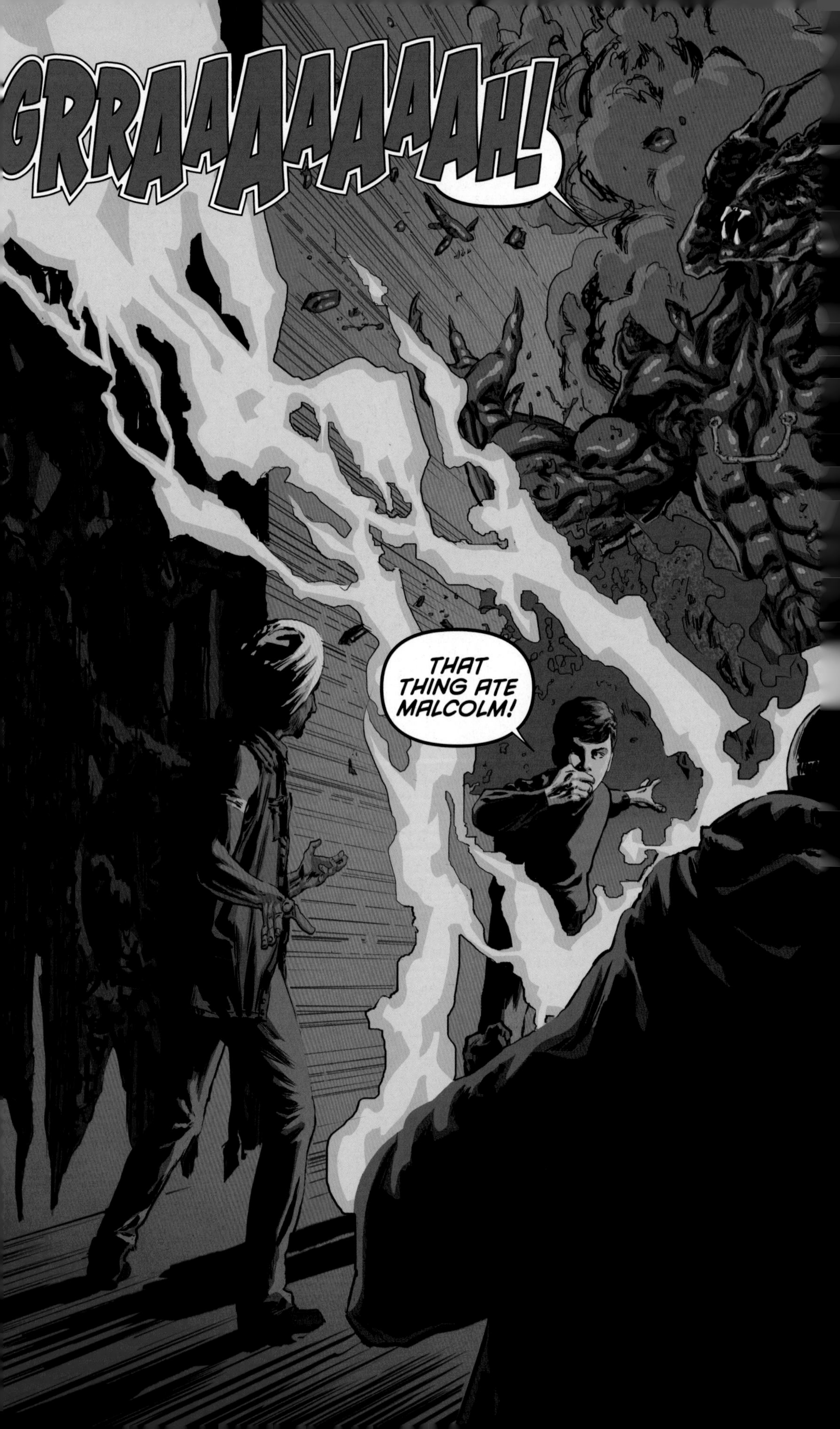
GRRAAAAAAAH!
THAT THING ATE MALCOLM!

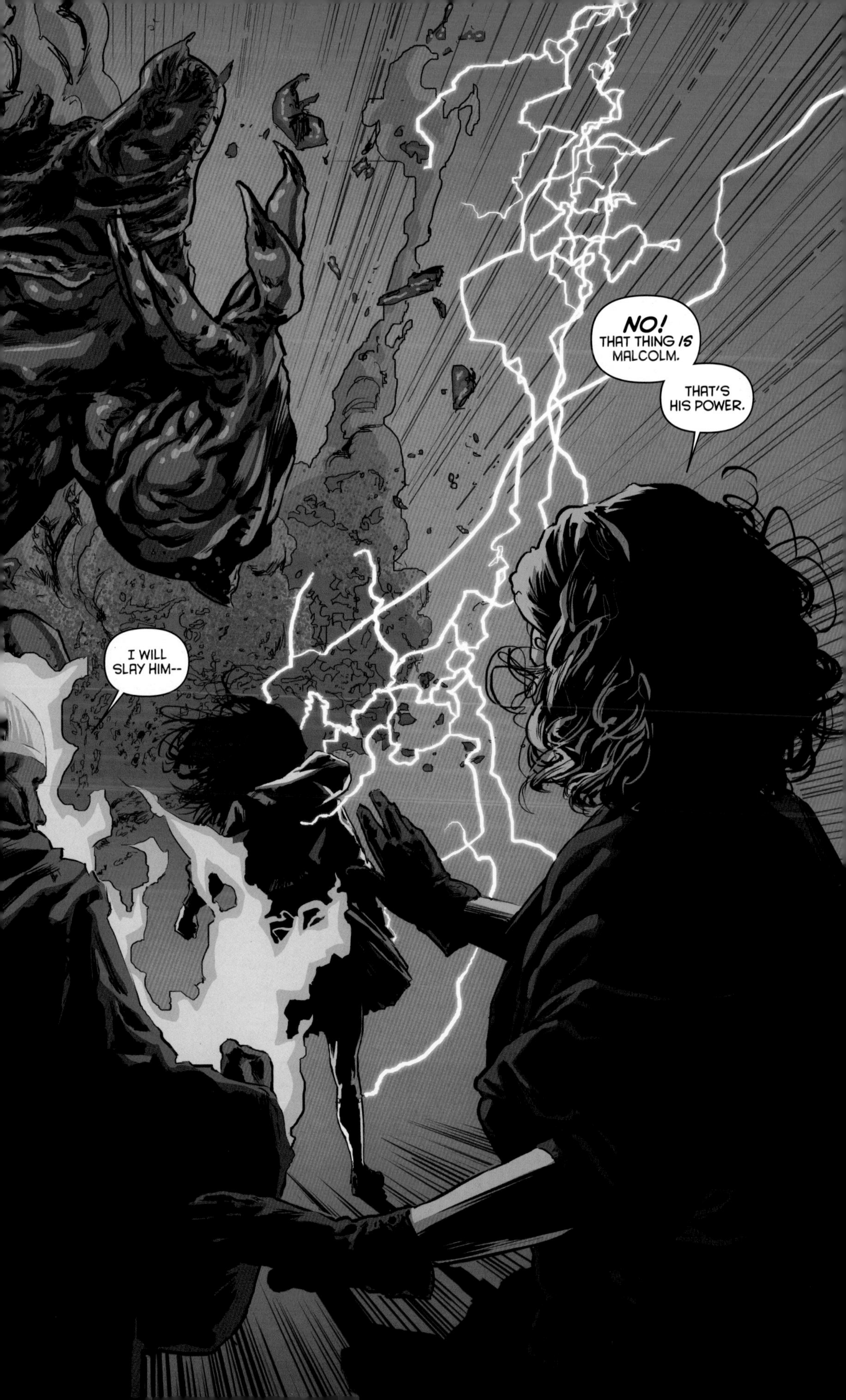
NO! THAT THING IS MALCOLM.
THAT'S HIS POWER.
I WILL SLAY HIM--

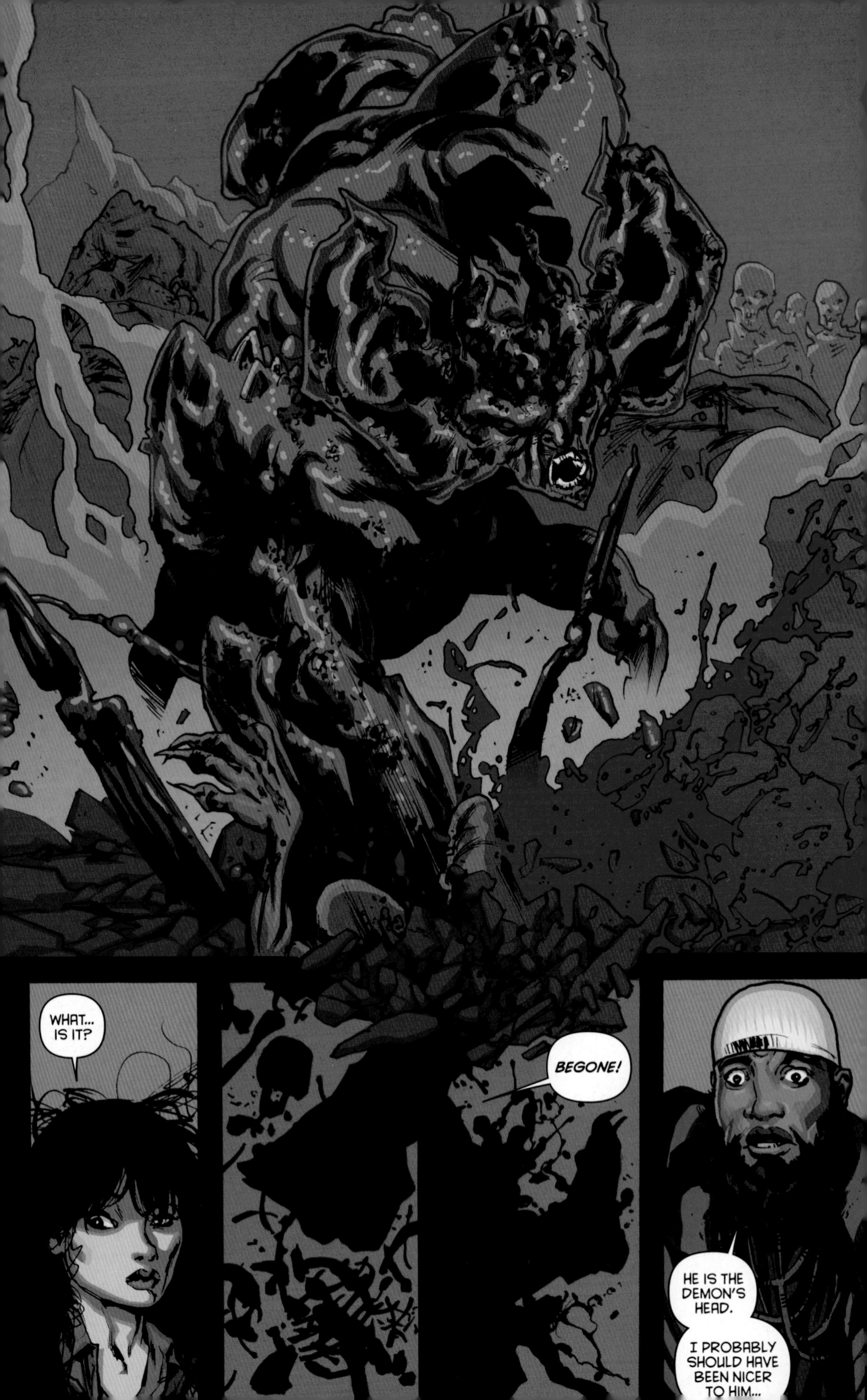
WHAT... IS IT?
BEGONE!
HE IS THE DEMON'S HEAD.
I PROBABLY SHOULD HAVE BEEN NICER TO HIM...

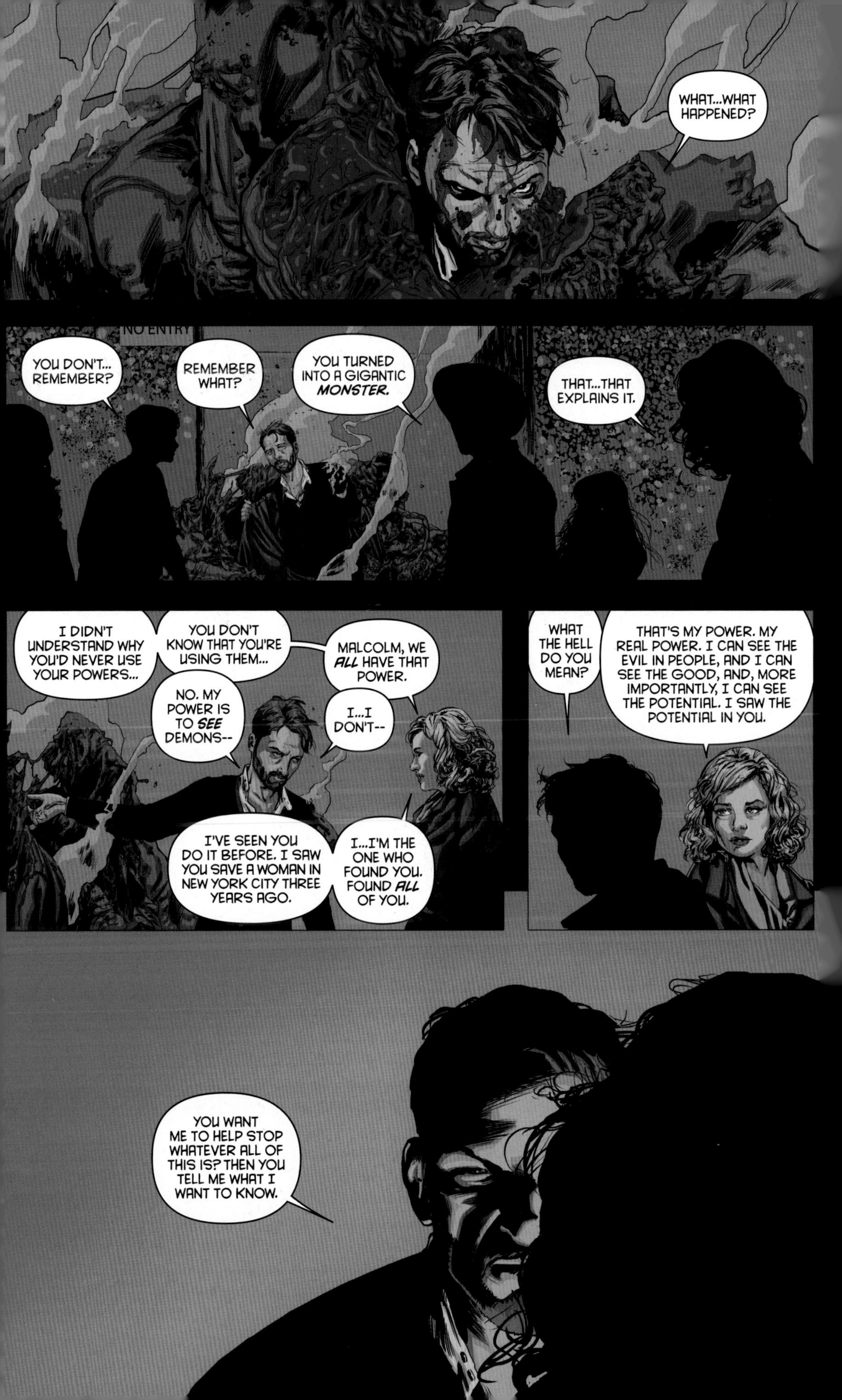
WHAT...WHAT HAPPENED?
NO ENTRY
YOU DON'T... REMEMBER?
REMEMBER WHAT?
YOU TURNED INTO A GIGANTIC **MONSTER.**
THAT...THAT EXPLAINS IT.
I DIDN'T UNDERSTAND WHY YOU'D NEVER USE YOUR POWERS...
YOU DON'T KNOW THAT YOU'RE USING THEM...
NO. MY POWER IS TO **SEE** DEMONS--
MALCOLM, WE **ALL** HAVE THAT POWER.
I...I DON'T--
I'VE SEEN YOU DO IT BEFORE. I SAW YOU SAVE A WOMAN IN NEW YORK CITY THREE YEARS AGO.
I...I'M THE ONE WHO FOUND YOU. FOUND **ALL** OF YOU.
WHAT THE HELL DO YOU MEAN?
THAT'S MY POWER. MY REAL POWER. I CAN SEE THE EVIL IN PEOPLE, AND I CAN SEE THE GOOD, AND, MORE IMPORTANTLY, I CAN SEE THE POTENTIAL. I SAW THE POTENTIAL IN YOU.
YOU WANT ME TO HELP STOP WHATEVER ALL OF THIS IS? THEN YOU TELL ME WHAT I WANT TO KNOW.

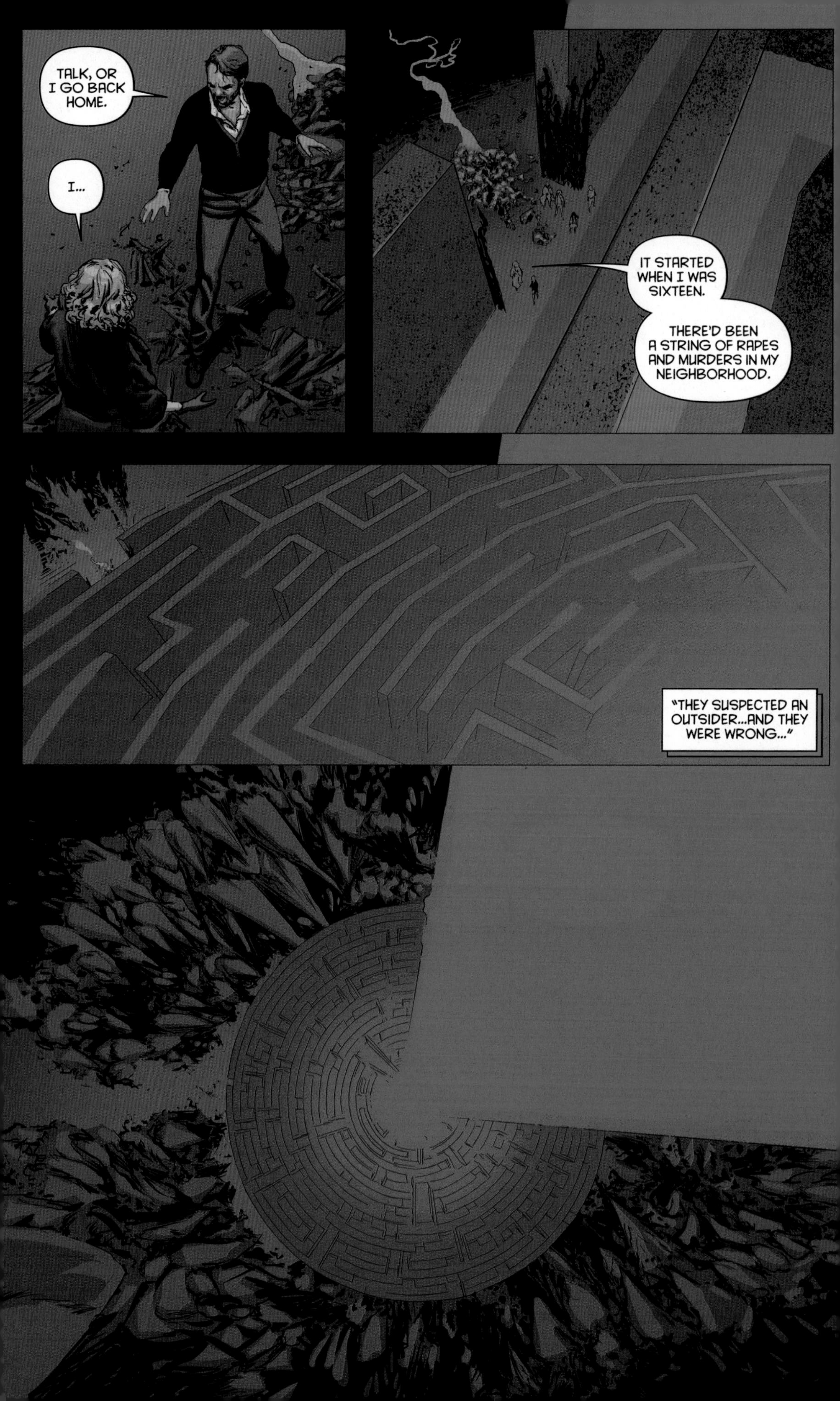
TALK, OR I GO BACK HOME.
I...
IT STARTED WHEN I WAS SIXTEEN.
THERE'D BEEN A STRING OF RAPES AND MURDERS IN MY NEIGHBORHOOD.
"THEY SUSPECTED AN OUTSIDER...AND THEY WERE WRONG..."

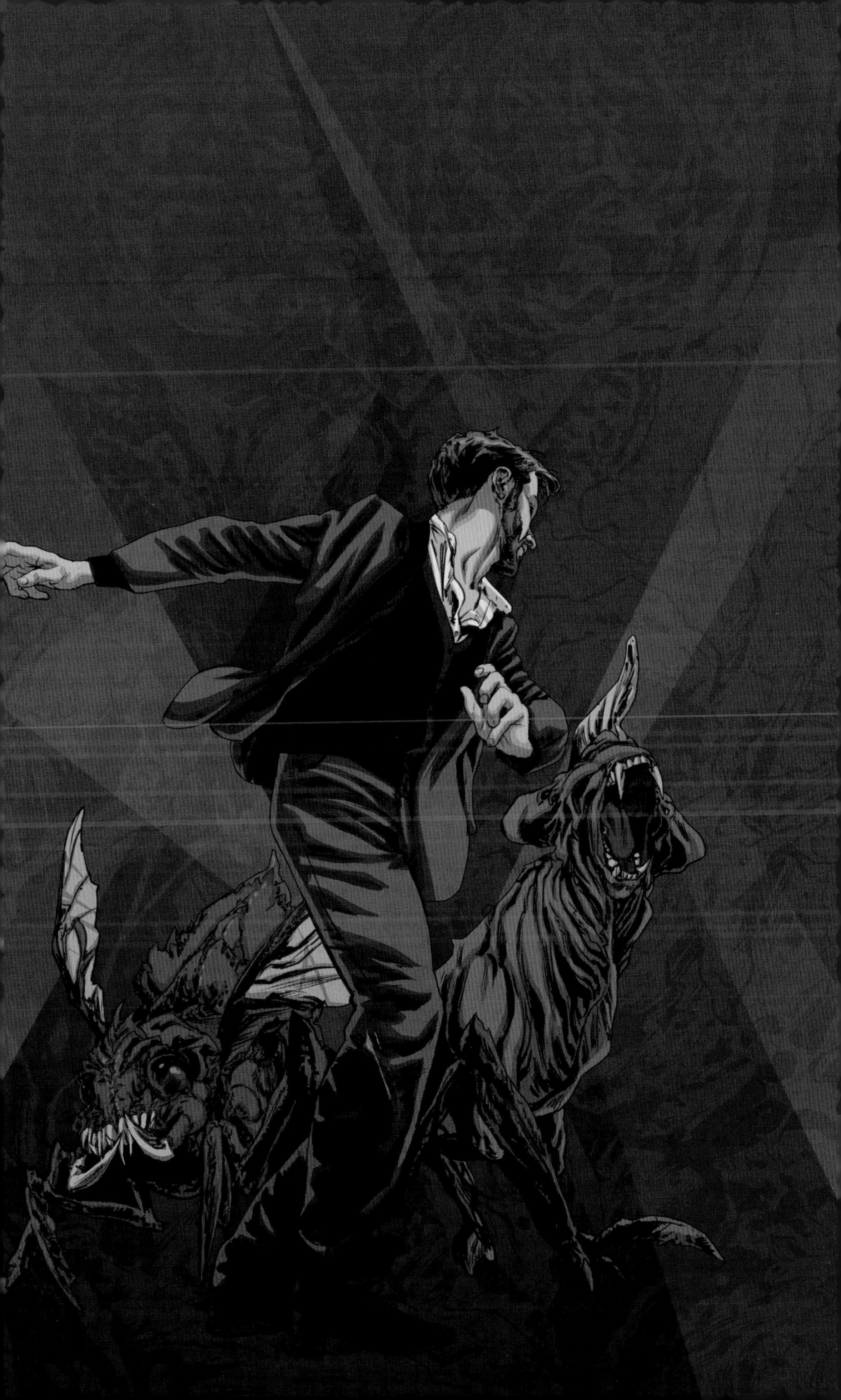

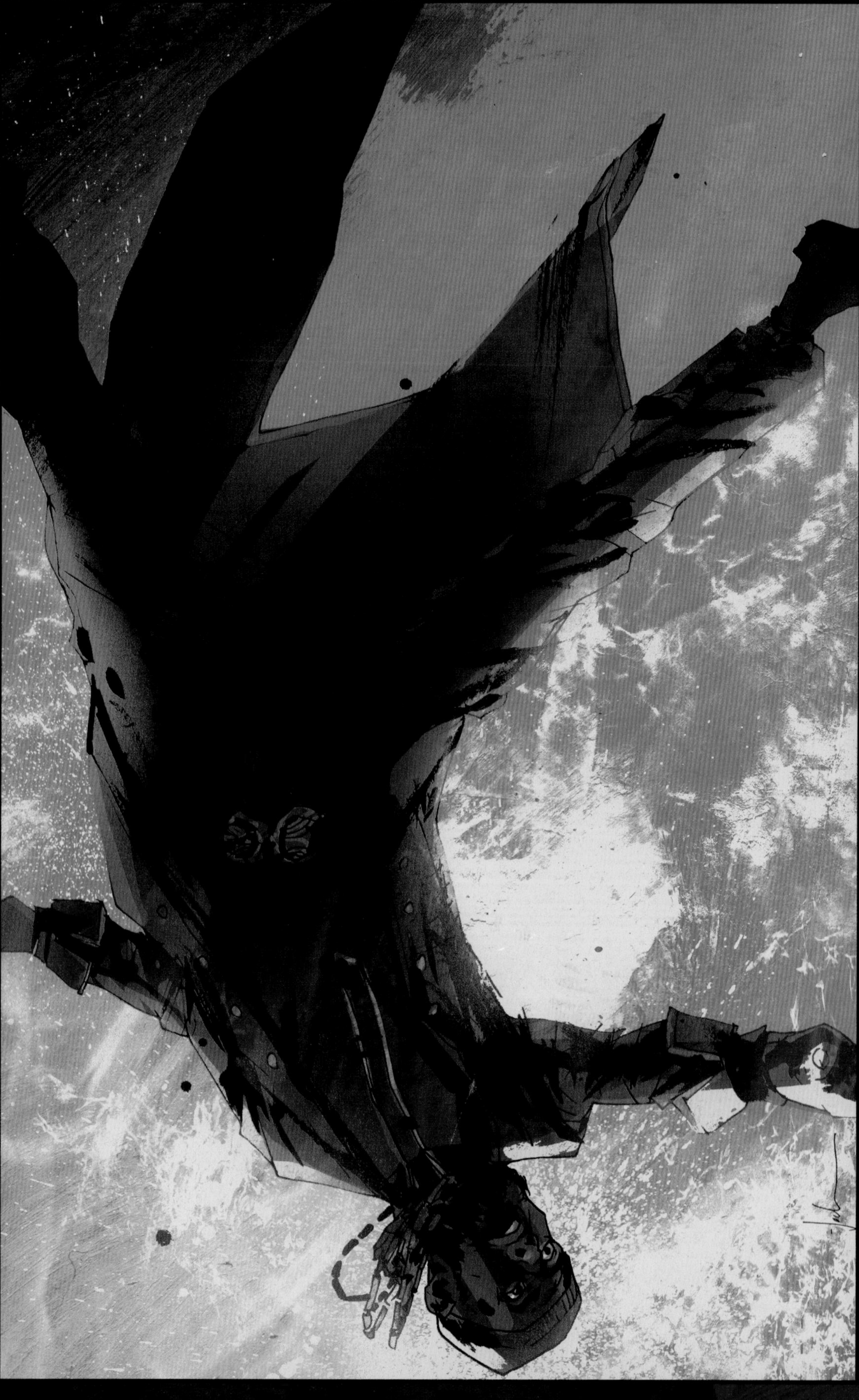

ISSUE #3 cover art by **JOCK**

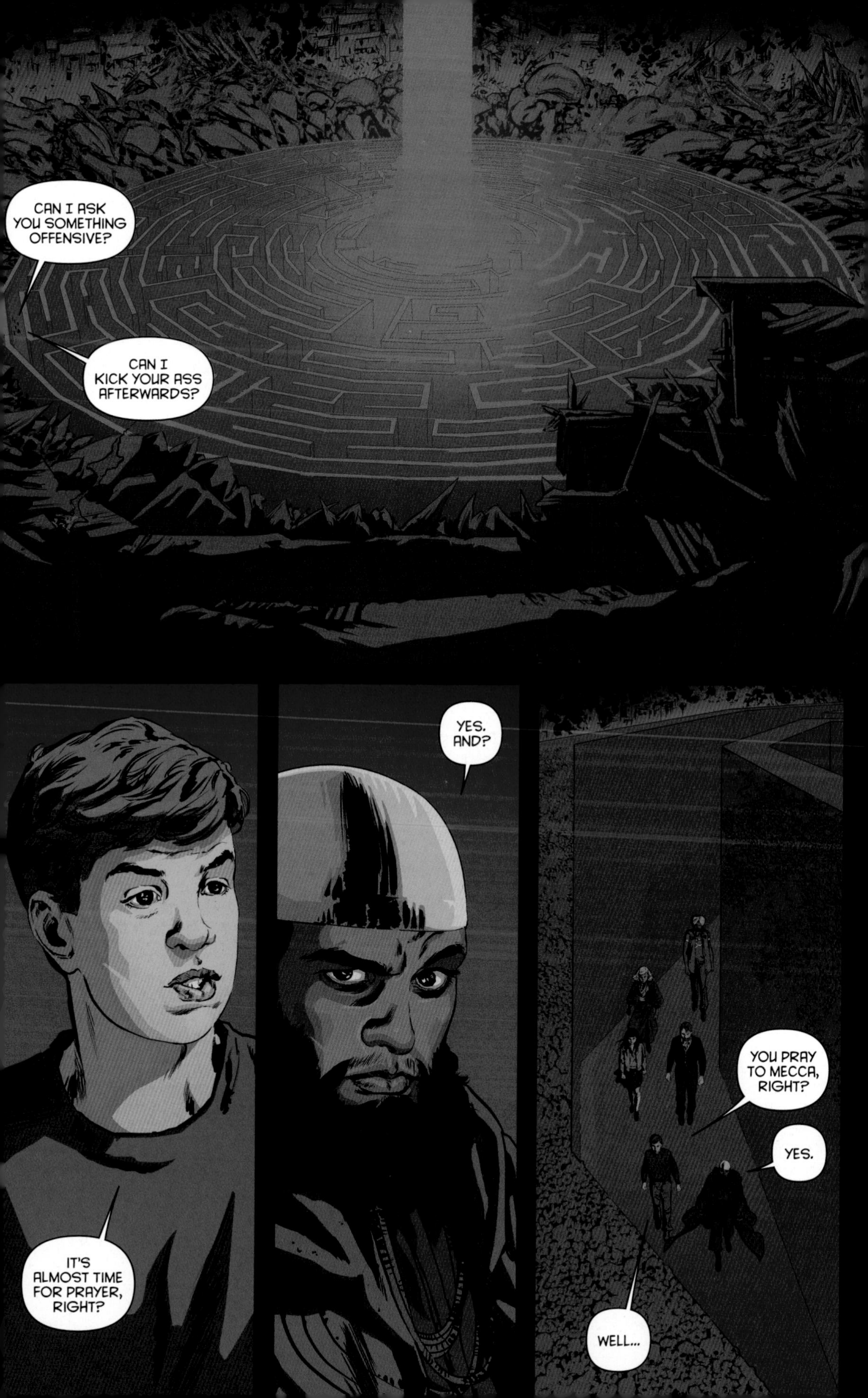
CAN I ASK YOU SOMETHING OFFENSIVE?
CAN I KICK YOUR ASS AFTERWARDS?
YES. AND?
IT'S ALMOST TIME FOR PRAYER, RIGHT?
YOU PRAY TO MECCA, RIGHT?
YES.
WELL...

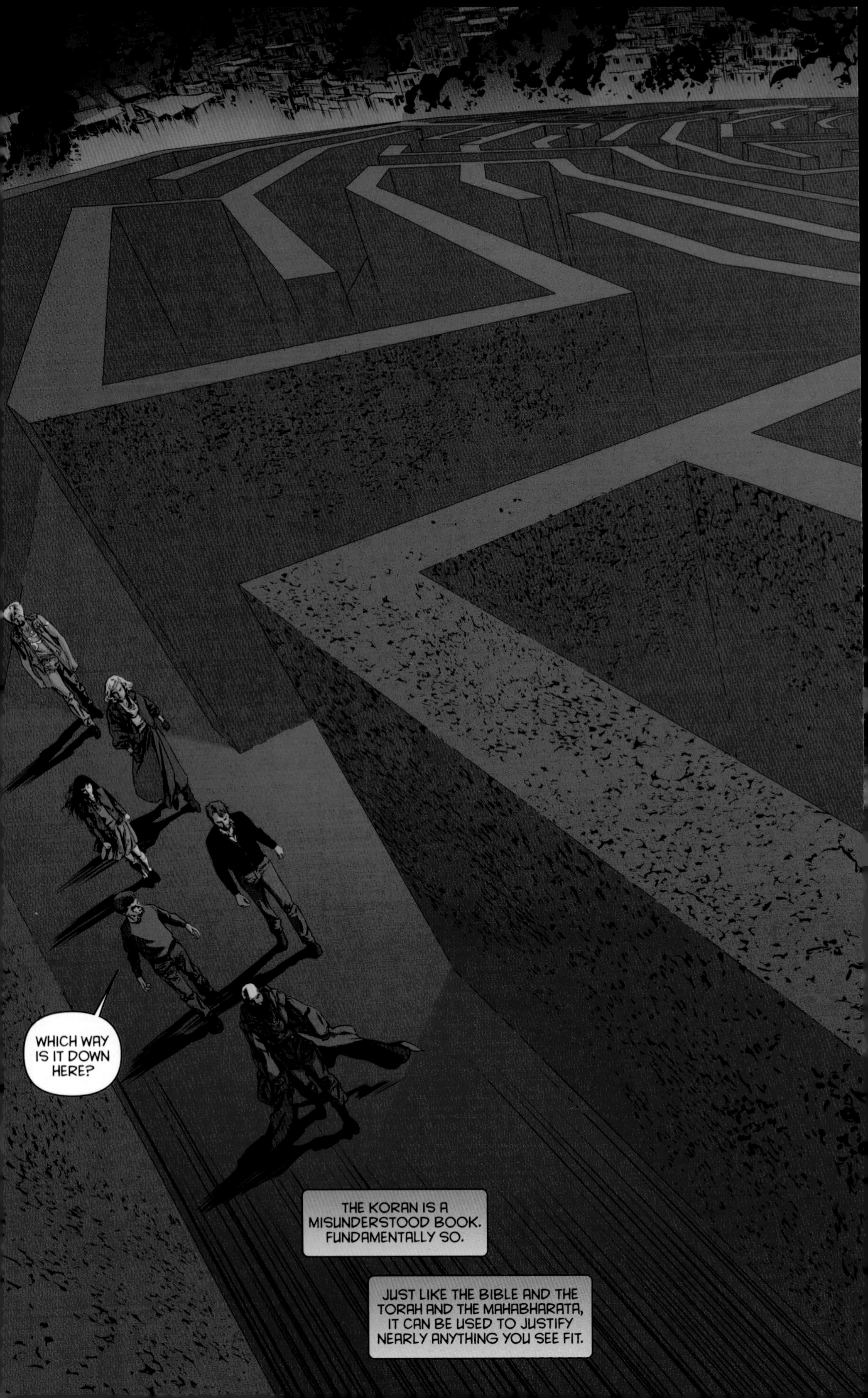
WHICH WAY IS IT DOWN HERE?
THE KORAN IS A MISUNDERSTOOD BOOK. FUNDAMENTALLY SO.
JUST LIKE THE BIBLE AND THE TORAH AND THE MAHABHARATA, IT CAN BE USED TO JUSTIFY NEARLY ANYTHING YOU SEE FIT.

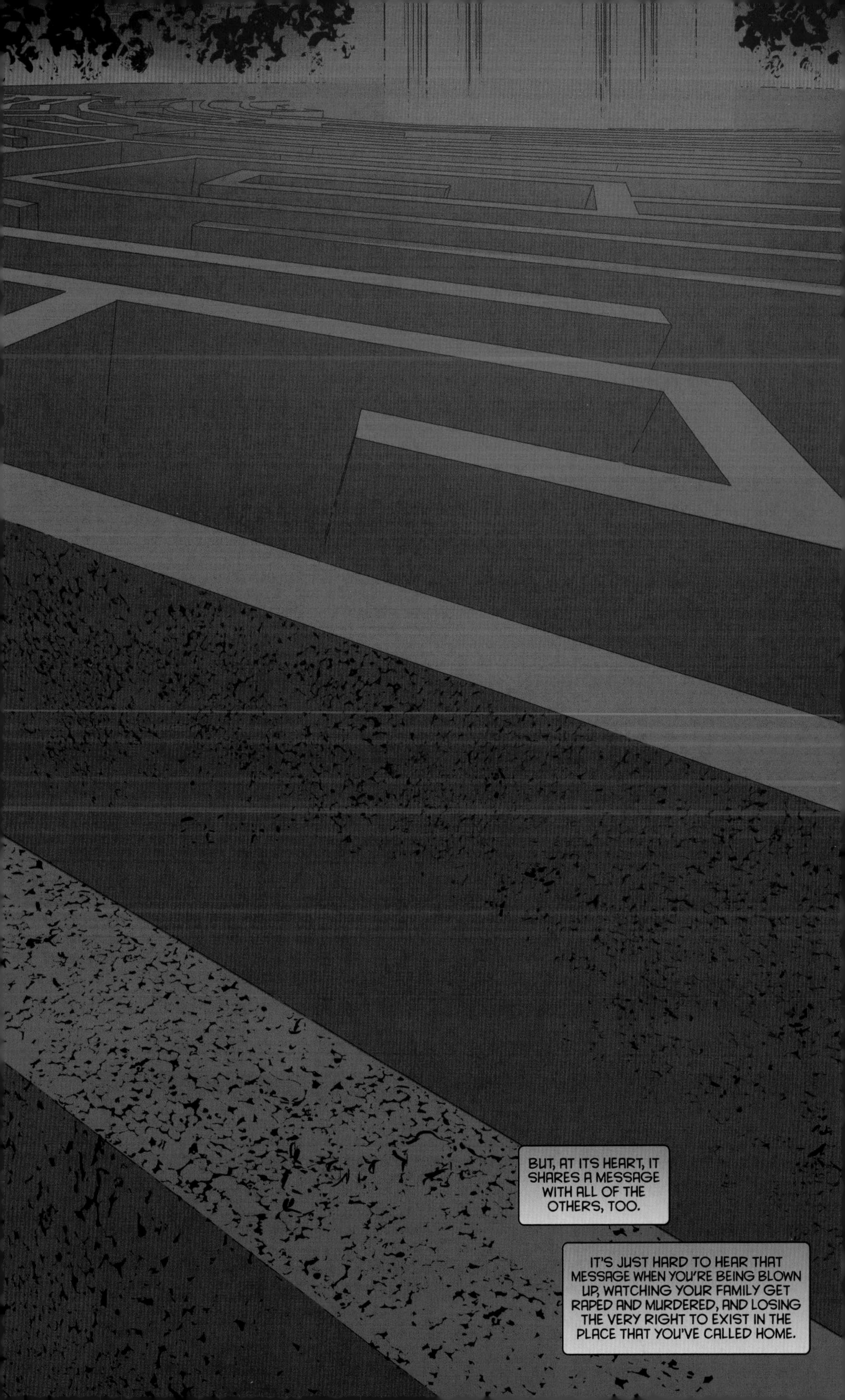
BUT, AT ITS HEART, IT SHARES A MESSAGE WITH ALL OF THE OTHERS, TOO.
IT'S JUST HARD TO HEAR THAT MESSAGE WHEN YOU'RE BEING BLOWN UP, WATCHING YOUR FAMILY GET RAPED AND MURDERED, AND LOSING THE VERY RIGHT TO EXIST IN THE PLACE THAT YOU'VE CALLED HOME.

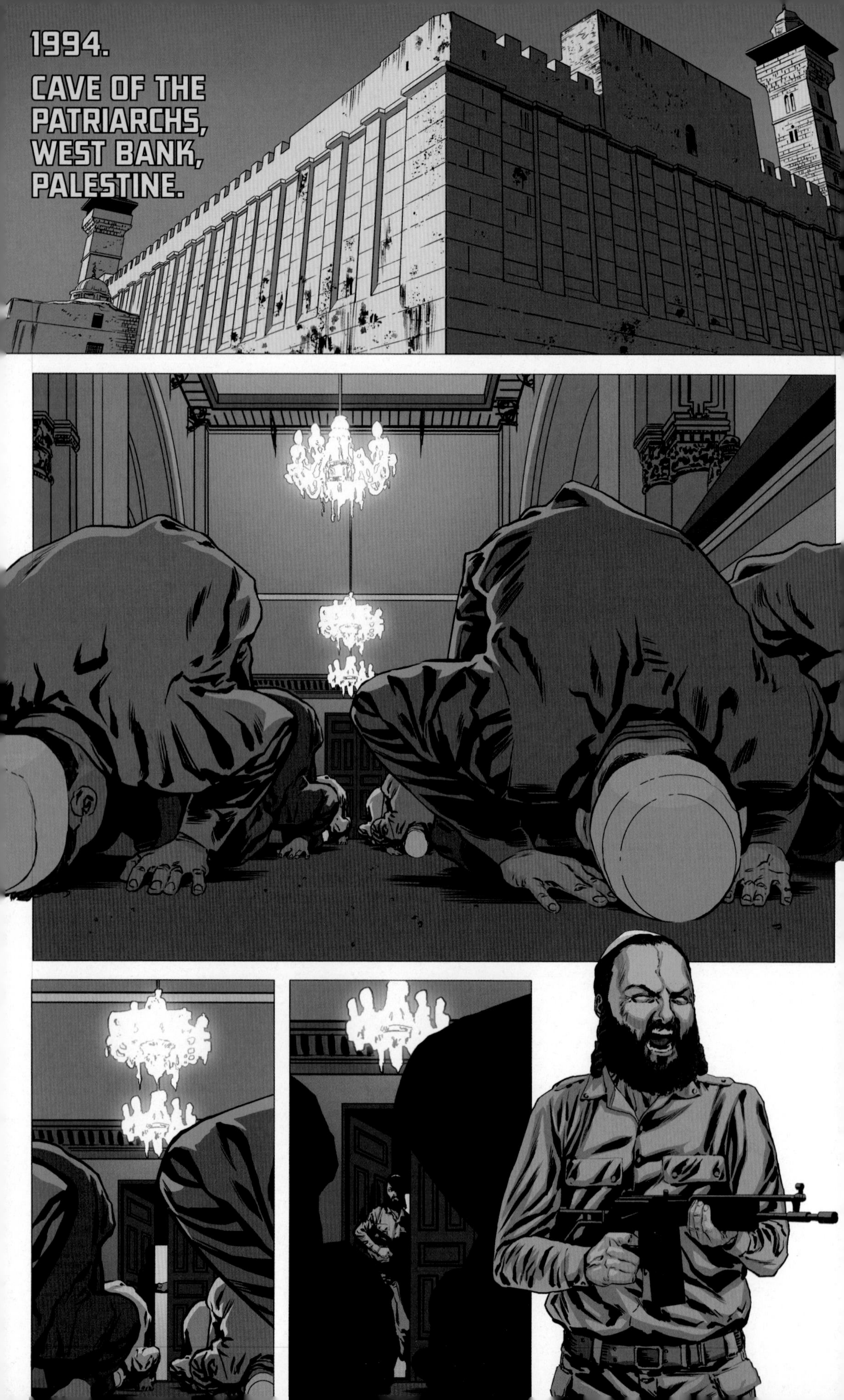
1994.
CAVE OF THE PATRIARCHS, WEST BANK, PALESTINE.

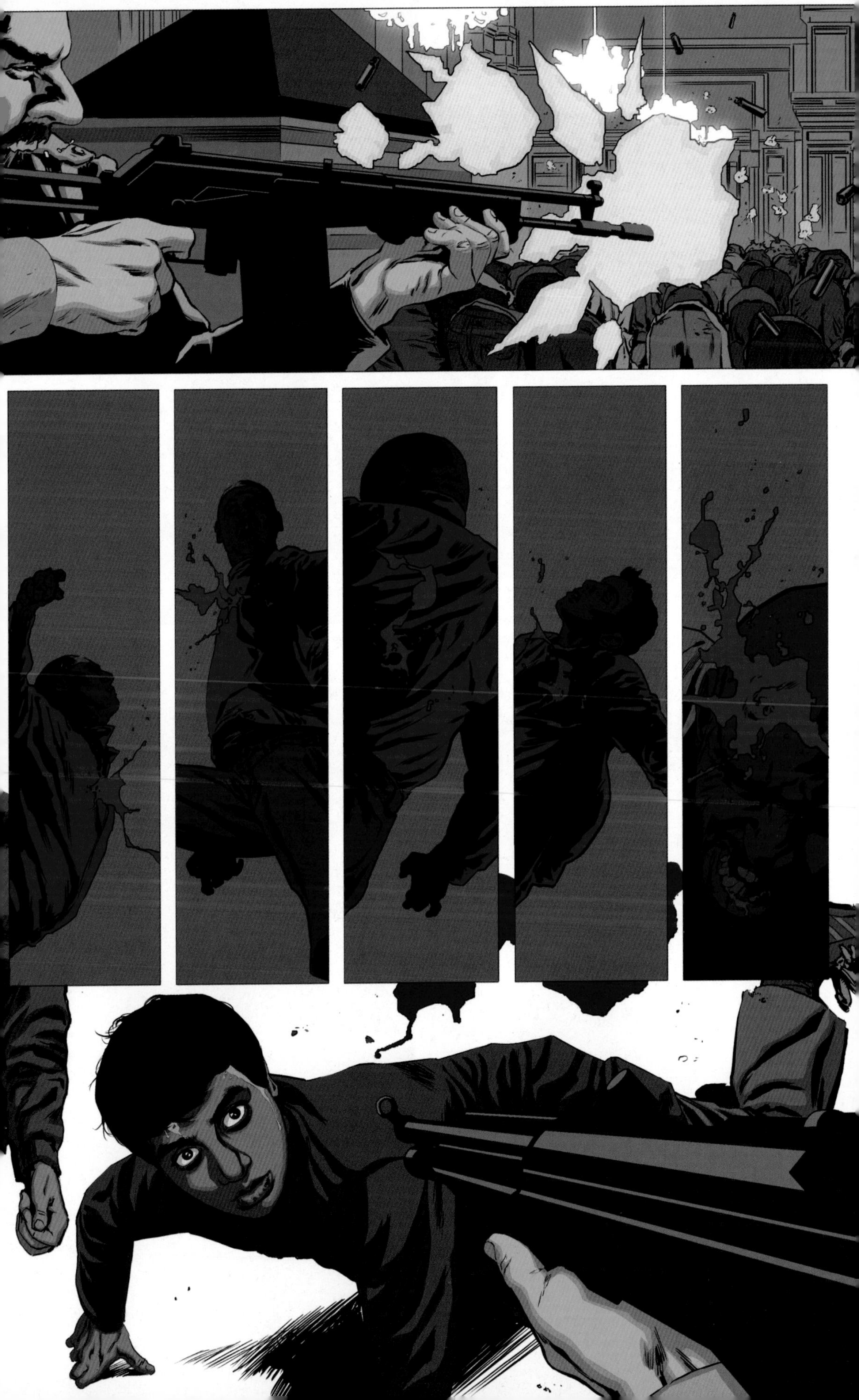

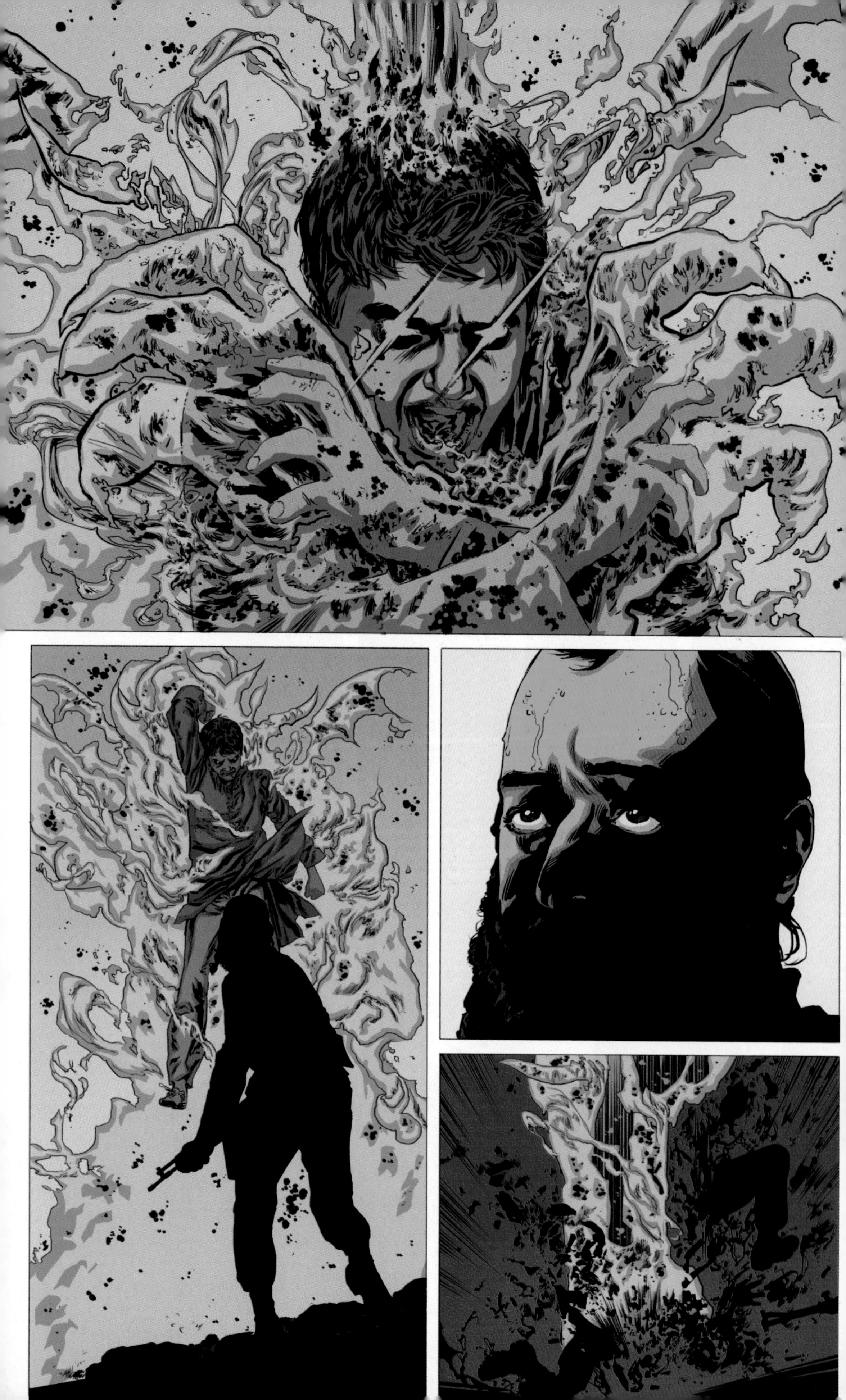

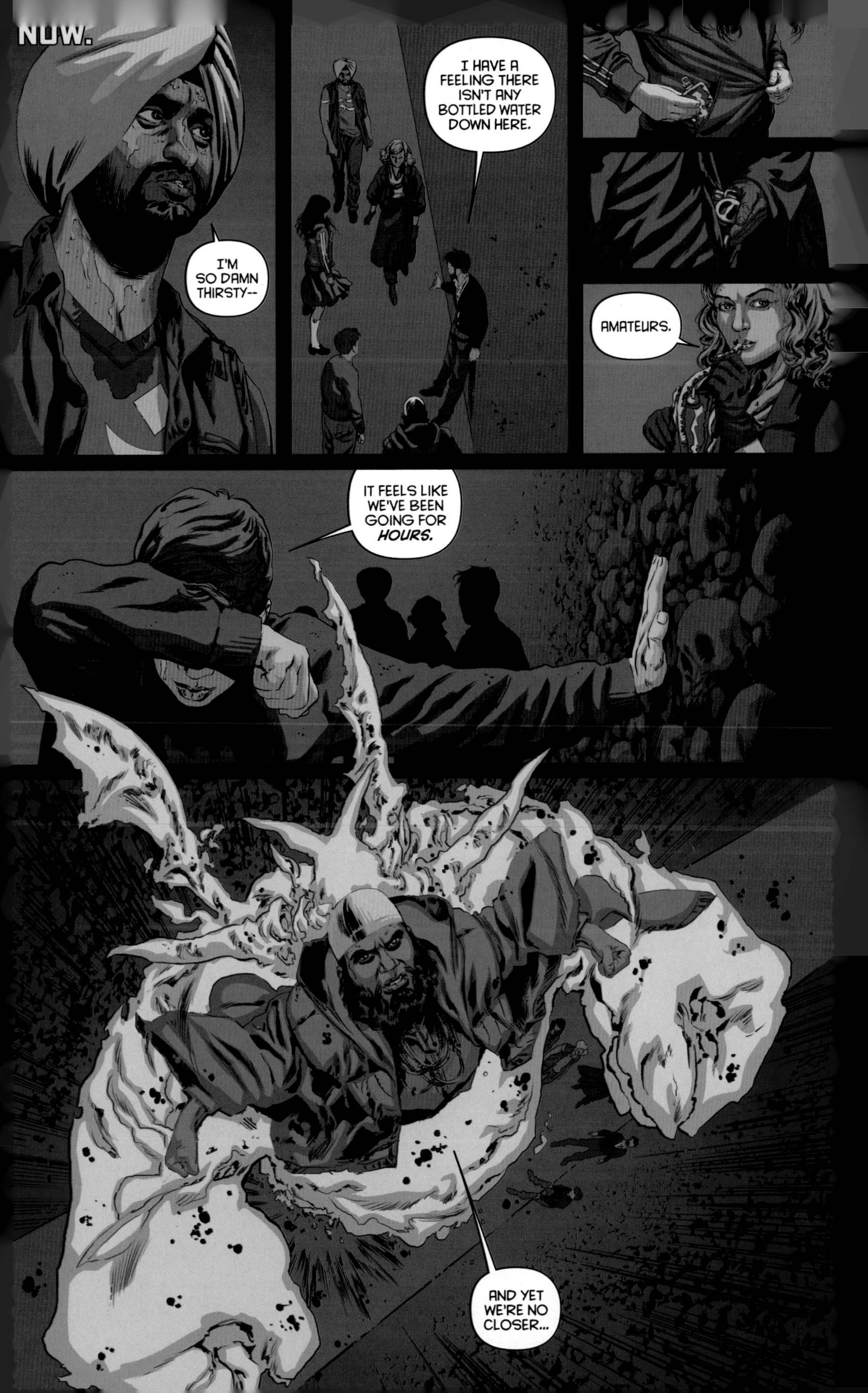
NOW.
I'M SO DAMN THIRSTY--
I HAVE A FEELING THERE ISN'T ANY BOTTLED WATER DOWN HERE.
AMATEURS.
IT FEELS LIKE WE'VE BEEN GOING FOR *HOURS.*
AND YET WE'RE NO CLOSER...

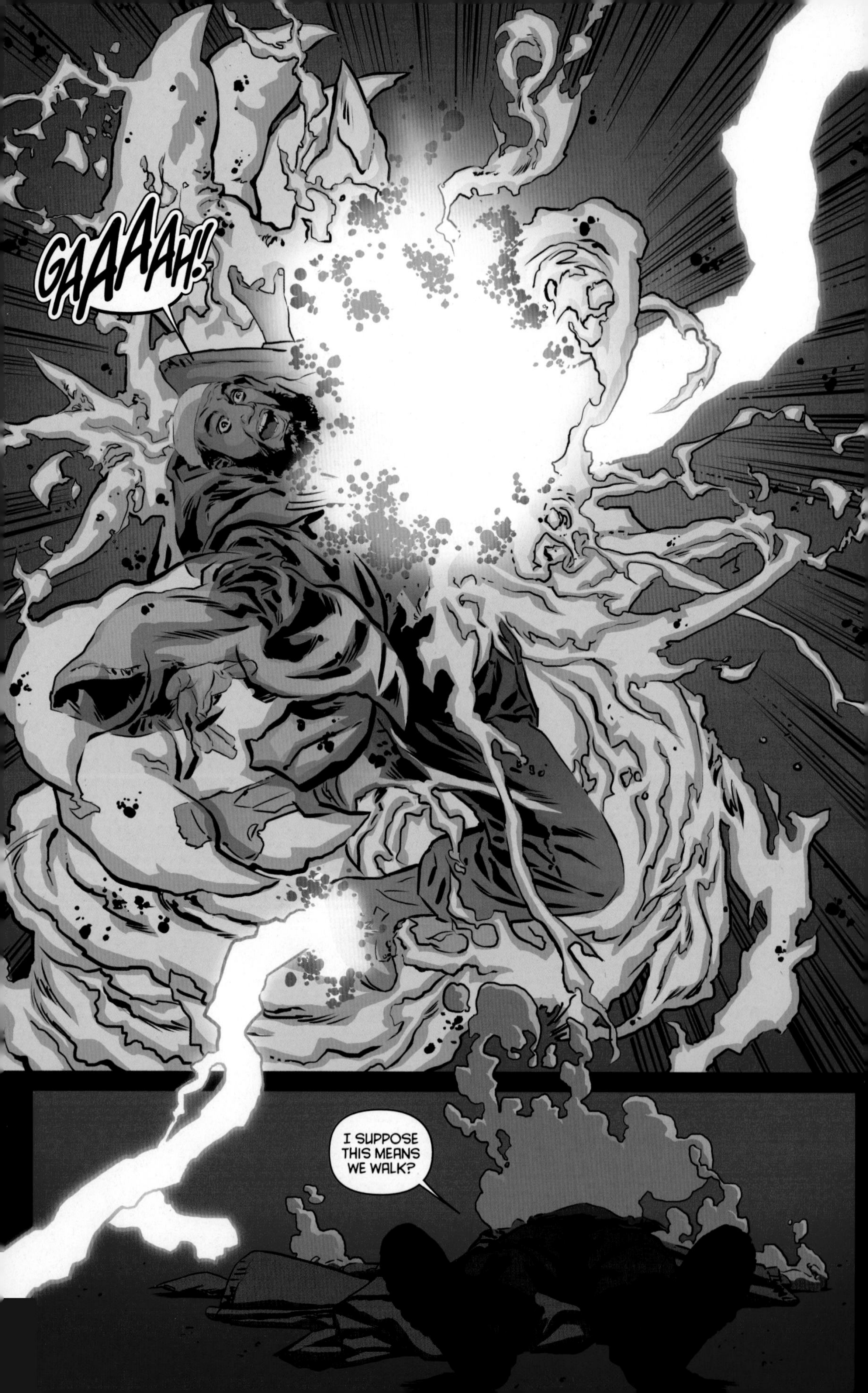
GAAAAH!
I SUPPOSE THIS MEANS WE WALK?

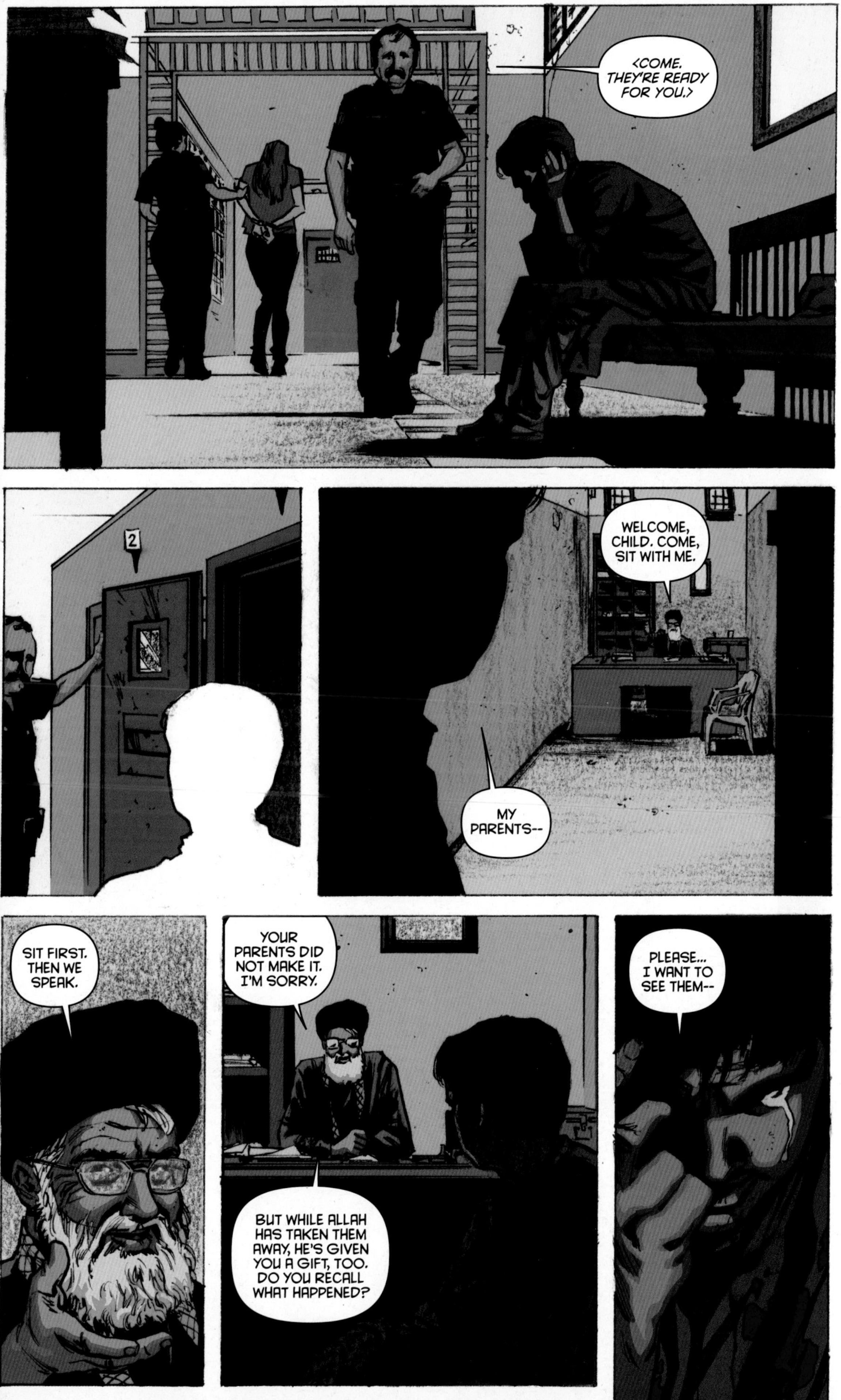

<COME. THEY'RE READY FOR YOU.>
WELCOME, CHILD. COME, SIT WITH ME.
MY PARENTS--
SIT FIRST. THEN WE SPEAK.
YOUR PARENTS DID NOT MAKE IT. I'M SORRY.
BUT WHILE ALLAH HAS TAKEN THEM AWAY, HE'S GIVEN YOU A GIFT, TOO. DO YOU RECALL WHAT HAPPENED?
PLEASE... I WANT TO SEE THEM--

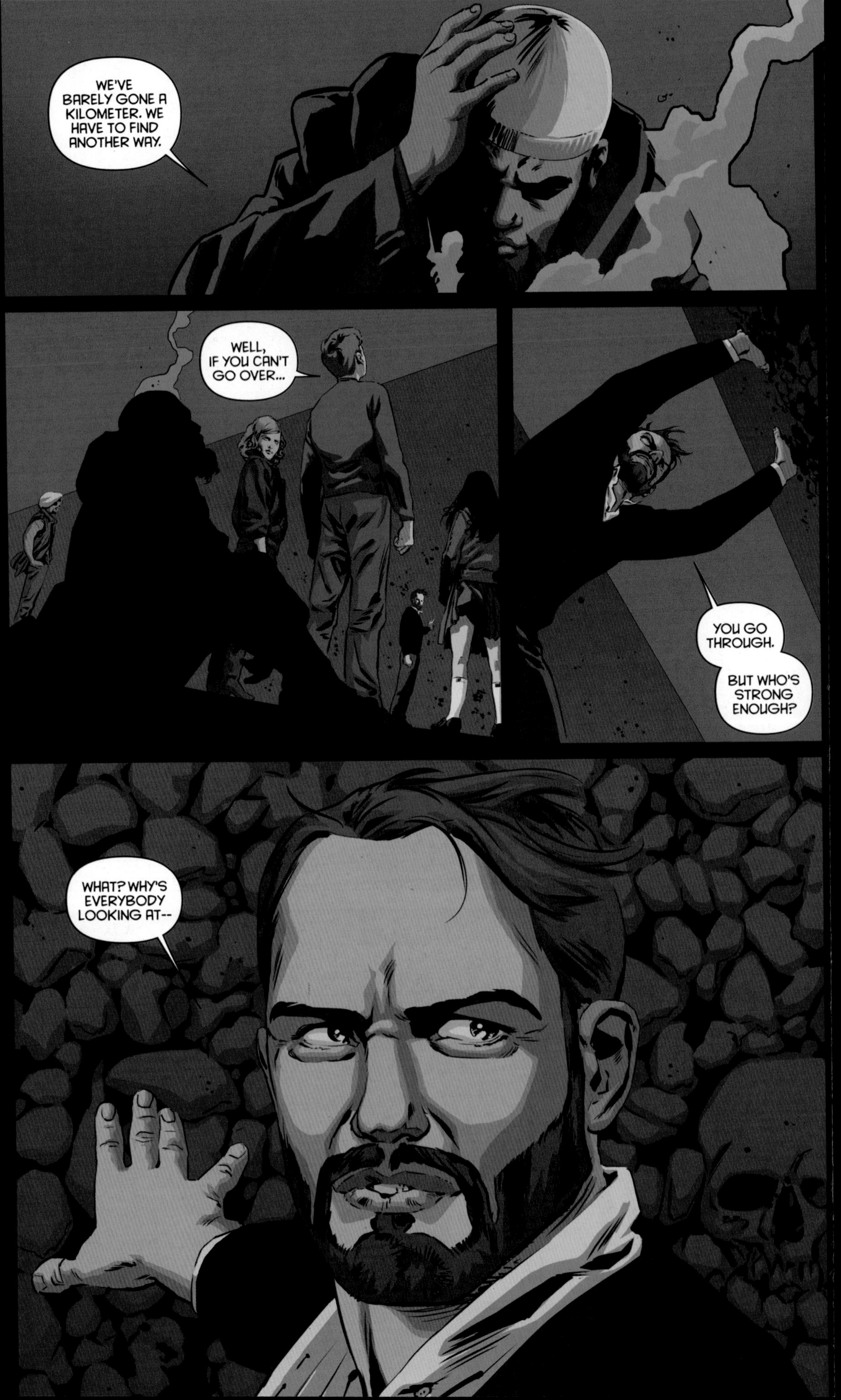
WE'VE BARELY GONE A KILOMETER. WE HAVE TO FIND ANOTHER WAY.
WELL, IF YOU CAN'T GO OVER...
YOU GO THROUGH.
BUT WHO'S STRONG ENOUGH?
WHAT? WHY'S EVERYBODY LOOKING AT--

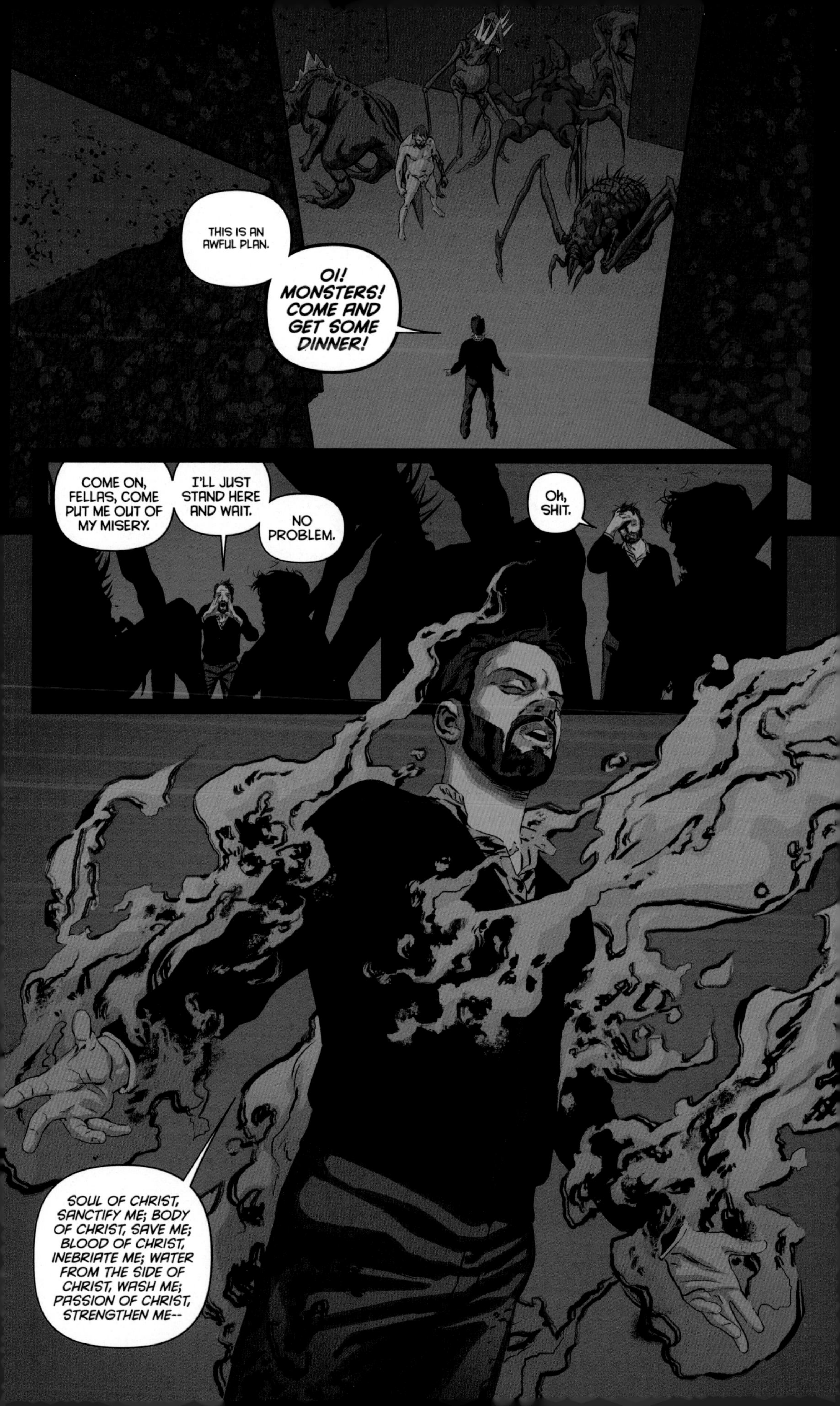

THIS IS AN AWFUL PLAN.
OI! MONSTERS! COME AND GET SOME DINNER!
COME ON, FELLAS, COME PUT ME OUT OF MY MISERY.
I'LL JUST STAND HERE AND WAIT.
NO PROBLEM.
Oh, SHIT.
SOUL OF CHRIST, SANCTIFY ME; BODY OF CHRIST, SAVE ME; BLOOD OF CHRIST, INEBRIATE ME; WATER FROM THE SIDE OF CHRIST, WASH ME; PASSION OF CHRIST, STRENGTHEN ME--

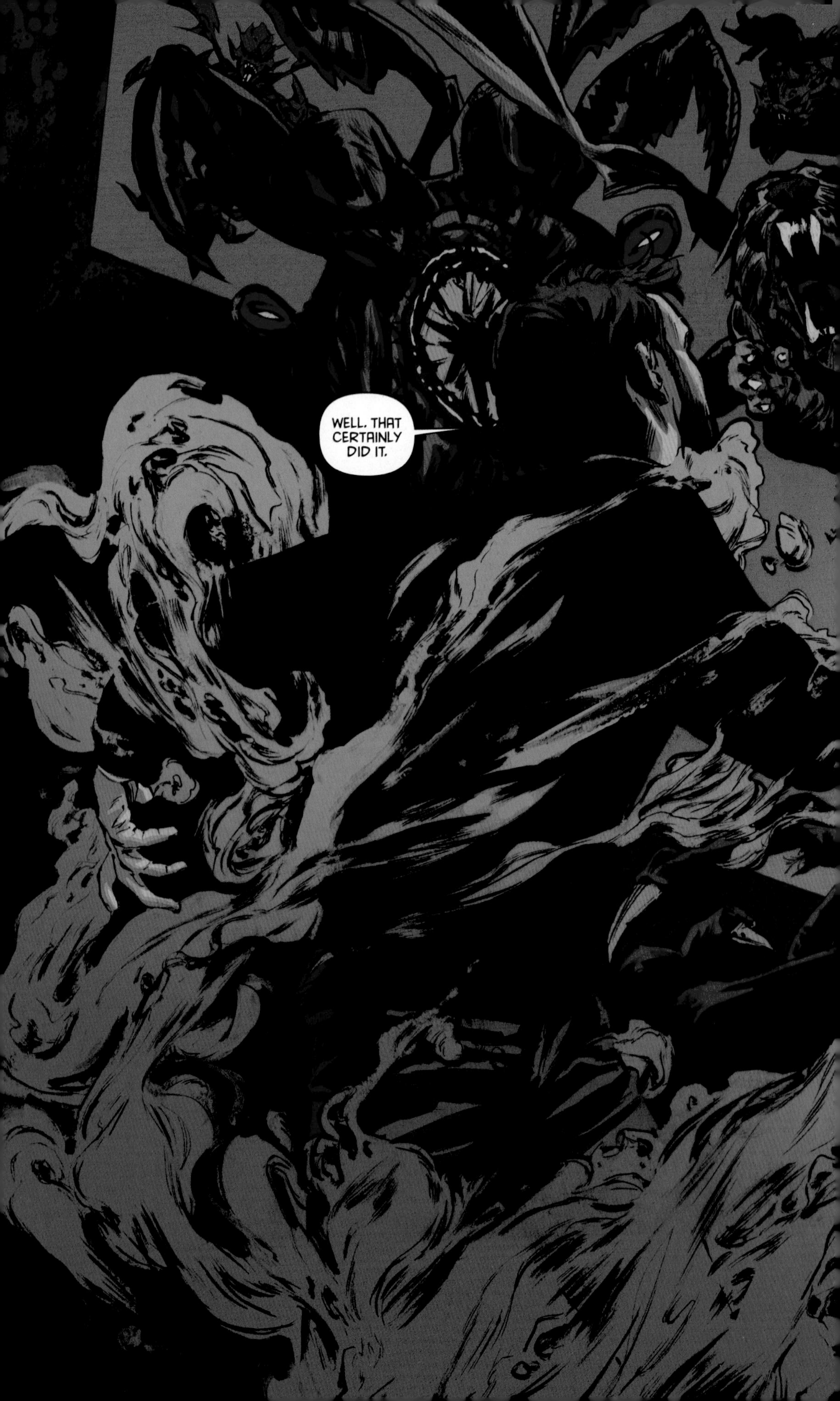
WELL. THAT CERTAINLY DID IT.

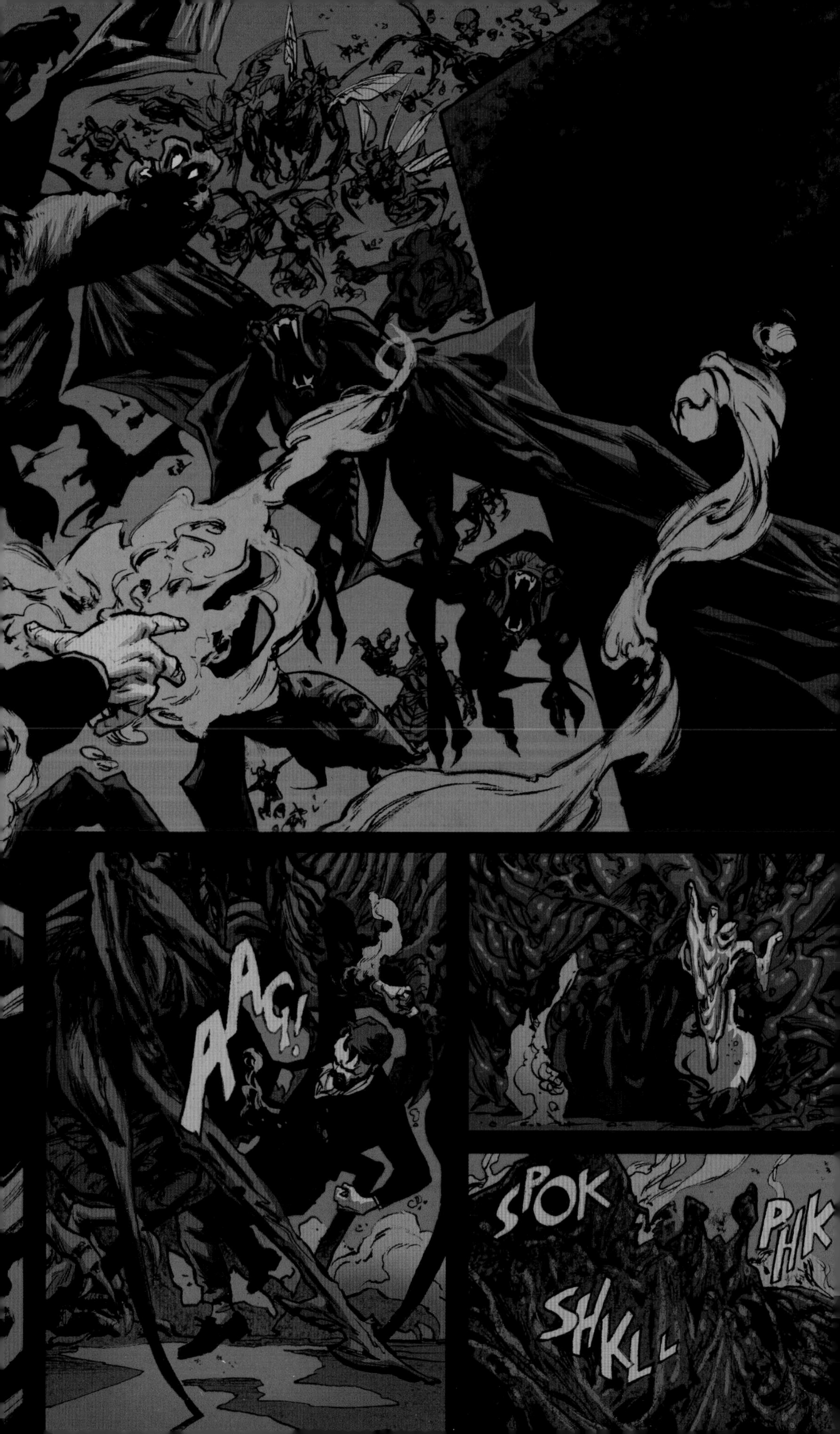
AAG!
SPOK
PHK
SHKLLL

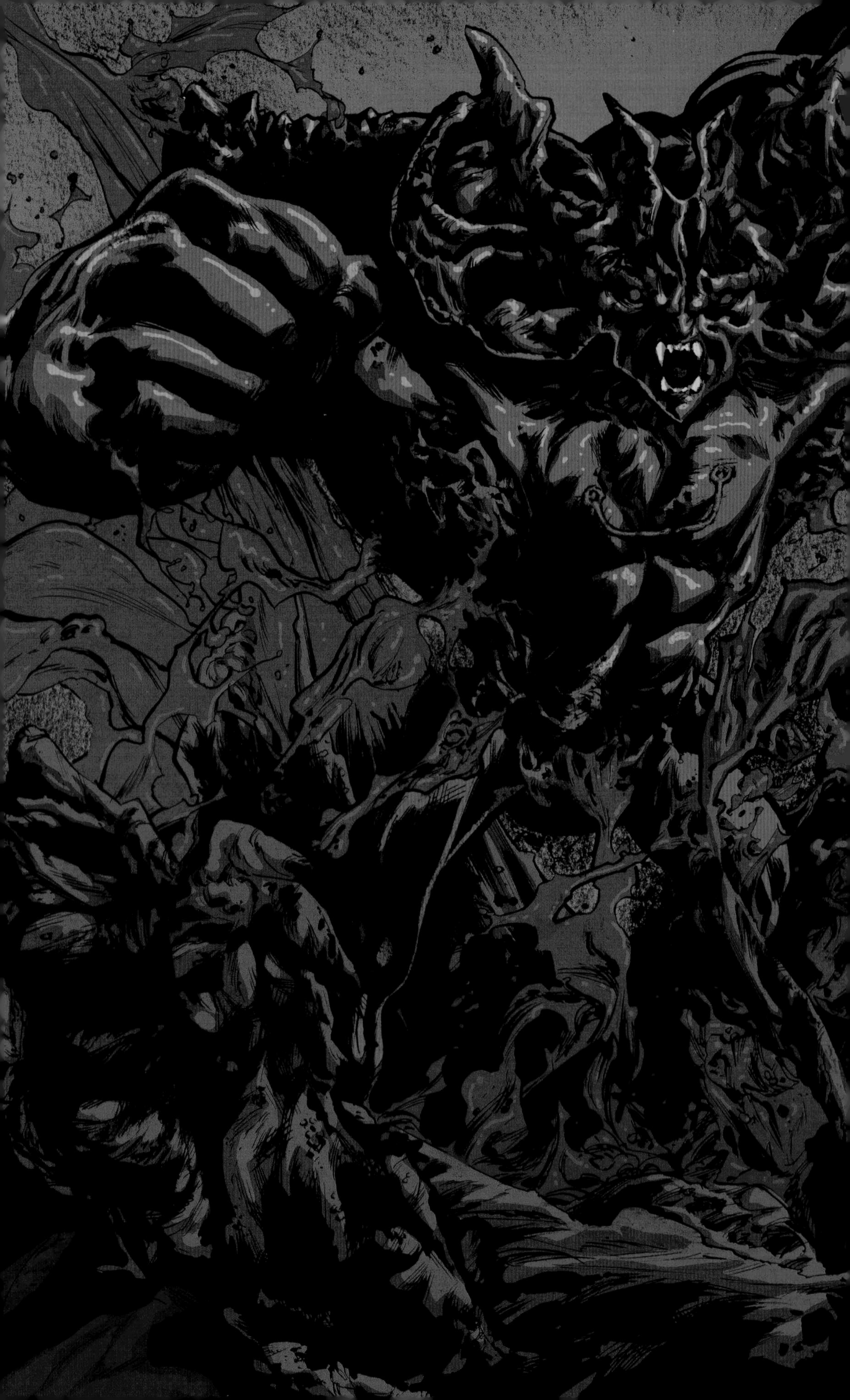

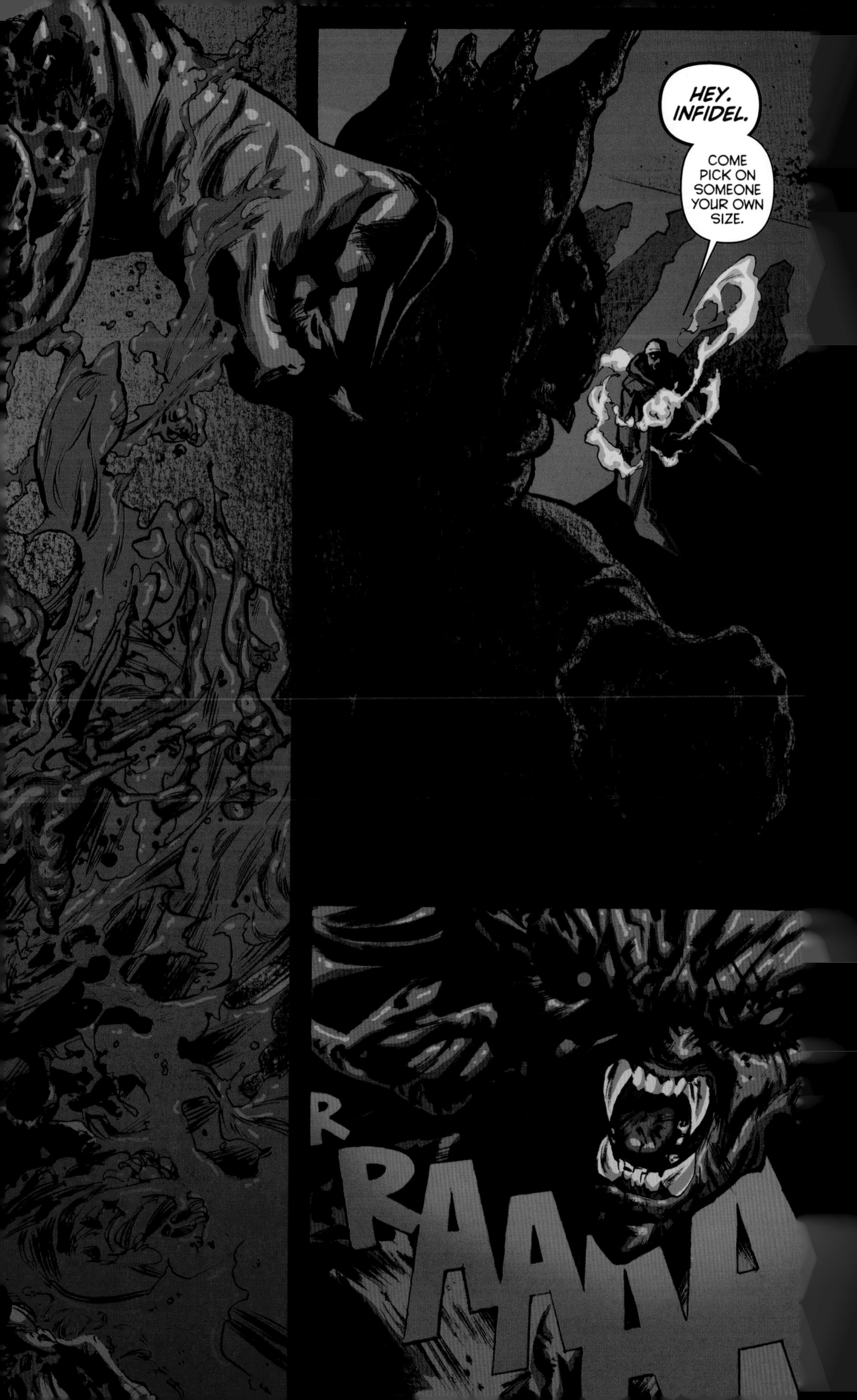
HEY. INFIDEL.
COME PICK ON SOMEONE YOUR OWN SIZE.
R
RAAAA

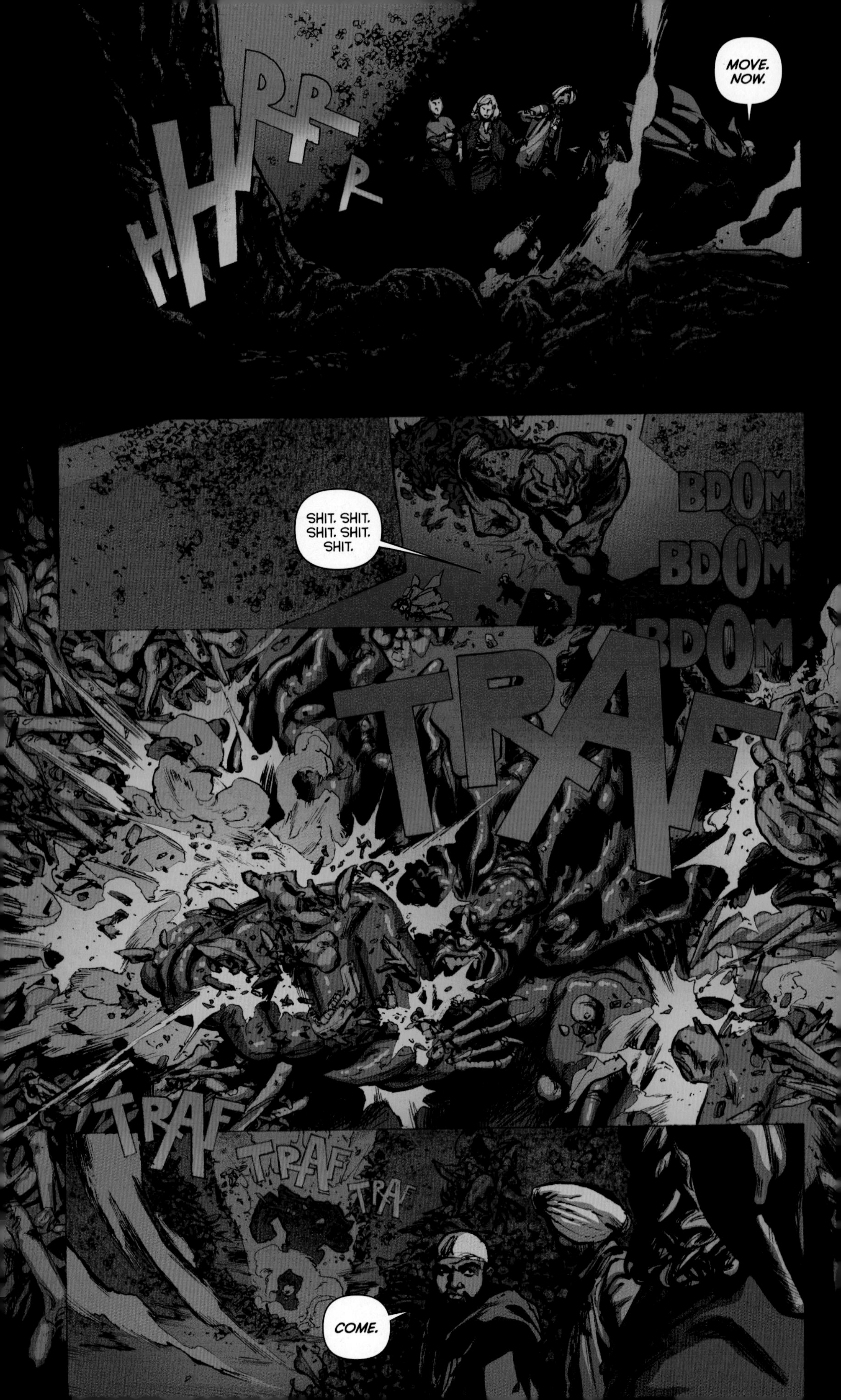
HHRRRR
MOVE. NOW.
SHIT. SHIT. SHIT. SHIT. SHIT.
BDOM
BDOM
BDOM
TRAF
TRAF
TRAF
TRAF
COME.

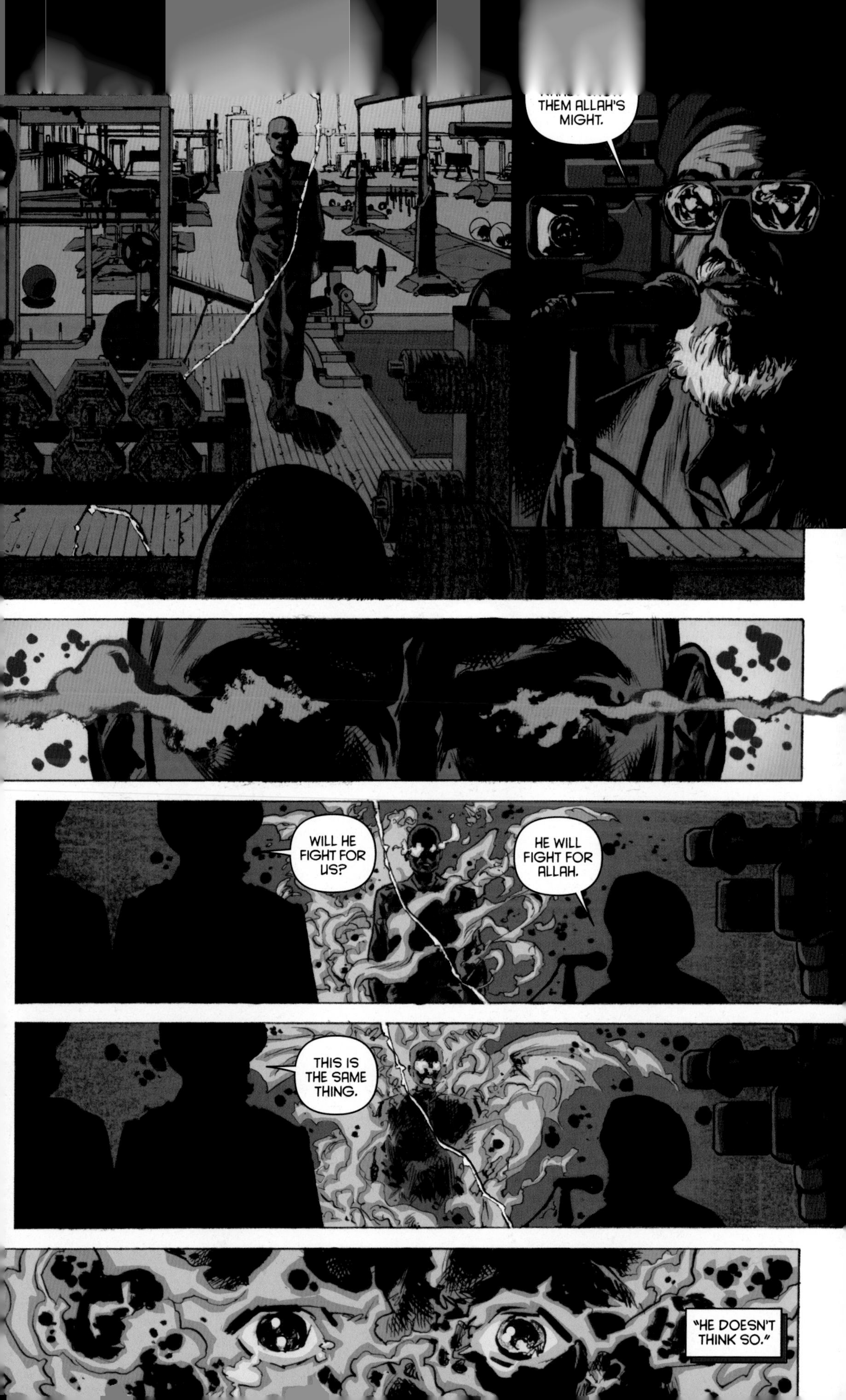
THEM ALLAH'S MIGHT.
WILL HE FIGHT FOR US?
HE WILL FIGHT FOR ALLAH.
THIS IS THE SAME THING.
"HE DOESN'T THINK SO."

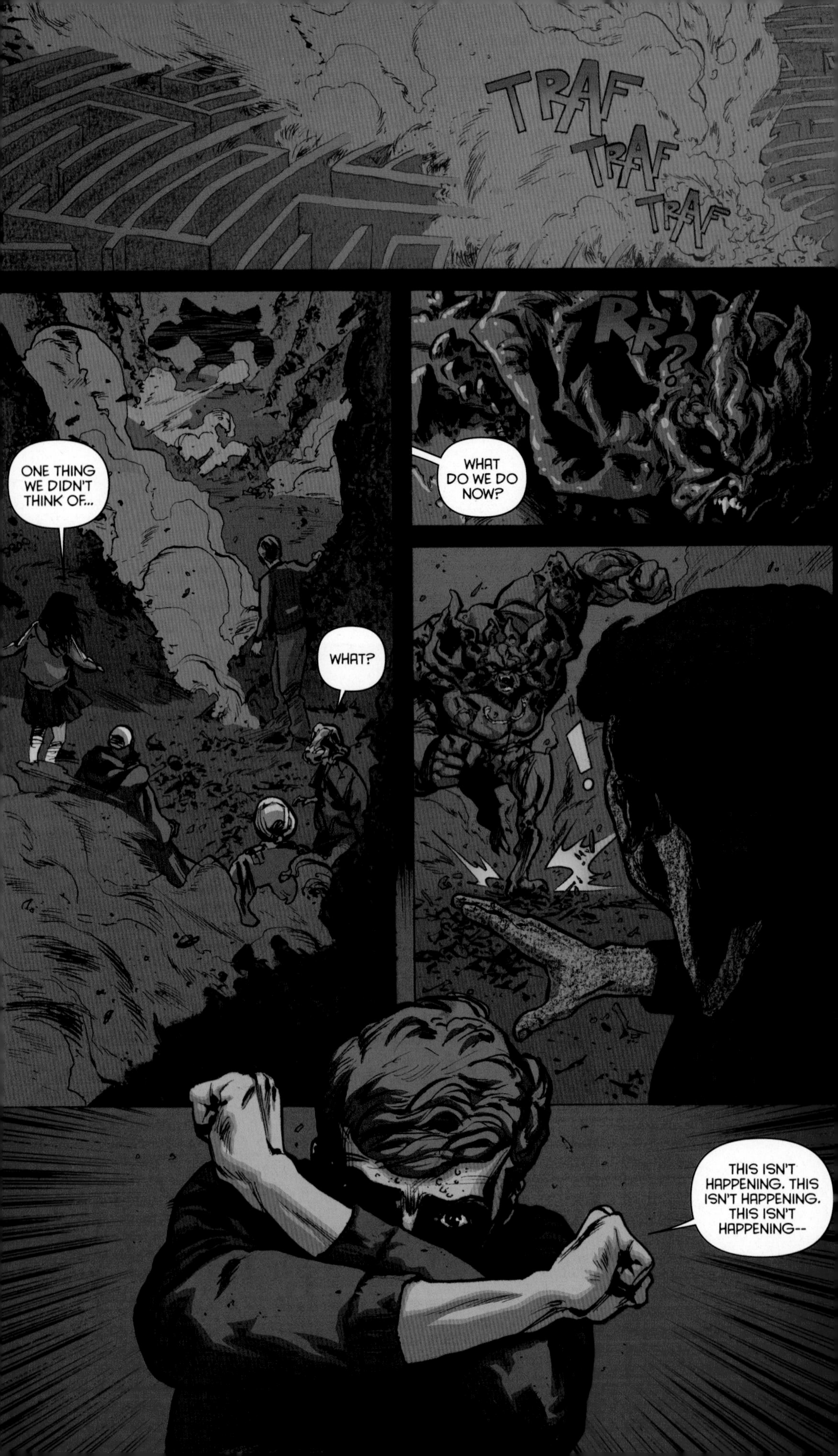
TRAF
TRAF
TRAF
ONE THING WE DIDN'T THINK OF...
WHAT?
RR??
WHAT DO WE DO NOW?
!
THIS ISN'T HAPPENING. THIS ISN'T HAPPENING. THIS ISN'T HAPPENING--

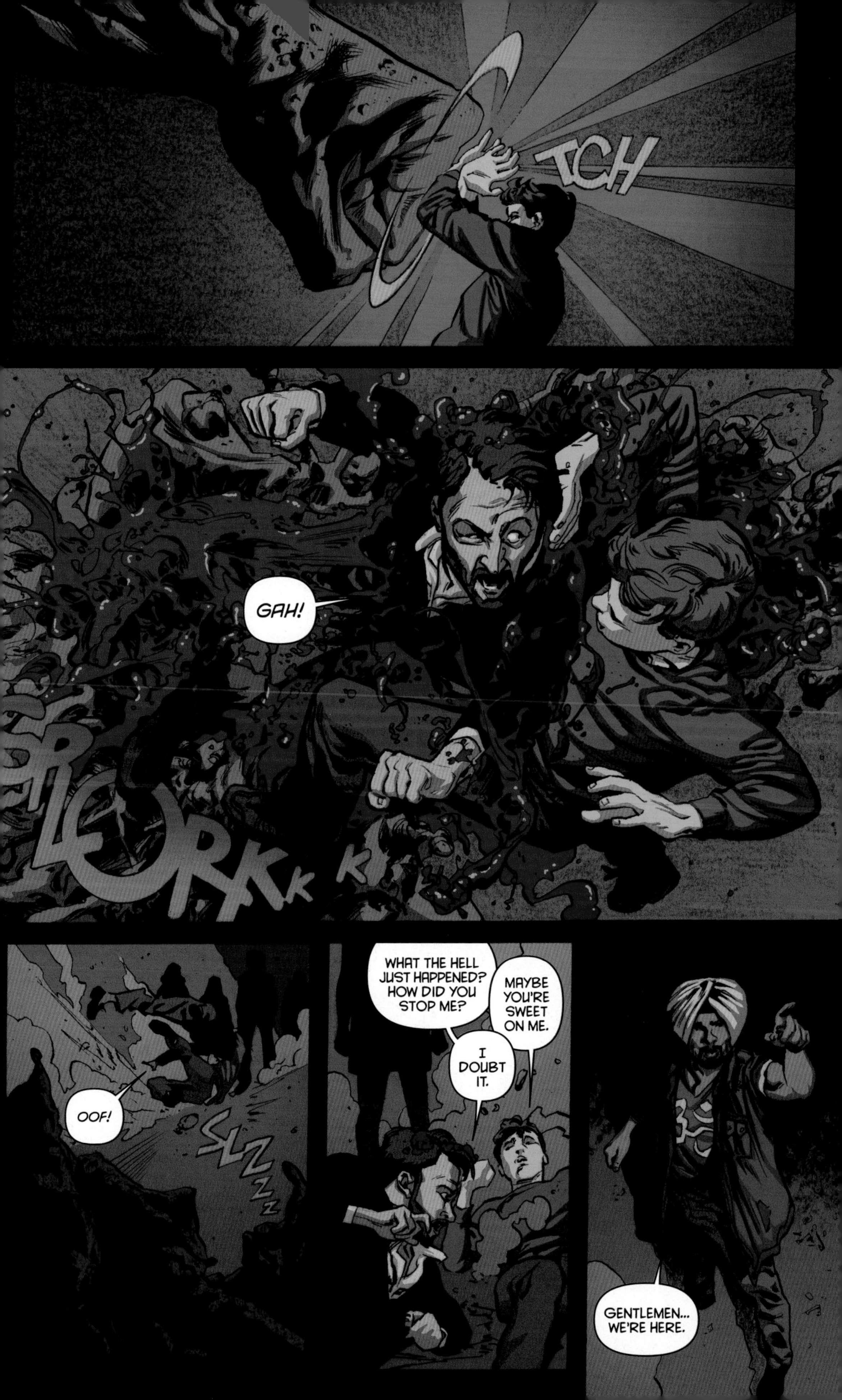
TCH
GAH!
SPLORKk k
OOF!
SLZZZ
WHAT THE HELL JUST HAPPENED? HOW DID YOU STOP ME?
MAYBE YOU'RE SWEET ON ME.
I DOUBT IT.
GENTLEMEN... WE'RE HERE.

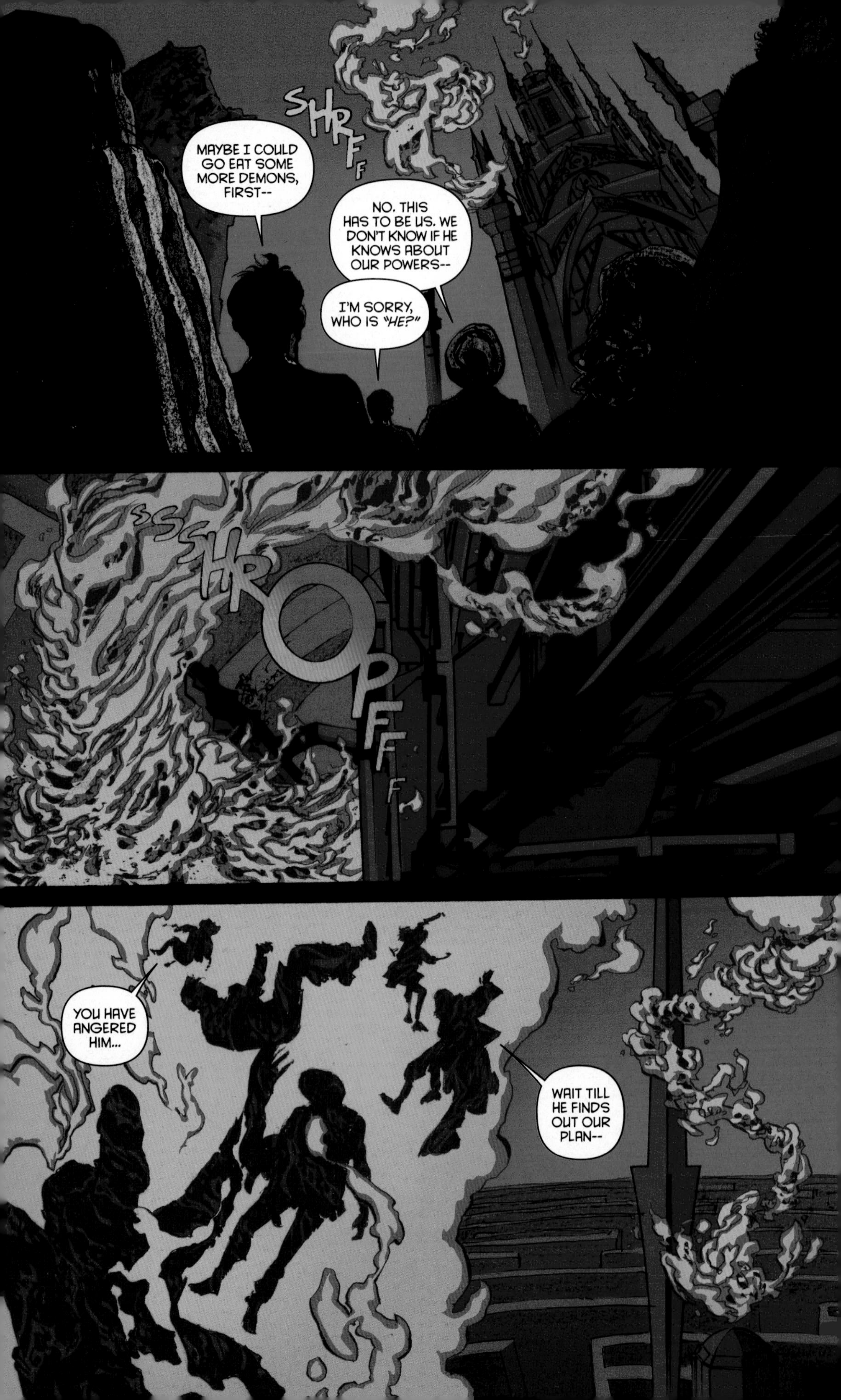
SHRFF
MAYBE I COULD GO EAT SOME MORE DEMONS, FIRST--
NO. THIS HAS TO BE US. WE DON'T KNOW IF HE KNOWS ABOUT OUR POWERS--
I'M SORRY, WHO IS *"HE?"*
SSSHROOPFFFF
YOU HAVE ANGERED HIM...
WAIT TILL HE FINDS OUT OUR PLAN--

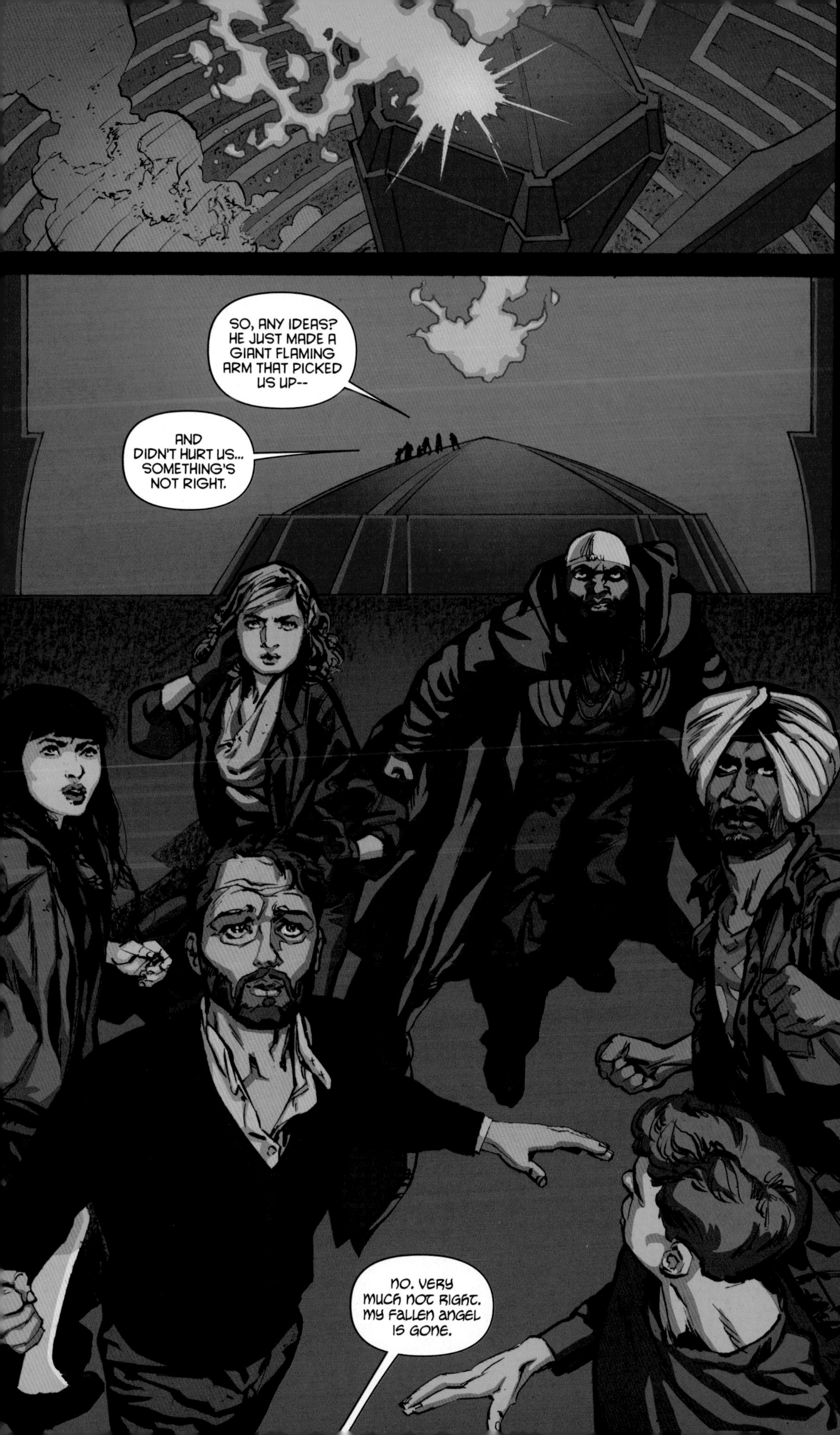
SO, ANY IDEAS? HE JUST MADE A GIANT FLAMING ARM THAT PICKED US UP--
AND DIDN'T HURT US... SOMETHING'S NOT RIGHT.
NO. VERY MUCH NOT RIGHT. MY FALLEN ANGEL IS GONE.

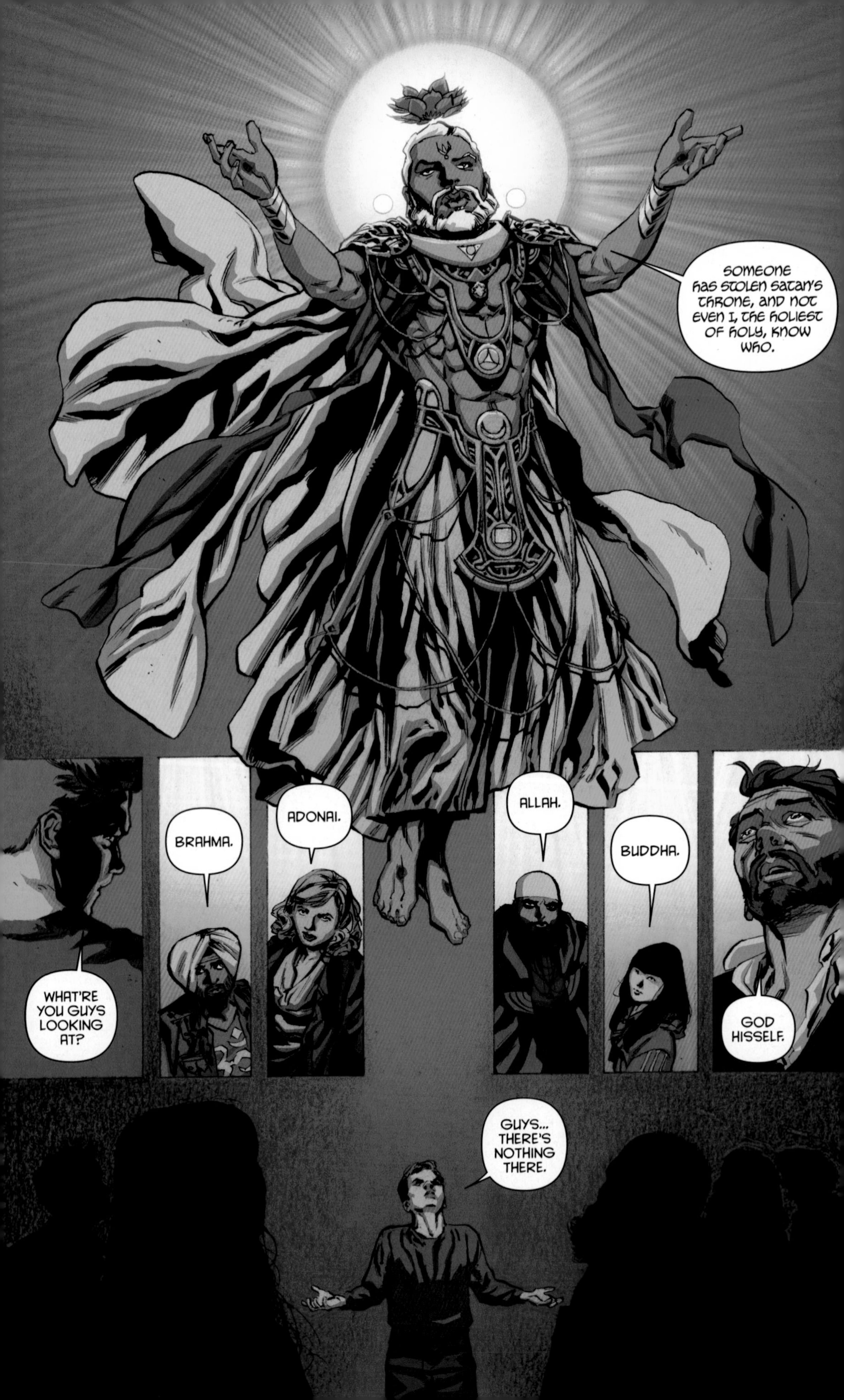
SOMEONE HAS STOLEN SATAN'S THRONE, AND NOT EVEN I, THE HOLIEST OF HOLY, KNOW WHO.
WHAT'RE YOU GUYS LOOKING AT?
BRAHMA.
ADONAI.
ALLAH.
BUDDHA.
GOD HISSELF.
GUYS... THERE'S NOTHING THERE.

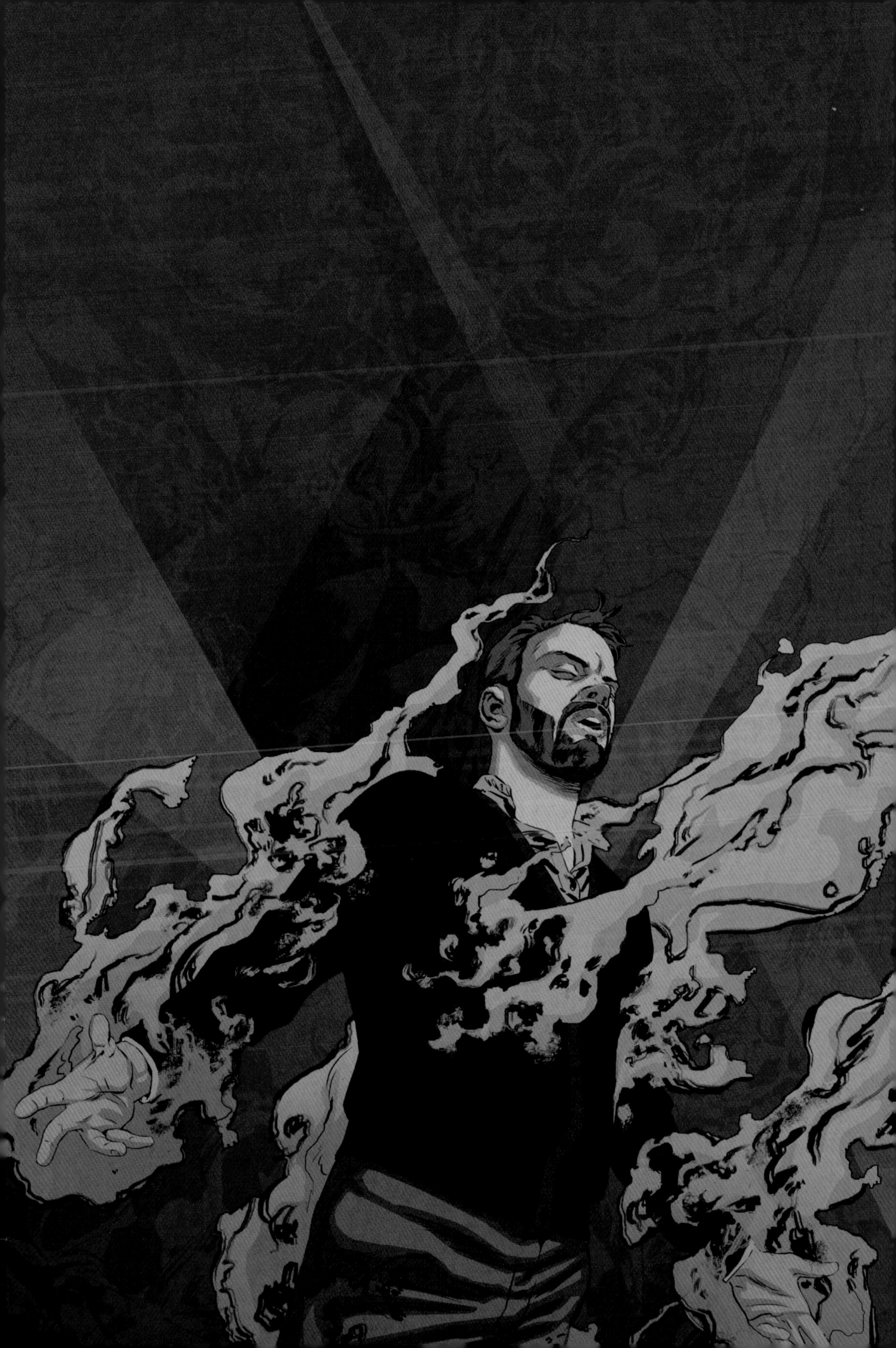

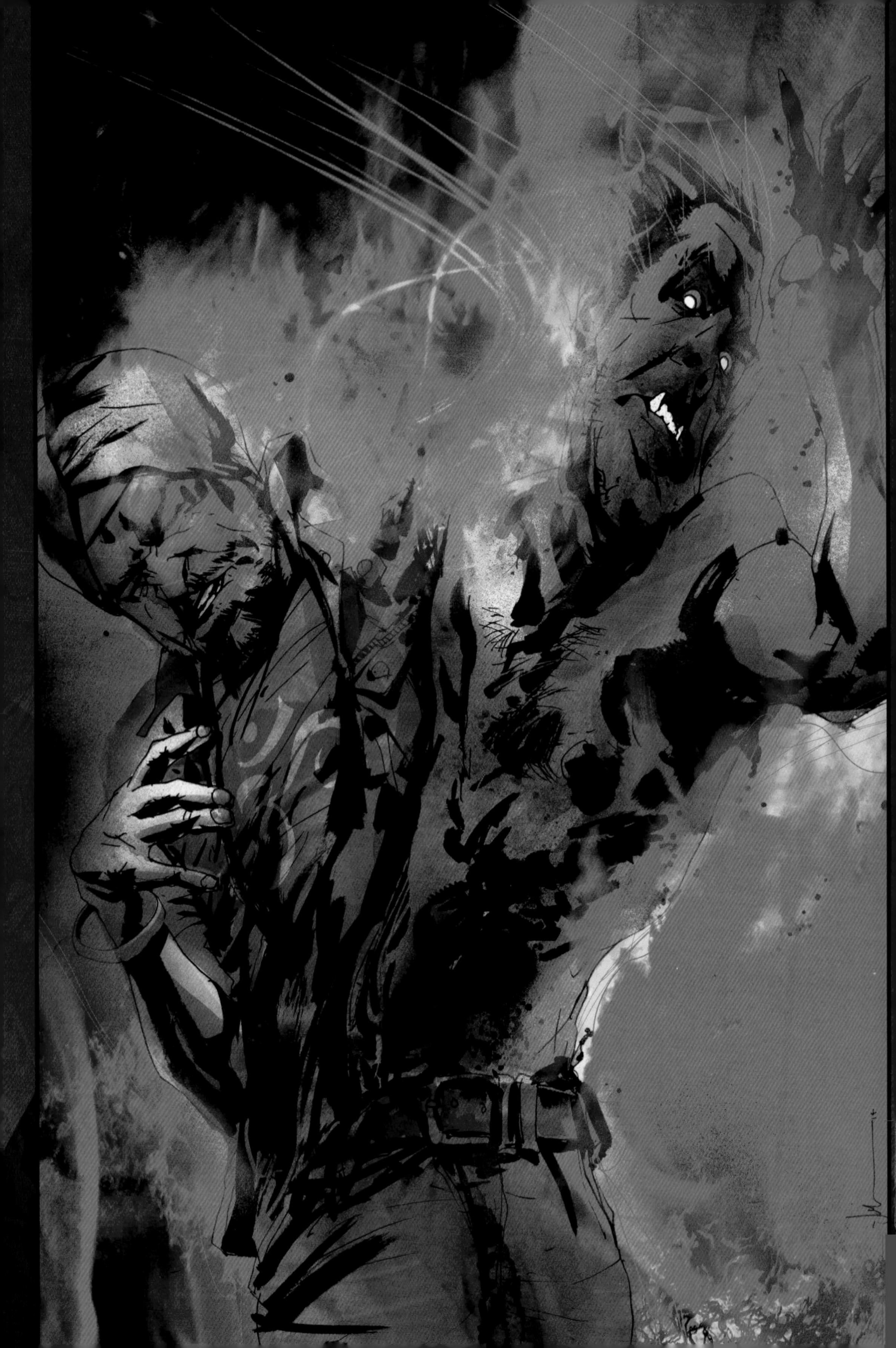

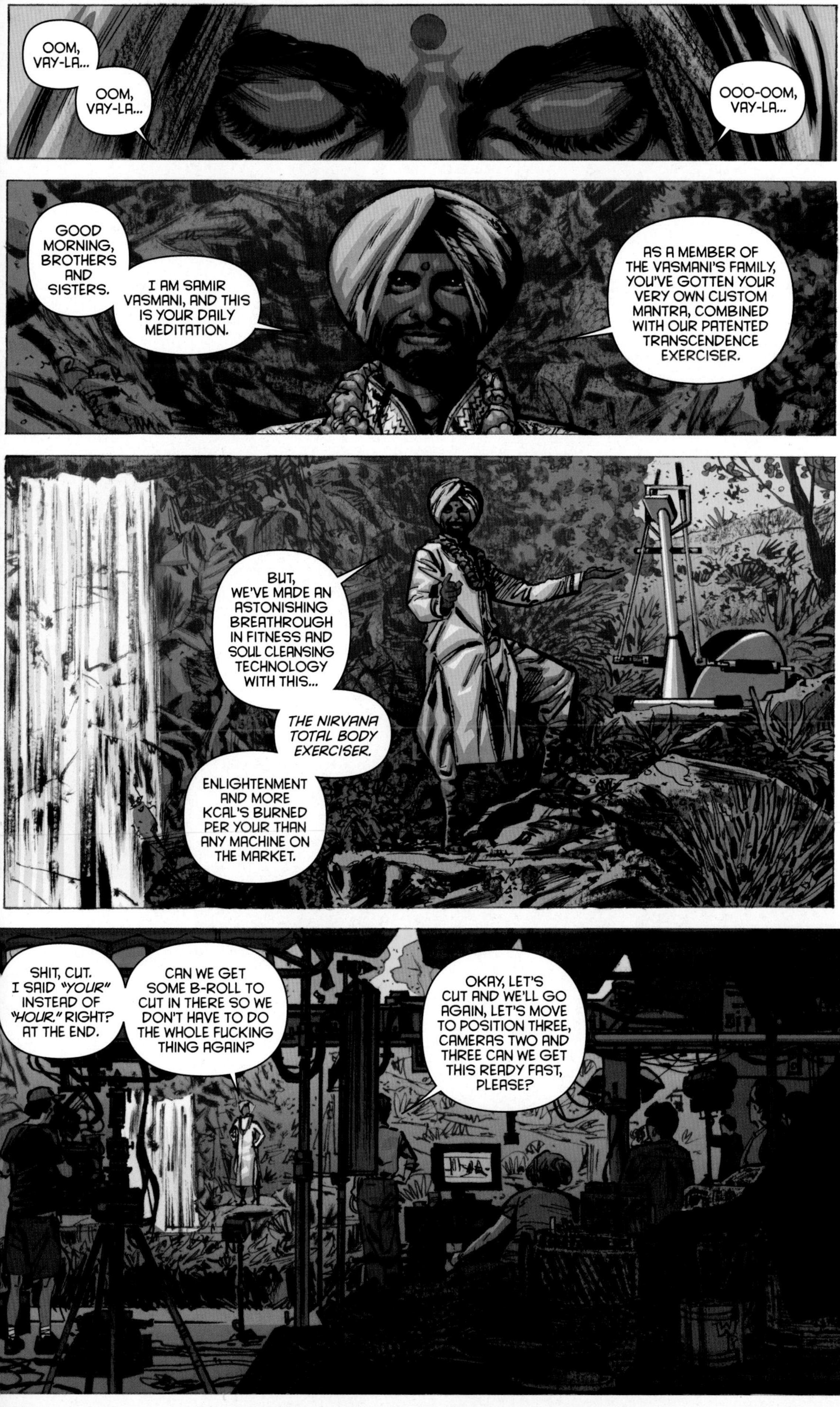
OOM, VAY-LA...
OOM, VAY-LA...
OOO-OOM, VAY-LA...
GOOD MORNING, BROTHERS AND SISTERS.
I AM SAMIR VASMANI, AND THIS IS YOUR DAILY MEDITATION.
AS A MEMBER OF THE VASMANI'S FAMILY, YOU'VE GOTTEN YOUR VERY OWN CUSTOM MANTRA, COMBINED WITH OUR PATENTED TRANSCENDENCE EXERCISER.
BUT, WE'VE MADE AN ASTONISHING BREATHROUGH IN FITNESS AND SOUL CLEANSING TECHNOLOGY WITH THIS...
THE NIRVANA TOTAL BODY EXERCISER.
ENLIGHTENMENT AND MORE KCAL'S BURNED PER YOUR THAN ANY MACHINE ON THE MARKET.
SHIT, CUT. I SAID *"YOUR"* INSTEAD OF *"HOUR,"* RIGHT? AT THE END.
CAN WE GET SOME B-ROLL TO CUT IN THERE SO WE DON'T HAVE TO DO THE WHOLE FUCKING THING AGAIN?
OKAY, LET'S CUT AND WE'LL GO AGAIN, LET'S MOVE TO POSITION THREE, CAMERAS TWO AND THREE CAN WE GET THIS READY FAST, PLEASE?

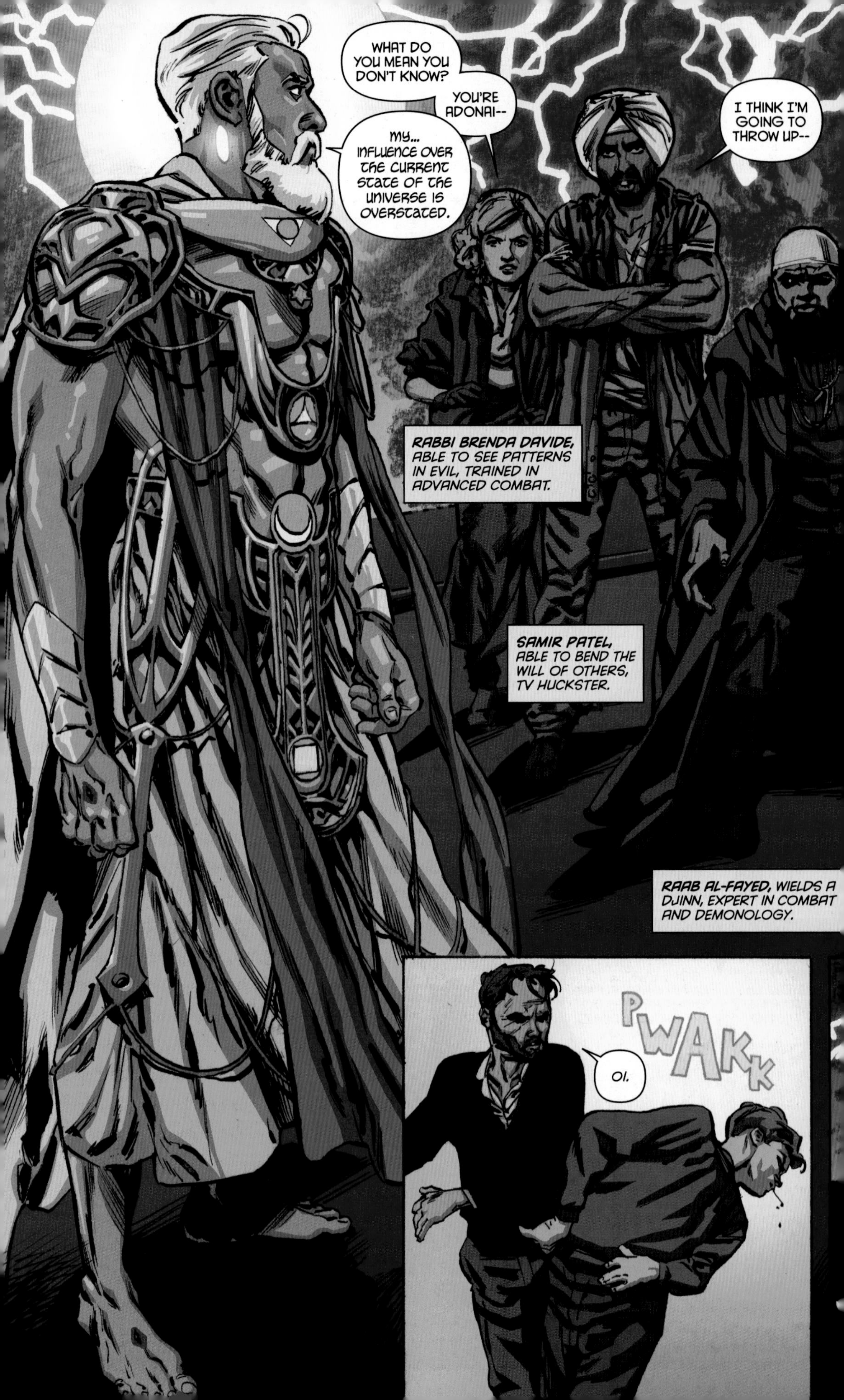
WHAT DO YOU MEAN YOU DON'T KNOW?
YOU'RE ADONAI--
MY... INFLUENCE OVER THE CURRENT STATE OF THE UNIVERSE IS OVERSTATED.
I THINK I'M GOING TO THROW UP--
RABBI BRENDA DAVIDE, ABLE TO SEE PATTERNS IN EVIL, TRAINED IN ADVANCED COMBAT.
SAMIR PATEL, ABLE TO BEND THE WILL OF OTHERS, TV HUCKSTER.
RAAB AL-FAYED, WIELDS A DJINN, EXPERT IN COMBAT AND DEMONOLOGY.
PWAKK
OI.

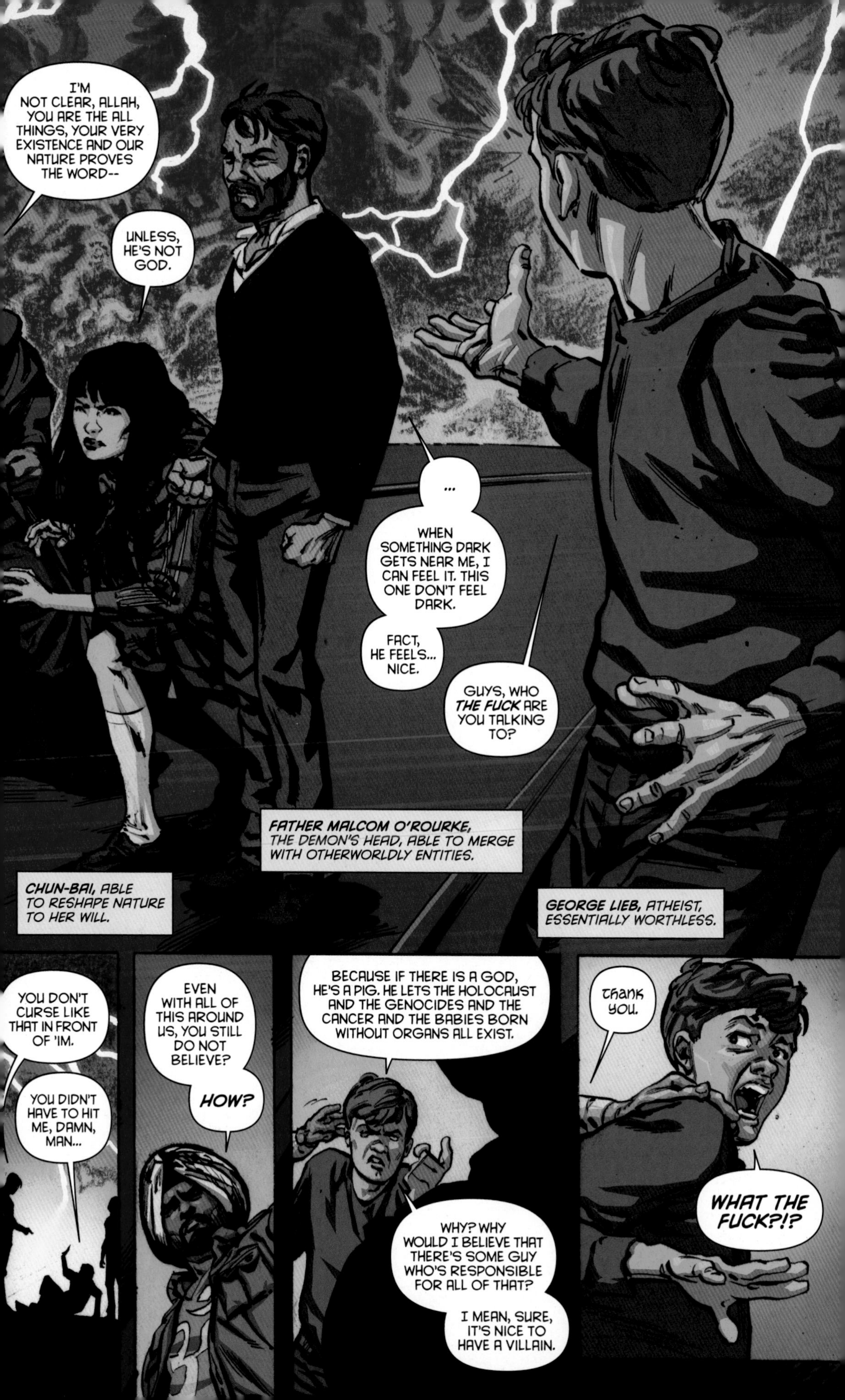

I'M NOT CLEAR, ALLAH, YOU ARE THE ALL THINGS, YOUR VERY EXISTENCE AND OUR NATURE PROVES THE WORD--
UNLESS, HE'S NOT GOD.
...
WHEN SOMETHING DARK GETS NEAR ME, I CAN FEEL IT. THIS ONE DON'T FEEL DARK.
FACT, HE FEELS... NICE.
GUYS, WHO THE FUCK ARE YOU TALKING TO?
FATHER MALCOM O'ROURKE, THE DEMON'S HEAD, ABLE TO MERGE WITH OTHERWORLDLY ENTITIES.
CHUN-BAI, ABLE TO RESHAPE NATURE TO HER WILL.
GEORGE LIEB, ATHEIST, ESSENTIALLY WORTHLESS.
YOU DON'T CURSE LIKE THAT IN FRONT OF 'IM.
YOU DIDN'T HAVE TO HIT ME, DAMN, MAN...
EVEN WITH ALL OF THIS AROUND US, YOU STILL DO NOT BELIEVE?
HOW?
BECAUSE IF THERE IS A GOD, HE'S A PIG. HE LETS THE HOLOCAUST AND THE GENOCIDES AND THE CANCER AND THE BABIES BORN WITHOUT ORGANS ALL EXIST.
WHY? WHY WOULD I BELIEVE THAT THERE'S SOME GUY WHO'S RESPONSIBLE FOR ALL OF THAT?
I MEAN, SURE, IT'S NICE TO HAVE A VILLAIN.
thank you.
WHAT THE FUCK?!?

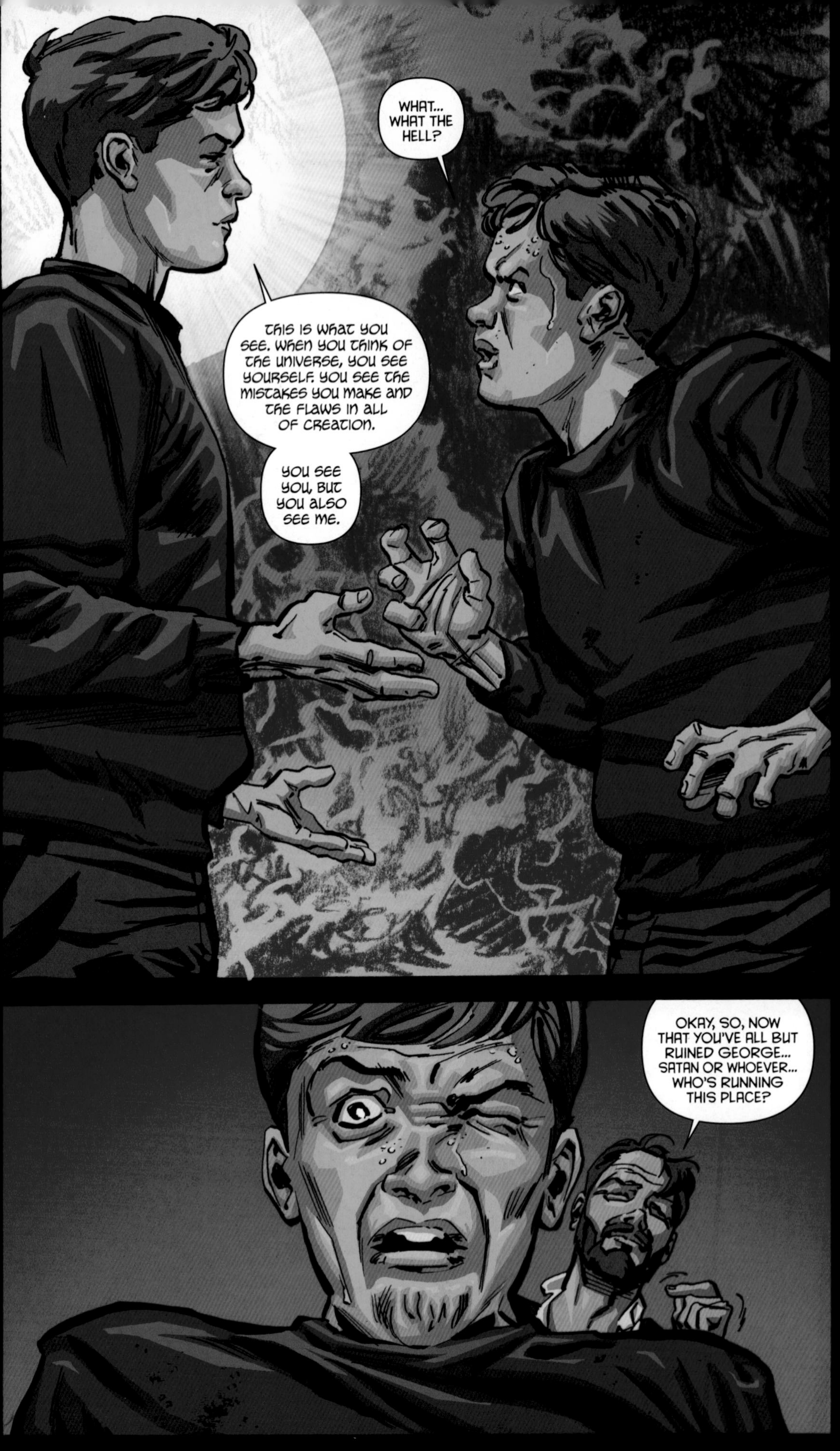
WHAT... WHAT THE HELL?
THIS IS WHAT YOU SEE. WHEN YOU THINK OF THE UNIVERSE, YOU SEE YOURSELF. YOU SEE THE MISTAKES YOU MAKE AND THE FLAWS IN ALL OF CREATION.
YOU SEE YOU, BUT YOU ALSO SEE ME.
OKAY, SO, NOW THAT YOU'VE ALL BUT RUINED GEORGE... SATAN OR WHOEVER... WHO'S RUNNING THIS PLACE?

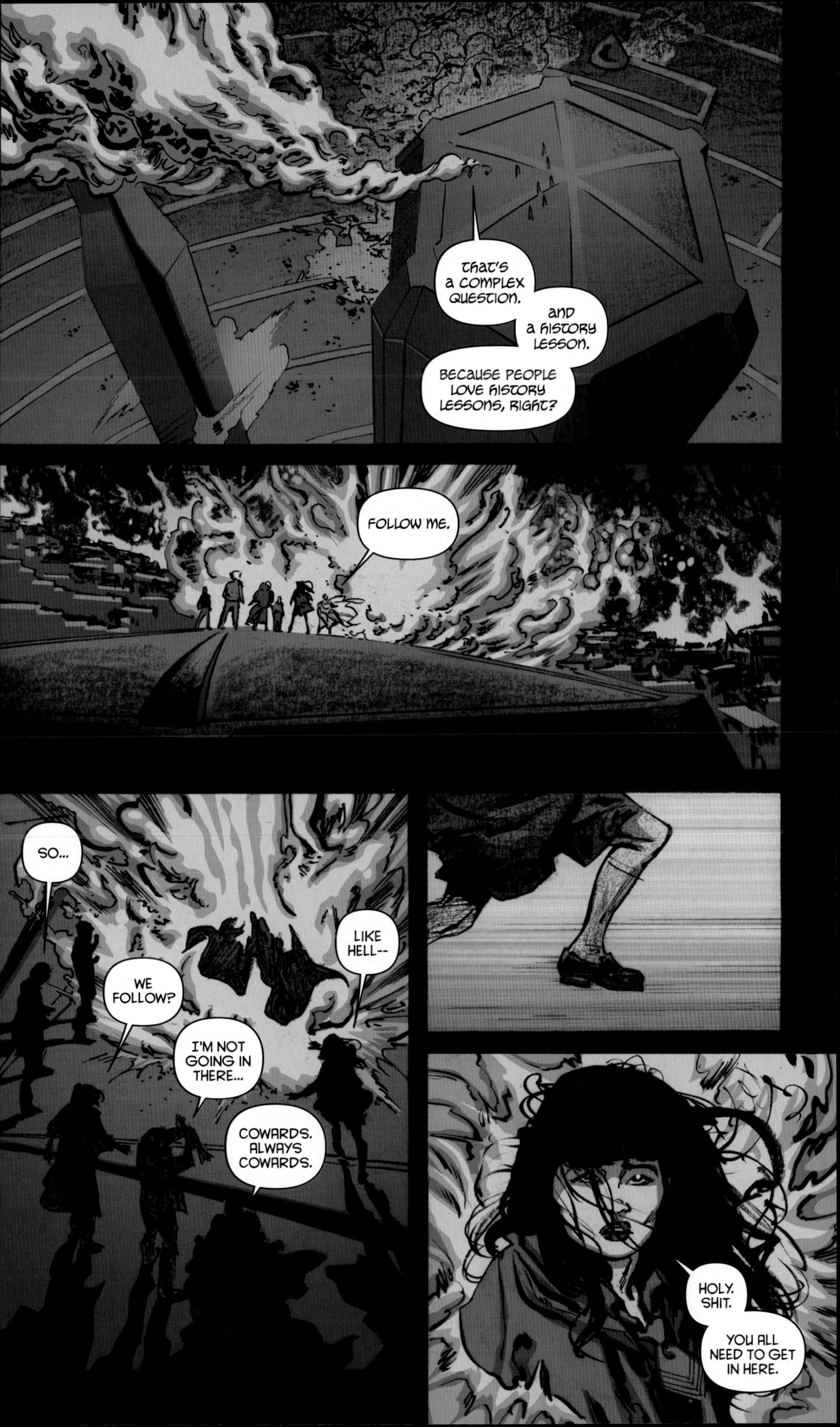
THAT'S A COMPLEX QUESTION.
AND A HISTORY LESSON.
BECAUSE PEOPLE LOVE HISTORY LESSONS, RIGHT?
FOLLOW ME.
SO...
WE FOLLOW?
I'M NOT GOING IN THERE...
LIKE HELL--
COWARDS. ALWAYS COWARDS.
HOLY. SHIT.
YOU ALL NEED TO GET IN HERE.

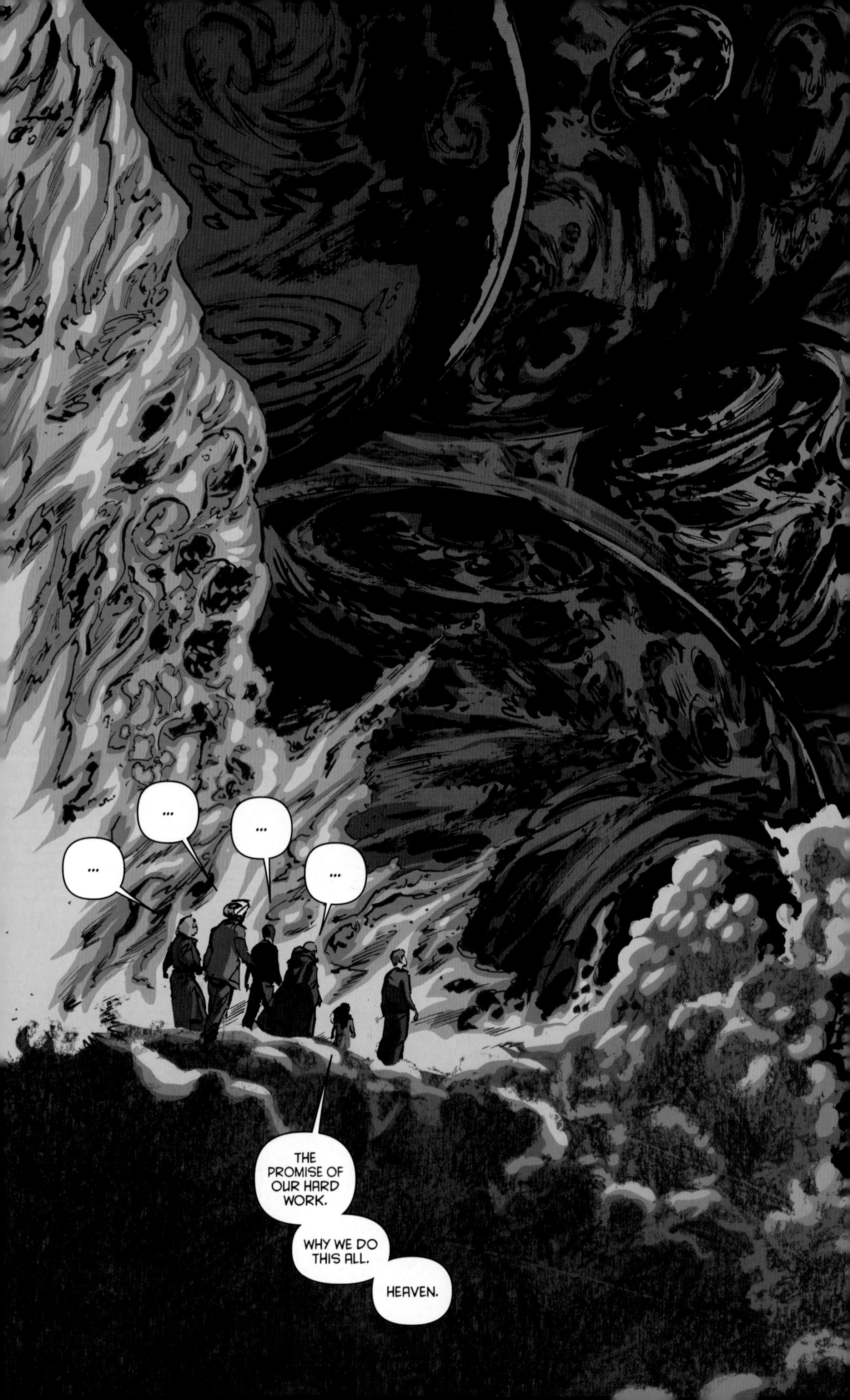
...
...
...
...
THE PROMISE OF OUR HARD WORK.
WHY WE DO THIS ALL.
HEAVEN.

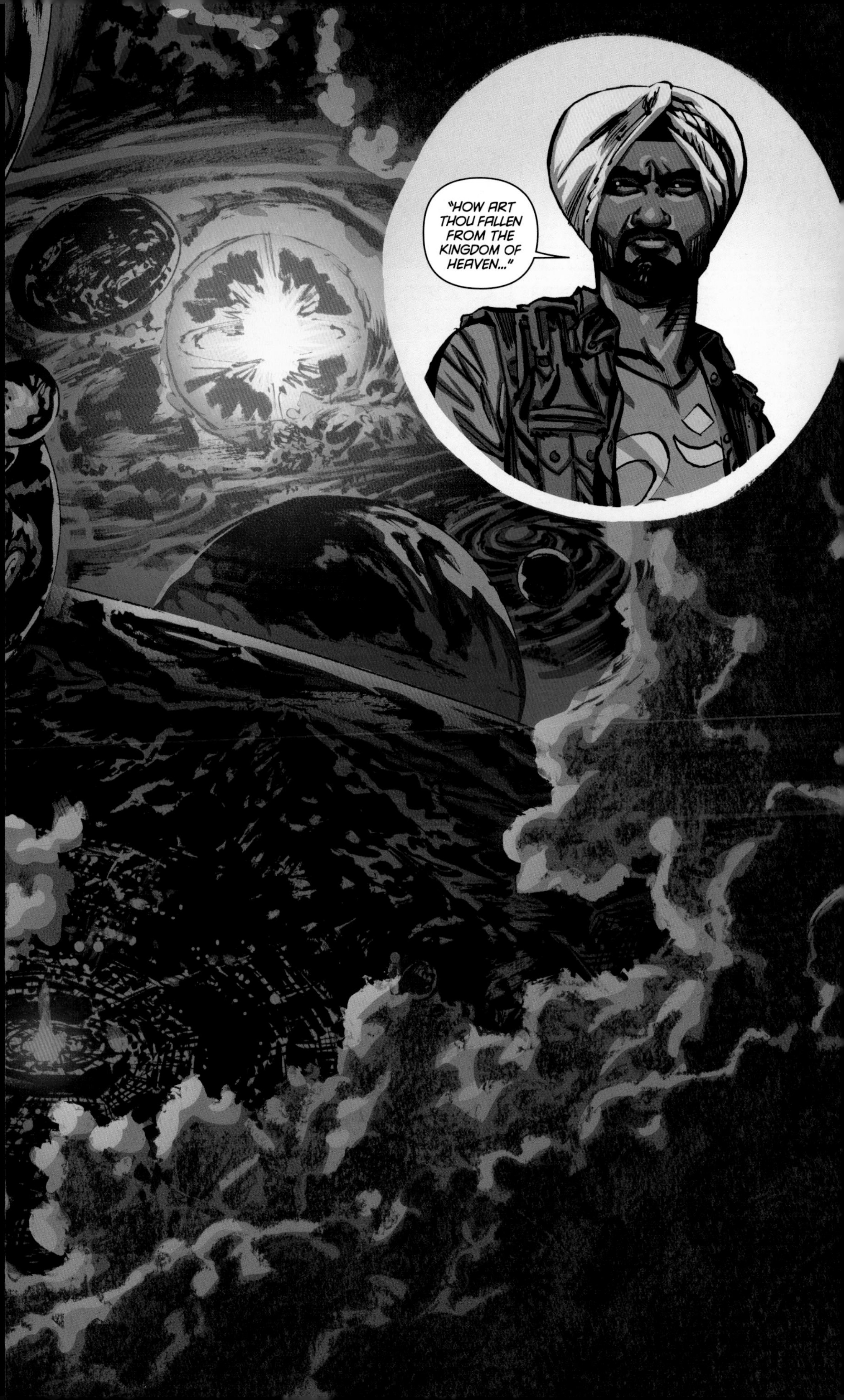
"HOW ART THOU FALLEN FROM THE KINGDOM OF HEAVEN..."

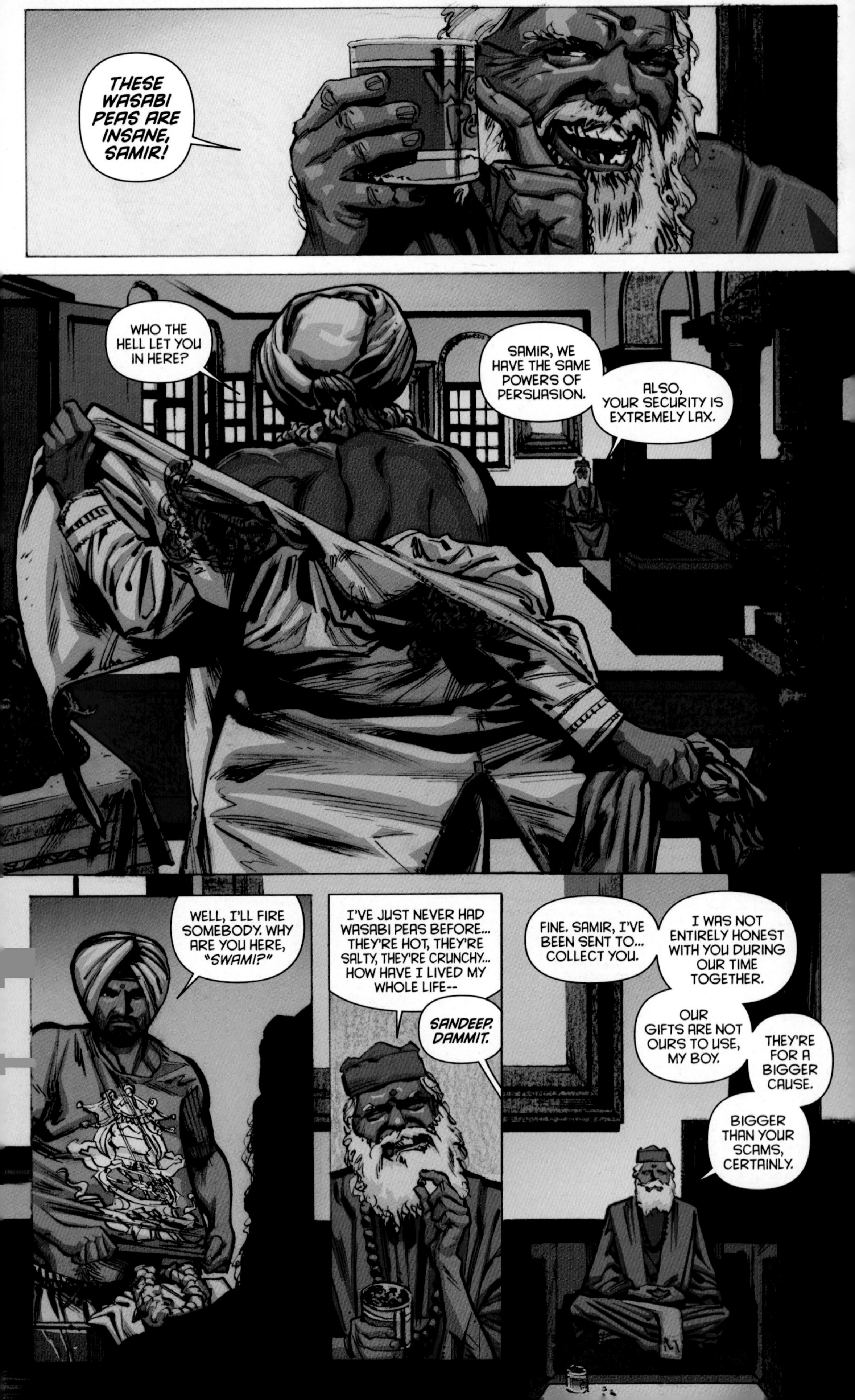
THESE WASABI PEAS ARE INSANE, SAMIR!
WHO THE HELL LET YOU IN HERE?
SAMIR, WE HAVE THE SAME POWERS OF PERSUASION.
ALSO, YOUR SECURITY IS EXTREMELY LAX.
WELL, I'LL FIRE SOMEBODY. WHY ARE YOU HERE, "SWAMI?"
I'VE JUST NEVER HAD WASABI PEAS BEFORE... THEY'RE HOT, THEY'RE SALTY, THEY'RE CRUNCHY... HOW HAVE I LIVED MY WHOLE LIFE--
SANDEEP. DAMMIT.
FINE. SAMIR, I'VE BEEN SENT TO... COLLECT YOU.
I WAS NOT ENTIRELY HONEST WITH YOU DURING OUR TIME TOGETHER.
OUR GIFTS ARE NOT OURS TO USE, MY BOY.
THEY'RE FOR A BIGGER CAUSE.
BIGGER THAN YOUR SCAMS, CERTAINLY.

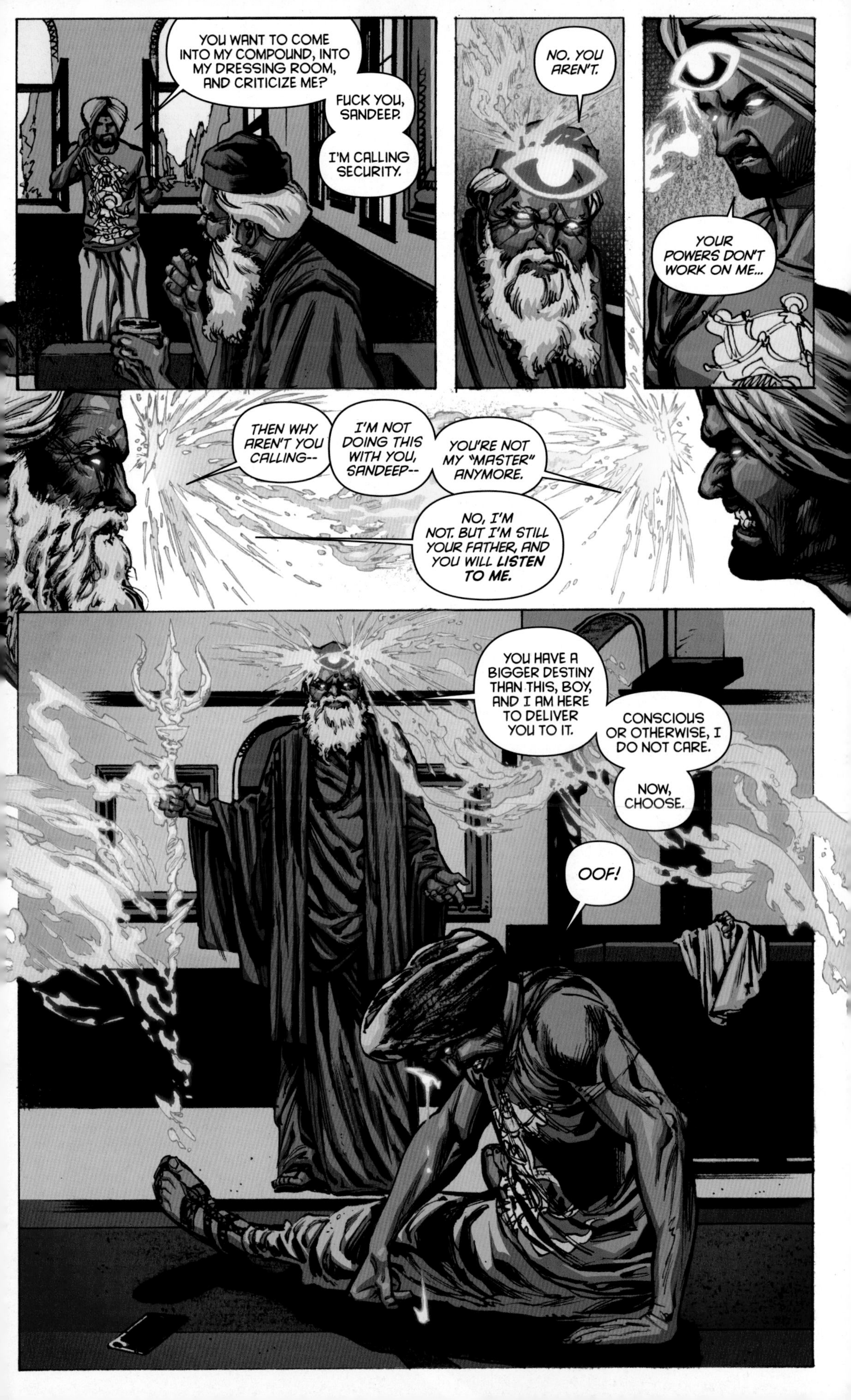
YOU WANT TO COME INTO MY COMPOUND, INTO MY DRESSING ROOM, AND CRITICIZE ME?
FUCK YOU, SANDEEP.
I'M CALLING SECURITY.
NO. YOU AREN'T.
YOUR POWERS DON'T WORK ON ME...
THEN WHY AREN'T YOU CALLING--
I'M NOT DOING THIS WITH YOU, SANDEEP--
YOU'RE NOT MY "MASTER" ANYMORE.
NO, I'M NOT. BUT I'M STILL YOUR FATHER, AND YOU WILL LISTEN TO ME.
YOU HAVE A BIGGER DESTINY THAN THIS, BOY, AND I AM HERE TO DELIVER YOU TO IT.
CONSCIOUS OR OTHERWISE, I DO NOT CARE.
NOW, CHOOSE.
OOF!

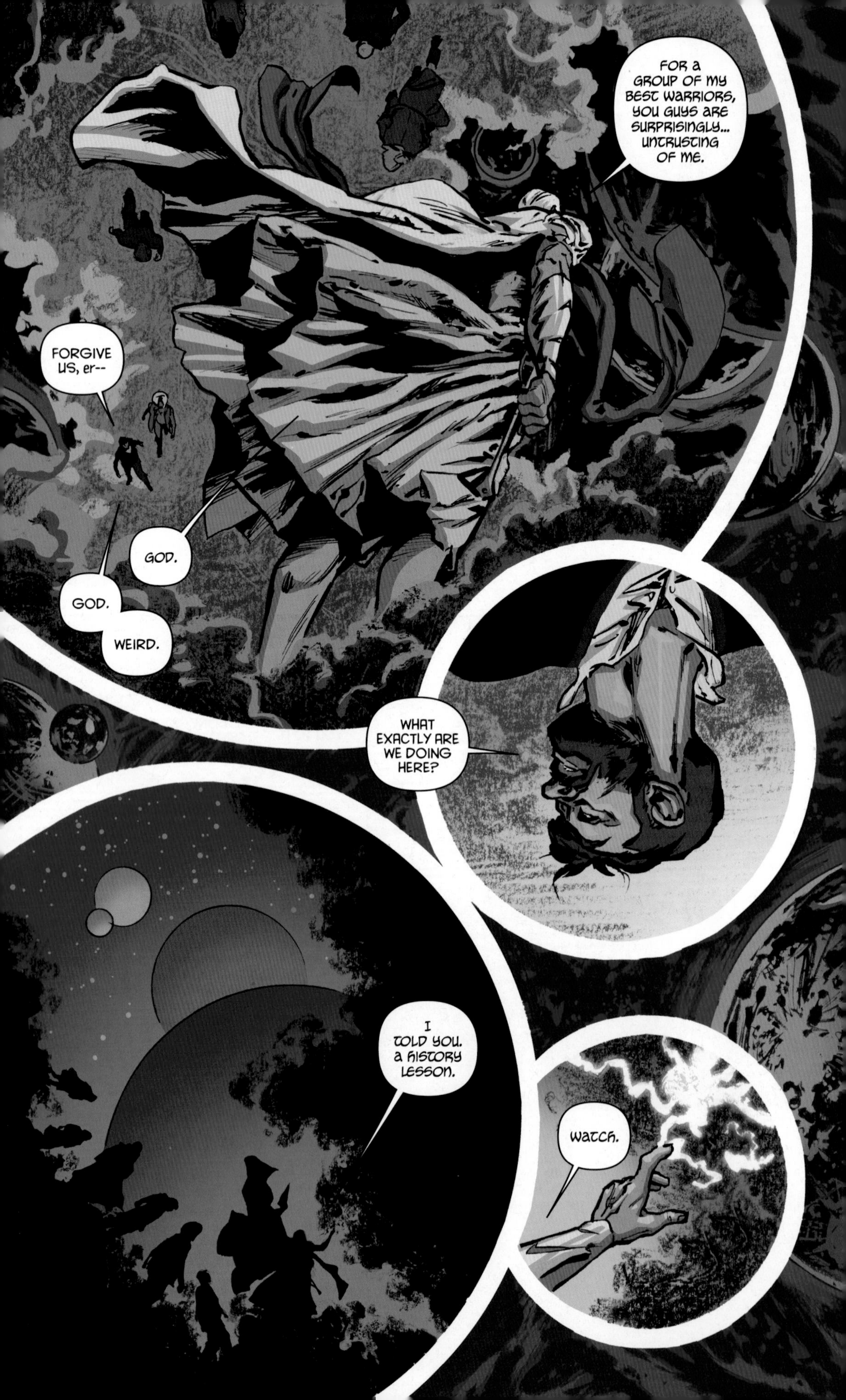
FOR A GROUP OF MY BEST WARRIORS, YOU GUYS ARE SURPRISINGLY... UNTRUSTING OF ME.
FORGIVE US, er--
GOD.
GOD.
WEIRD.
WHAT EXACTLY ARE WE DOING HERE?
I TOLD YOU. A HISTORY LESSON.
WATCH.

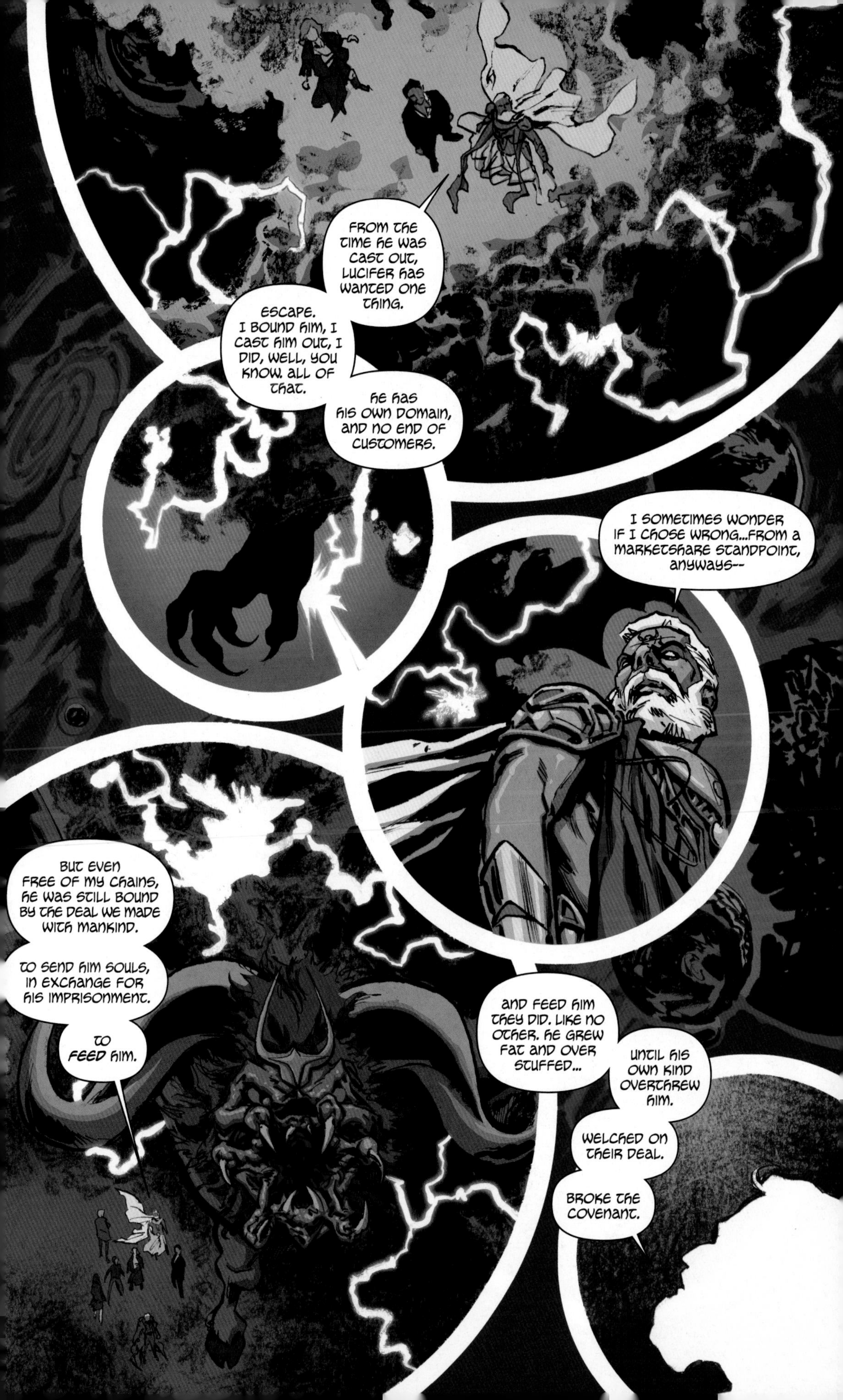
FROM THE TIME HE WAS CAST OUT, LUCIFER HAS WANTED ONE THING.
ESCAPE. I BOUND HIM, I CAST HIM OUT, I DID, WELL, YOU KNOW. ALL OF THAT.
HE HAS HIS OWN DOMAIN, AND NO END OF CUSTOMERS.
I SOMETIMES WONDER IF I CHOSE WRONG...FROM A MARKETSHARE STANDPOINT, ANYWAYS--
BUT EVEN FREE OF MY CHAINS, HE WAS STILL BOUND BY THE DEAL WE MADE WITH MANKIND.
TO SEND HIM SOULS, IN EXCHANGE FOR HIS IMPRISONMENT.
TO *FEED* HIM.
AND FEED HIM THEY DID. LIKE NO OTHER. HE GREW FAT AND OVER STUFFED...
UNTIL HIS OWN KIND OVERTHREW HIM.
WELCHED ON THEIR DEAL.
BROKE THE COVENANT.

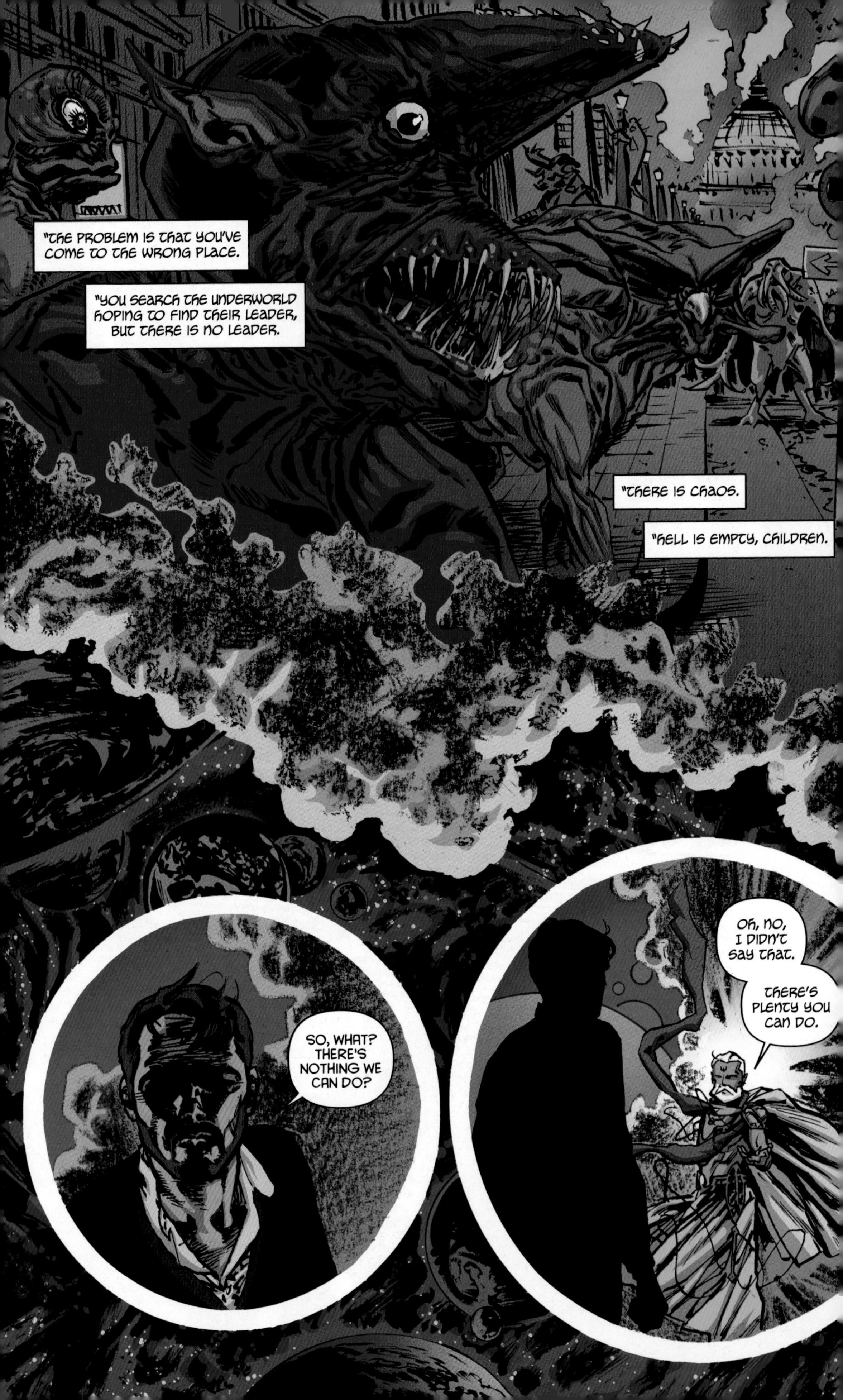
"THE PROBLEM IS THAT YOU'VE COME TO THE WRONG PLACE.
"YOU SEARCH THE UNDERWORLD HOPING TO FIND THEIR LEADER, BUT THERE IS NO LEADER.
"THERE IS CHAOS.
"HELL IS EMPTY, CHILDREN.
SO, WHAT? THERE'S NOTHING WE CAN DO?
OH, NO, I DIDN'T SAY THAT.
THERE'S PLENTY YOU CAN DO.

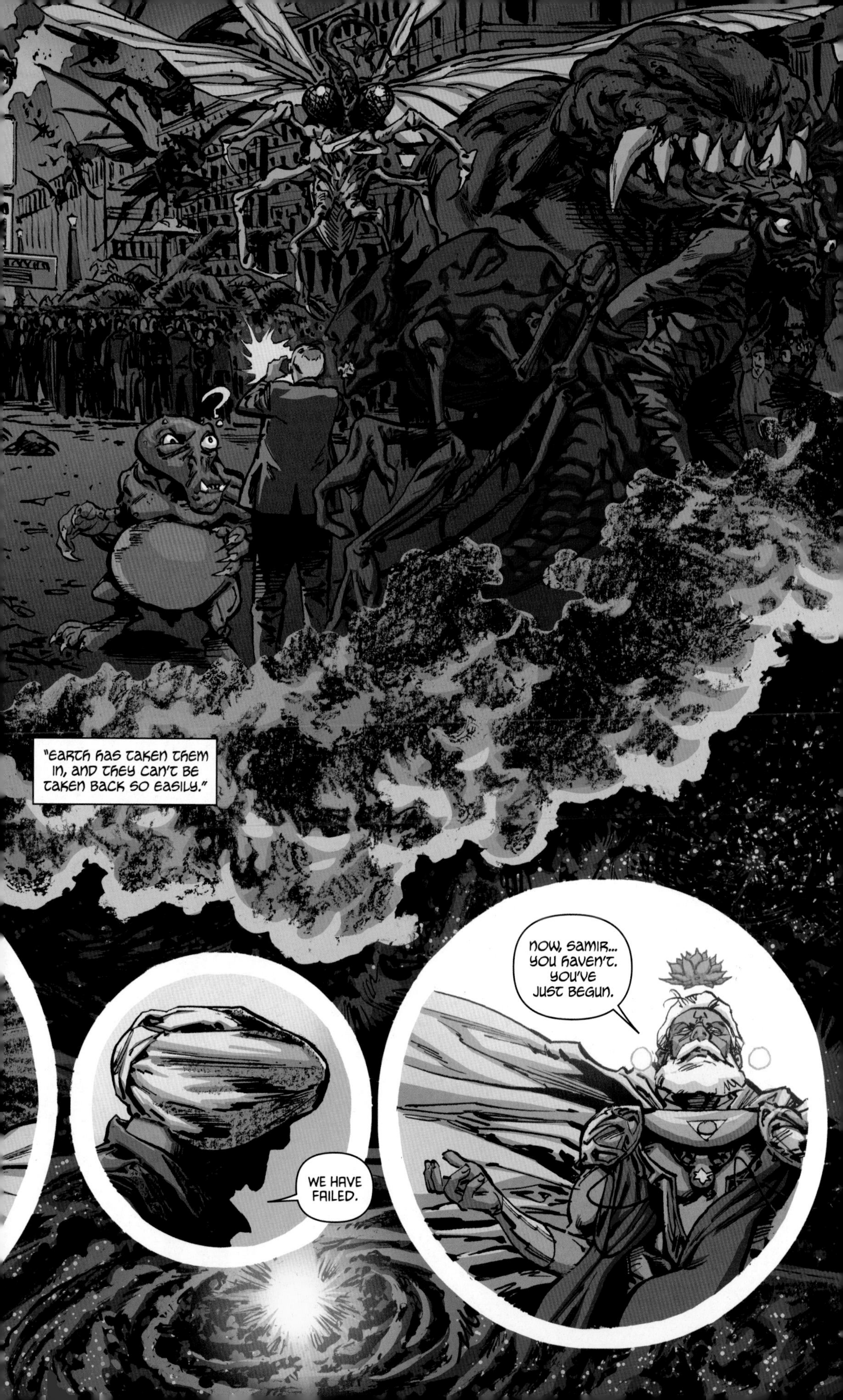
"EARTH HAS TAKEN THEM IN, AND THEY CAN'T BE TAKEN BACK SO EASILY."
WE HAVE FAILED.
NOW, SAMIR... YOU HAVEN'T. YOU'VE JUST BEGUN.

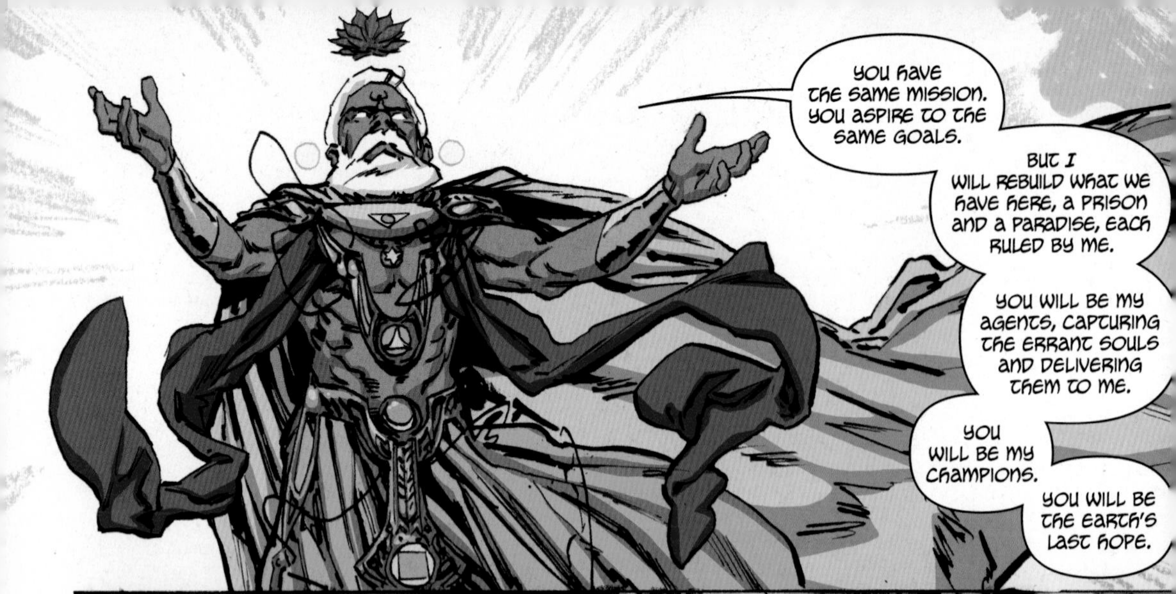
YOU HAVE THE SAME MISSION. YOU ASPIRE TO THE SAME GOALS.
BUT I WILL REBUILD WHAT WE HAVE HERE, A PRISON AND A PARADISE, EACH RULED BY ME.
YOU WILL BE MY AGENTS, CAPTURING THE ERRANT SOULS AND DELIVERING THEM TO ME.
YOU WILL BE MY CHAMPIONS.
YOU WILL BE THE EARTH'S LAST HOPE.

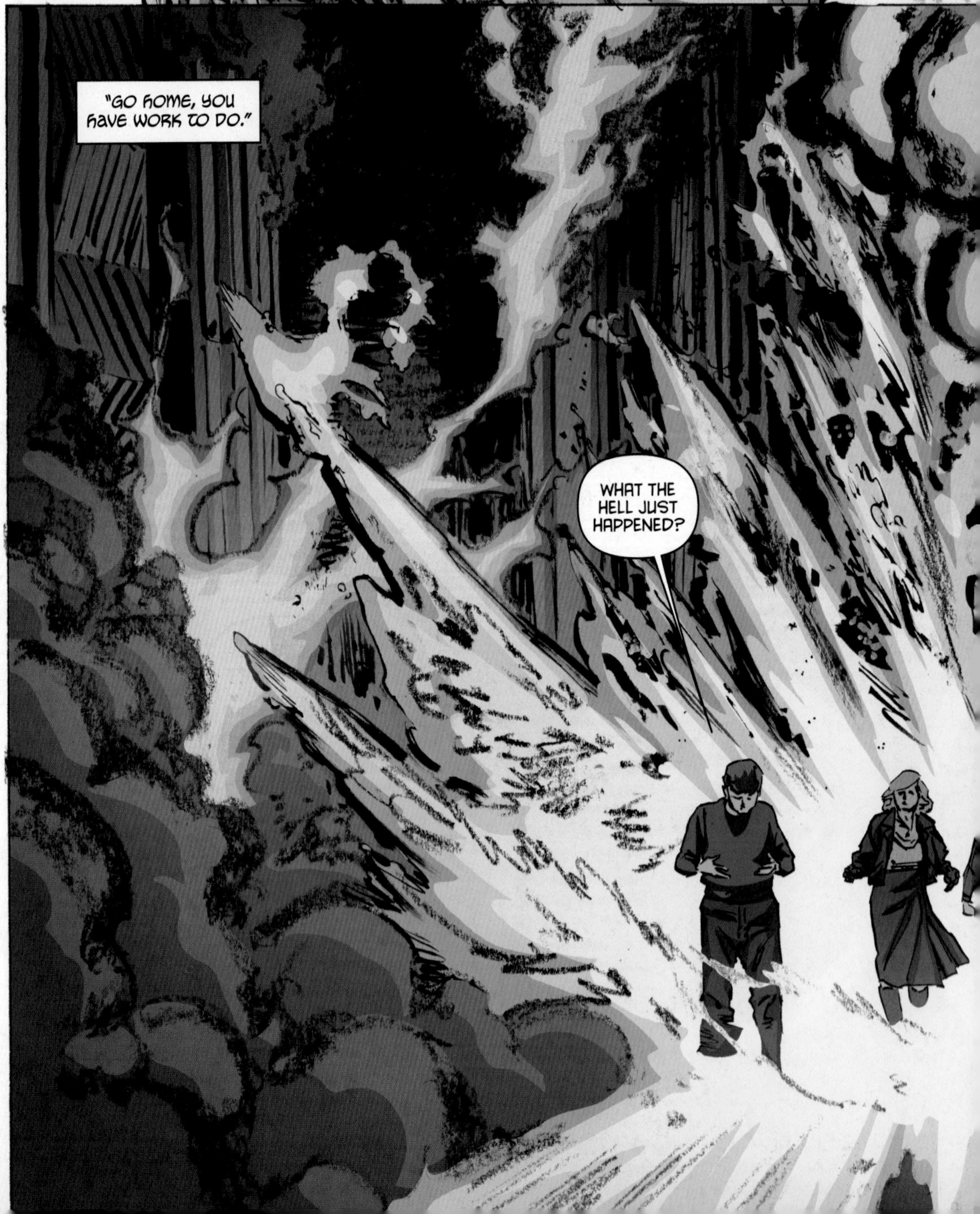
"GO HOME, YOU HAVE WORK TO DO."
WHAT THE HELL JUST HAPPENED?

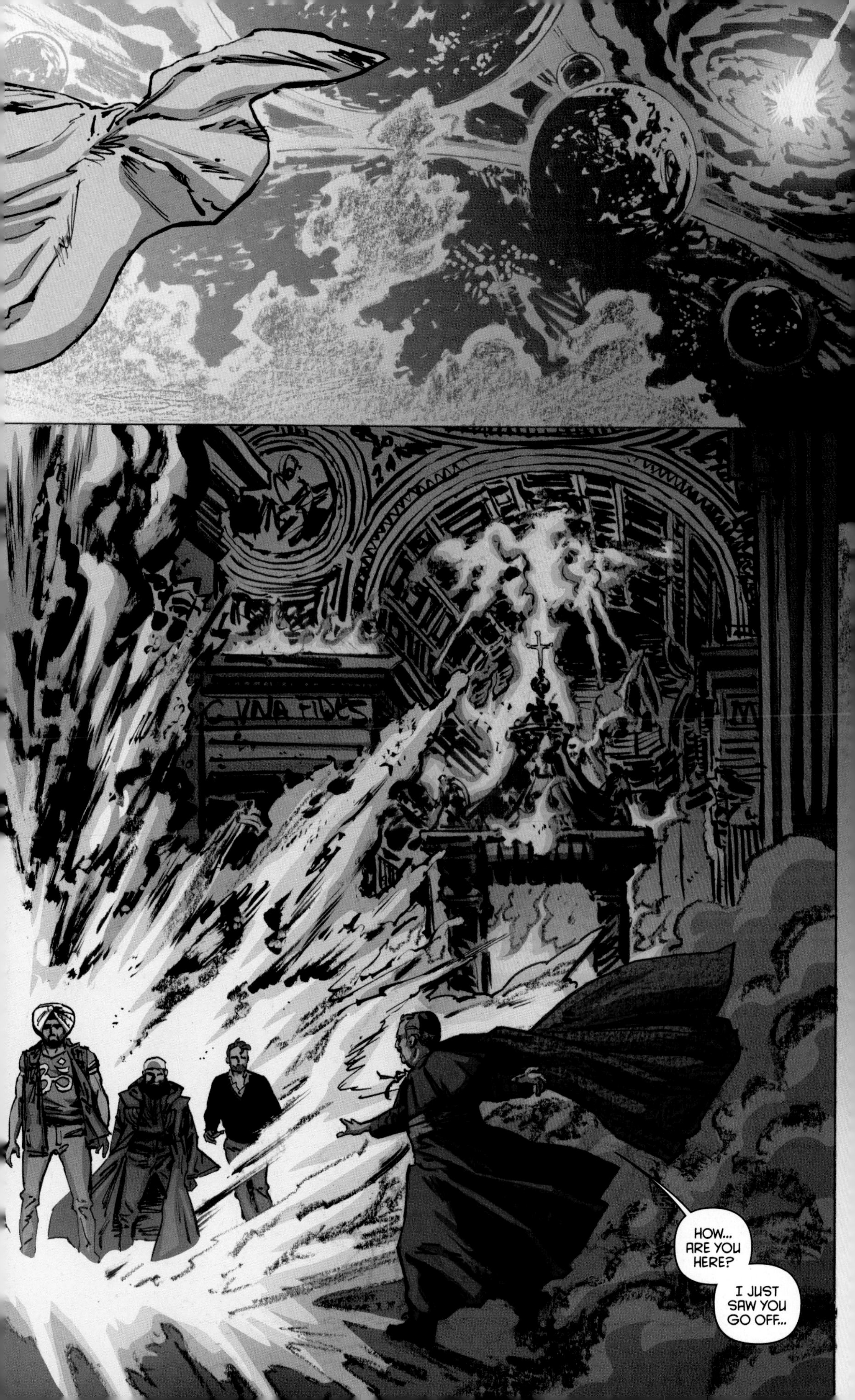
HOW... ARE YOU HERE?
I JUST SAW YOU GO OFF...

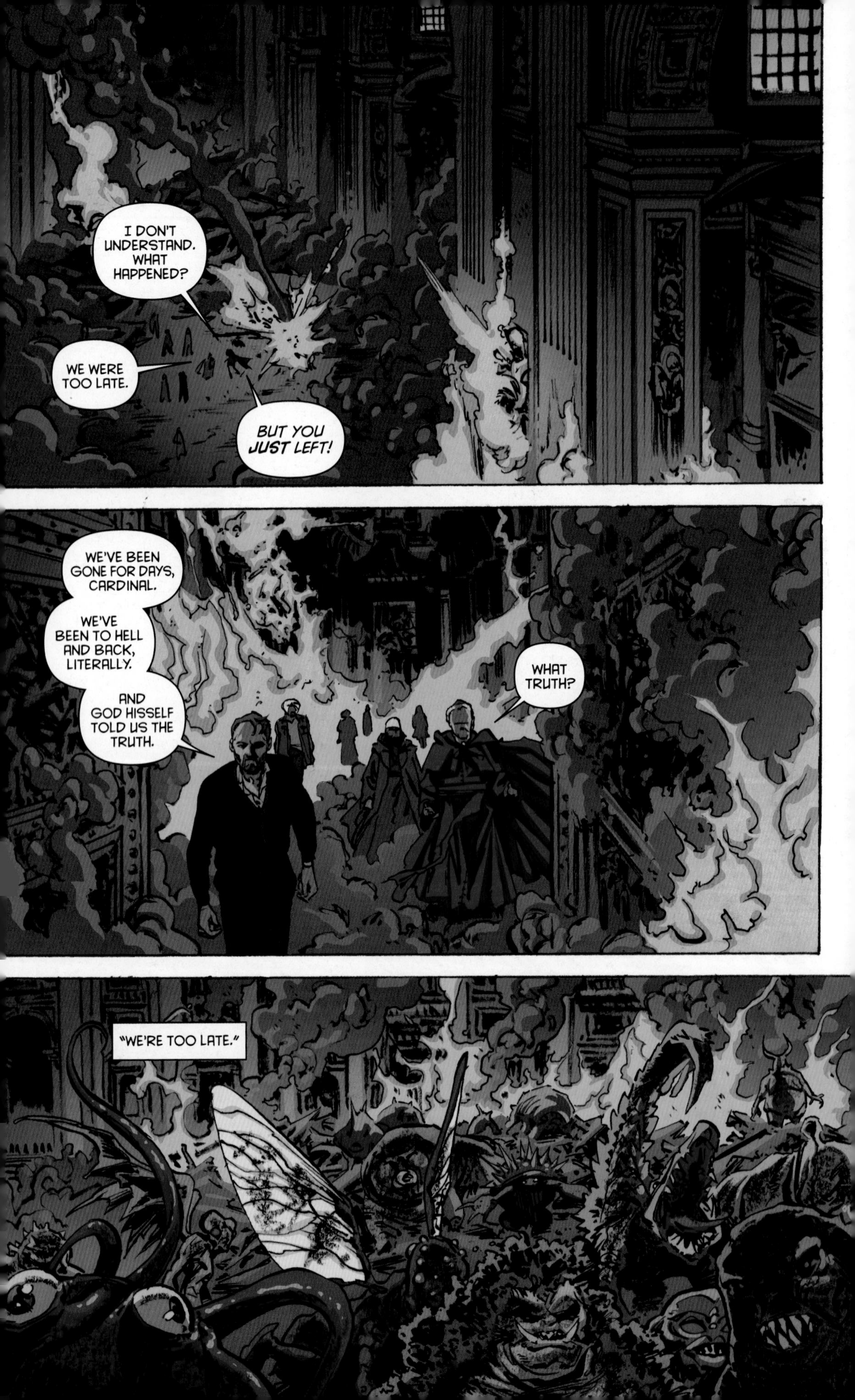
I DON'T UNDERSTAND. WHAT HAPPENED?
WE WERE TOO LATE.
BUT YOU JUST LEFT!
WE'VE BEEN GONE FOR DAYS, CARDINAL.
WE'VE BEEN TO HELL AND BACK, LITERALLY.
AND GOD HISSELF TOLD US THE TRUTH.
WHAT TRUTH?
"WE'RE TOO LATE."

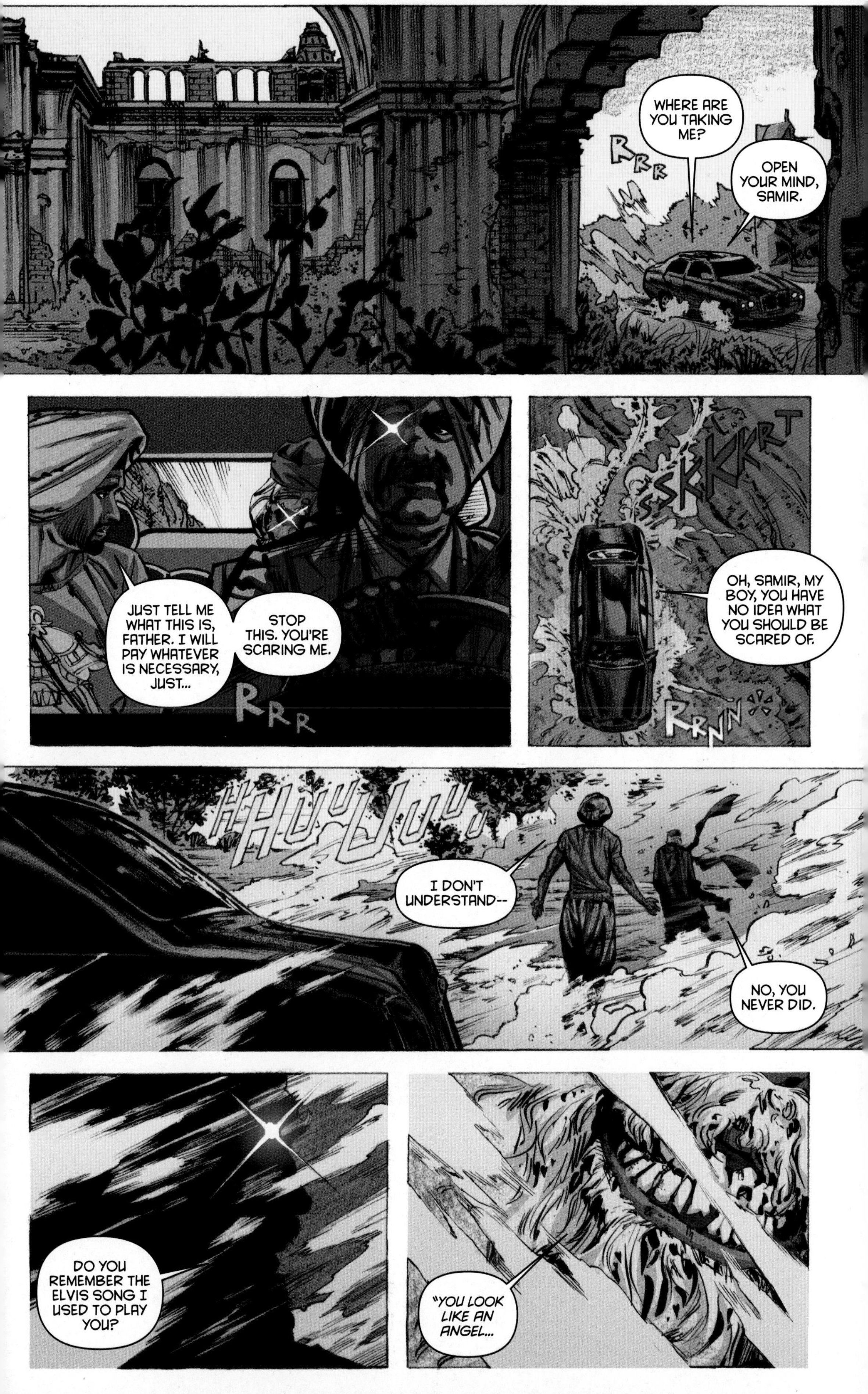
WHERE ARE YOU TAKING ME?
RRR
OPEN YOUR MIND, SAMIR.
JUST TELL ME WHAT THIS IS, FATHER. I WILL PAY WHATEVER IS NECESSARY, JUST...
STOP THIS. YOU'RE SCARING ME.
RRR
SSKKKRT
OH, SAMIR, MY BOY, YOU HAVE NO IDEA WHAT YOU SHOULD BE SCARED OF.
RRNN
HHUUUUUU
I DON'T UNDERSTAND--
NO, YOU NEVER DID.
DO YOU REMEMBER THE ELVIS SONG I USED TO PLAY YOU?
"YOU LOOK LIKE AN ANGEL...

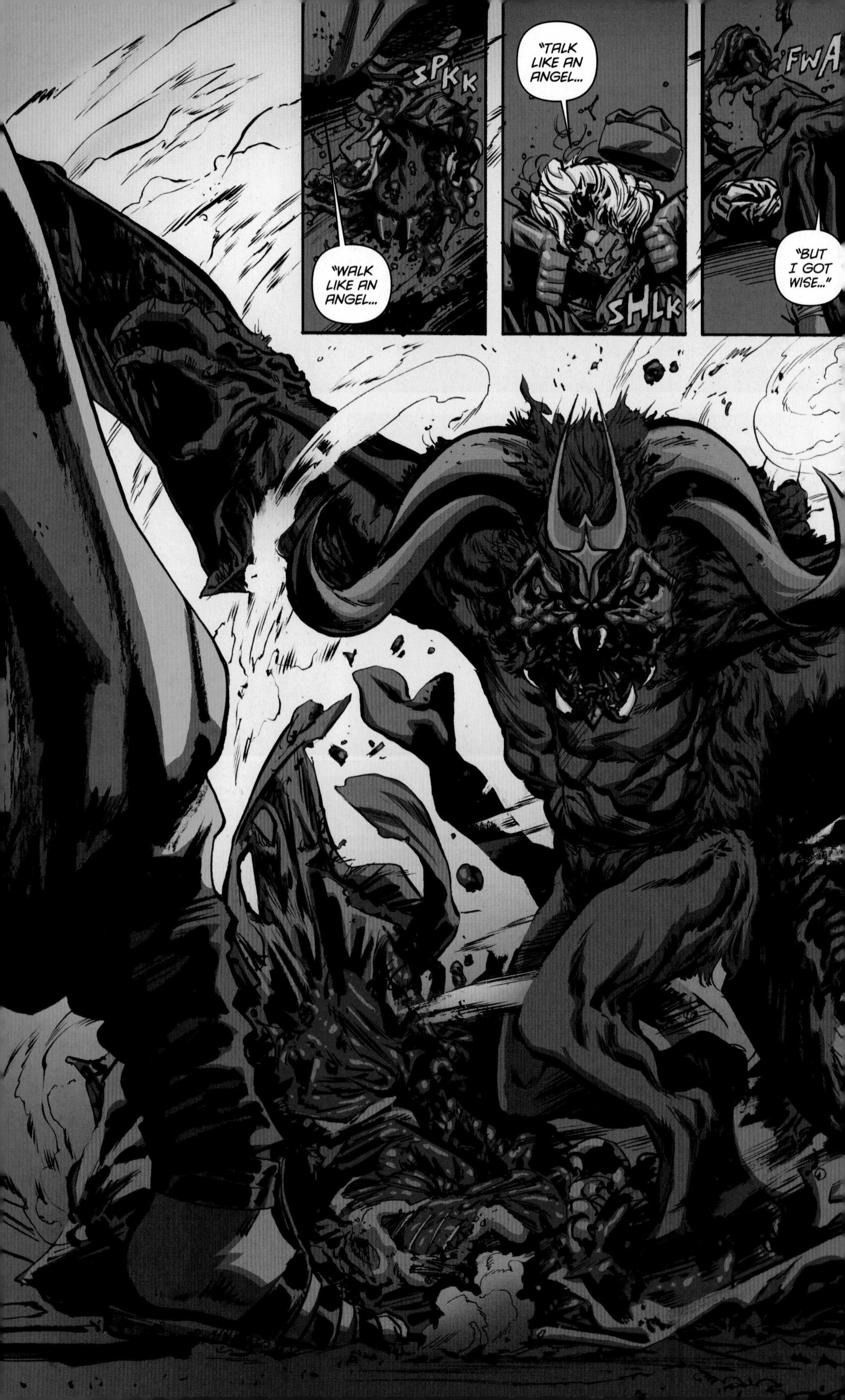
SPKK
"WALK LIKE AN ANGEL...
"TALK LIKE AN ANGEL...
SHLK
FWA
"BUT I GOT WISE..."

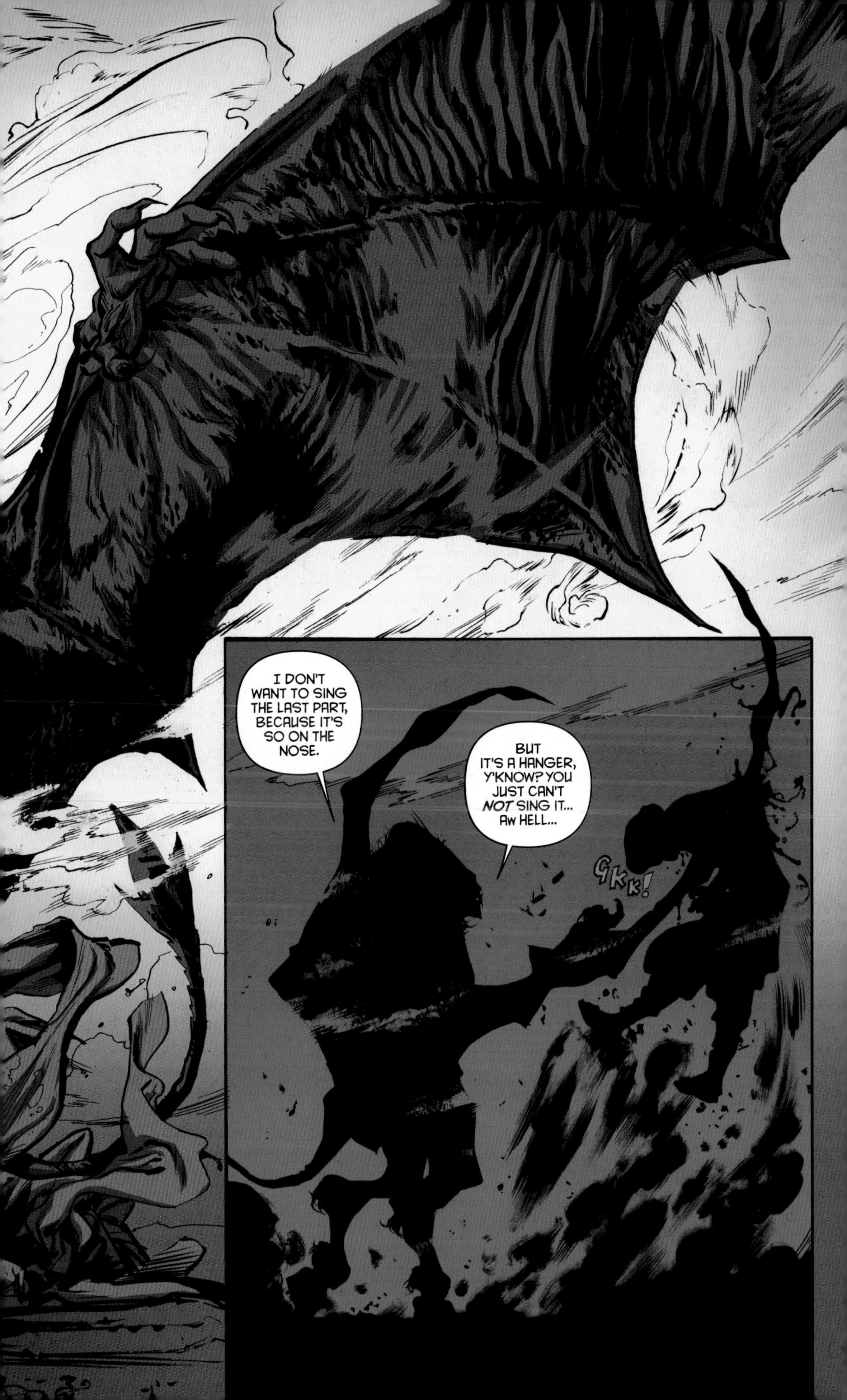
I DON'T WANT TO SING THE LAST PART, BECAUSE IT'S SO ON THE NOSE.
BUT IT'S A HANGER, Y'KNOW? YOU JUST CAN'T *NOT* SING IT... AW HELL...
GKK!

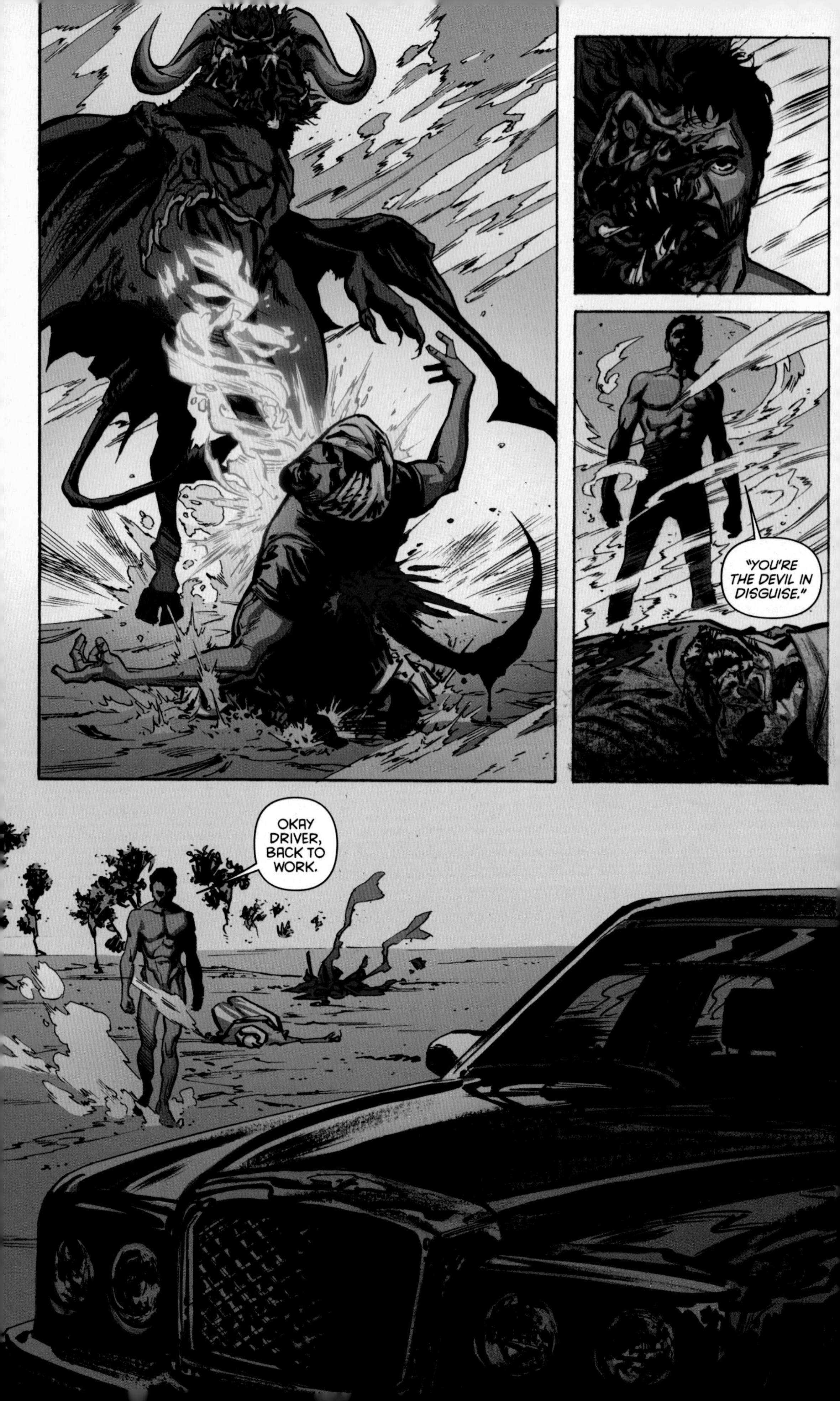
"YOU'RE THE DEVIL IN DISGUISE."
OKAY DRIVER, BACK TO WORK.

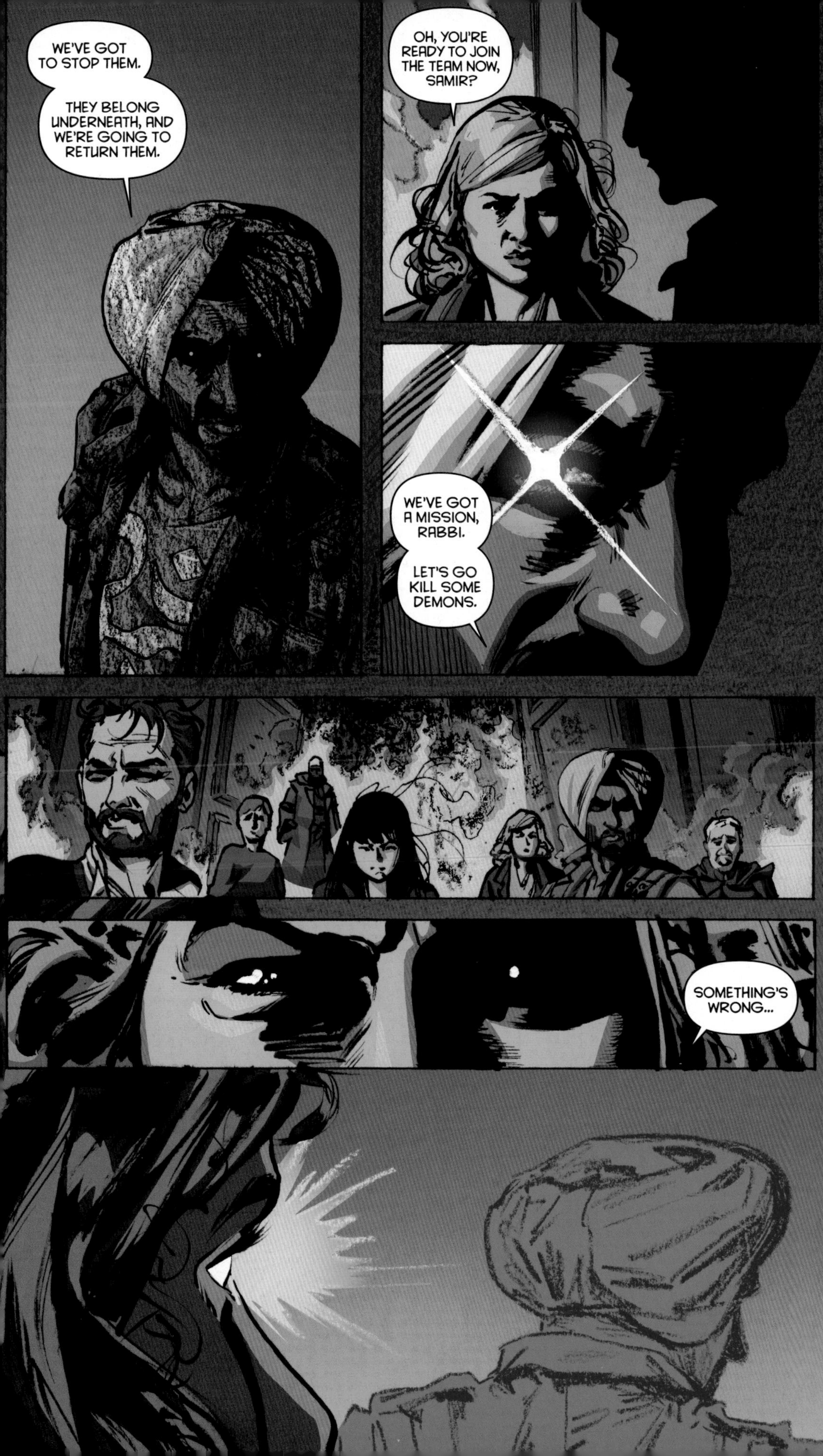
WE'VE GOT TO STOP THEM.
THEY BELONG UNDERNEATH, AND WE'RE GOING TO RETURN THEM.
OH, YOU'RE READY TO JOIN THE TEAM NOW, SAMIR?
WE'VE GOT A MISSION, RABBI.
LET'S GO KILL SOME DEMONS.
SOMETHING'S WRONG...

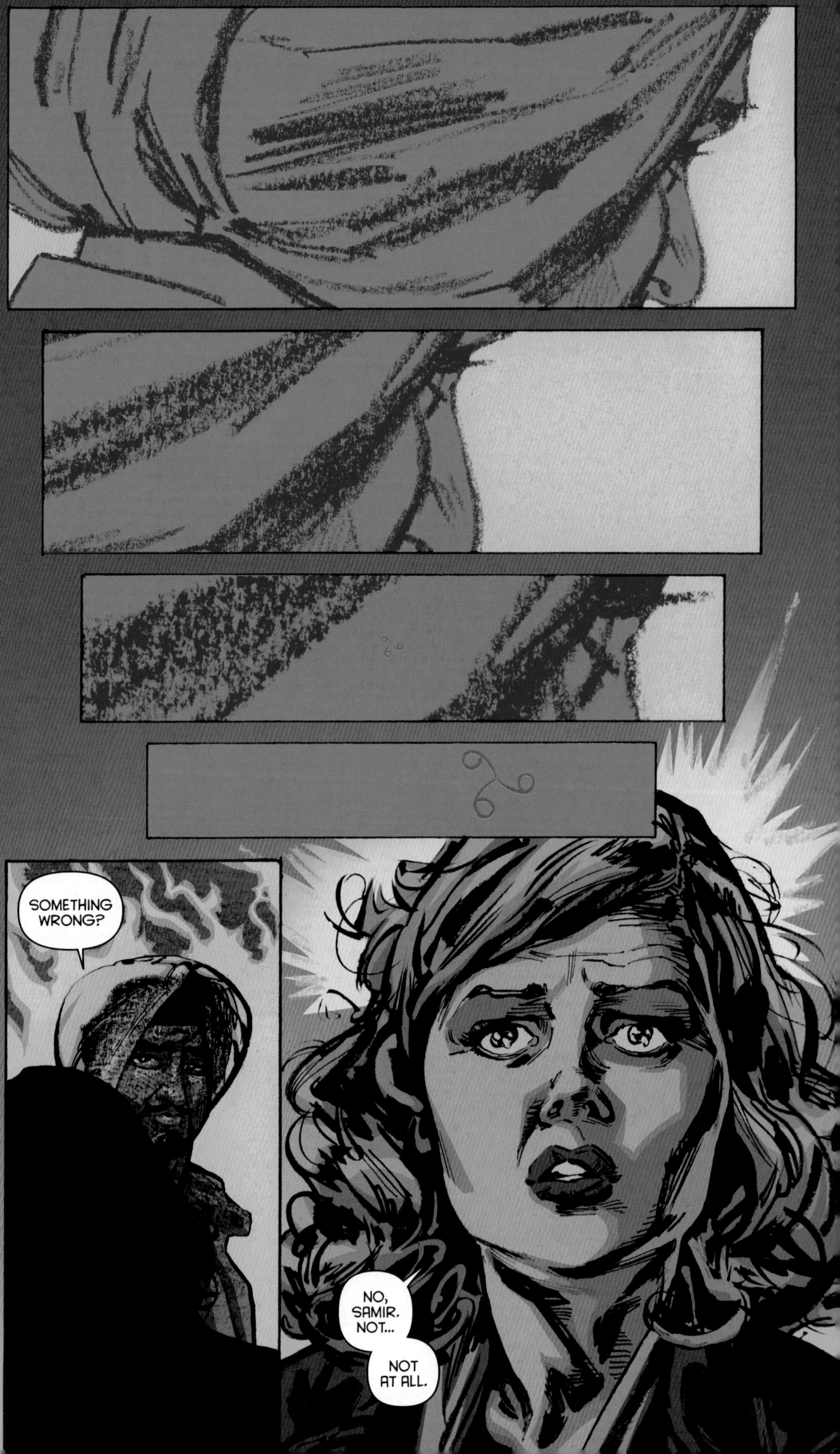
SOMETHING WRONG?
NO, SAMIR. NOT...
NOT AT ALL.

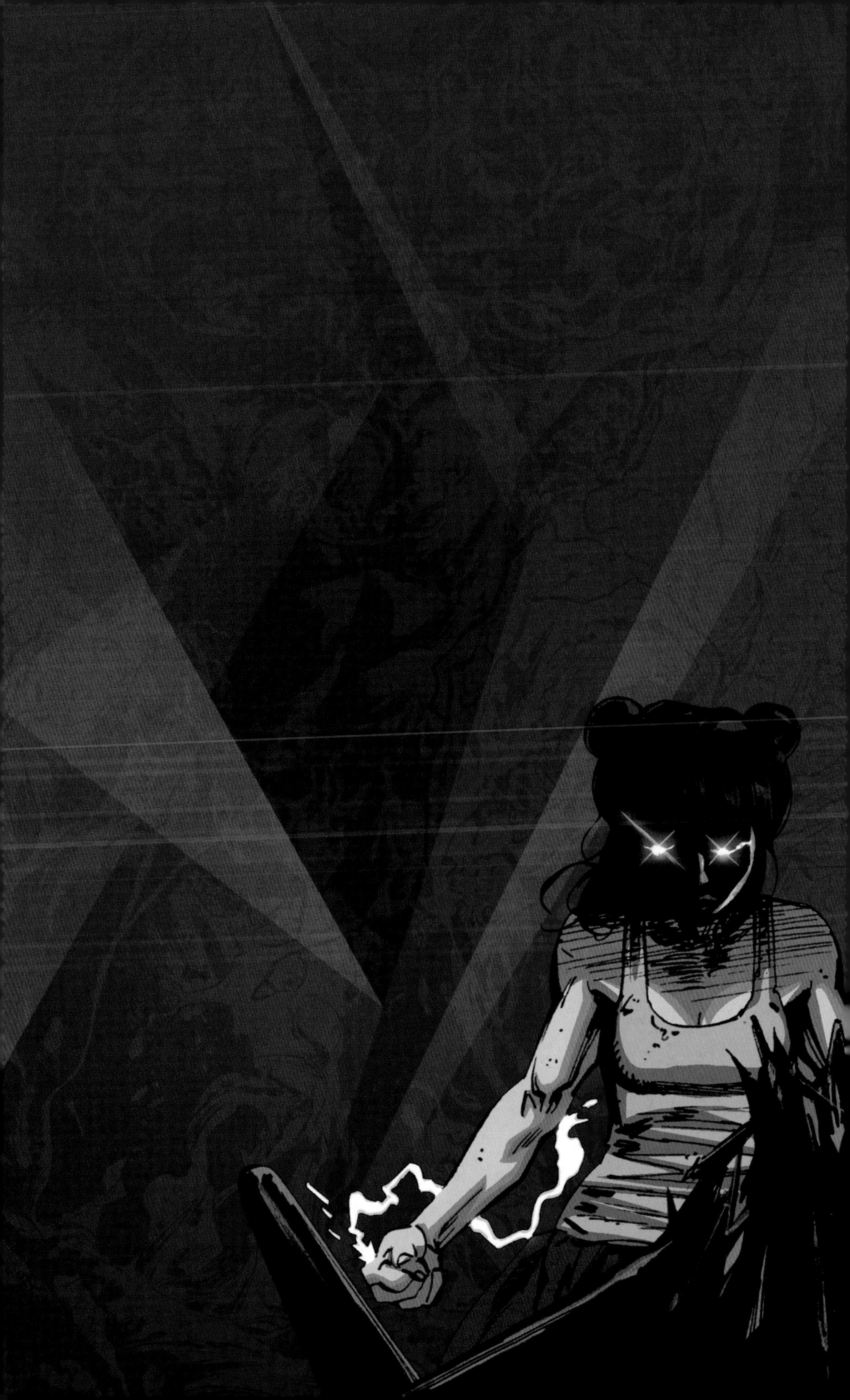

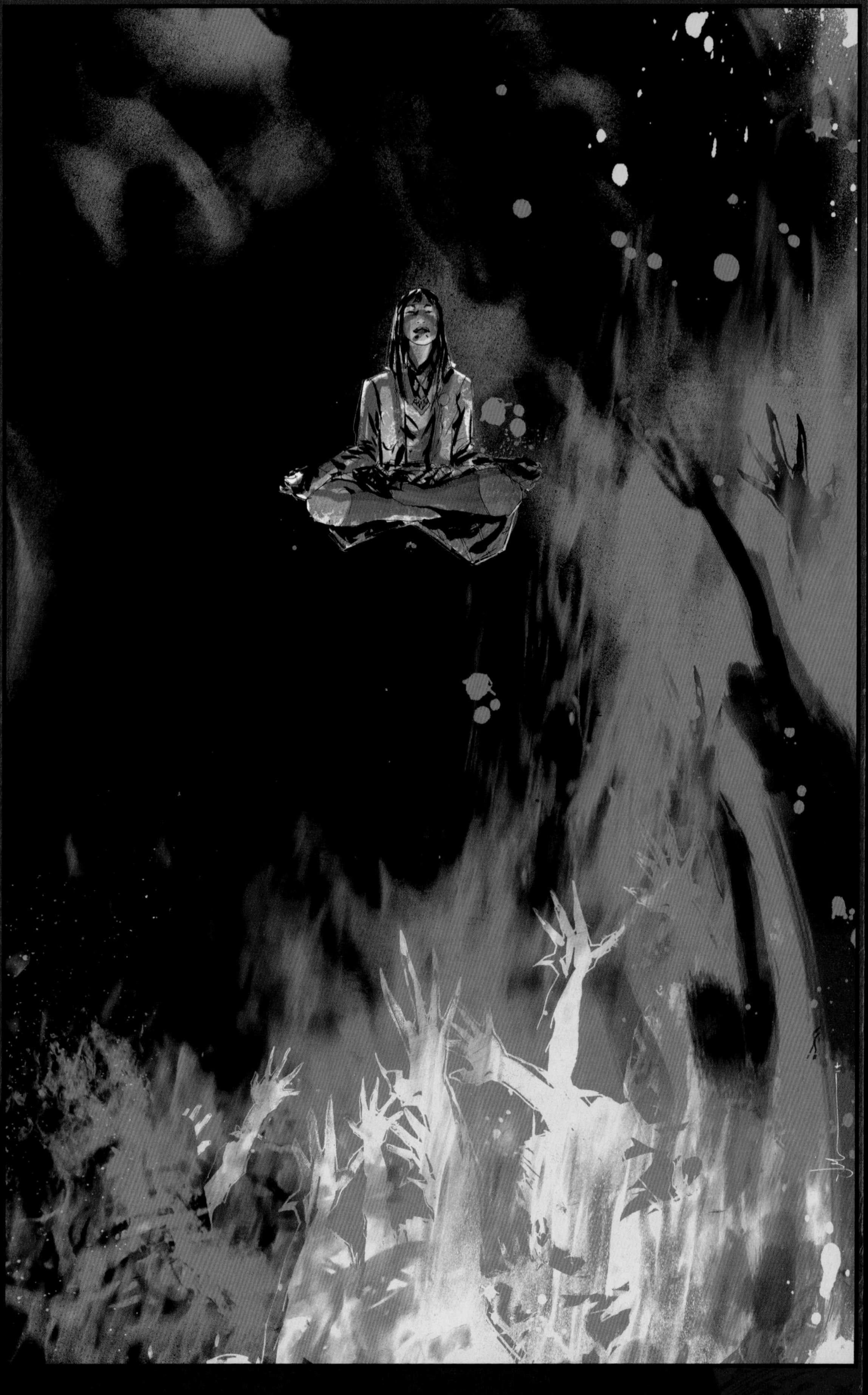

ISSUE #5 cover art by JOCK

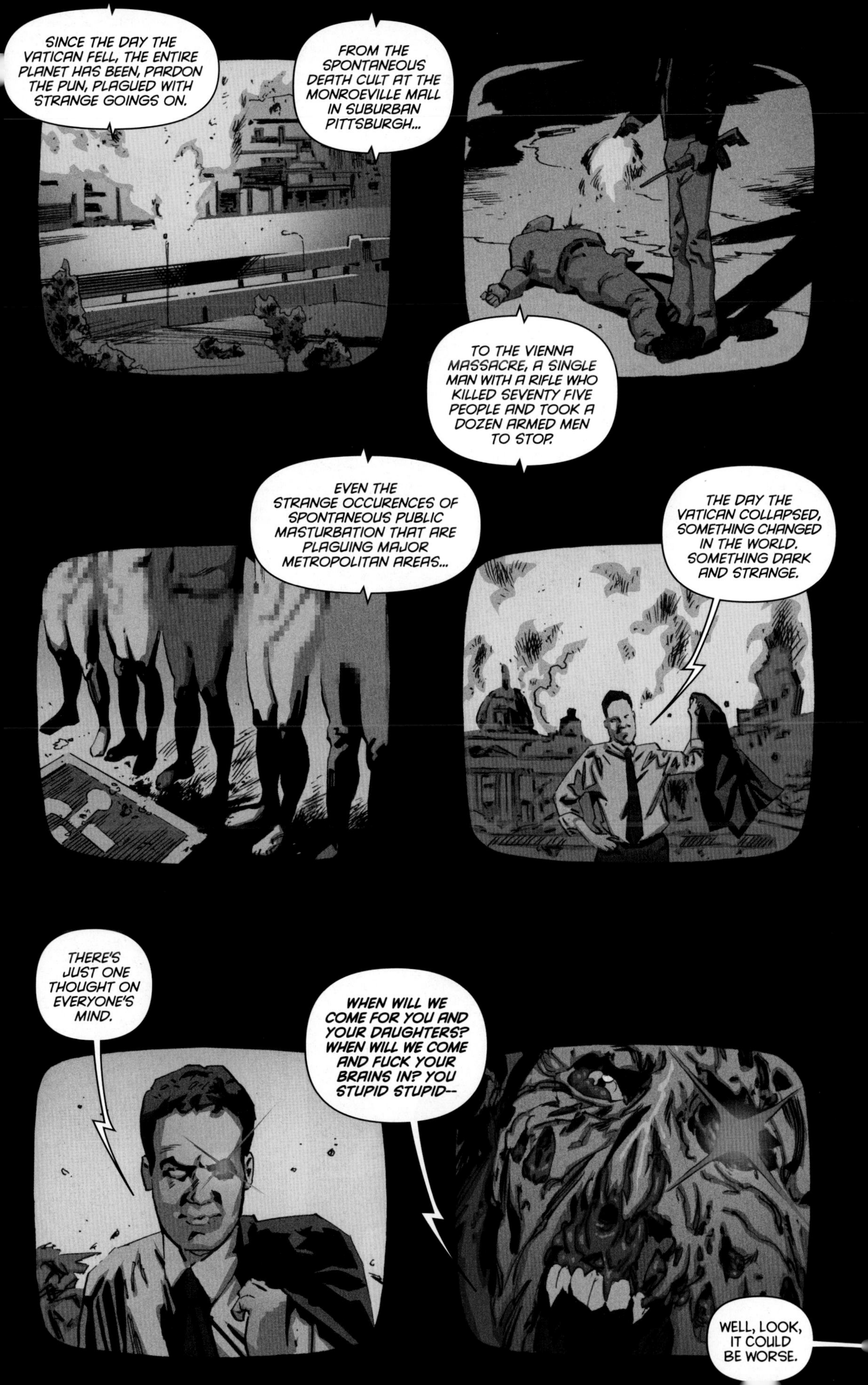
SINCE THE DAY THE VATICAN FELL, THE ENTIRE PLANET HAS BEEN, PARDON THE PUN, PLAGUED WITH STRANGE GOINGS ON.
FROM THE SPONTANEOUS DEATH CULT AT THE MONROEVILLE MALL IN SUBURBAN PITTSBURGH...
TO THE VIENNA MASSACRE, A SINGLE MAN WITH A RIFLE WHO KILLED SEVENTY FIVE PEOPLE AND TOOK A DOZEN ARMED MEN TO STOP.
EVEN THE STRANGE OCCURENCES OF SPONTANEOUS PUBLIC MASTURBATION THAT ARE PLAGUING MAJOR METROPOLITAN AREAS...
THE DAY THE VATICAN COLLAPSED, SOMETHING CHANGED IN THE WORLD. SOMETHING DARK AND STRANGE.
THERE'S JUST ONE THOUGHT ON EVERYONE'S MIND.
WHEN WILL WE COME FOR YOU AND YOUR DAUGHTERS? WHEN WILL WE COME AND FUCK YOUR BRAINS IN? YOU STUPID STUPID--
WELL, LOOK, IT COULD BE WORSE.

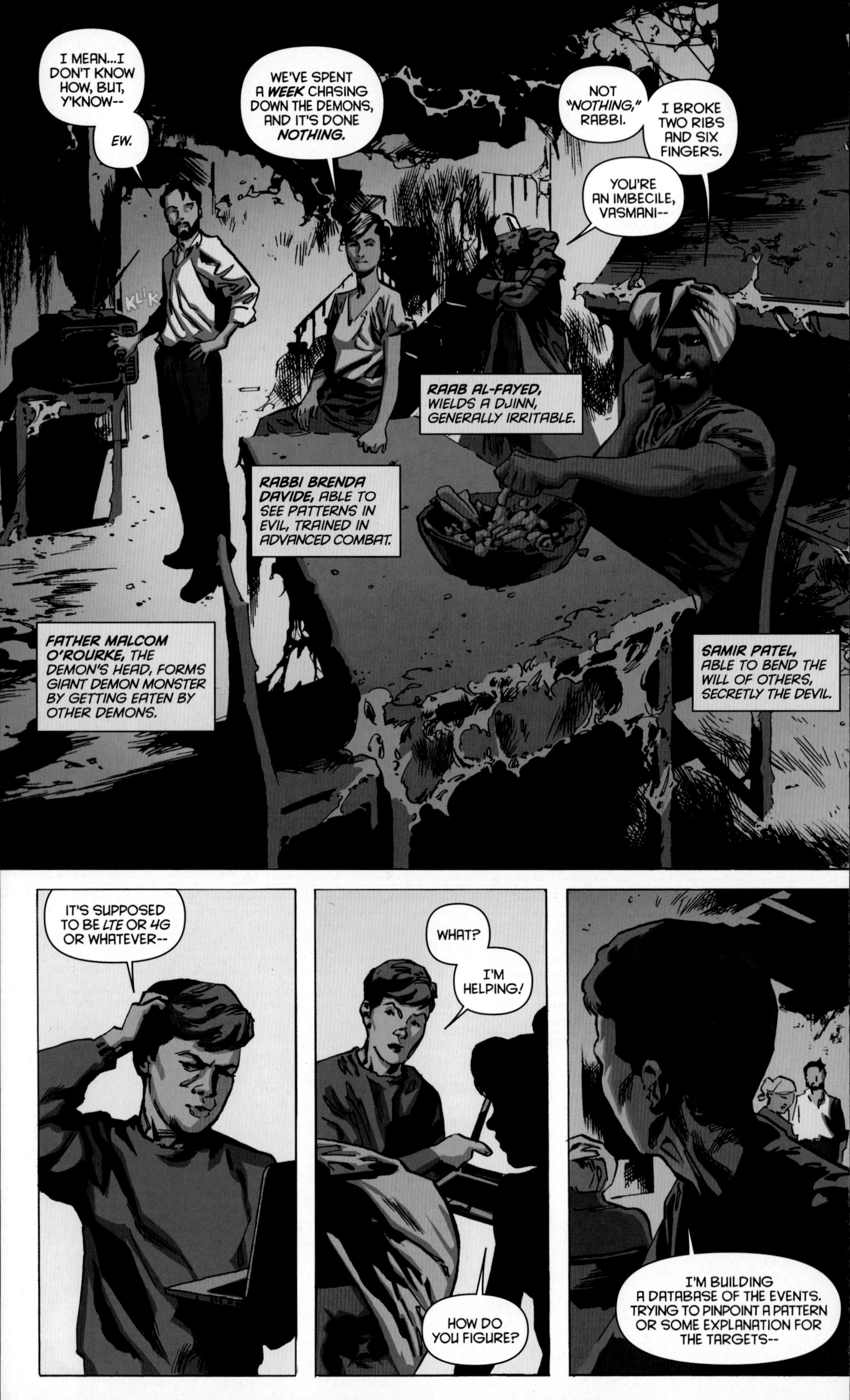
I MEAN...I DON'T KNOW HOW, BUT, Y'KNOW--
EW.
WE'VE SPENT A WEEK CHASING DOWN THE DEMONS, AND IT'S DONE NOTHING.
NOT "NOTHING," RABBI.
I BROKE TWO RIBS AND SIX FINGERS.
YOU'RE AN IMBECILE, VASMANI--
KLIK
RAAB AL-FAYED, WIELDS A DJINN, GENERALLY IRRITABLE.
RABBI BRENDA DAVIDE, ABLE TO SEE PATTERNS IN EVIL, TRAINED IN ADVANCED COMBAT.
FATHER MALCOM O'ROURKE, THE DEMON'S HEAD, FORMS GIANT DEMON MONSTER BY GETTING EATEN BY OTHER DEMONS.
SAMIR PATEL, ABLE TO BEND THE WILL OF OTHERS, SECRETLY THE DEVIL.
IT'S SUPPOSED TO BE LTE OR 4G OR WHATEVER--
WHAT?
I'M HELPING!
HOW DO YOU FIGURE?
I'M BUILDING A DATABASE OF THE EVENTS. TRYING TO PINPOINT A PATTERN OR SOME EXPLANATION FOR THE TARGETS--

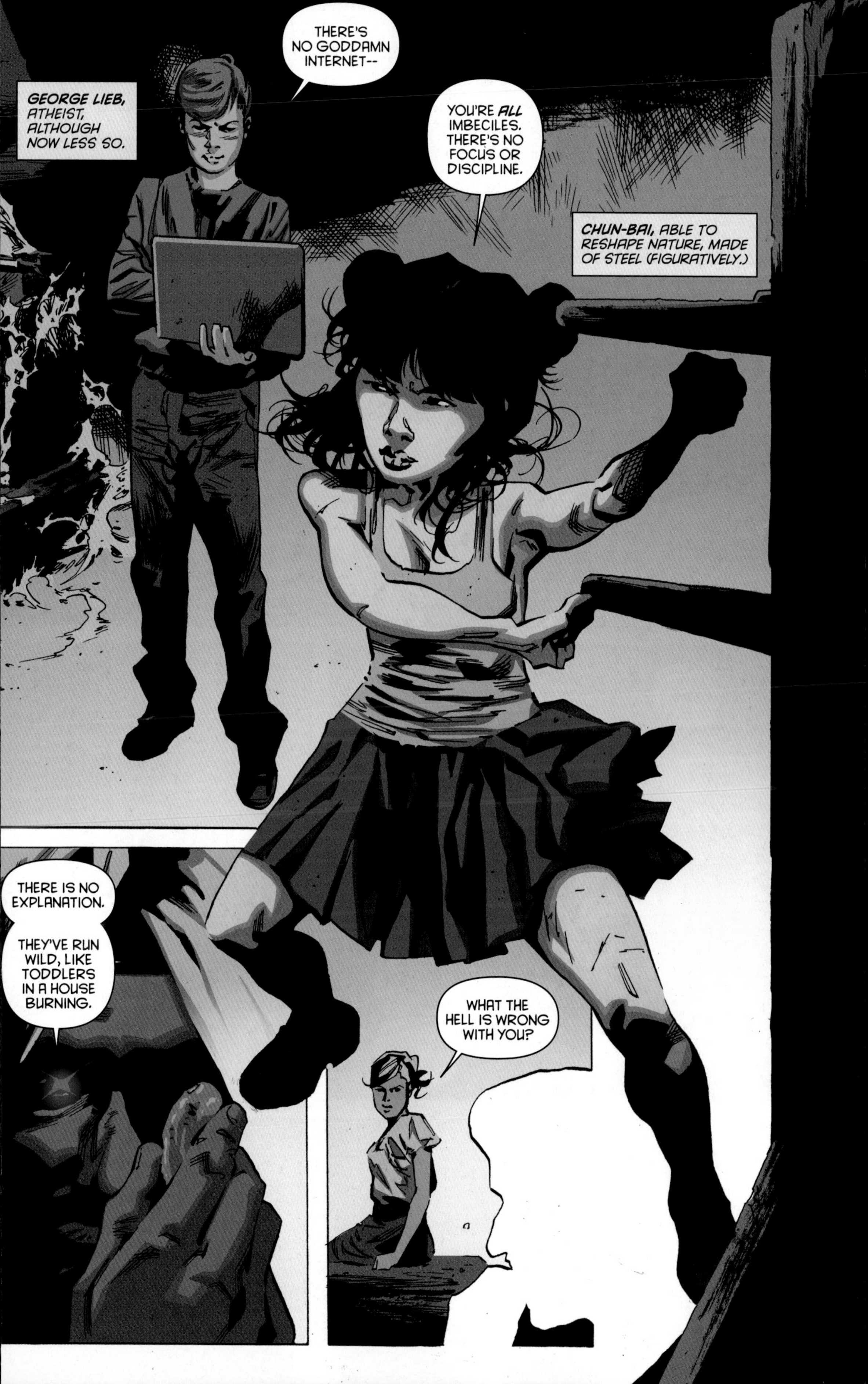
GEORGE LIEB, ATHEIST, ALTHOUGH NOW LESS SO.
THERE'S NO GODDAMN INTERNET--
YOU'RE ALL IMBECILES. THERE'S NO FOCUS OR DISCIPLINE.
CHUN-BAI, ABLE TO RESHAPE NATURE, MADE OF STEEL (FIGURATIVELY.)
THERE IS NO EXPLANATION.
THEY'VE RUN WILD, LIKE TODDLERS IN A HOUSE BURNING.
WHAT THE HELL IS WRONG WITH YOU?

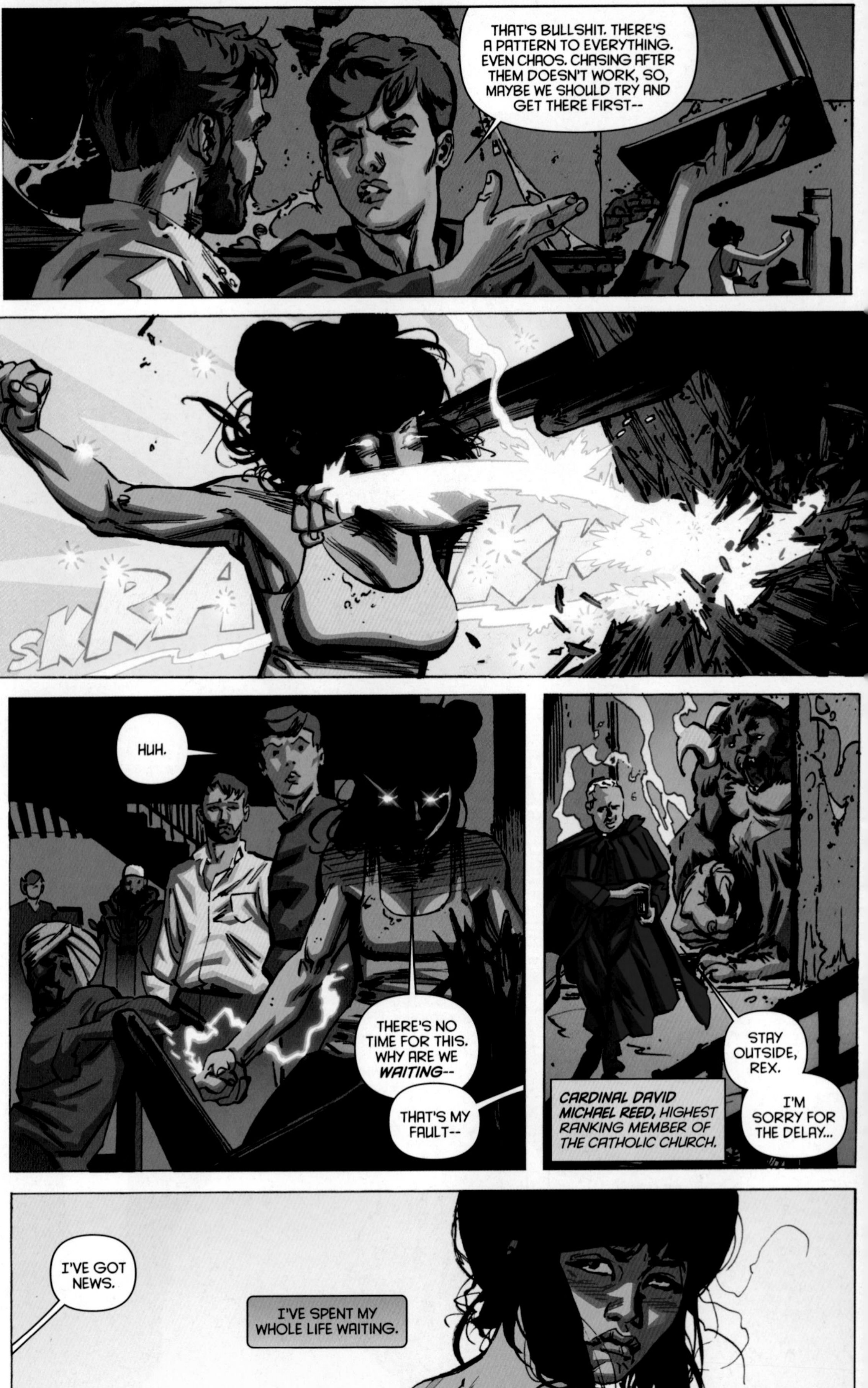
THAT'S BULLSHIT. THERE'S A PATTERN TO EVERYTHING. EVEN CHAOS. CHASING AFTER THEM DOESN'T WORK, SO, MAYBE WE SHOULD TRY AND GET THERE FIRST--
SKRAAKK
HUH.
THERE'S NO TIME FOR THIS. WHY ARE WE WAITING--
THAT'S MY FAULT--
CARDINAL DAVID MICHAEL REED, HIGHEST RANKING MEMBER OF THE CATHOLIC CHURCH.
STAY OUTSIDE, REX.
I'M SORRY FOR THE DELAY...
I'VE GOT NEWS.
I'VE SPENT MY WHOLE LIFE WAITING.

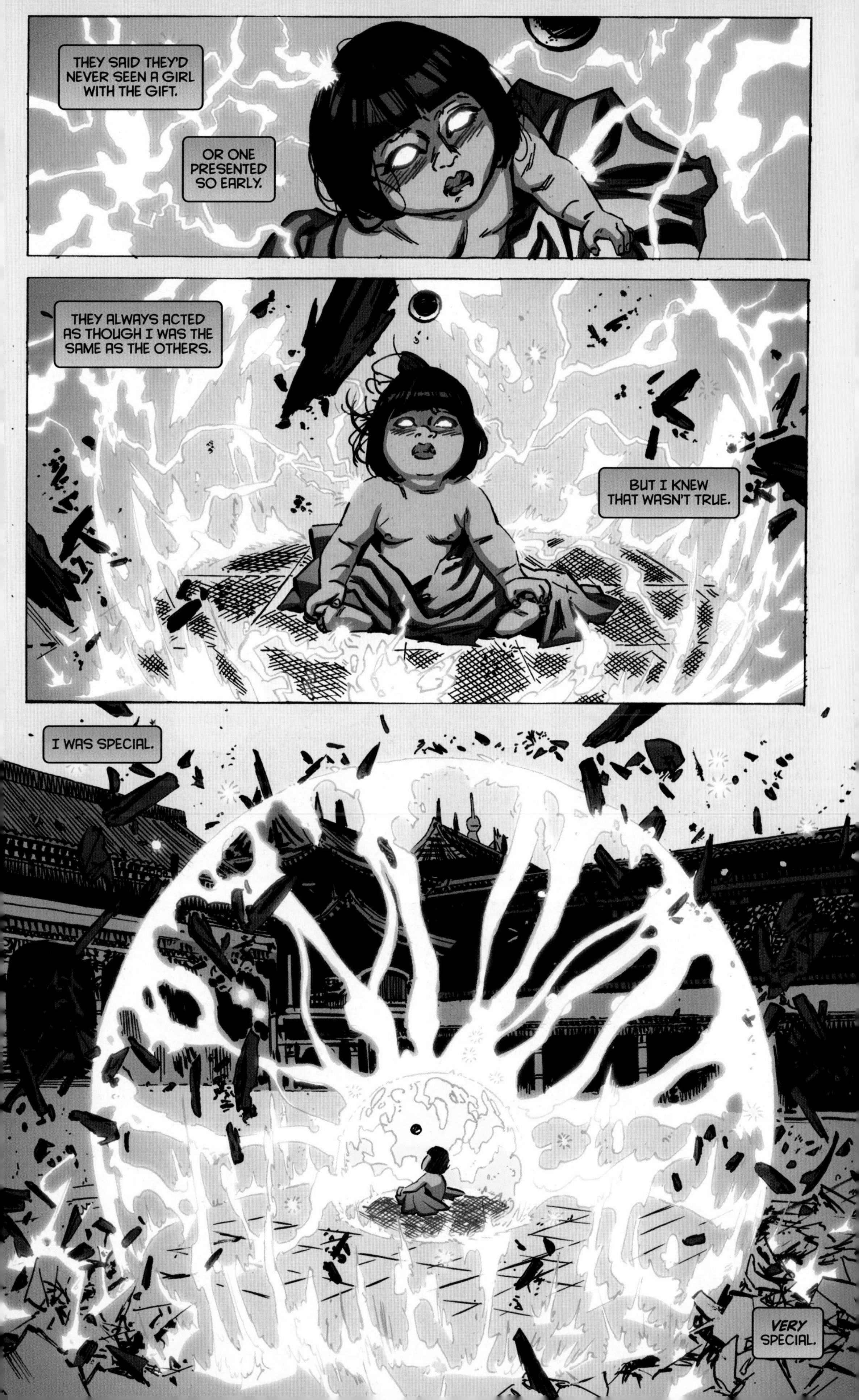
THEY SAID THEY'D NEVER SEEN A GIRL WITH THE GIFT.
OR ONE PRESENTED SO EARLY.
THEY ALWAYS ACTED AS THOUGH I WAS THE SAME AS THE OTHERS.
BUT I KNEW THAT WASN'T TRUE.
I WAS SPECIAL.
VERY SPECIAL.

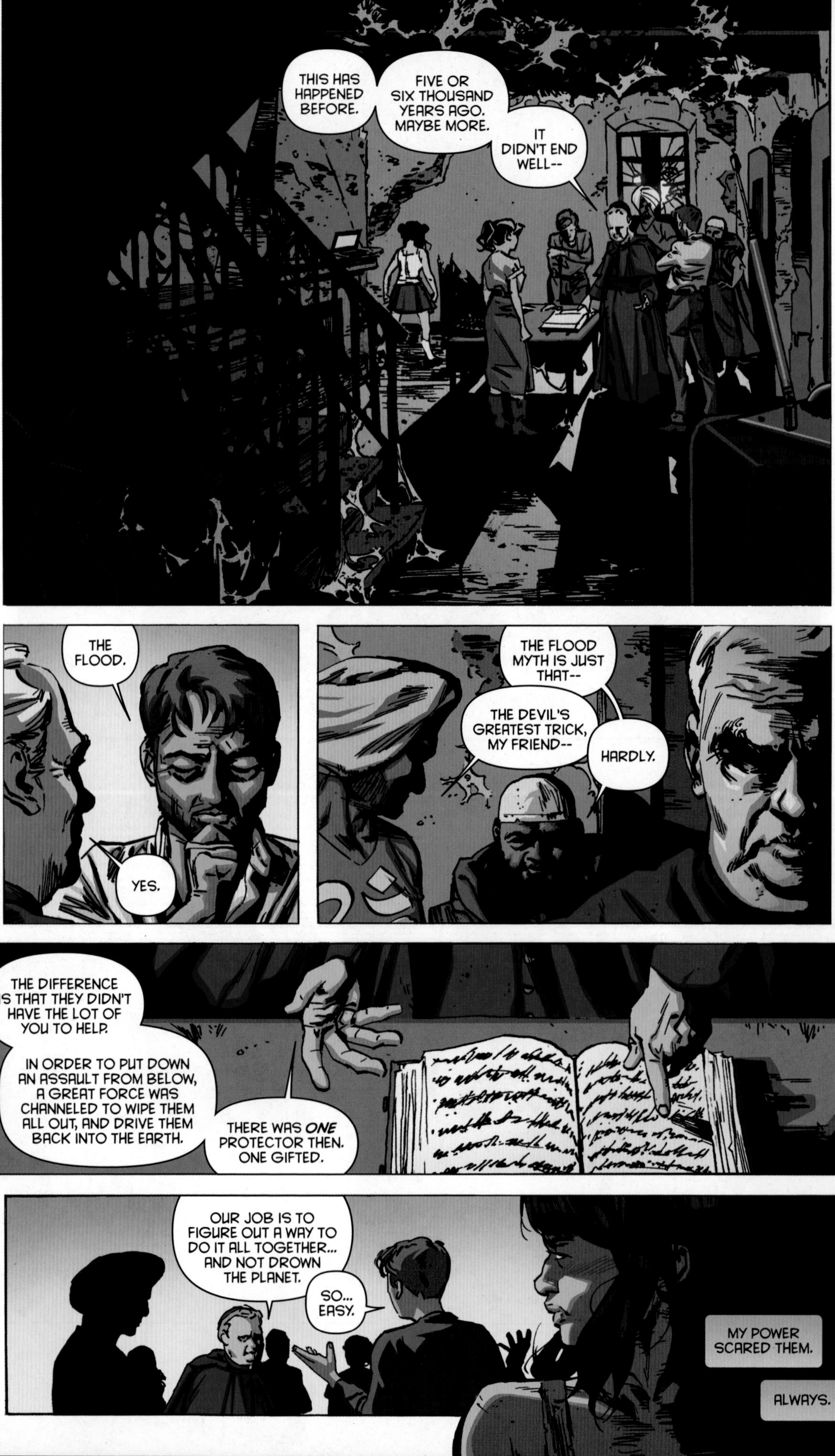
THIS HAS HAPPENED BEFORE.
FIVE OR SIX THOUSAND YEARS AGO. MAYBE MORE.
IT DIDN'T END WELL--
THE FLOOD.
YES.
THE FLOOD MYTH IS JUST THAT--
THE DEVIL'S GREATEST TRICK, MY FRIEND--
HARDLY.
THE DIFFERENCE IS THAT THEY DIDN'T HAVE THE LOT OF YOU TO HELP.
IN ORDER TO PUT DOWN AN ASSAULT FROM BELOW, A GREAT FORCE WAS CHANNELED TO WIPE THEM ALL OUT, AND DRIVE THEM BACK INTO THE EARTH.
THERE WAS *ONE* PROTECTOR THEN. ONE GIFTED.
OUR JOB IS TO FIGURE OUT A WAY TO DO IT ALL TOGETHER... AND NOT DROWN THE PLANET.
SO... EASY.
MY POWER SCARED THEM.
ALWAYS.

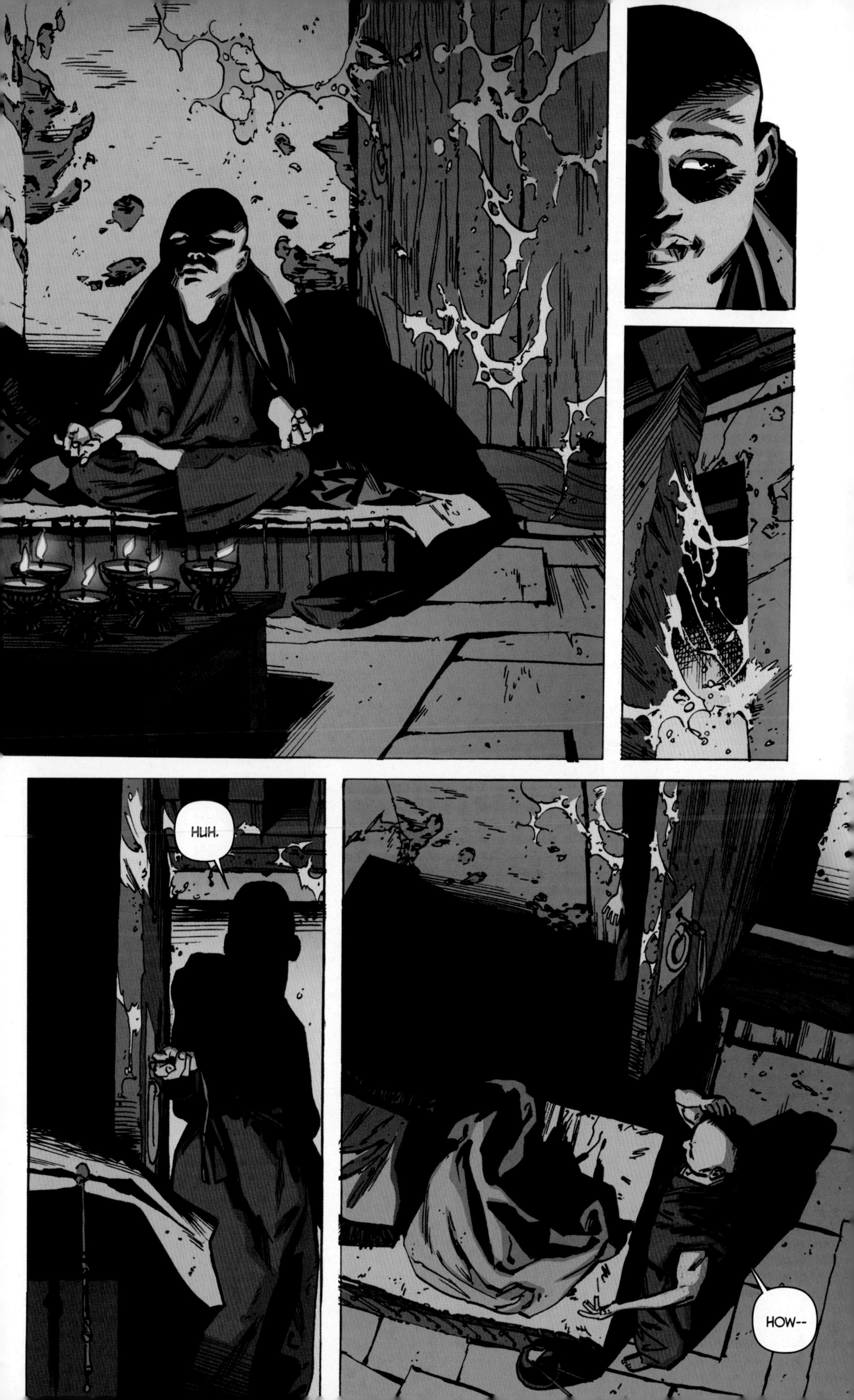
HUH.
HOW--

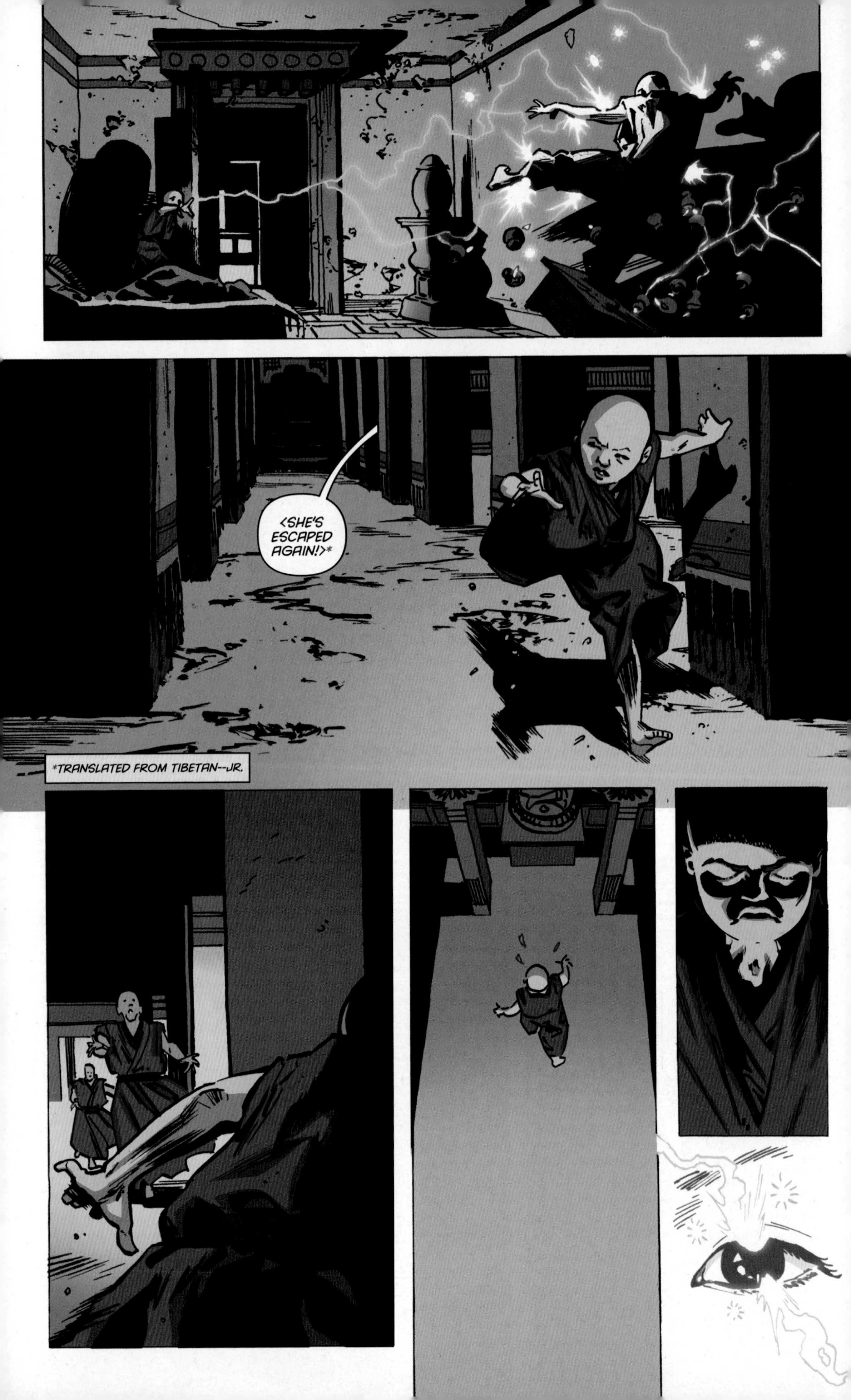

<SHE'S ESCAPED AGAIN!>*
*TRANSLATED FROM TIBETAN--JR.

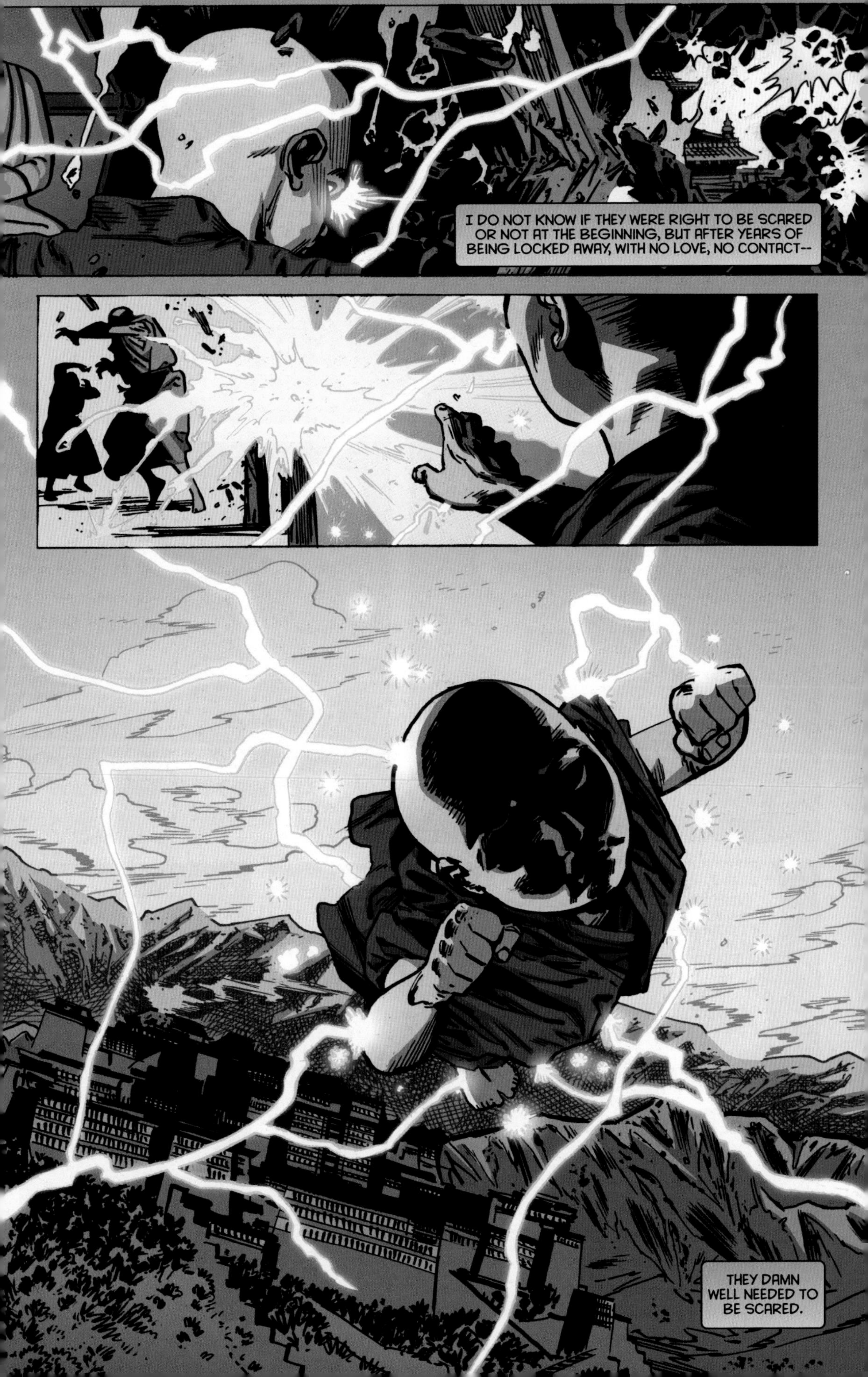

I DO NOT KNOW IF THEY WERE RIGHT TO BE SCARED OR NOT AT THE BEGINNING, BUT AFTER YEARS OF BEING LOCKED AWAY, WITH NO LOVE, NO CONTACT--
THEY DAMN WELL NEEDED TO BE SCARED.

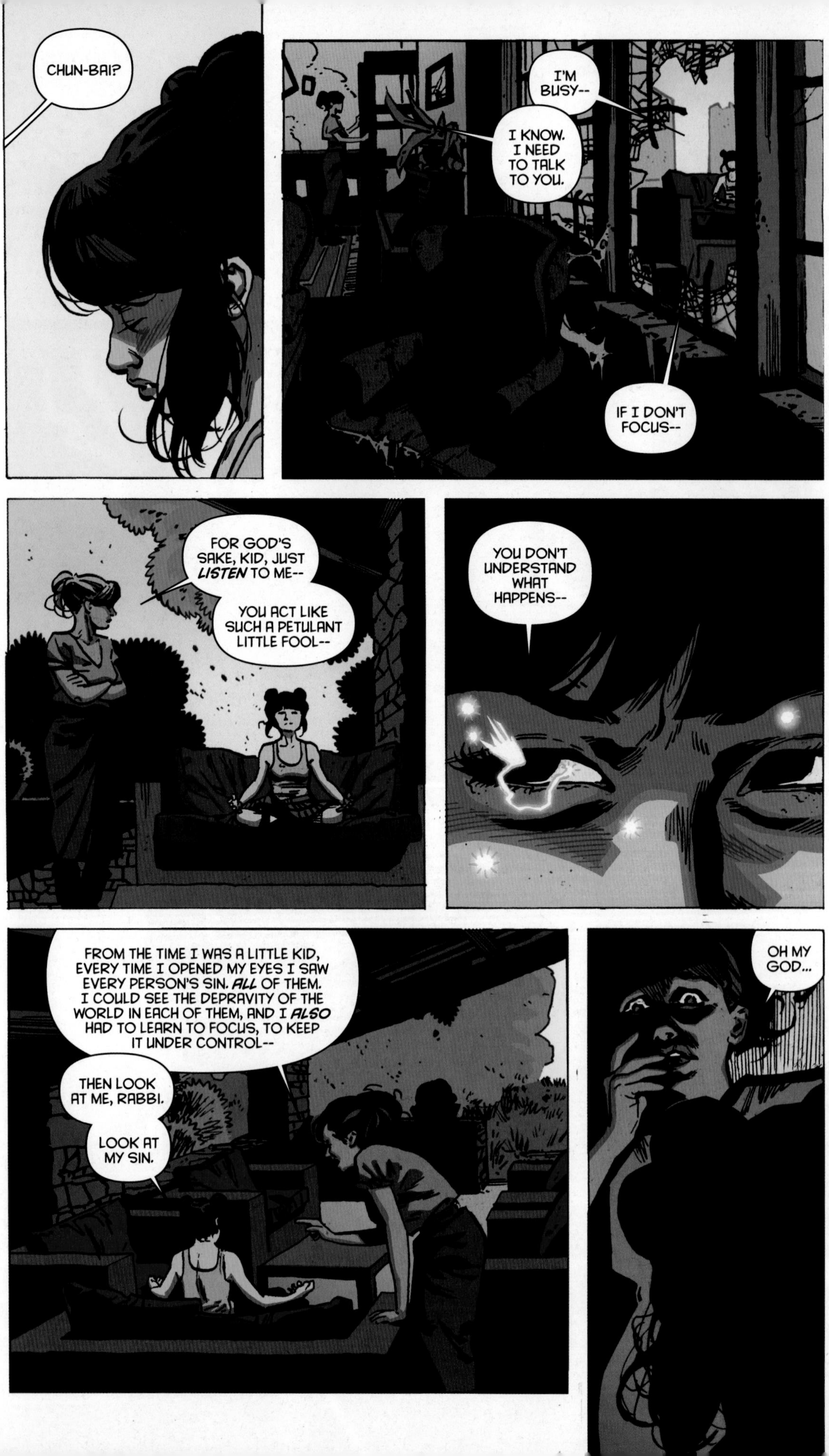
CHUN-BAI?
I'M BUSY--
I KNOW. I NEED TO TALK TO YOU.
IF I DON'T FOCUS--
FOR GOD'S SAKE, KID, JUST *LISTEN* TO ME--
YOU ACT LIKE SUCH A PETULANT LITTLE FOOL--
YOU DON'T UNDERSTAND WHAT HAPPENS--
FROM THE TIME I WAS A LITTLE KID, EVERY TIME I OPENED MY EYES I SAW EVERY PERSON'S SIN. *ALL* OF THEM. I COULD SEE THE DEPRAVITY OF THE WORLD IN EACH OF THEM, AND I *ALSO* HAD TO LEARN TO FOCUS, TO KEEP IT UNDER CONTROL--
THEN LOOK AT ME, RABBI.
LOOK AT MY SIN.
OH MY GOD...

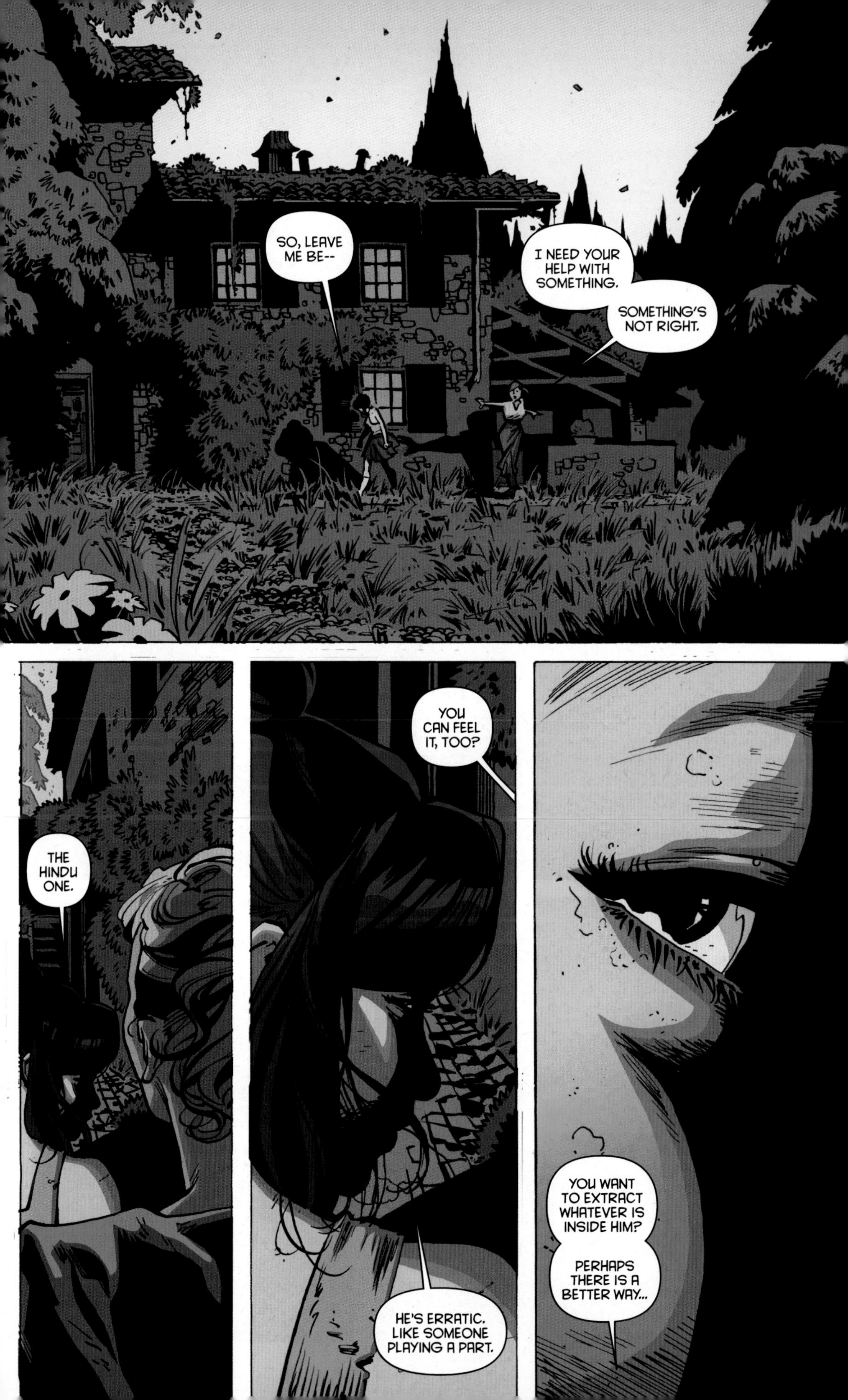
SO, LEAVE ME BE--
I NEED YOUR HELP WITH SOMETHING.
SOMETHING'S NOT RIGHT.
THE HINDU ONE.
YOU CAN FEEL IT, TOO?
HE'S ERRATIC. LIKE SOMEONE PLAYING A PART.
YOU WANT TO EXTRACT WHATEVER IS INSIDE HIM?
PERHAPS THERE IS A BETTER WAY...

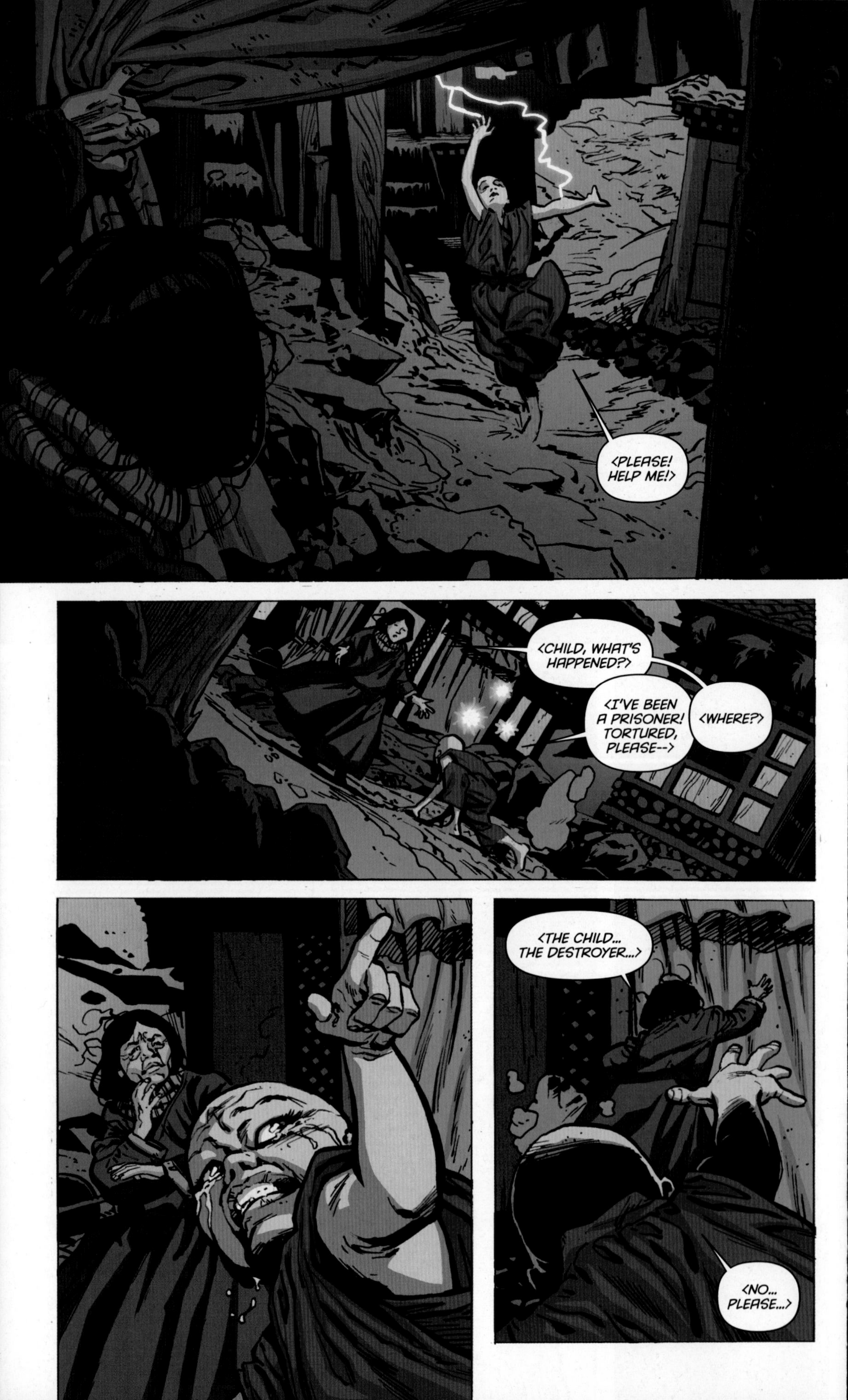
<PLEASE! HELP ME!>
<CHILD, WHAT'S HAPPENED?>
<WHERE?>
<I'VE BEEN A PRISONER! TORTURED, PLEASE-->
<THE CHILD... THE DESTROYER...>
<NO... PLEASE...>

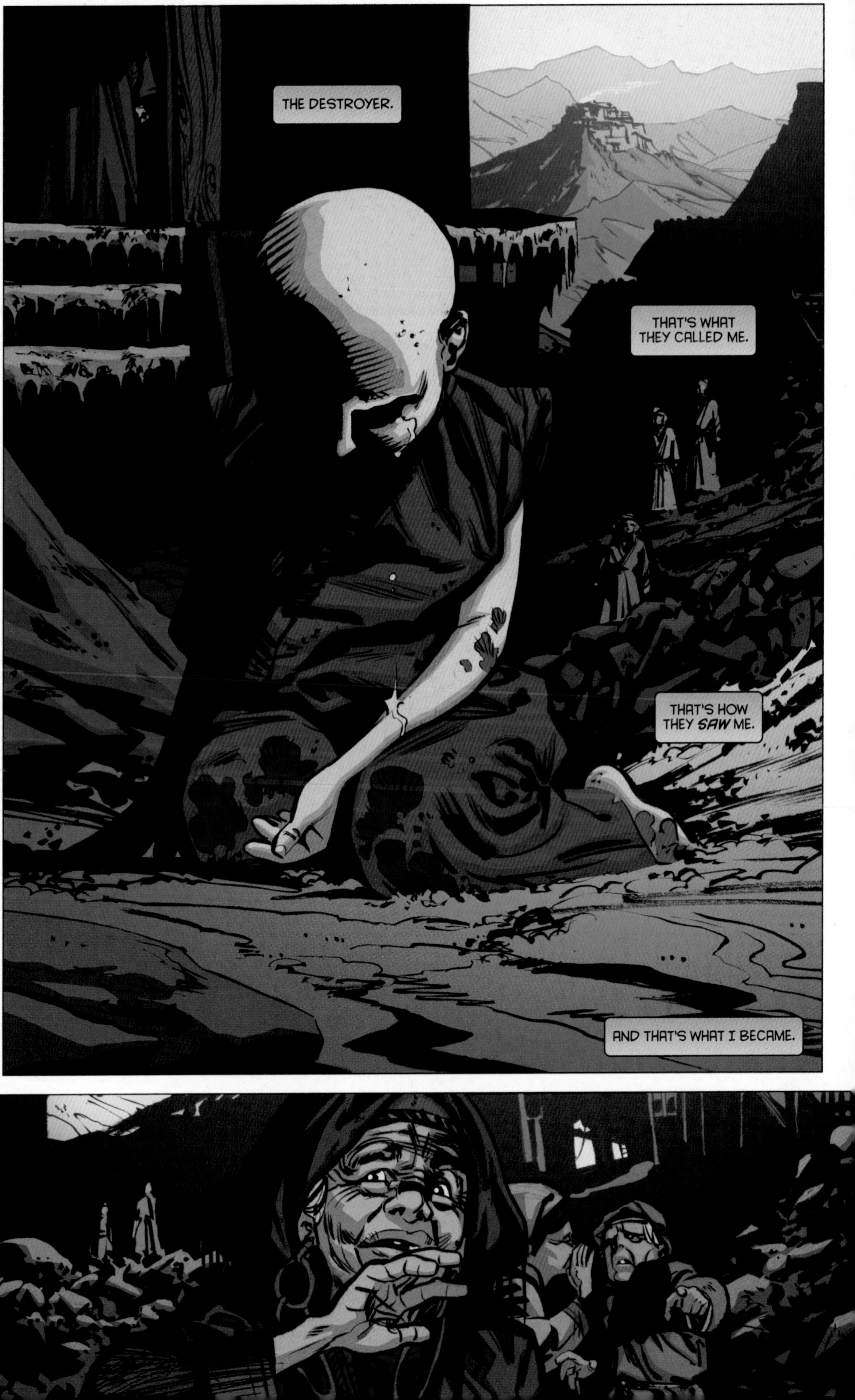
THE DESTROYER.
THAT'S WHAT THEY CALLED ME.
THAT'S HOW THEY SAW ME.
AND THAT'S WHAT I BECAME.

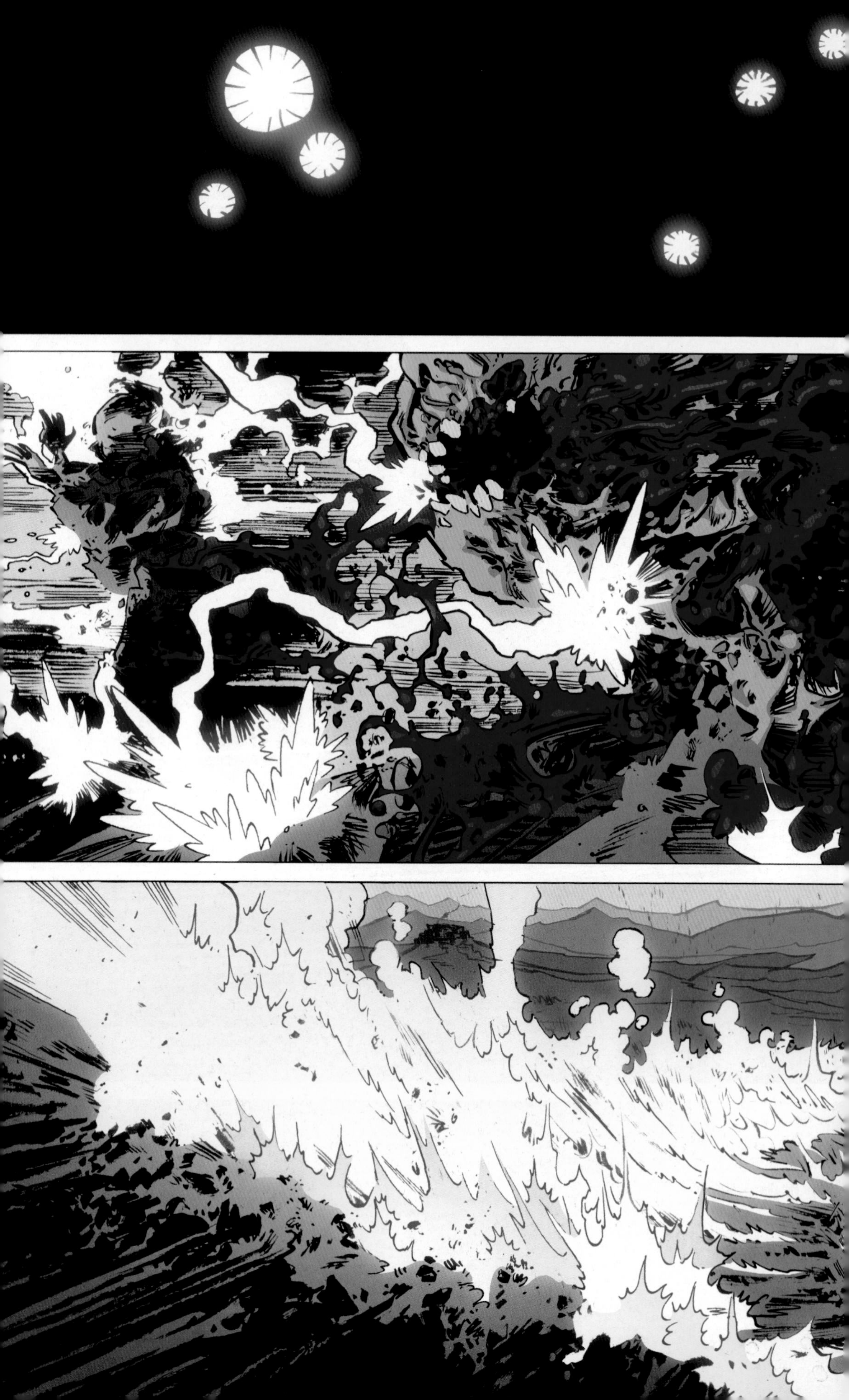

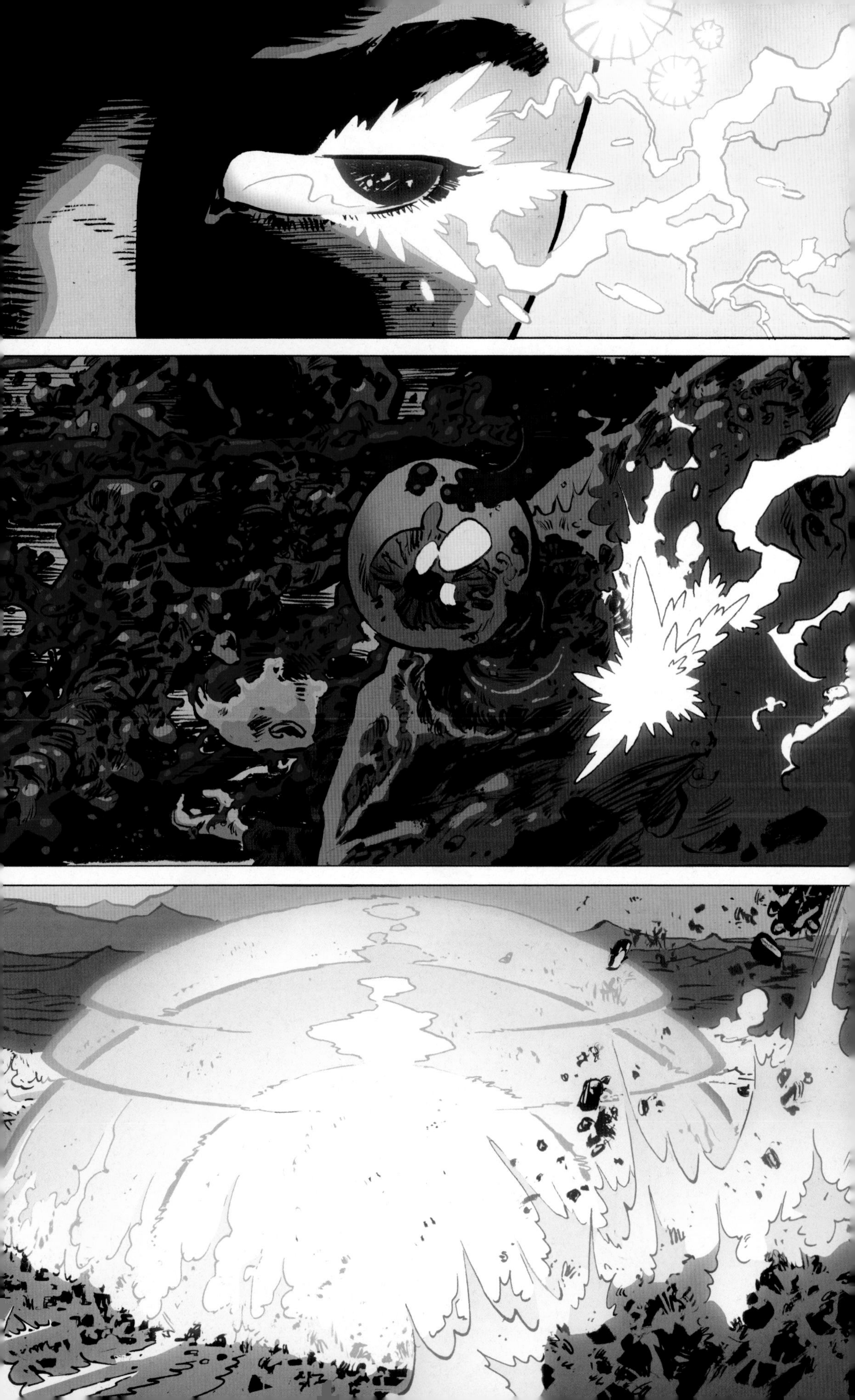

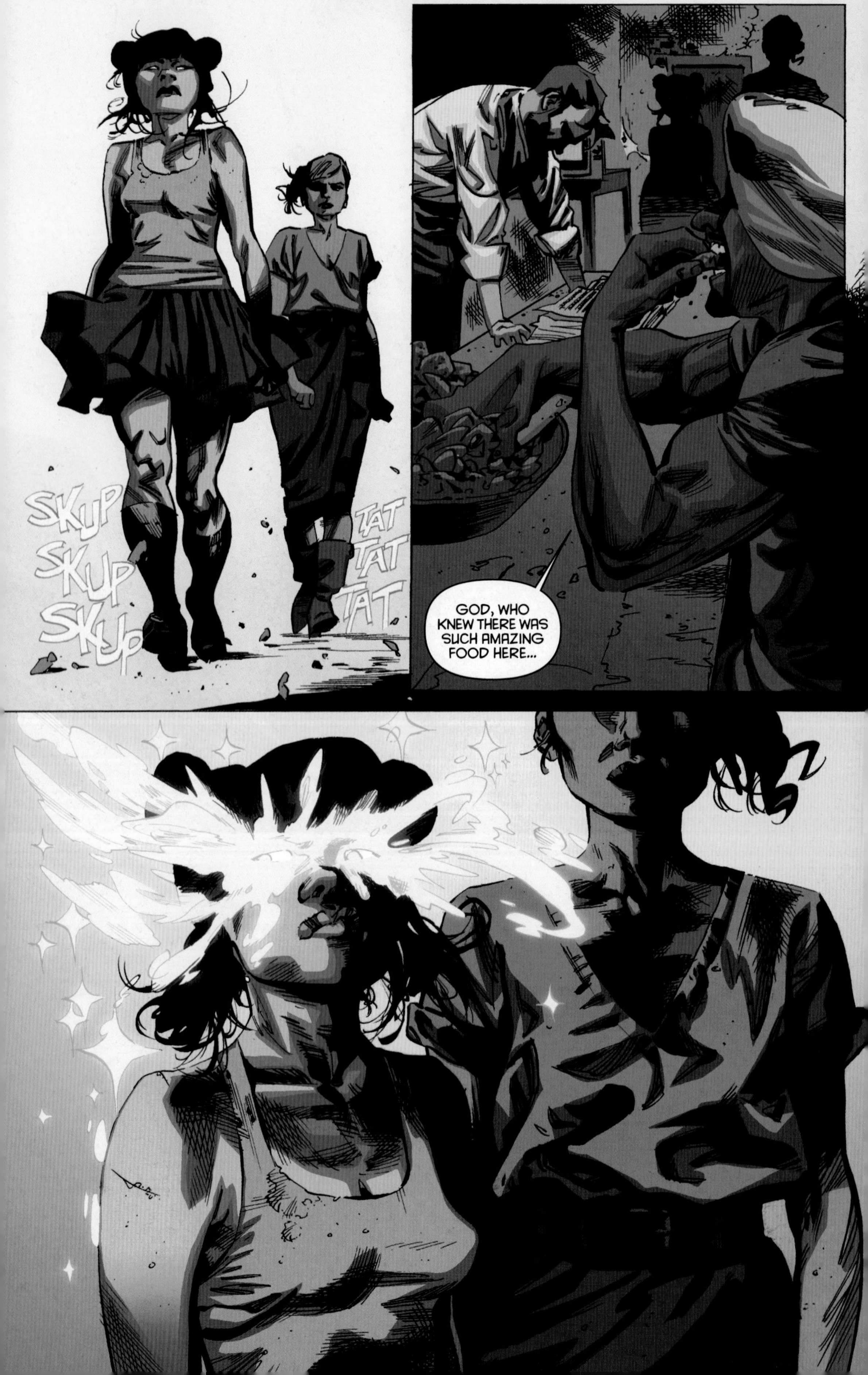
SKUP SKUP SKUP
TAT TAT TAT
GOD, WHO KNEW THERE WAS SUCH AMAZING FOOD HERE...

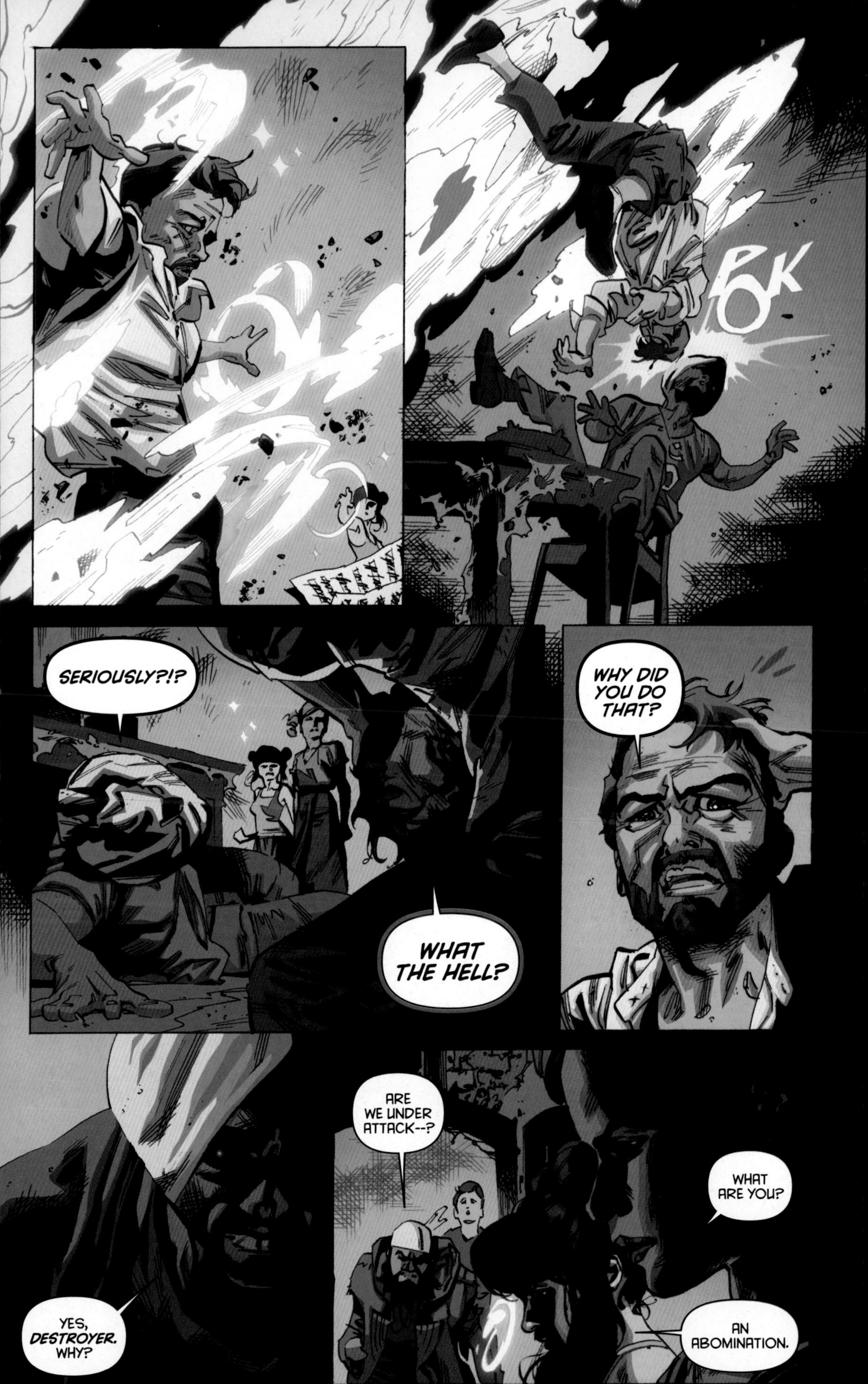
POK
SERIOUSLY?!?
WHAT THE HELL?
WHY DID YOU DO THAT?
ARE WE UNDER ATTACK--?
WHAT ARE YOU?
YES, DESTROYER. WHY?
AN ABOMINATION.

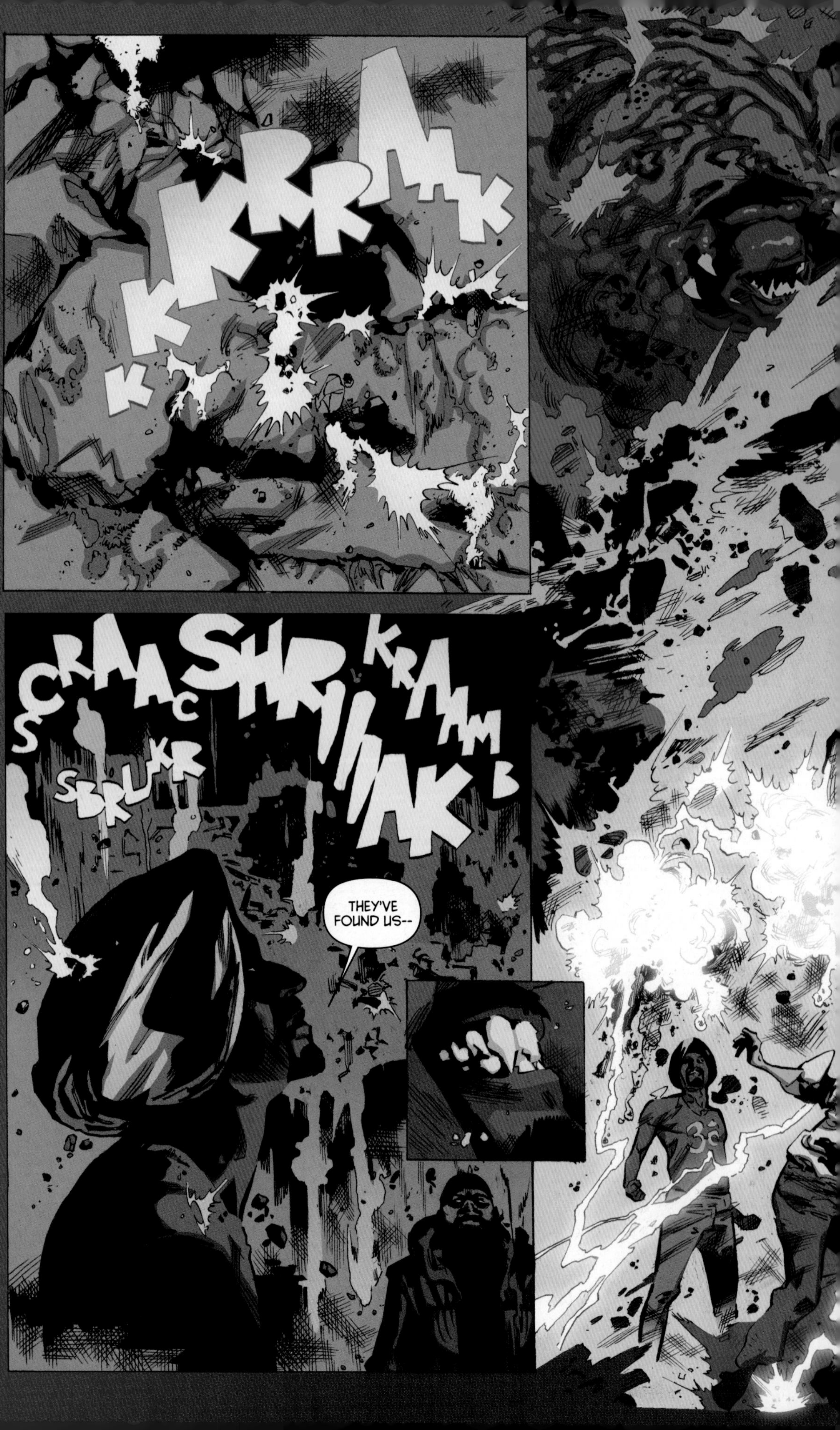
KRRAKK
SCRAASH
KRAAMB
SBRUKR
THEY'VE FOUND US--

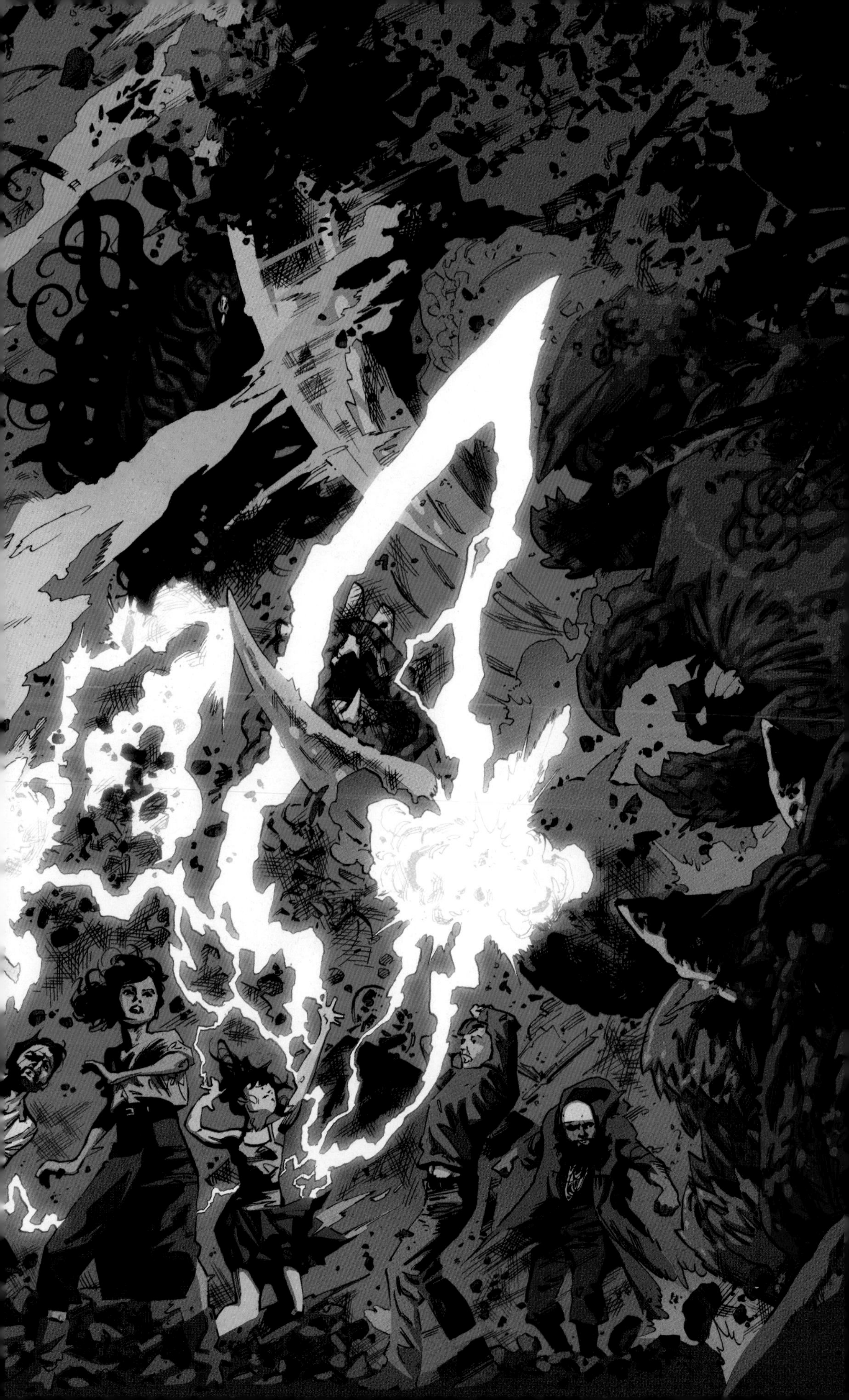

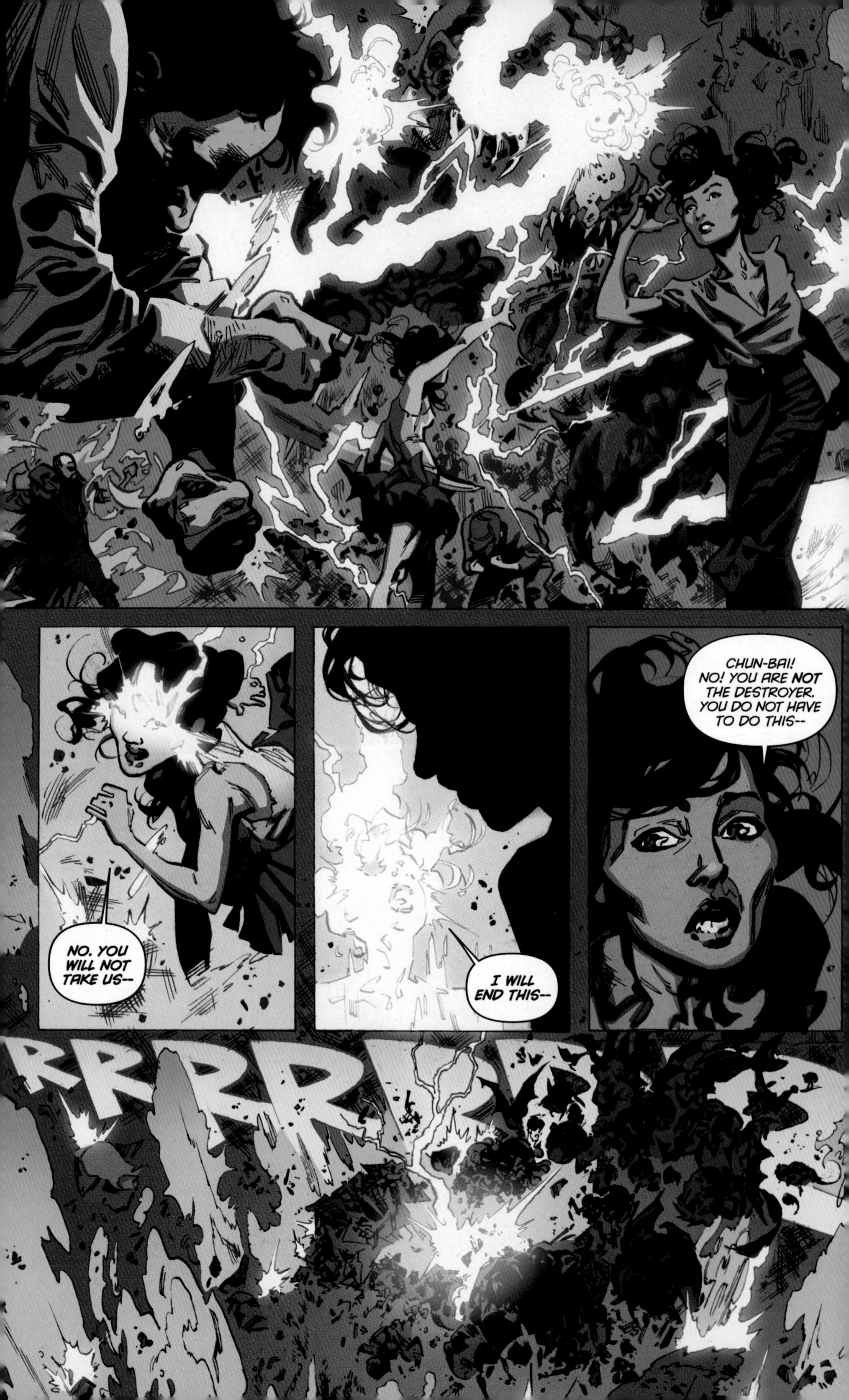
NO. YOU WILL NOT TAKE US--
I WILL END THIS--
CHUN-BAI! NO! YOU ARE NOT THE DESTROYER. YOU DO NOT HAVE TO DO THIS--
RRRR

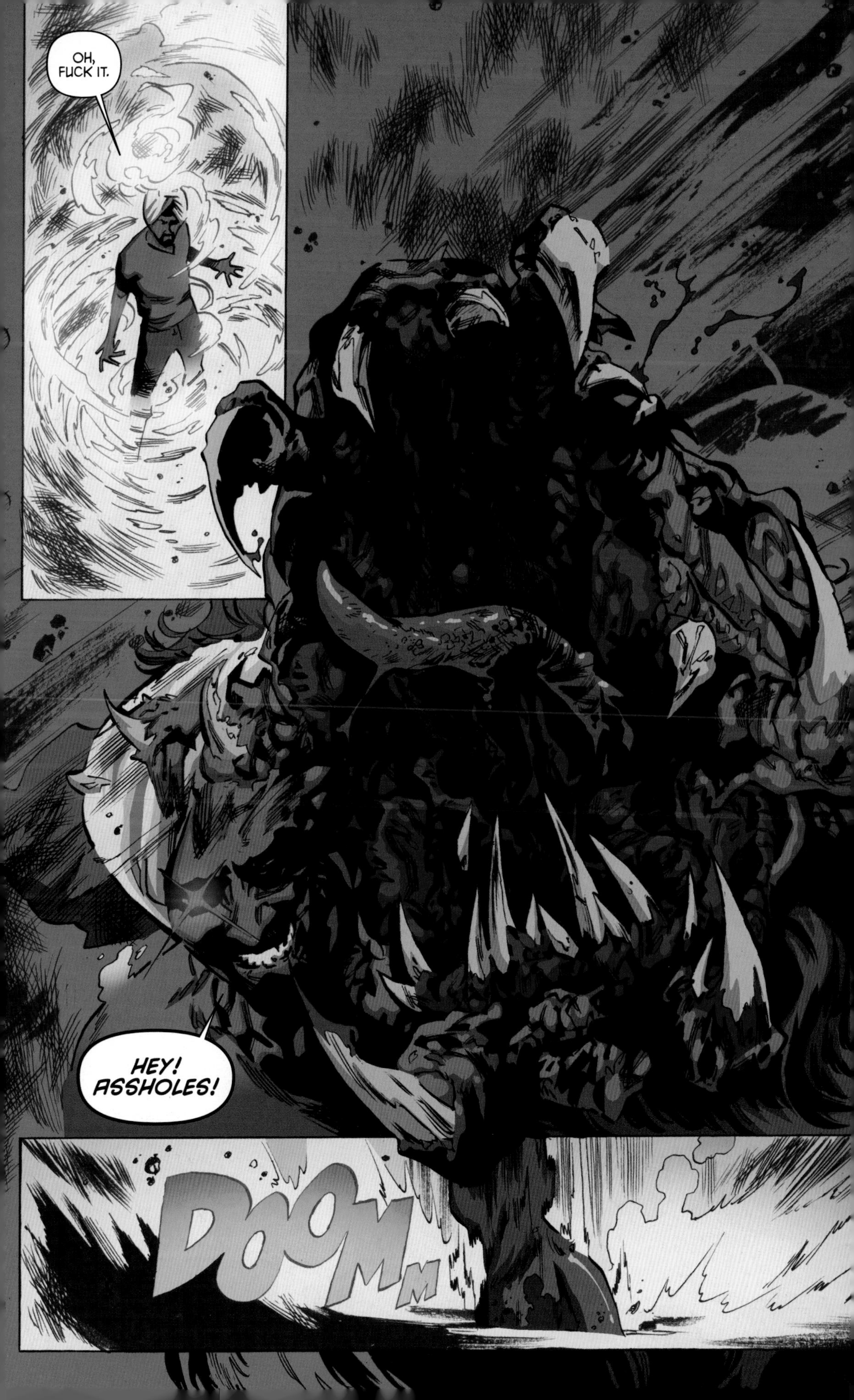
OH, FUCK IT.
HEY! ASSHOLES!
DOOMM

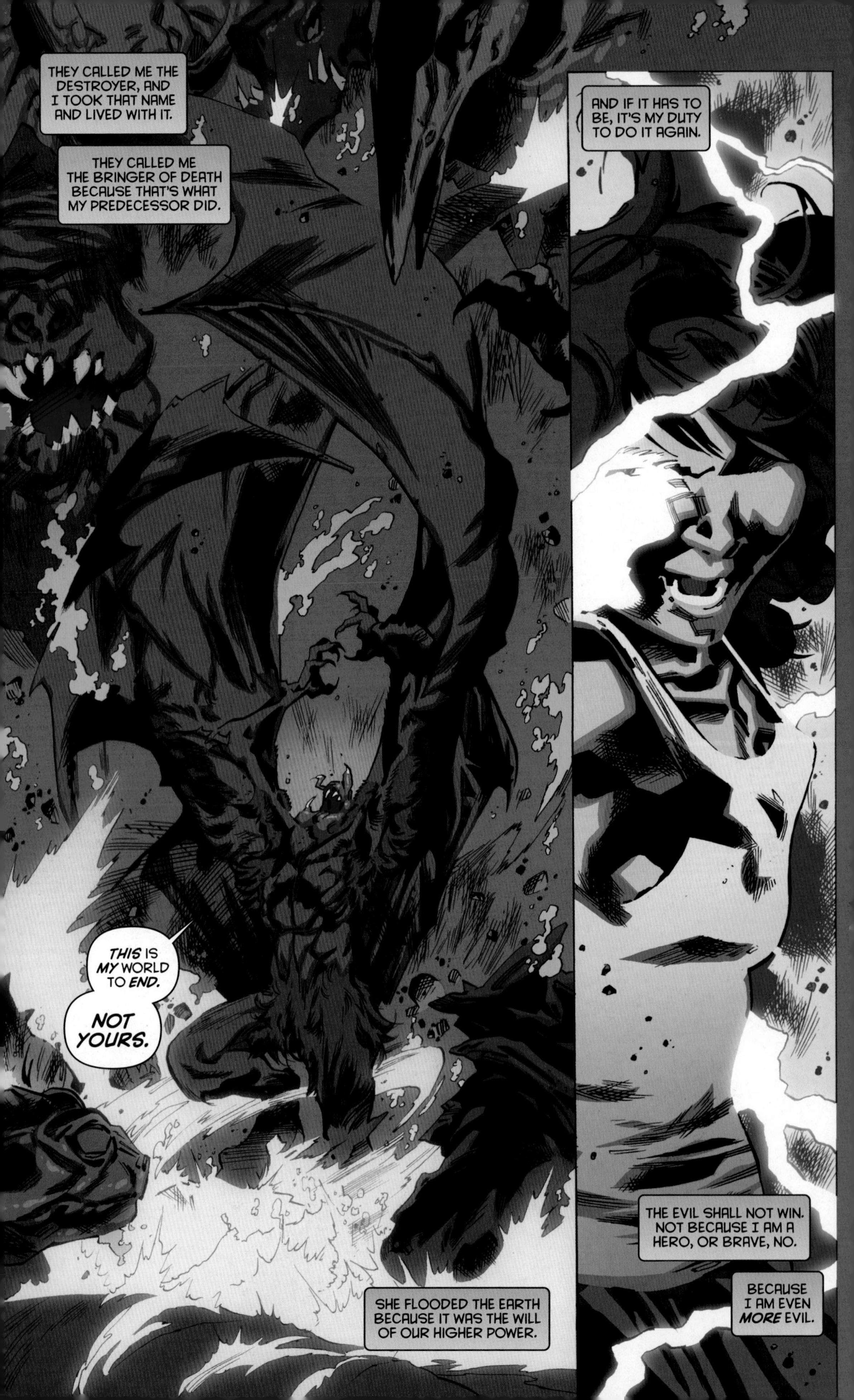
THEY CALLED ME THE DESTROYER, AND I TOOK THAT NAME AND LIVED WITH IT.
THEY CALLED ME THE BRINGER OF DEATH BECAUSE THAT'S WHAT MY PREDECESSOR DID.
THIS IS MY WORLD TO END.
NOT YOURS.
SHE FLOODED THE EARTH BECAUSE IT WAS THE WILL OF OUR HIGHER POWER.
AND IF IT HAS TO BE, IT'S MY DUTY TO DO IT AGAIN.
THE EVIL SHALL NOT WIN. NOT BECAUSE I AM A HERO, OR BRAVE, NO.
BECAUSE I AM EVEN MORE EVIL.

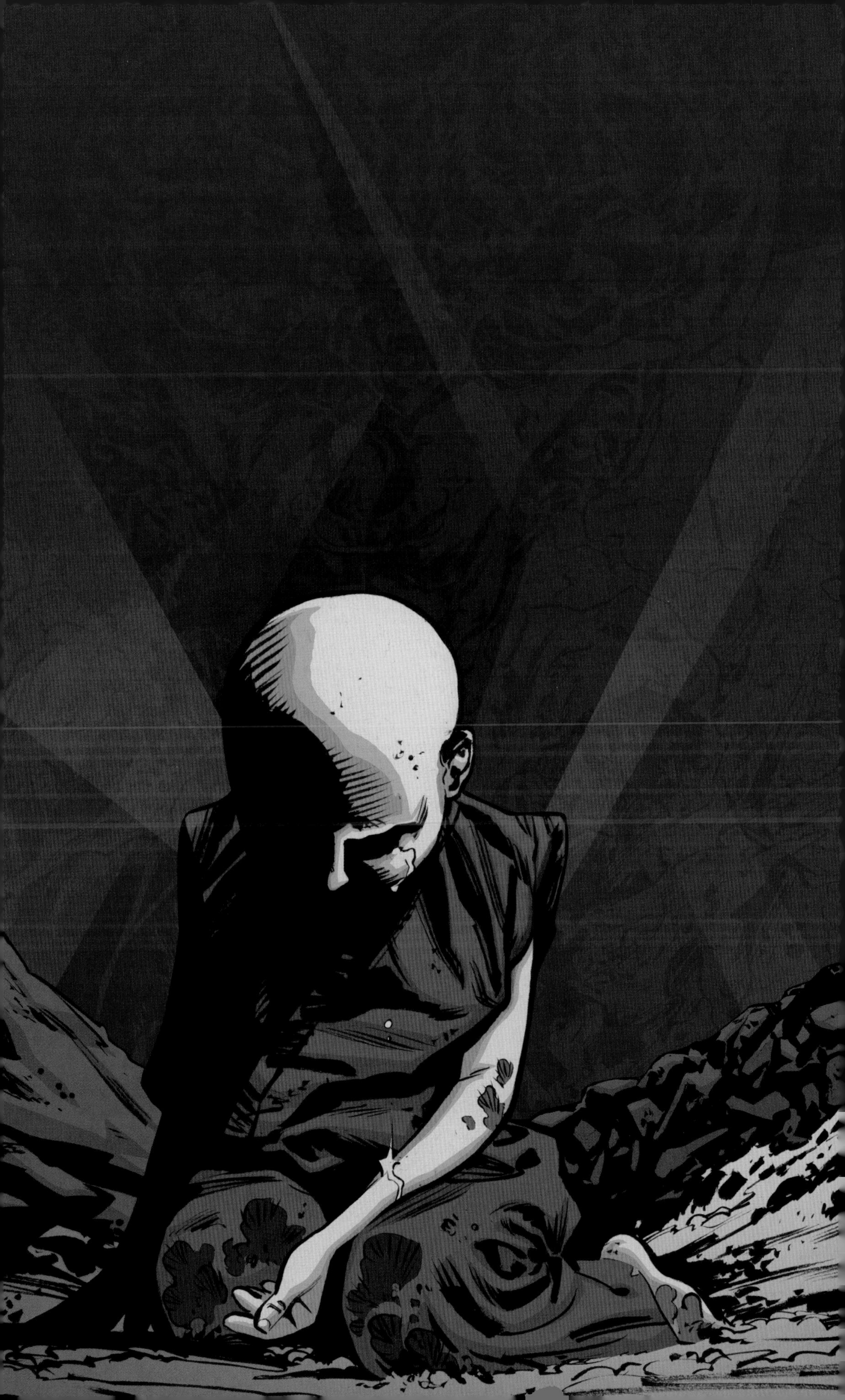

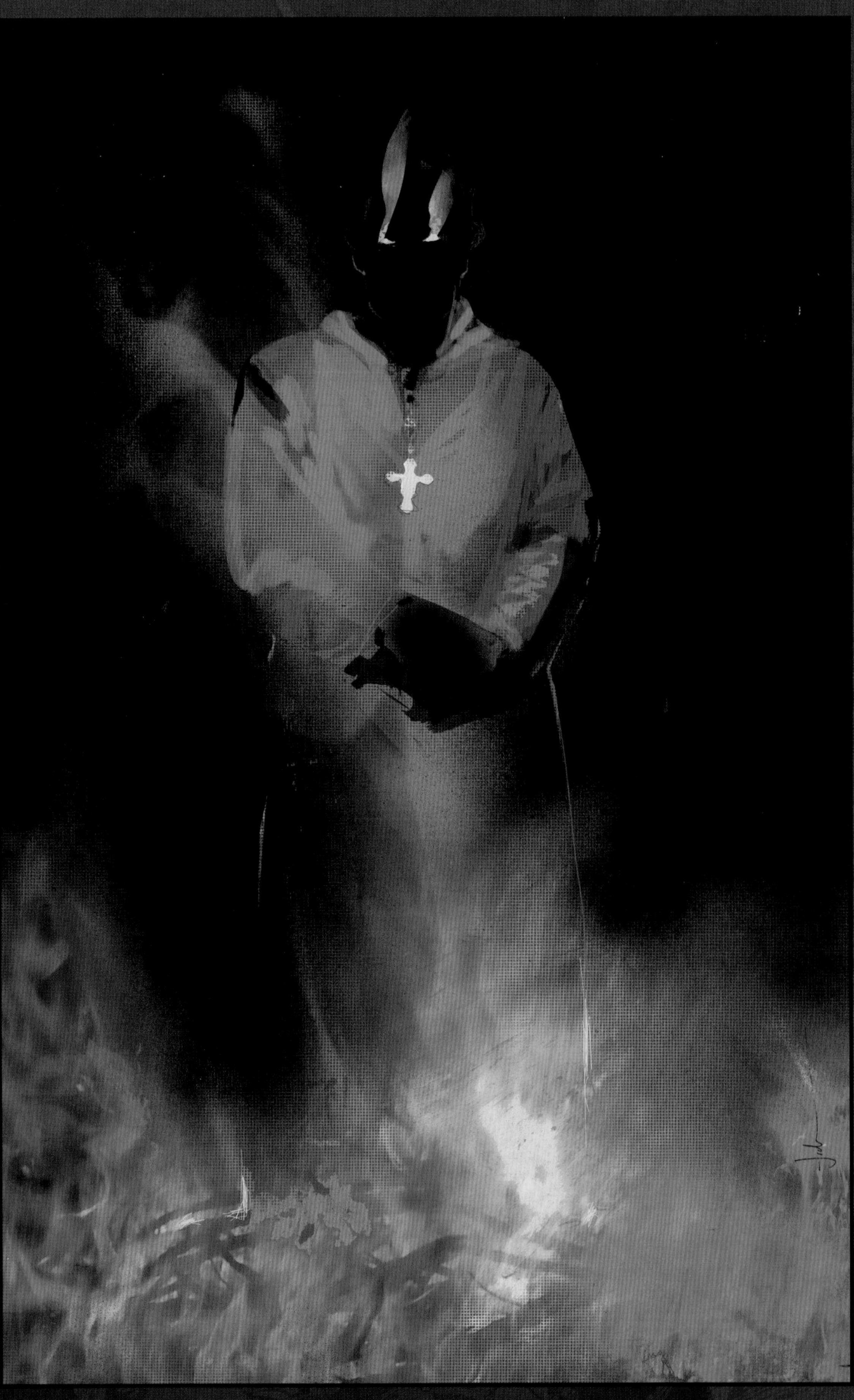

ISSUE #6 cover art by **JOCK**

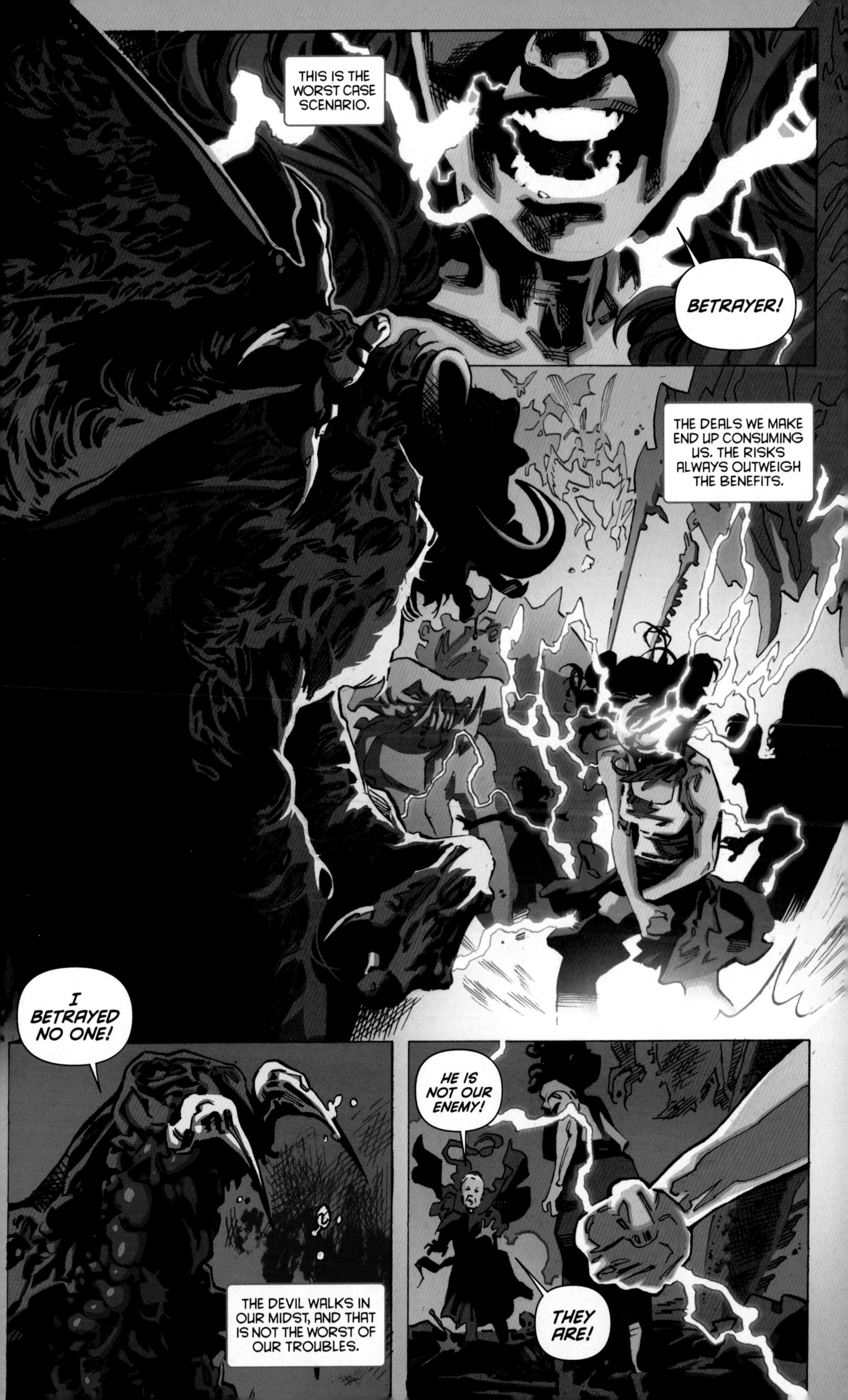
THIS IS THE WORST CASE SCENARIO.
BETRAYER!
THE DEALS WE MAKE END UP CONSUMING US. THE RISKS ALWAYS OUTWEIGH THE BENEFITS.
I BETRAYED NO ONE!
THE DEVIL WALKS IN OUR MIDST, AND THAT IS NOT THE WORST OF OUR TROUBLES.
HE IS NOT OUR ENEMY!
THEY ARE!

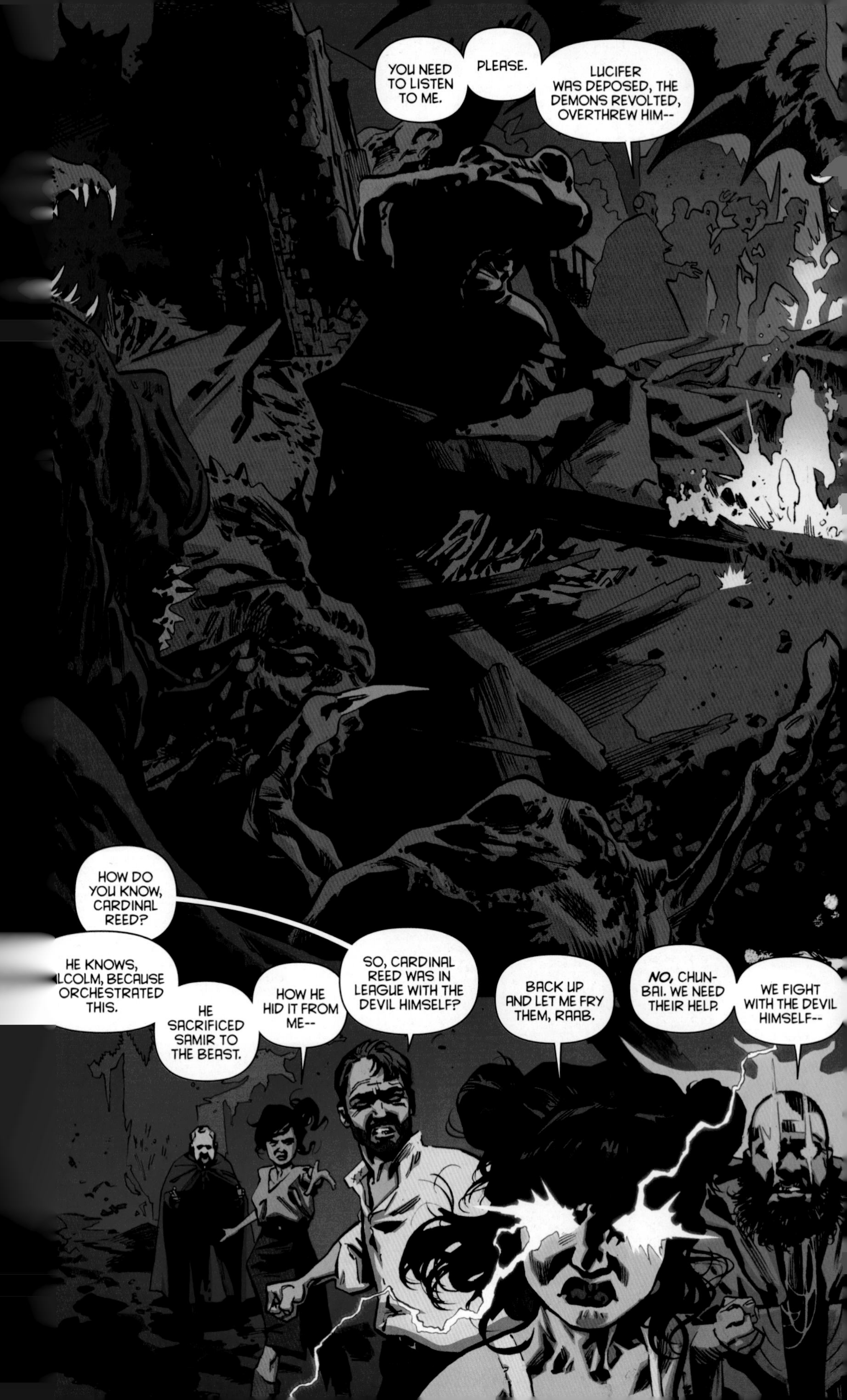
YOU NEED TO LISTEN TO ME.
PLEASE.
LUCIFER WAS DEPOSED, THE DEMONS REVOLTED, OVERTHREW HIM--
HOW DO YOU KNOW, CARDINAL REED?
HE KNOWS, LCOLM, BECAUSE ORCHESTRATED THIS.
HE SACRIFICED SAMIR TO THE BEAST.
HOW HE HID IT FROM ME--
SO, CARDINAL REED WAS IN LEAGUE WITH THE DEVIL HIMSELF?
BACK UP AND LET ME FRY THEM, RAAB.
NO, CHUN-BAI. WE NEED THEIR HELP.
WE FIGHT WITH THE DEVIL HIMSELF--

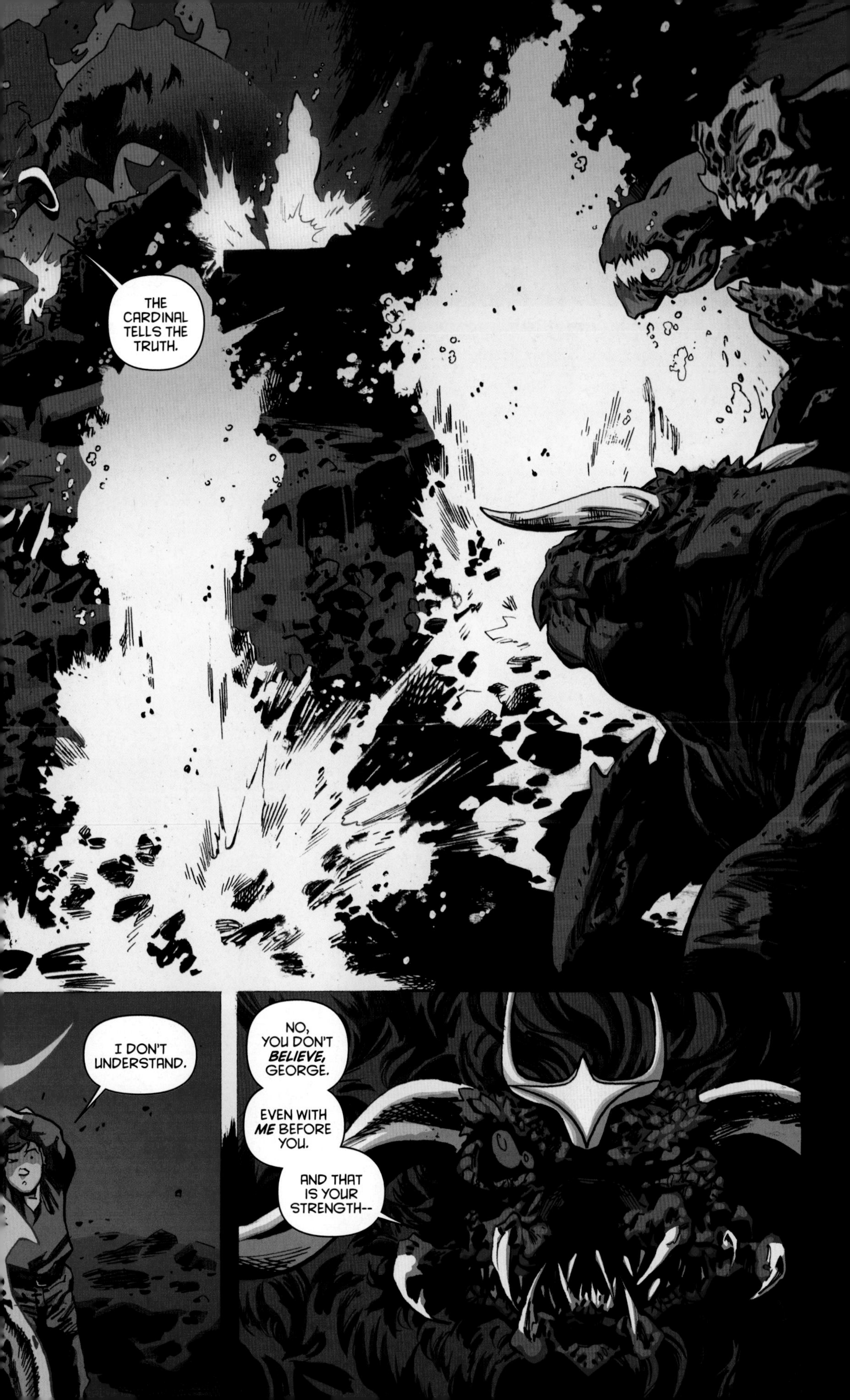
THE CARDINAL TELLS THE TRUTH.
I DON'T UNDERSTAND.
NO, YOU DON'T *BELIEVE,* GEORGE.
EVEN WITH *ME* BEFORE YOU.
AND THAT IS YOUR STRENGTH--

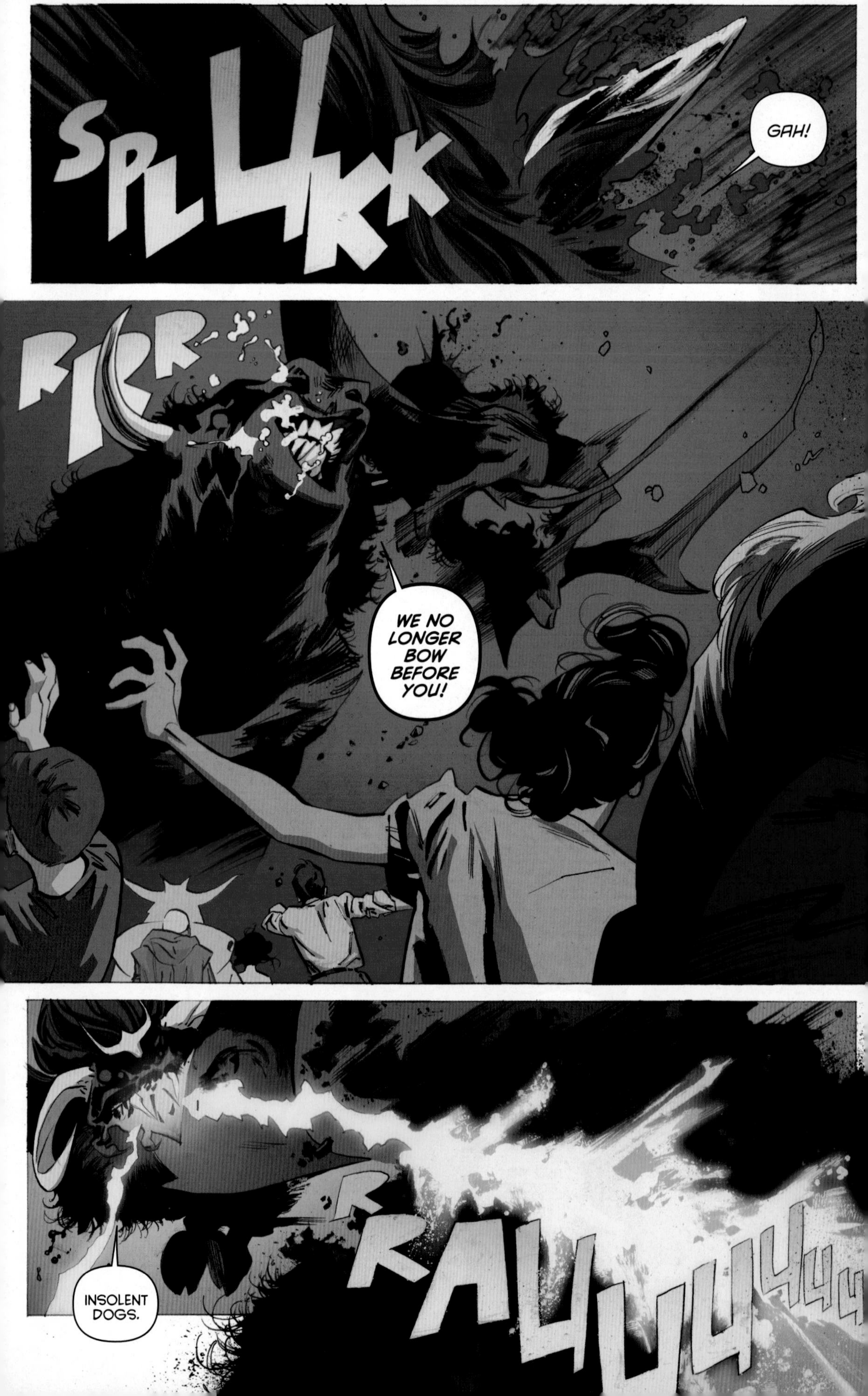
GAH!
WE NO LONGER BOW BEFORE YOU!
INSOLENT DOGS.

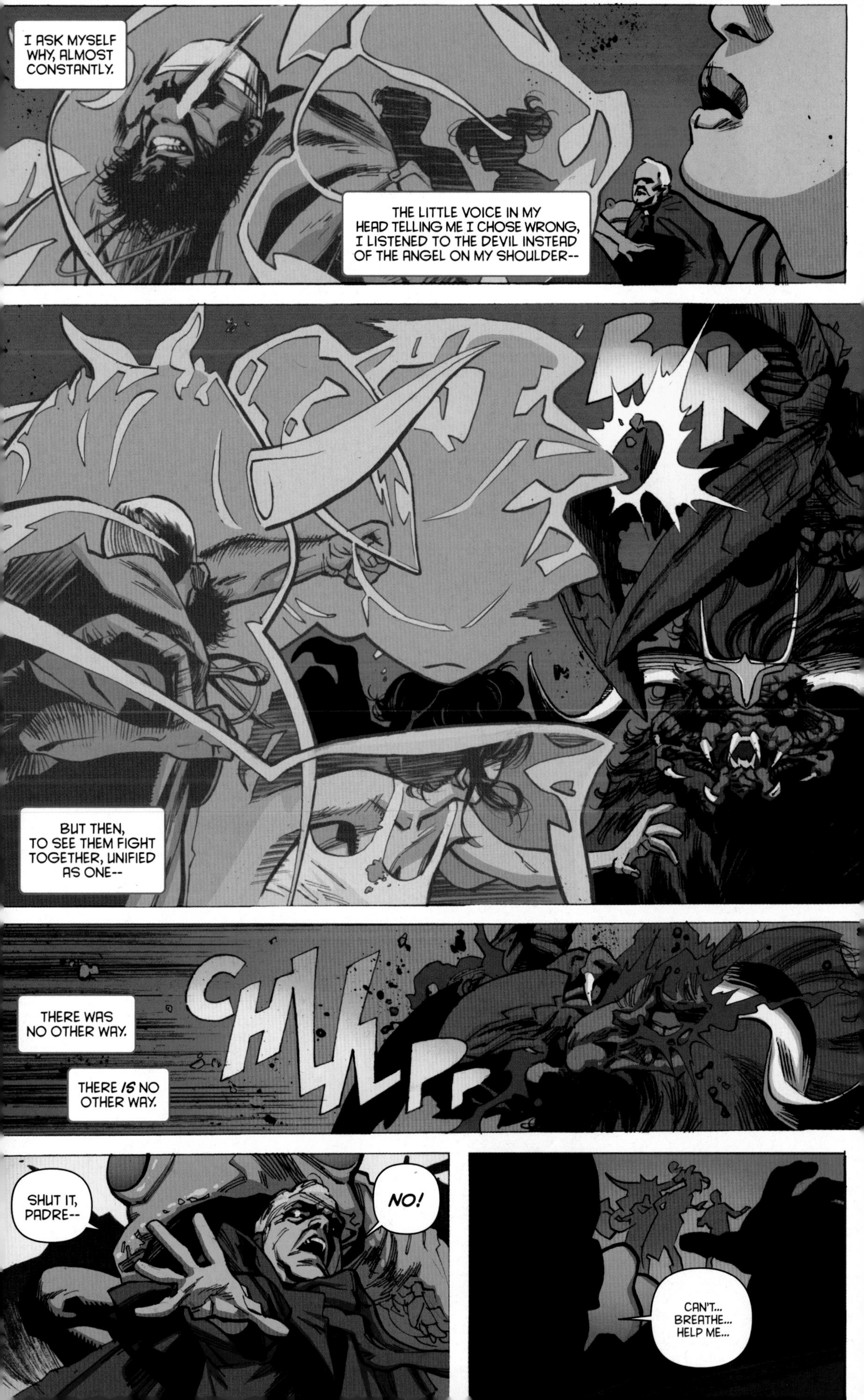
I ASK MYSELF WHY, ALMOST CONSTANTLY.
THE LITTLE VOICE IN MY HEAD TELLING ME I CHOSE WRONG, I LISTENED TO THE DEVIL INSTEAD OF THE ANGEL ON MY SHOULDER--
BUT THEN, TO SEE THEM FIGHT TOGETHER, UNIFIED AS ONE--
THERE WAS NO OTHER WAY.
THERE *IS* NO OTHER WAY.
SHUT IT, PADRE--
NO!
CAN'T... BREATHE... HELP ME...

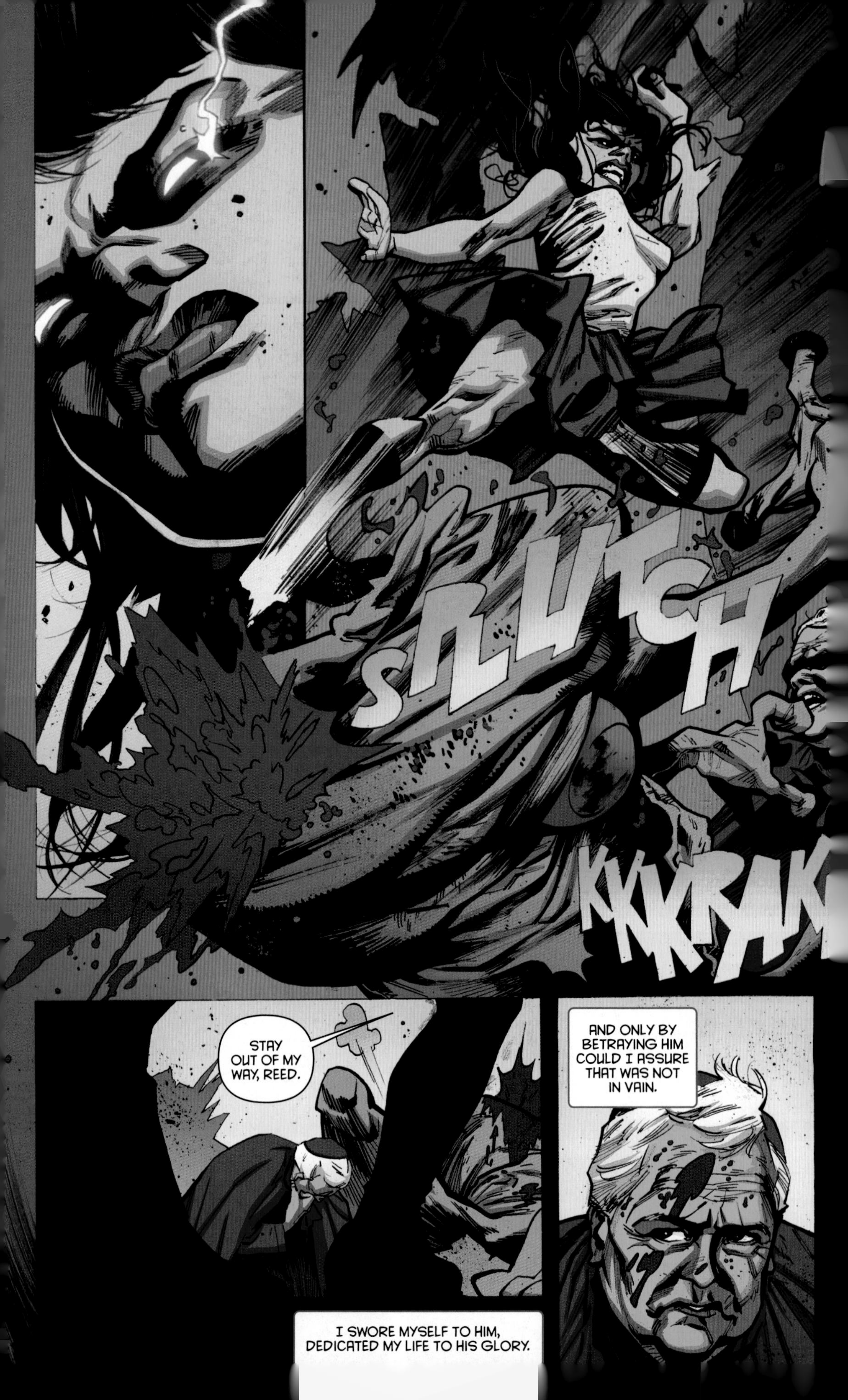
SHLUCH
KKKRAK
STAY OUT OF MY WAY, REED.
AND ONLY BY BETRAYING HIM COULD I ASSURE THAT WAS NOT IN VAIN.
I SWORE MYSELF TO HIM, DEDICATED MY LIFE TO HIS GLORY.

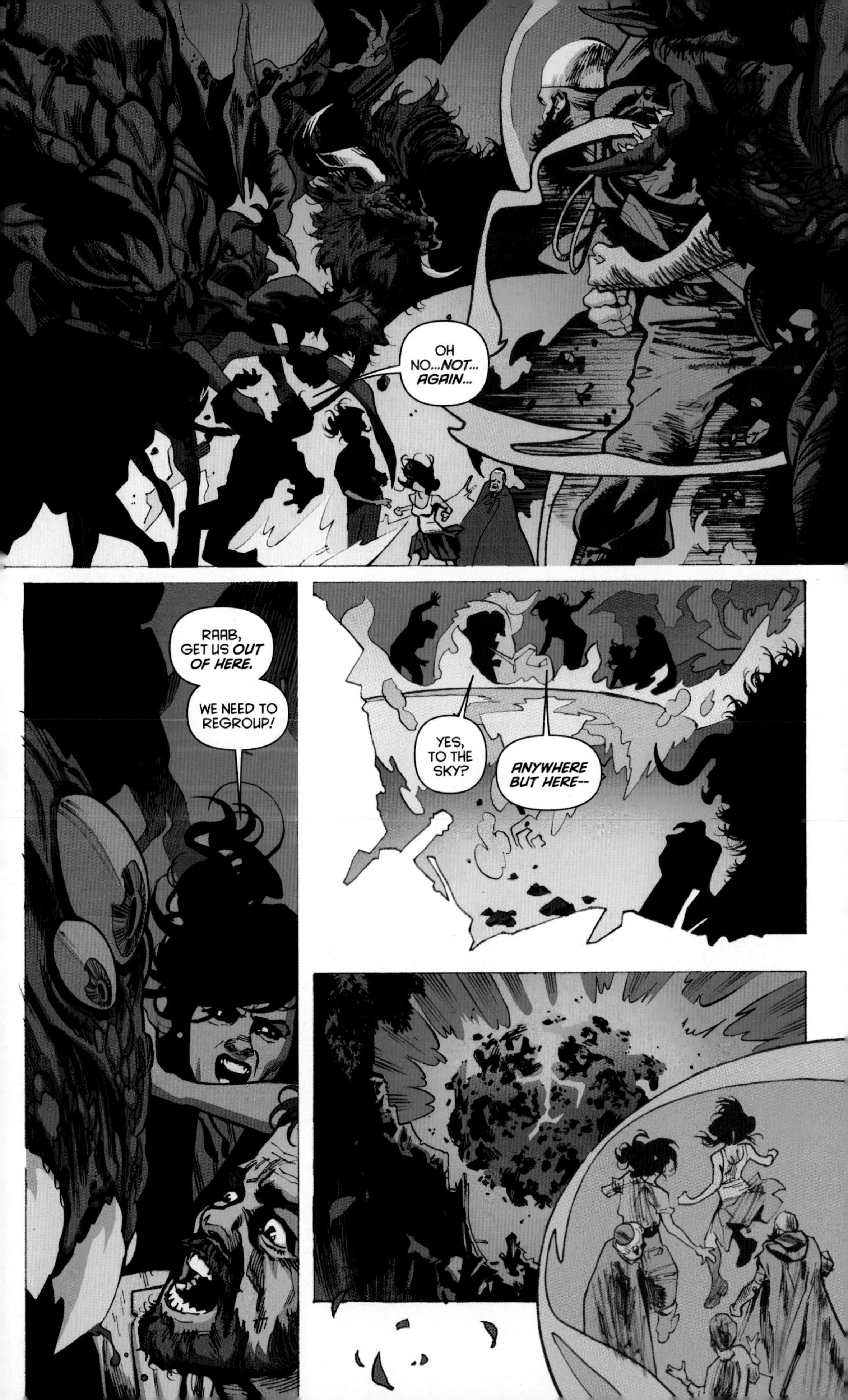
OH NO...NOT... AGAIN...
RAAB, GET US OUT OF HERE.
WE NEED TO REGROUP!
YES, TO THE SKY?
ANYWHERE BUT HERE--

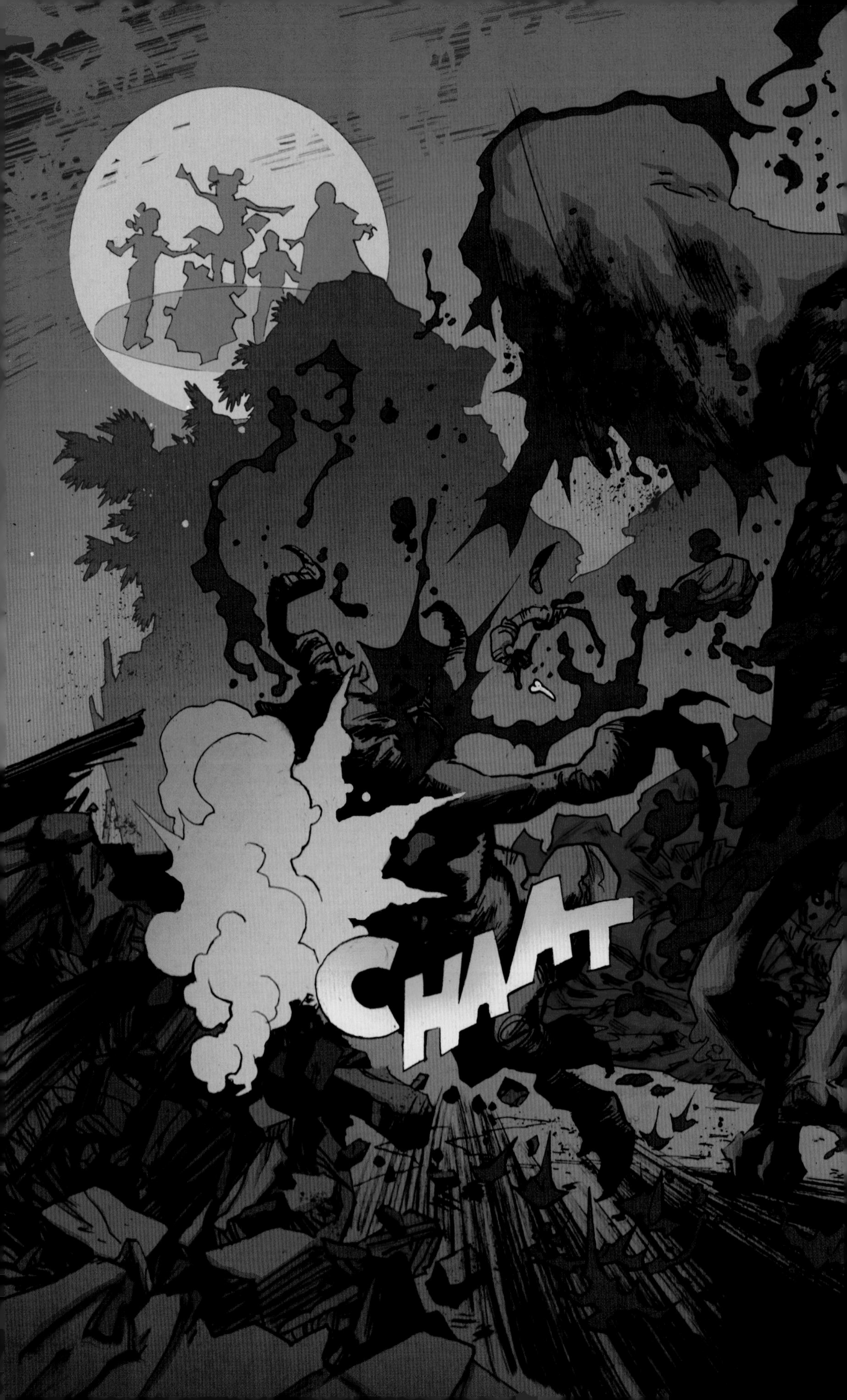
CHAAT

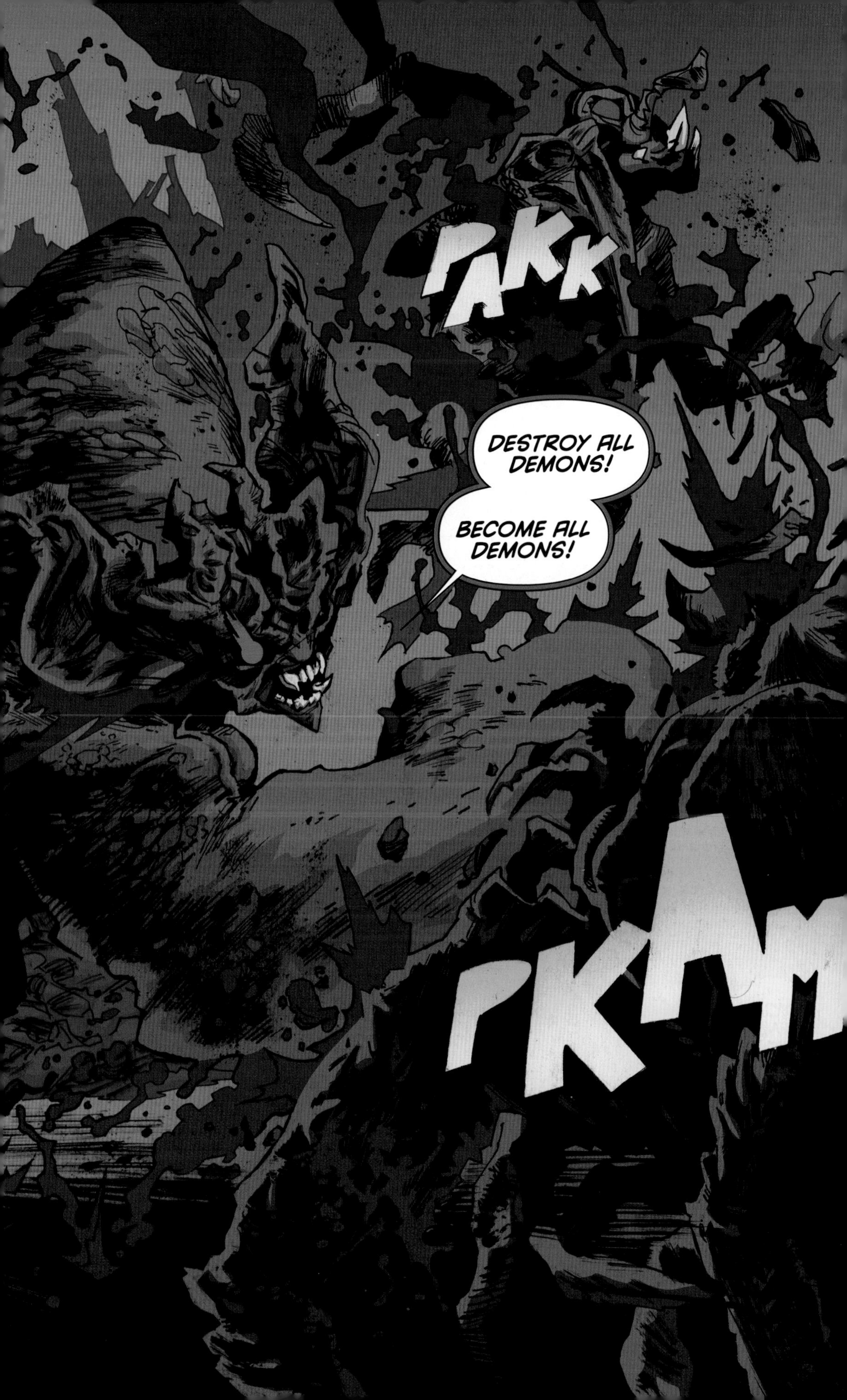
PAKK
DESTROY ALL DEMONS!
BECOME ALL DEMONS!
PKAM

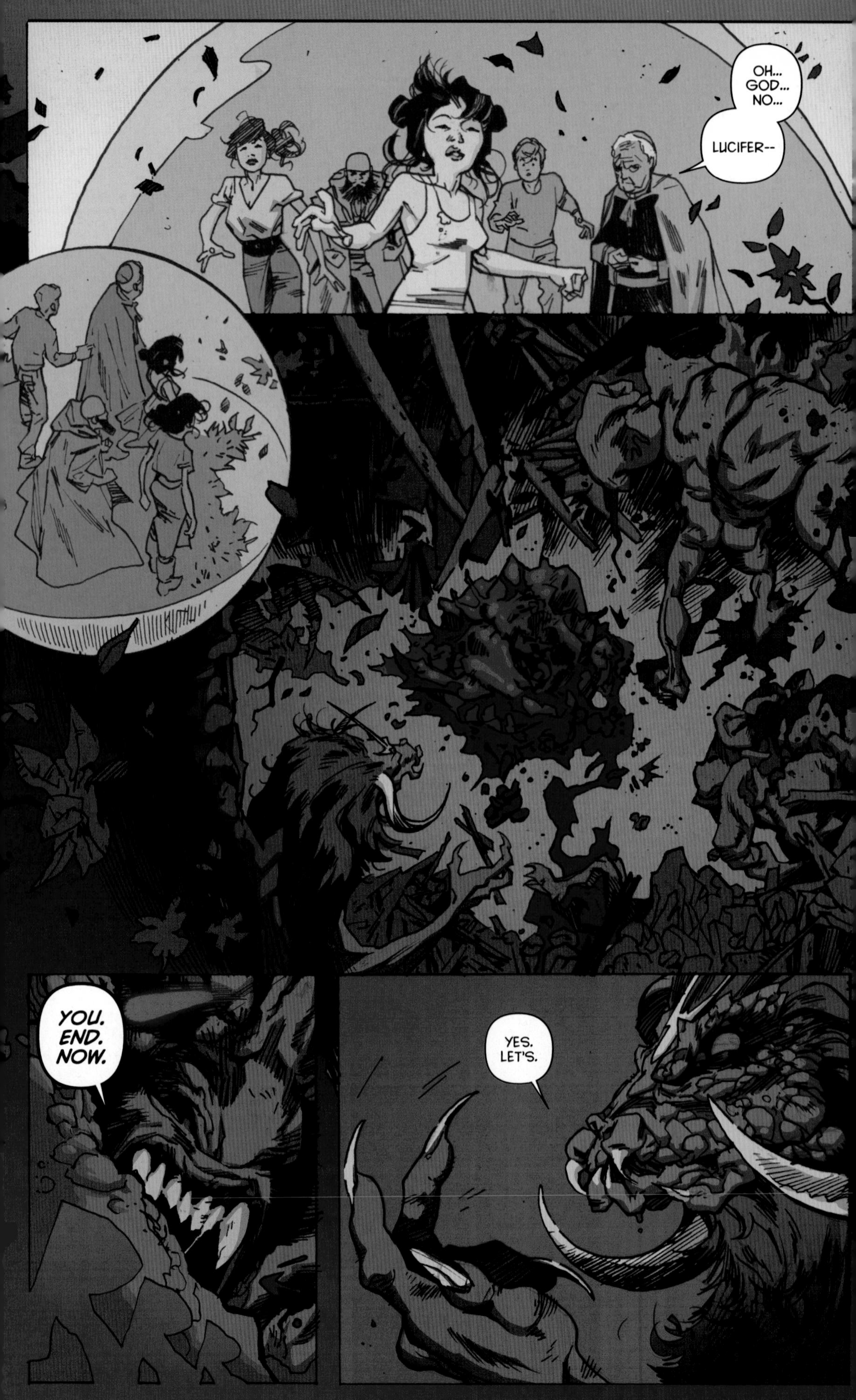
OH... GOD... NO...
LUCIFER--
YOU. END. NOW.
YES. LET'S.

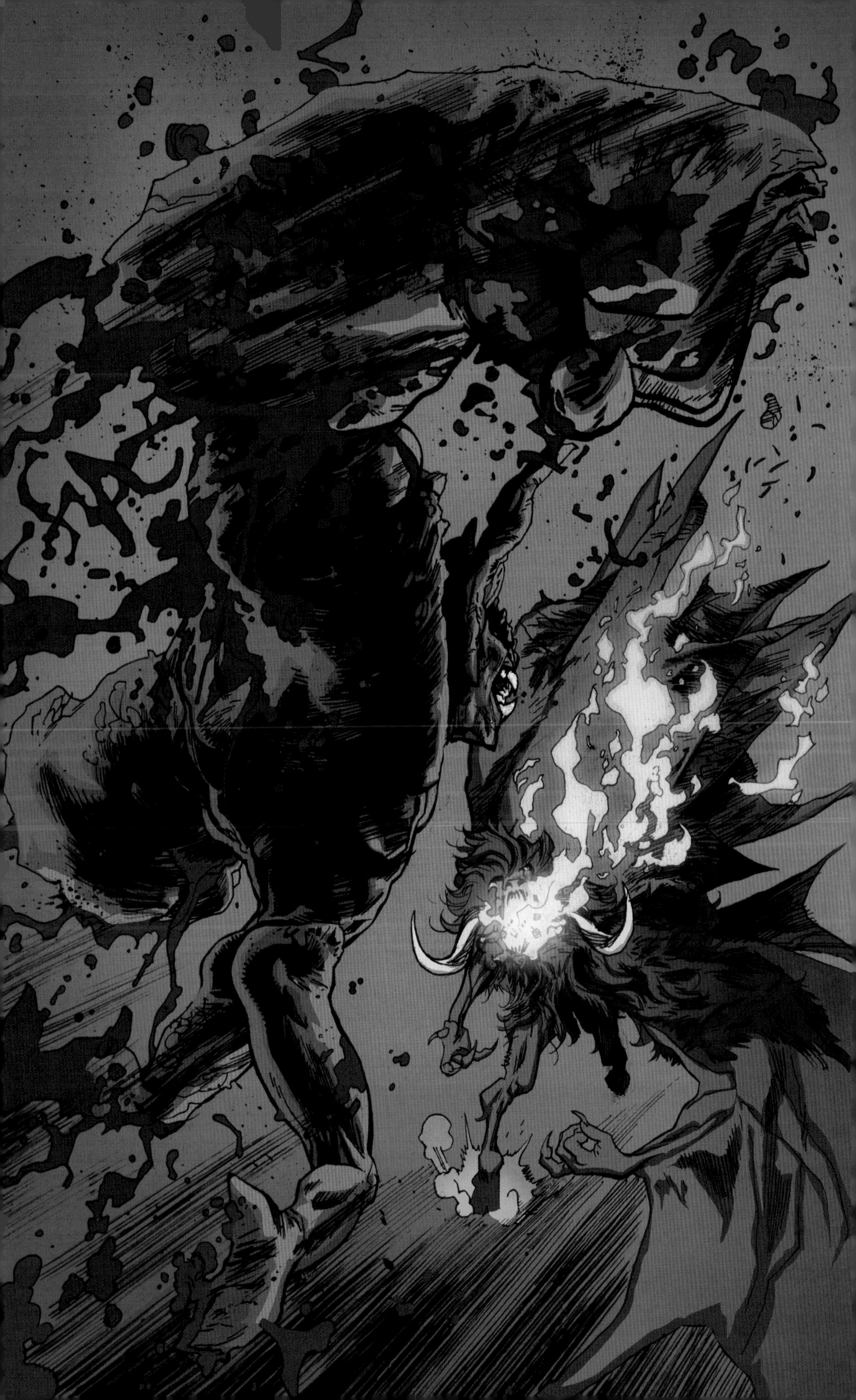

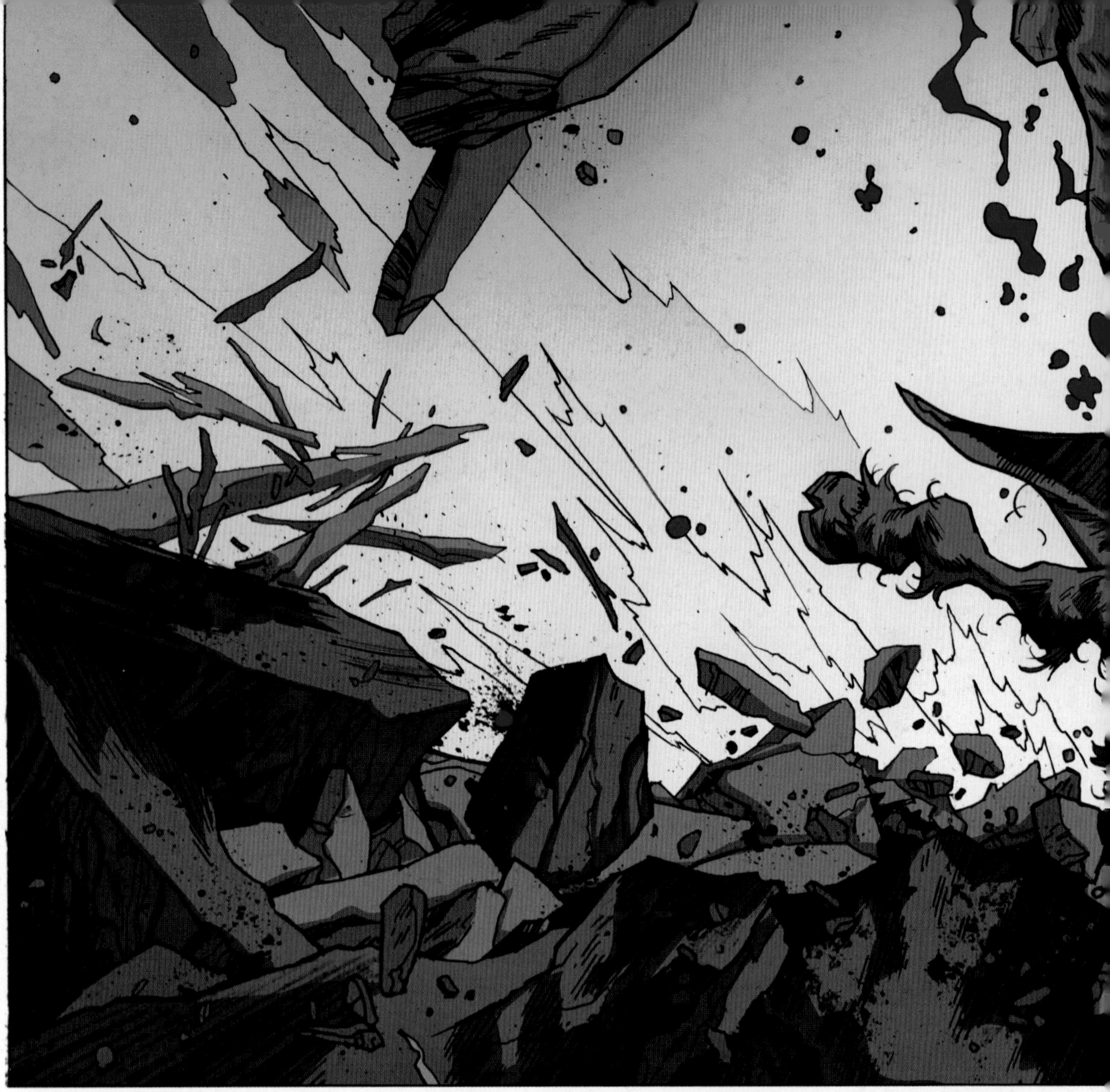

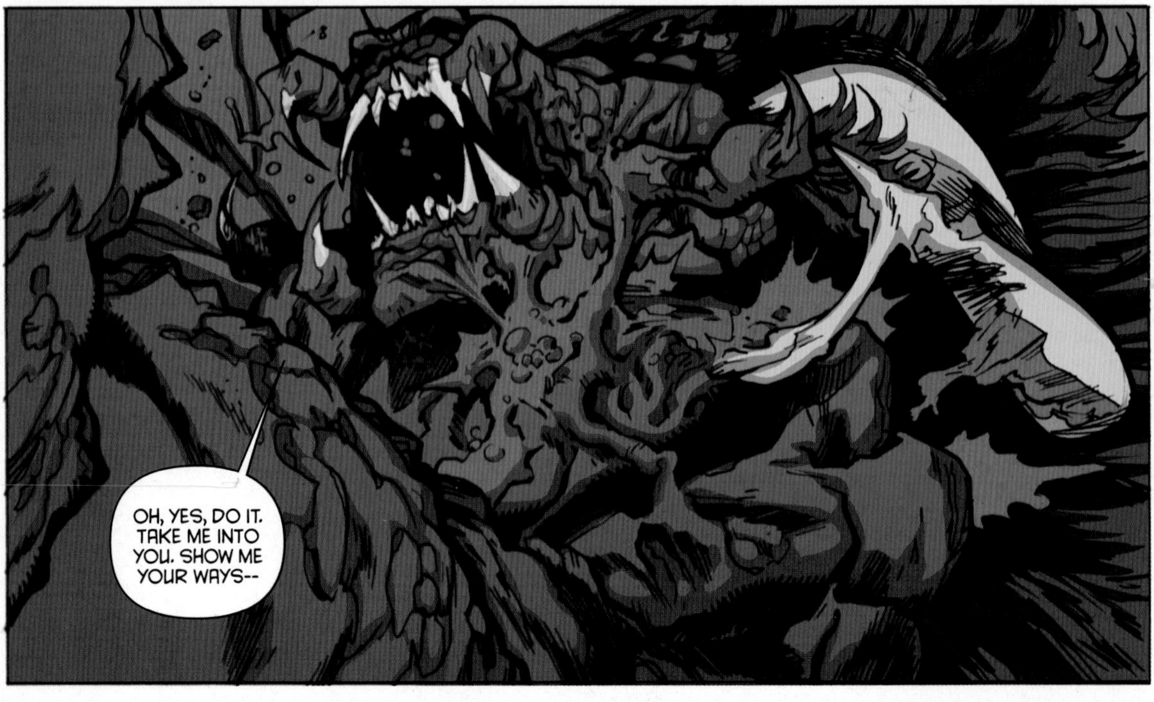
OH, YES, DO IT. TAKE ME INTO YOU. SHOW ME YOUR WAYS--

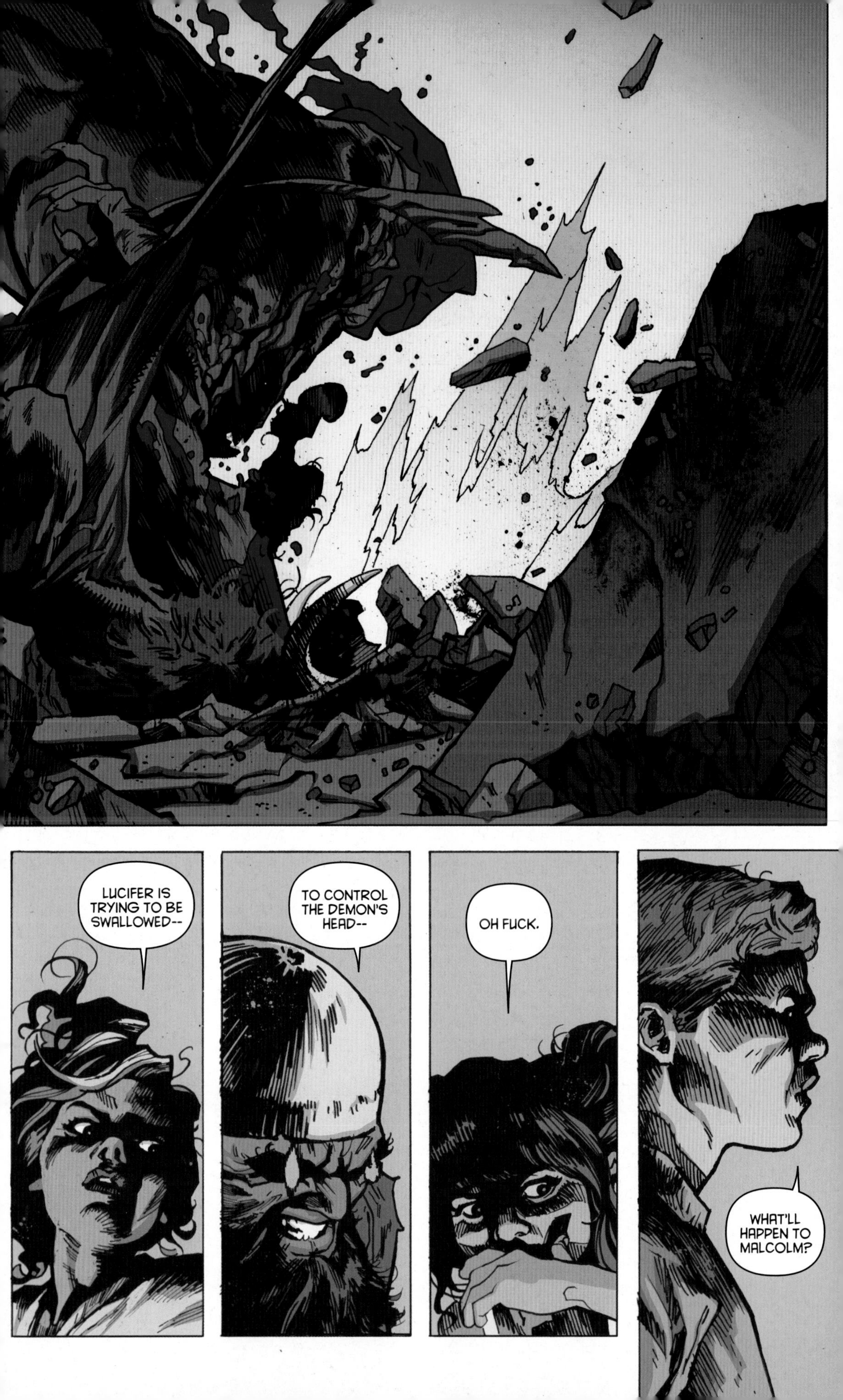
LUCIFER IS TRYING TO BE SWALLOWED--
TO CONTROL THE DEMON'S HEAD--
OH FUCK.
WHAT'LL HAPPEN TO MALCOLM?

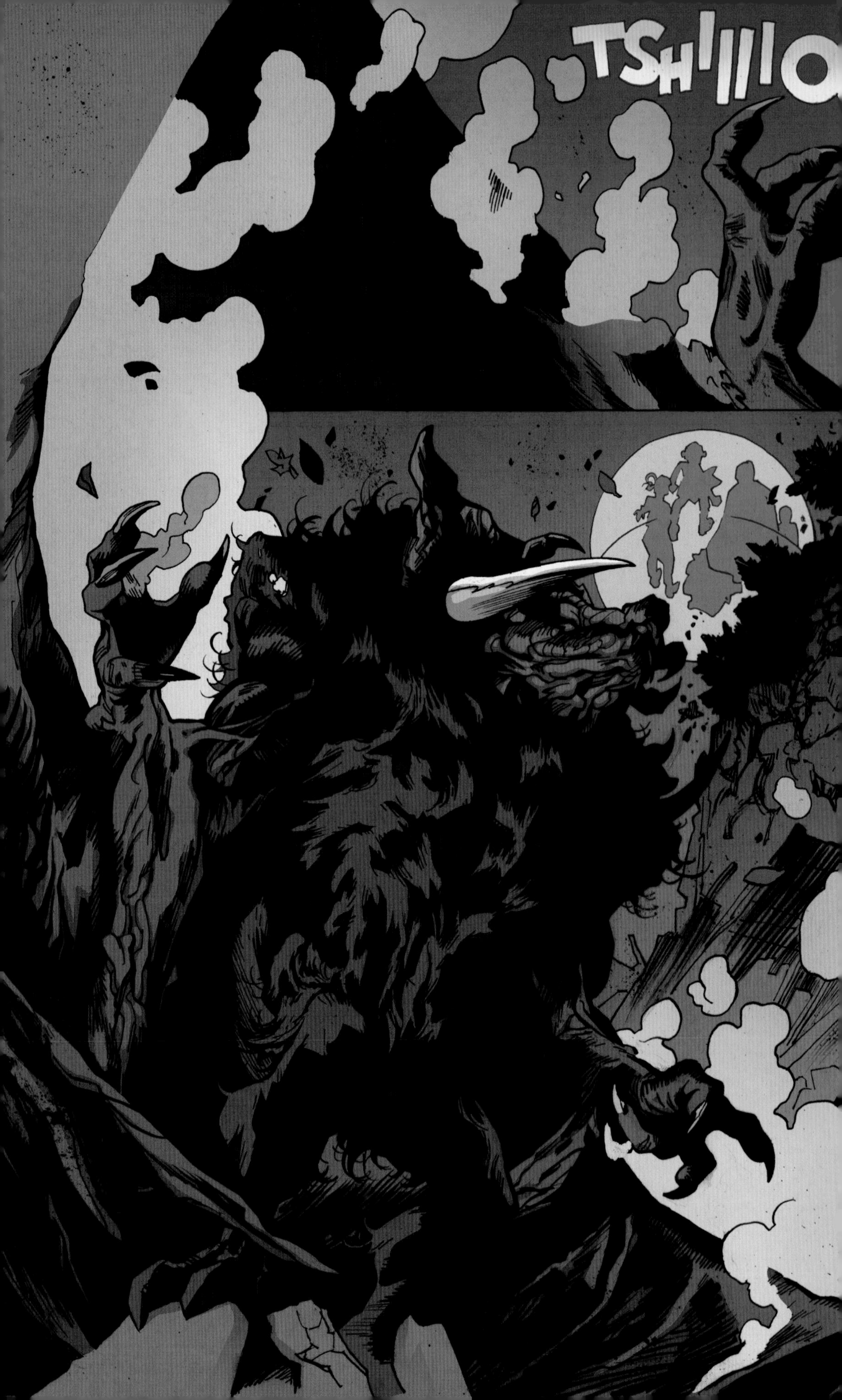
TSHIIIIO

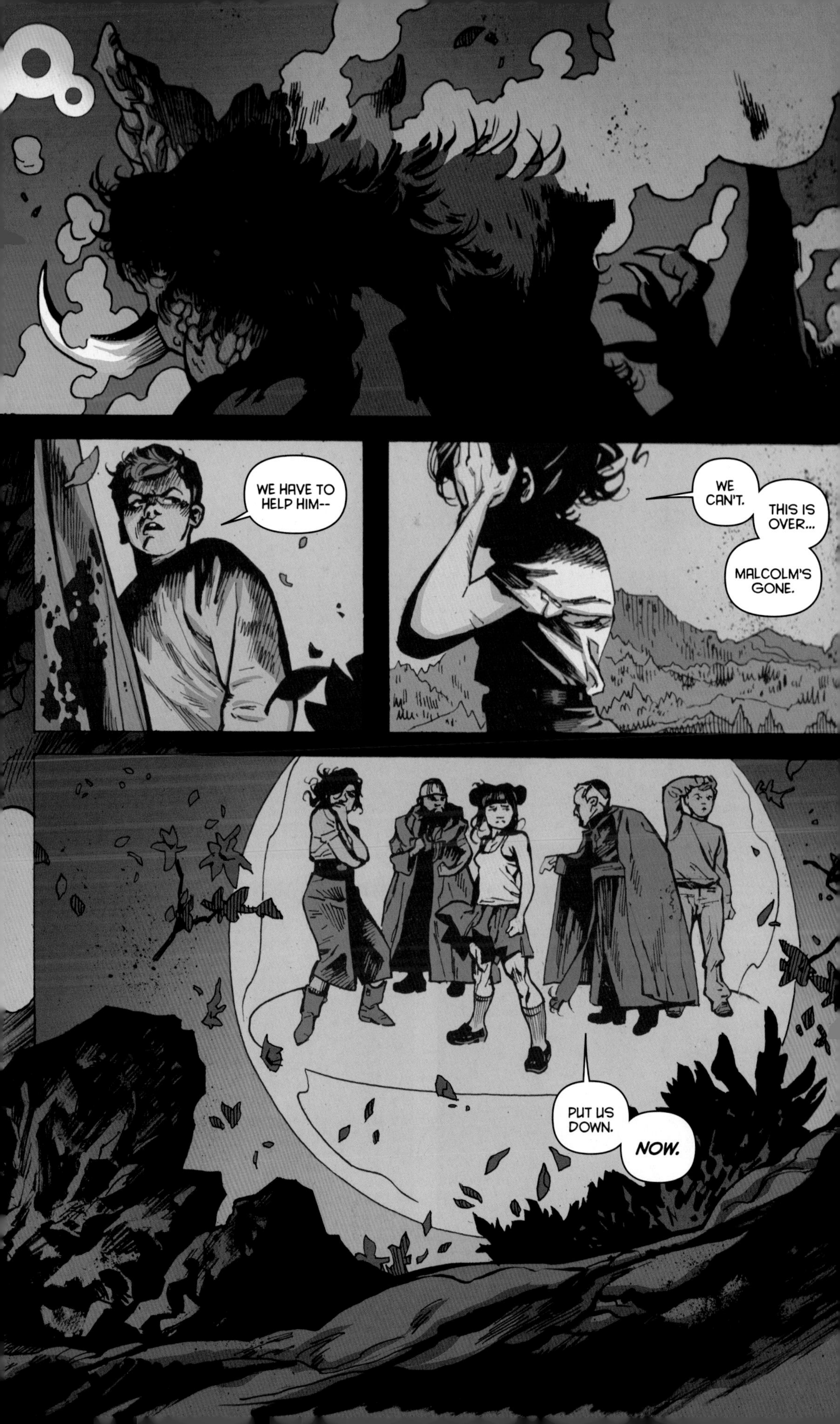
WE HAVE TO HELP HIM--
WE CAN'T.
THIS IS OVER...
MALCOLM'S GONE.
PUT US DOWN.
NOW.

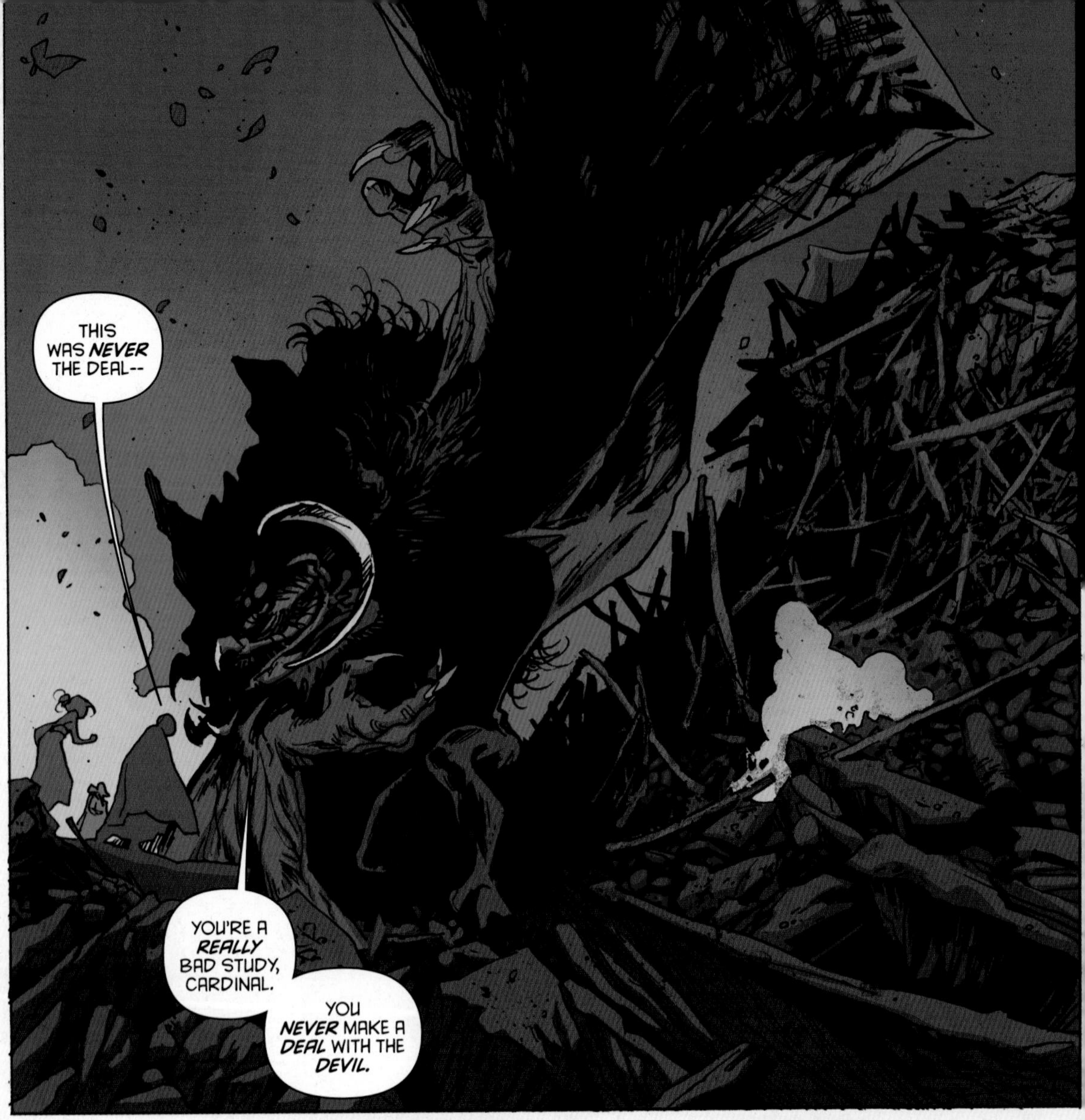
THIS WAS NEVER THE DEAL--
YOU'RE A REALLY BAD STUDY, CARDINAL.
YOU NEVER MAKE A DEAL WITH THE DEVIL.

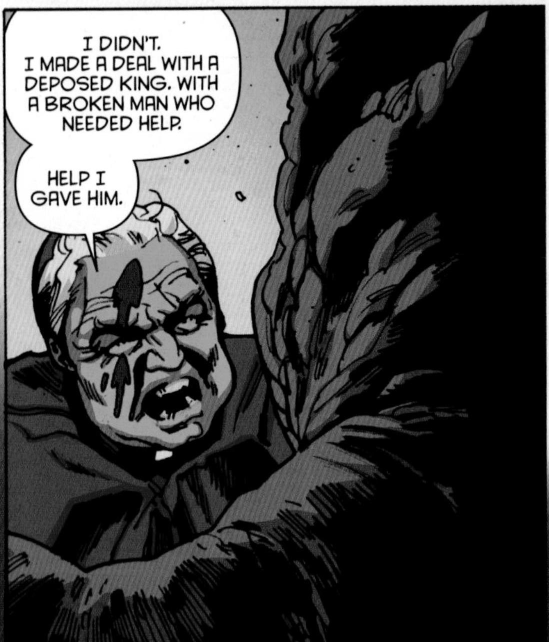
I DIDN'T. I MADE A DEAL WITH A DEPOSED KING. WITH A BROKEN MAN WHO NEEDED HELP.
HELP I GAVE HIM.

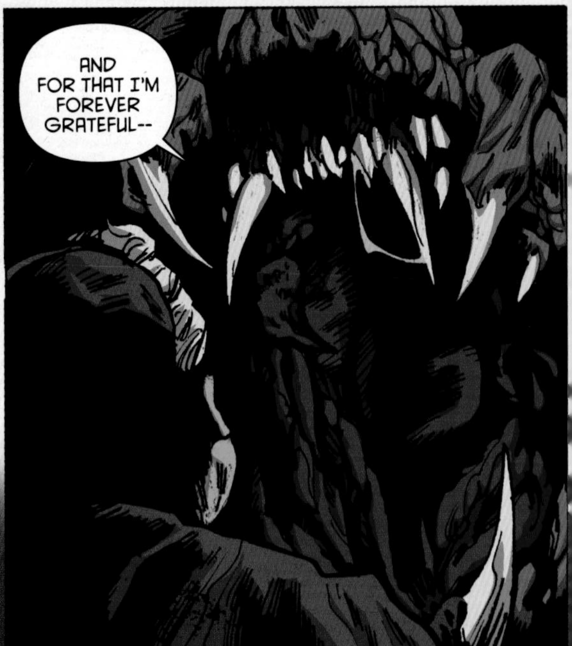
AND FOR THAT I'M FOREVER GRATEFUL--

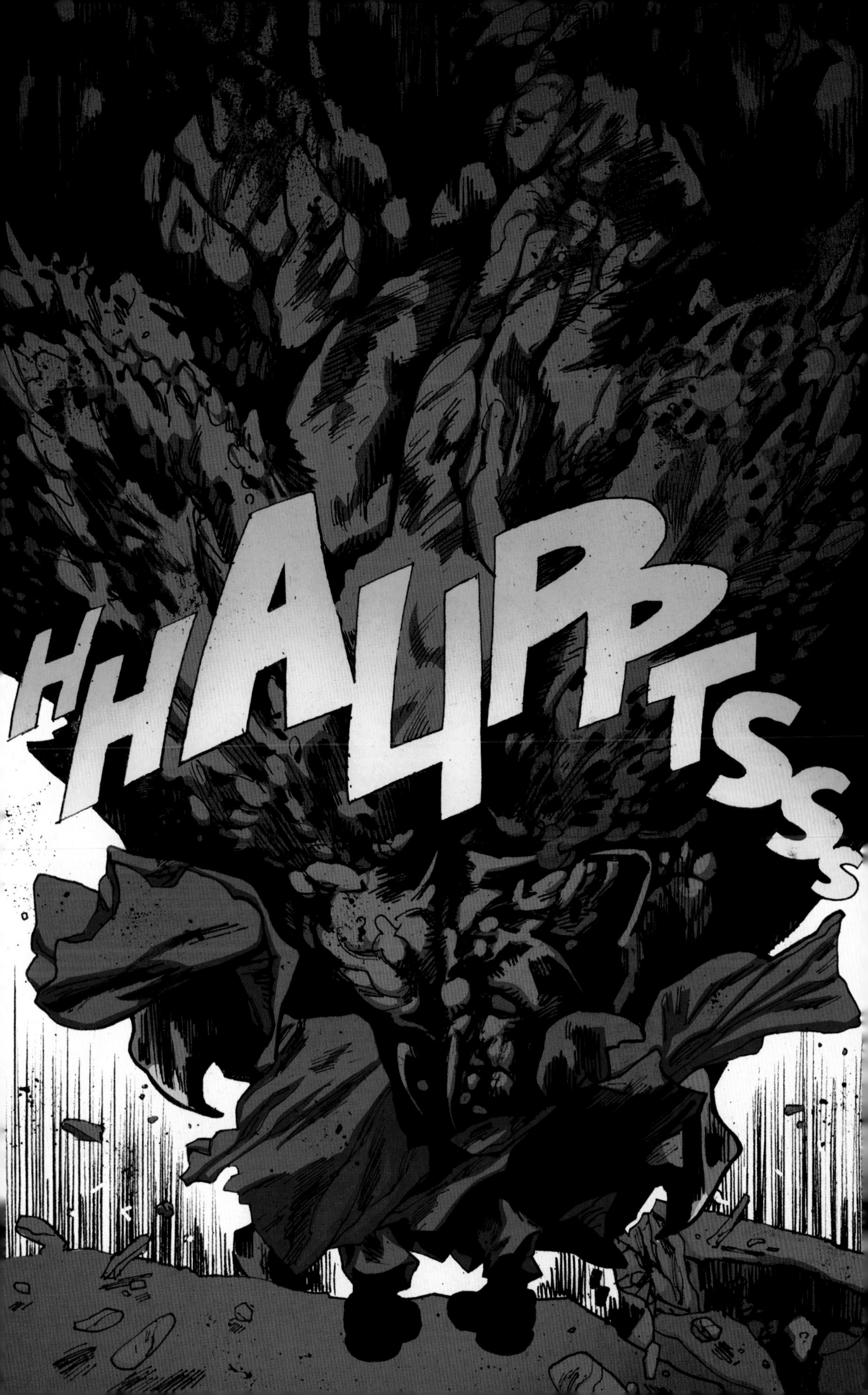
HHAUPPTSSS

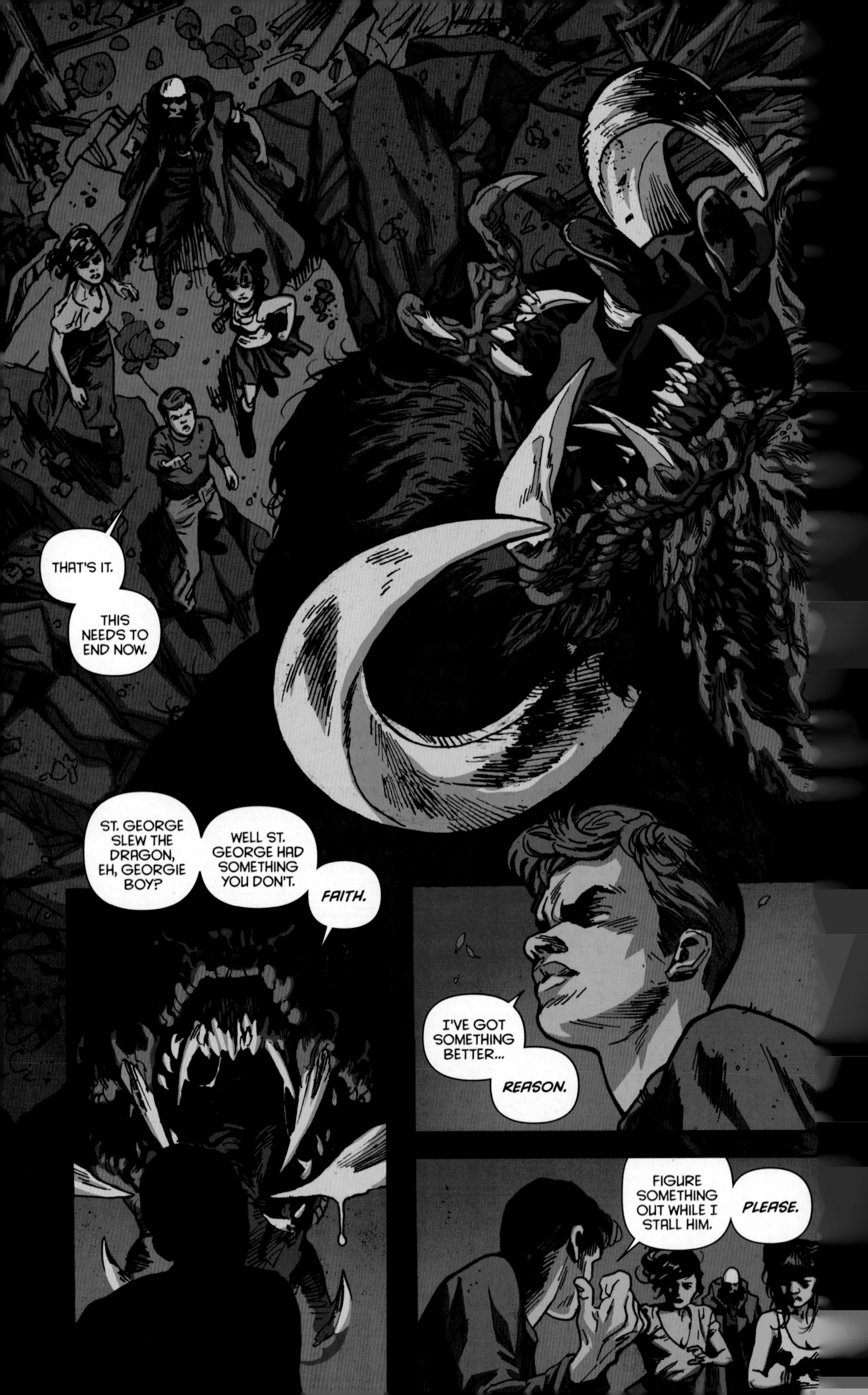
THAT'S IT.
THIS NEEDS TO END NOW.
ST. GEORGE SLEW THE DRAGON, EH, GEORGIE BOY?
WELL ST. GEORGE HAD SOMETHING YOU DON'T.
FAITH.
I'VE GOT SOMETHING BETTER...
REASON.
FIGURE SOMETHING OUT WHILE I STALL HIM.
PLEASE.

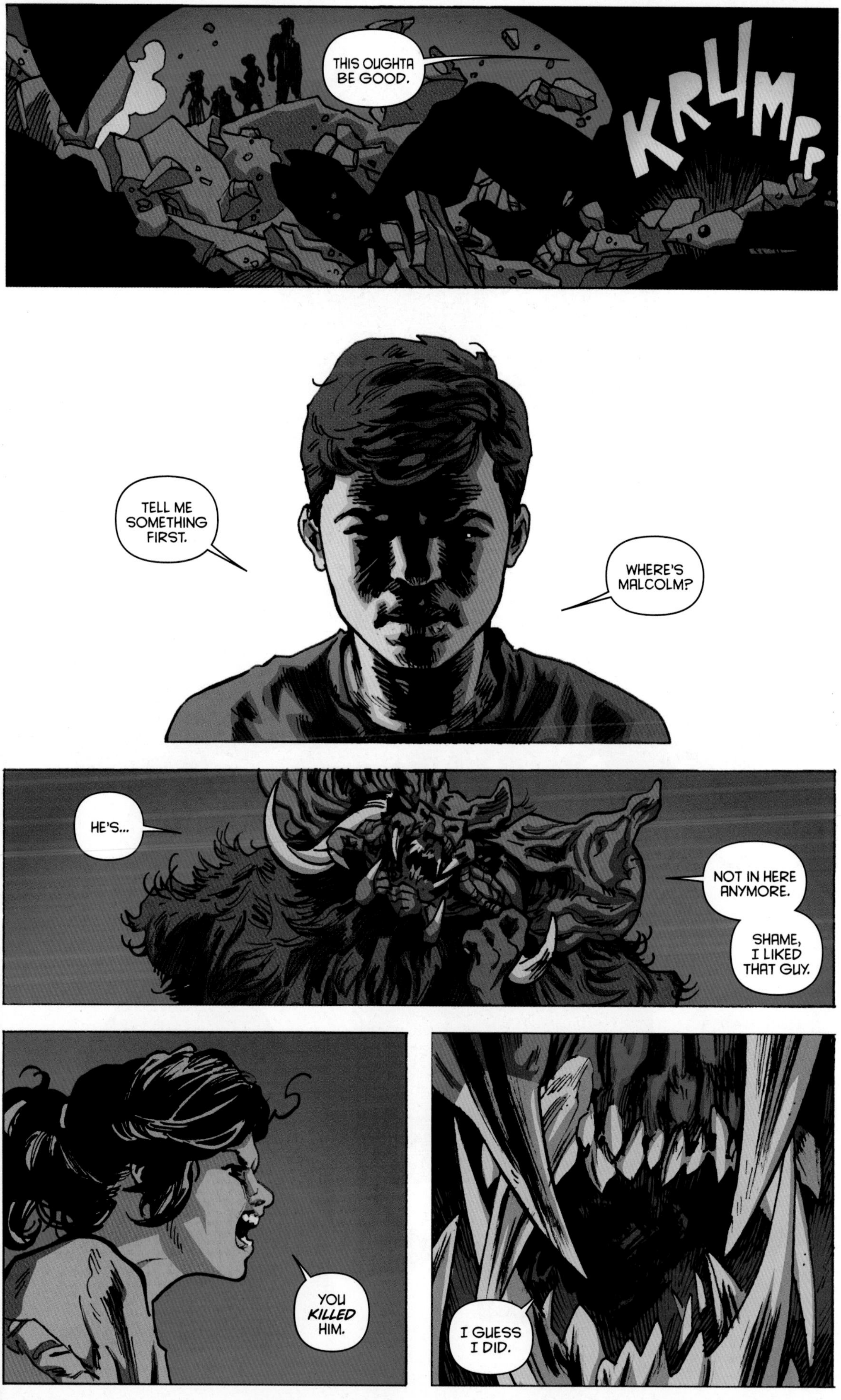
THIS OUGHTA BE GOOD.
KRUMPP
TELL ME SOMETHING FIRST.
WHERE'S MALCOLM?
HE'S...
NOT IN HERE ANYMORE.
SHAME, I LIKED THAT GUY.
YOU *KILLED* HIM.
I GUESS I DID.

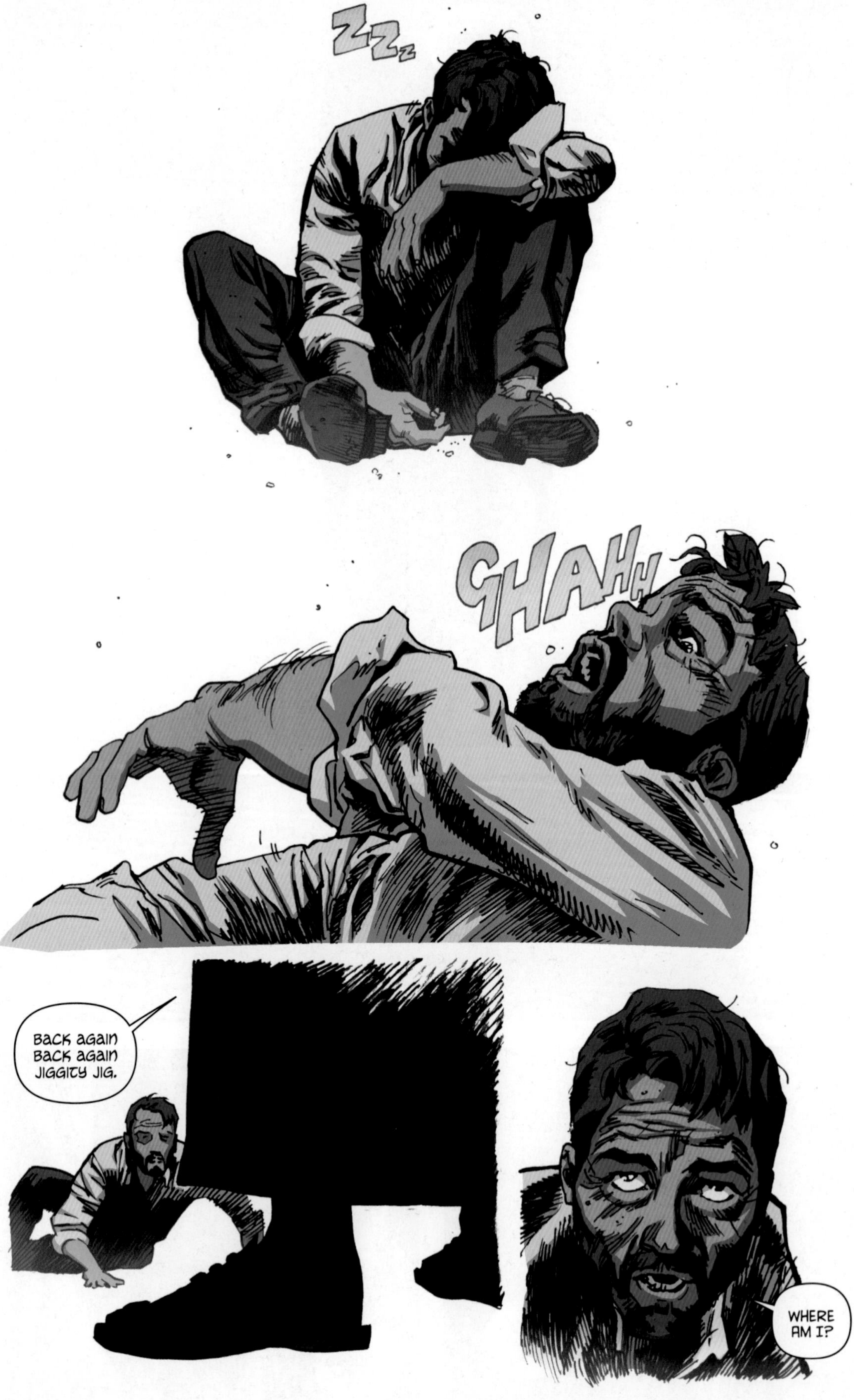
ZZz
GHAHH
BACK AGAIN
BACK AGAIN
JIGGITY JIG.
WHERE
AM I?

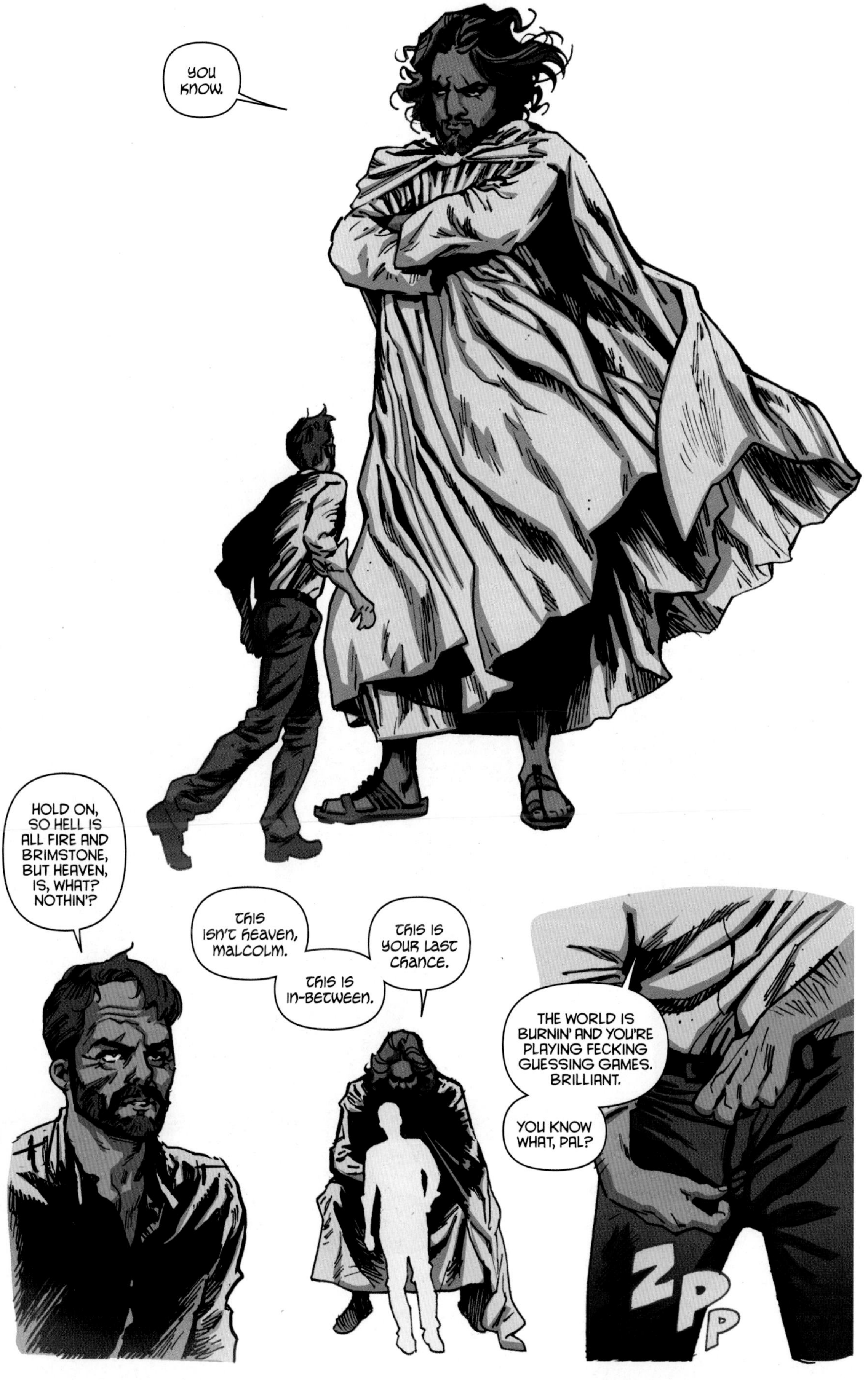
YOU KNOW.
HOLD ON, SO HELL IS ALL FIRE AND BRIMSTONE, BUT HEAVEN, IS, WHAT? NOTHIN'?
THIS ISN'T HEAVEN, MALCOLM.
THIS IS IN-BETWEEN.
THIS IS YOUR LAST CHANCE.
THE WORLD IS BURNIN' AND YOU'RE PLAYING FECKING GUESSING GAMES. BRILLIANT.
YOU KNOW WHAT, PAL?
ZPP

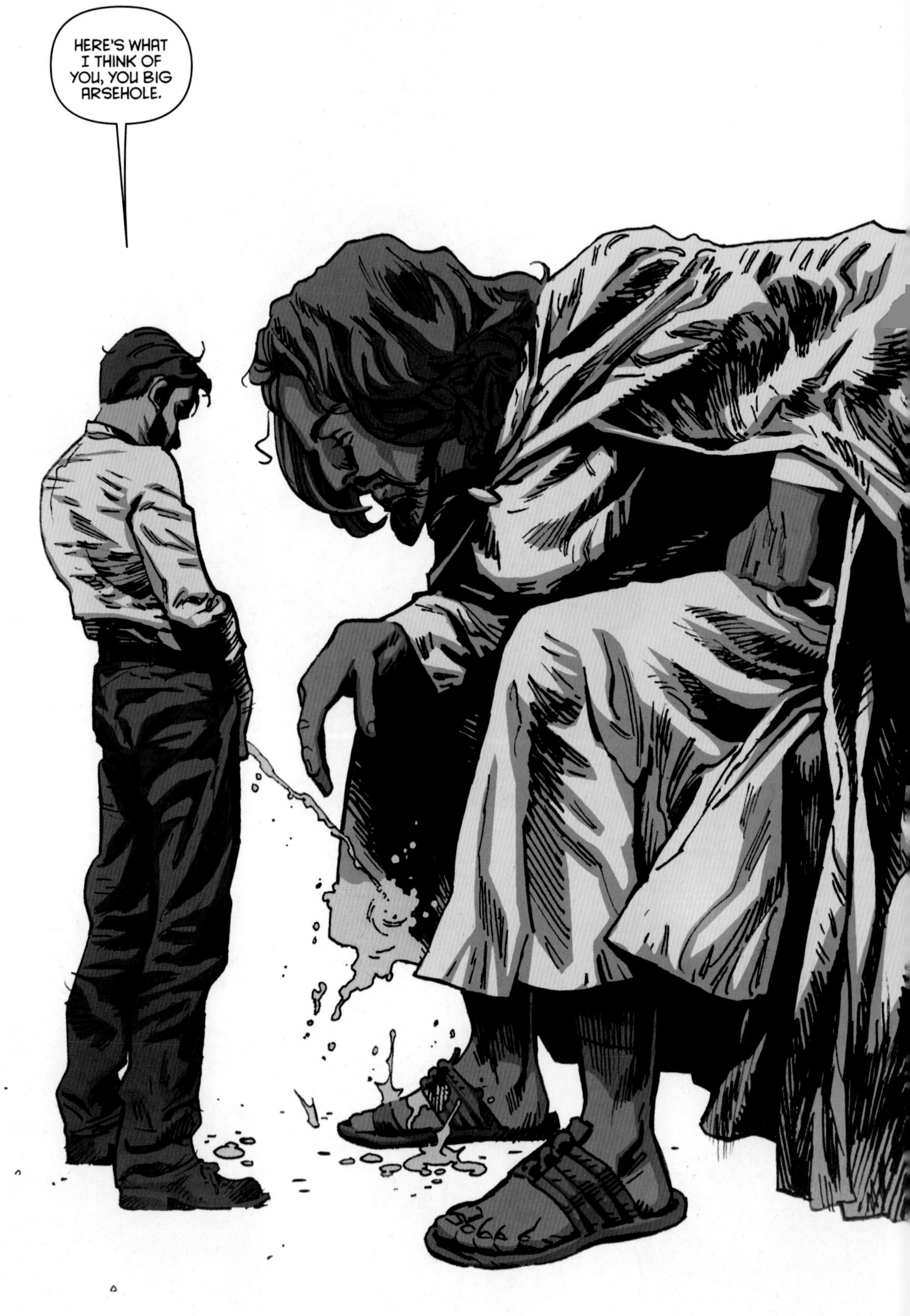
HERE'S WHAT I THINK OF YOU, YOU BIG ARSEHOLE.

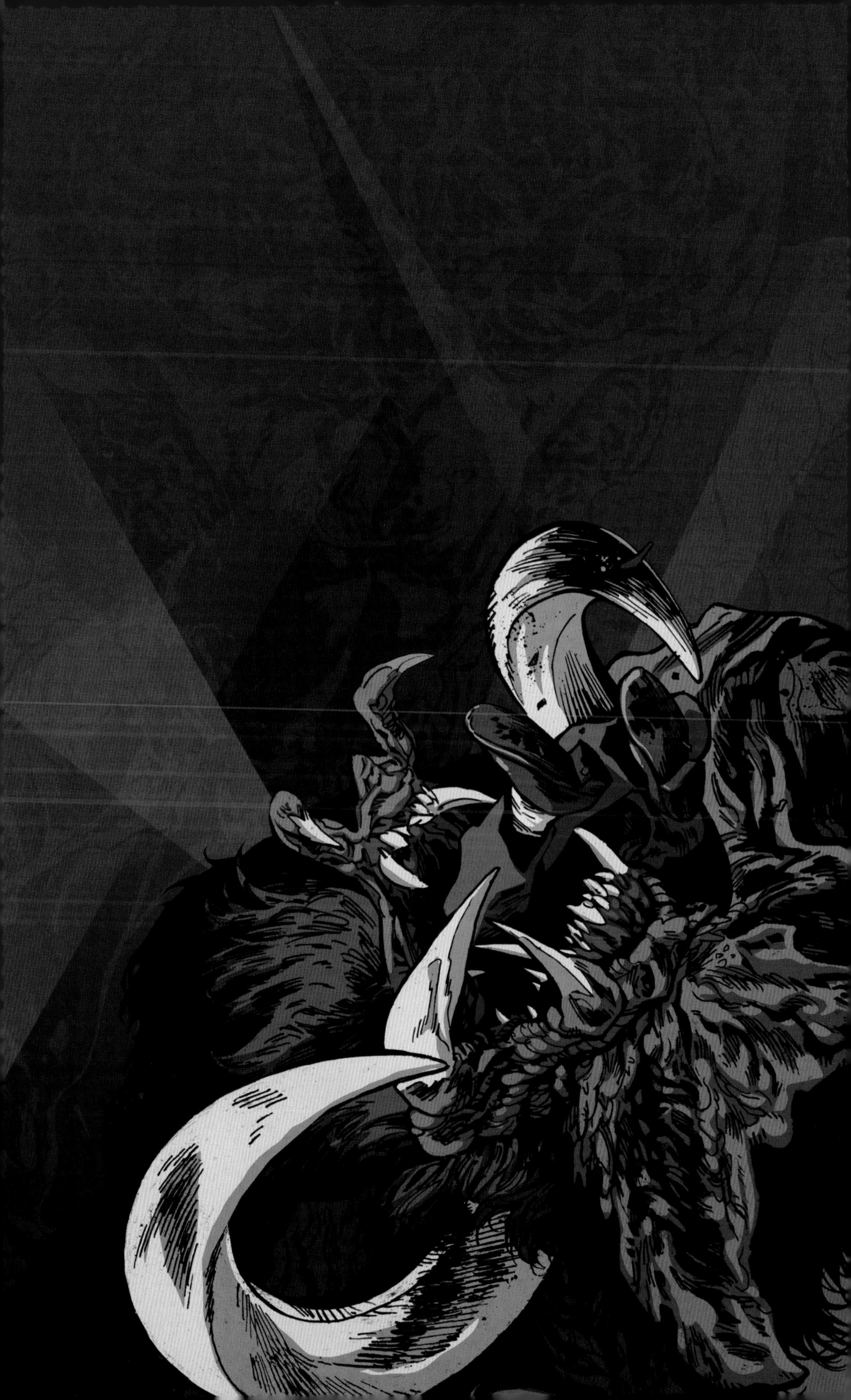

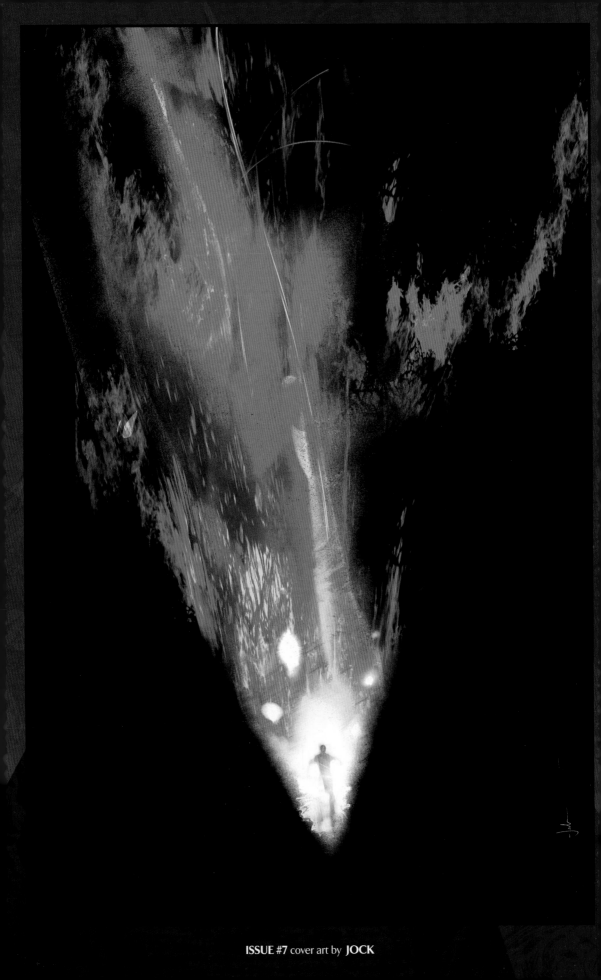

ISSUE #7 cover art by **JOCK**

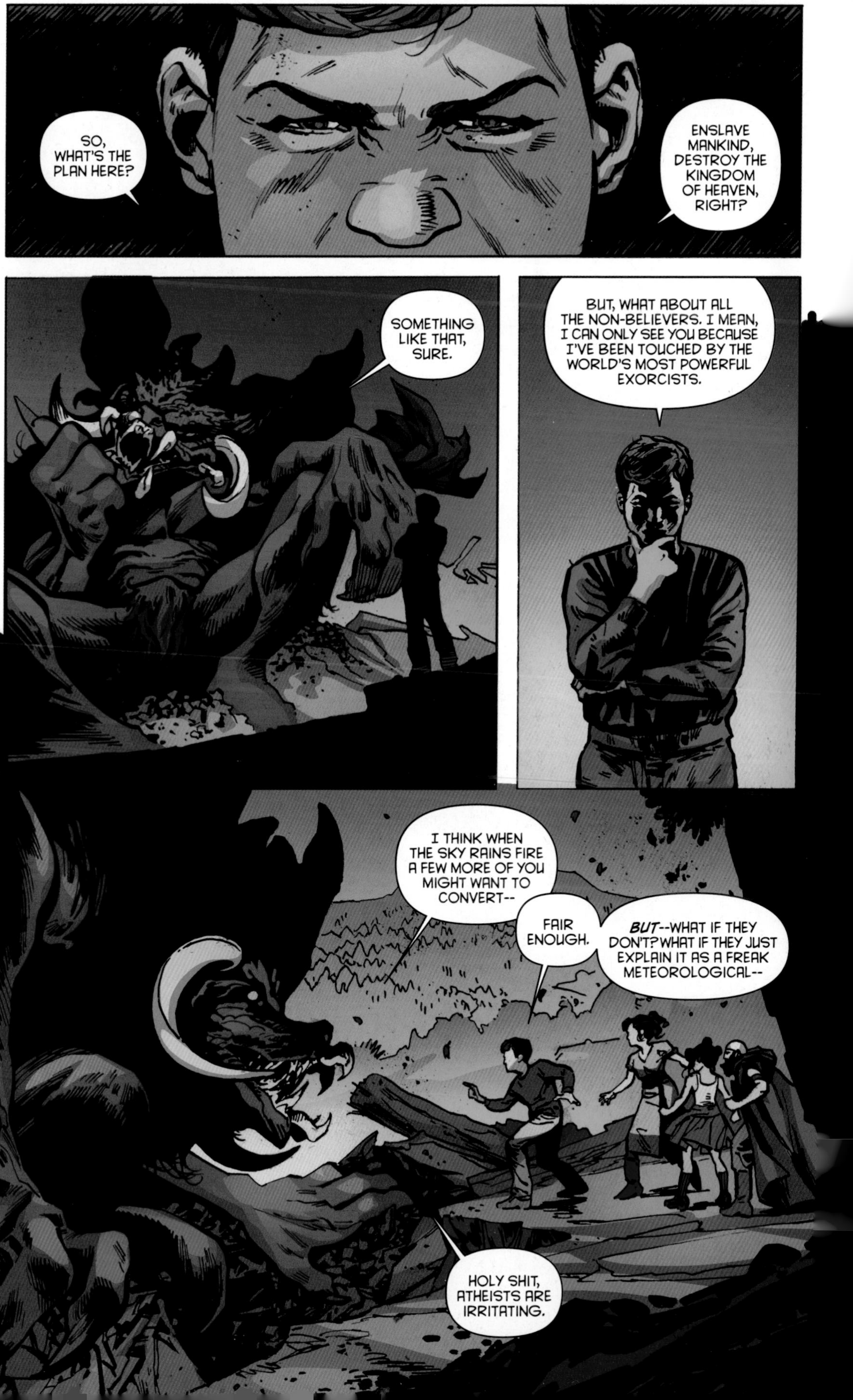
SO, WHAT'S THE PLAN HERE?
ENSLAVE MANKIND, DESTROY THE KINGDOM OF HEAVEN, RIGHT?
SOMETHING LIKE THAT, SURE.
BUT, WHAT ABOUT ALL THE NON-BELIEVERS. I MEAN, I CAN ONLY SEE YOU BECAUSE I'VE BEEN TOUCHED BY THE WORLD'S MOST POWERFUL EXORCISTS.
I THINK WHEN THE SKY RAINS FIRE A FEW MORE OF YOU MIGHT WANT TO CONVERT--
FAIR ENOUGH.
BUT--WHAT IF THEY DON'T? WHAT IF THEY JUST EXPLAIN IT AS A FREAK METEOROLOGICAL--
HOLY SHIT, ATHEISTS ARE IRRITATING.

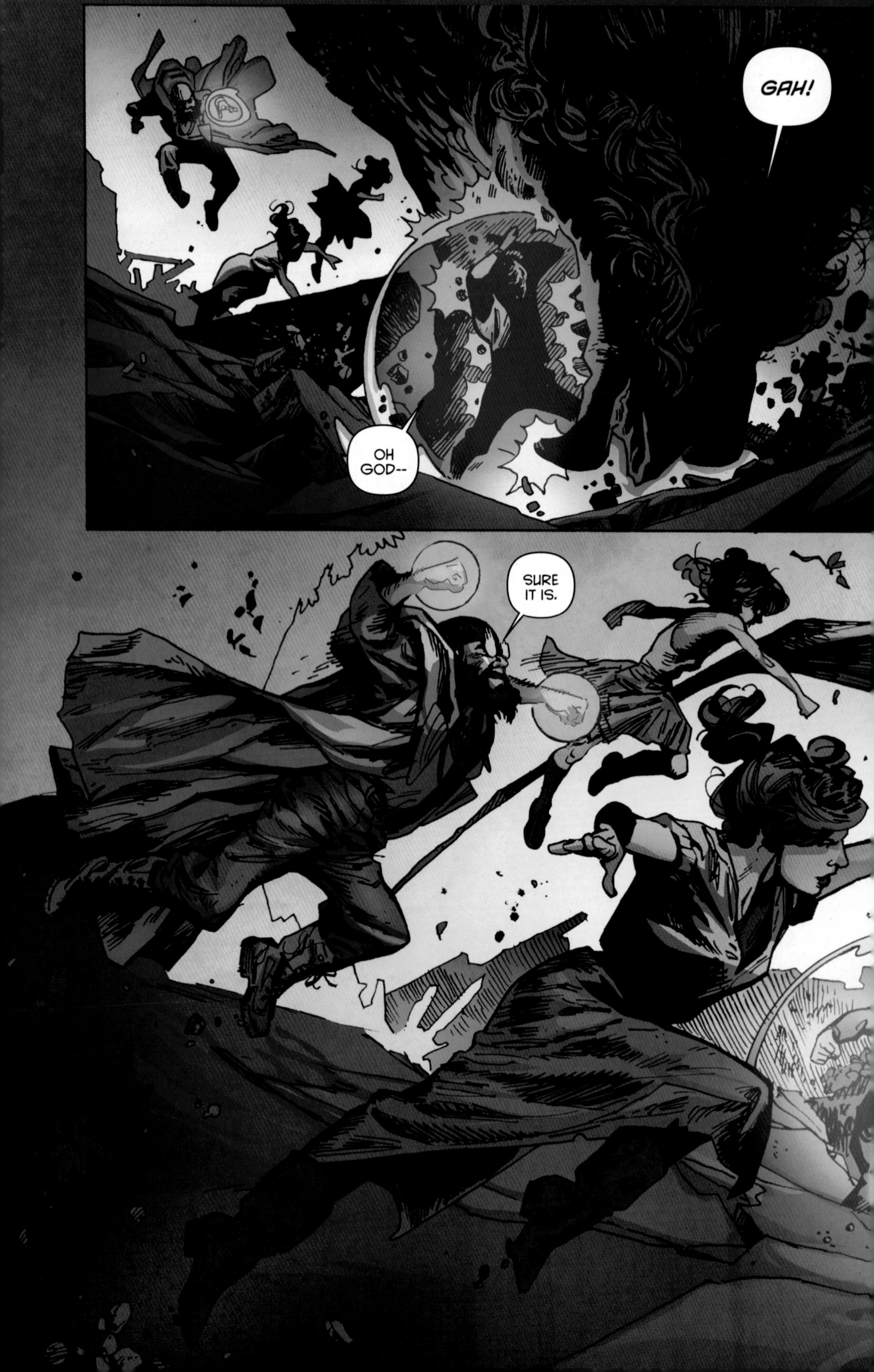
GAH!
OH GOD--
SURE IT IS.

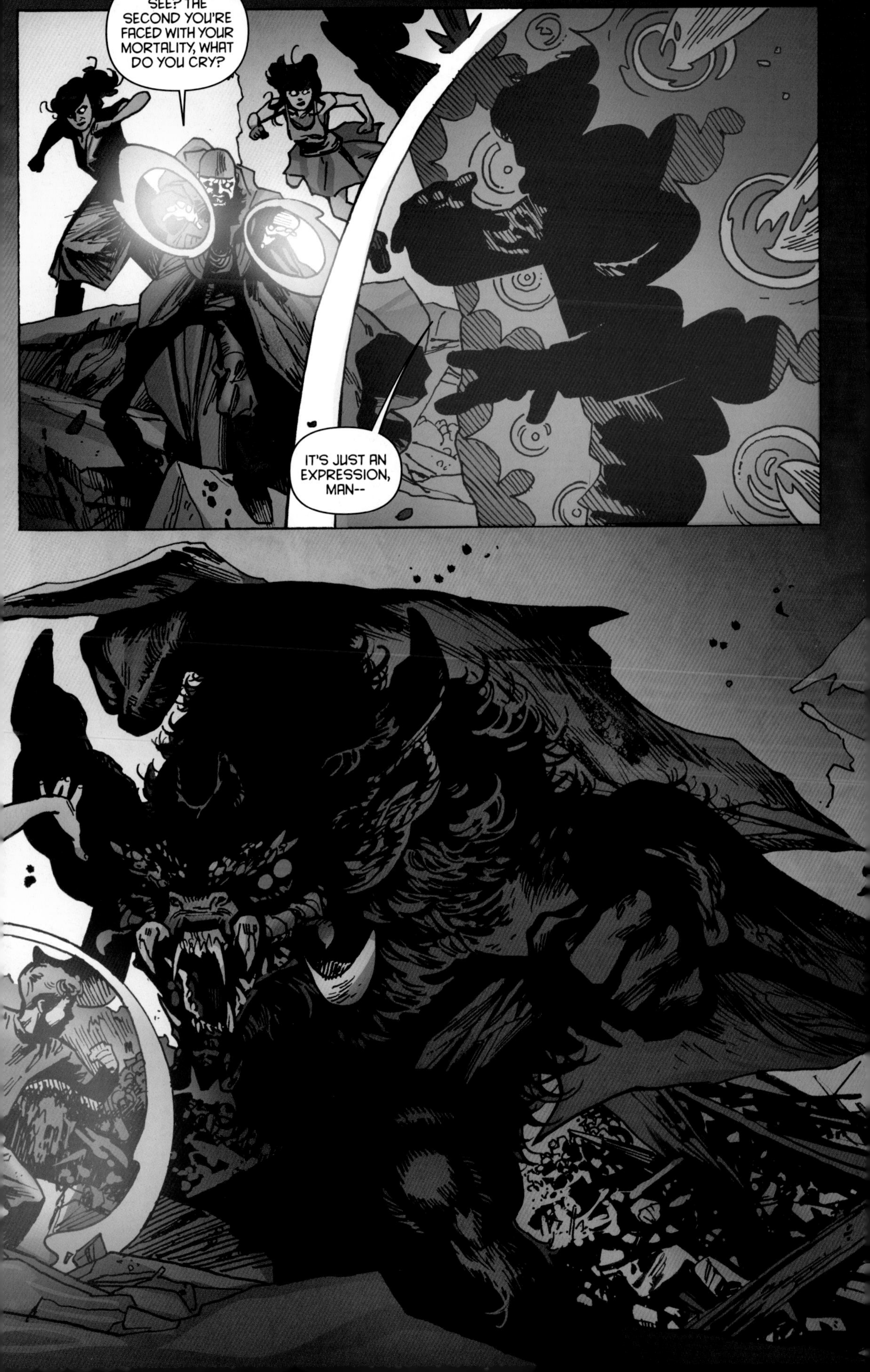
SEE? THE SECOND YOU'RE FACED WITH YOUR MORTALITY, WHAT DO YOU CRY?
IT'S JUST AN EXPRESSION, MAN--

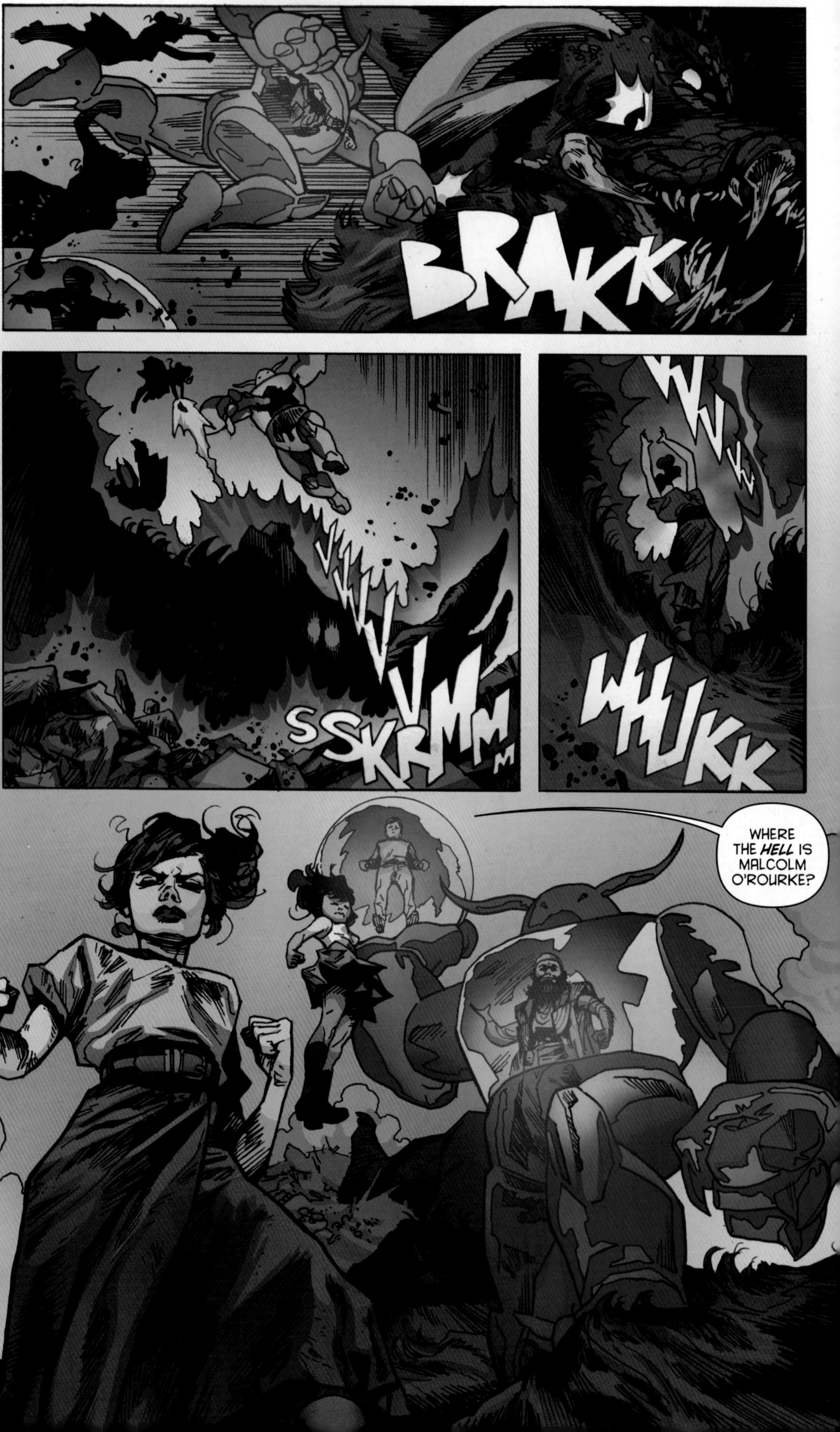
BRAKK
SSKRMMM
WHUKK
WHERE THE *HELL* IS MALCOLM O'ROURKE?

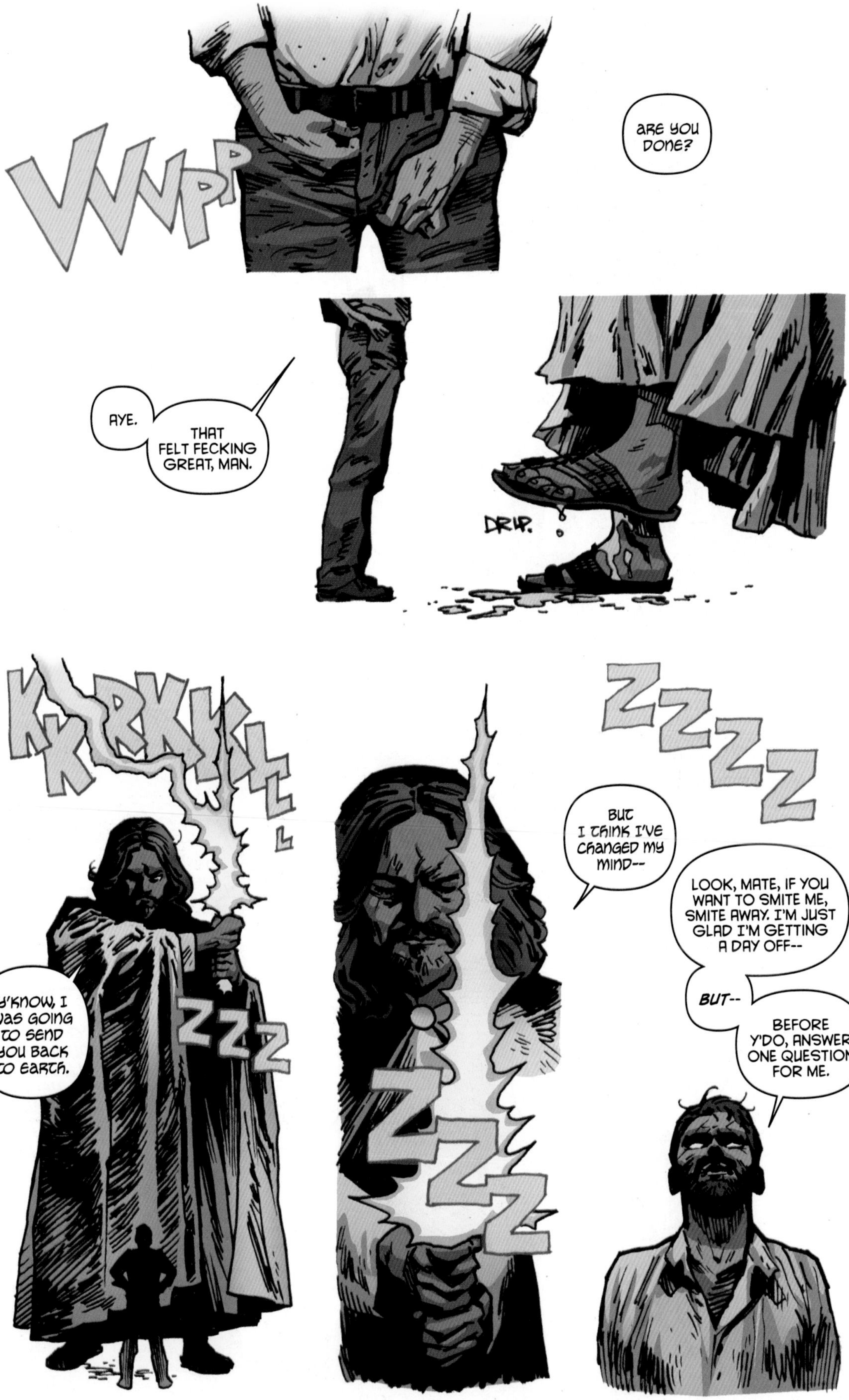
VVVPP
ARE YOU DONE?
AYE.
THAT FELT FECKING GREAT, MAN.
DRIP.
KKRKKLLL
Y'KNOW, I WAS GOING TO SEND YOU BACK TO EARTH.
ZZZ
ZZZ
BUT I THINK I'VE CHANGED MY MIND--
ZZZZ
LOOK, MATE, IF YOU WANT TO SMITE ME, SMITE AWAY. I'M JUST GLAD I'M GETTING A DAY OFF--
BUT--
BEFORE Y'DO, ANSWER ONE QUESTION FOR ME.

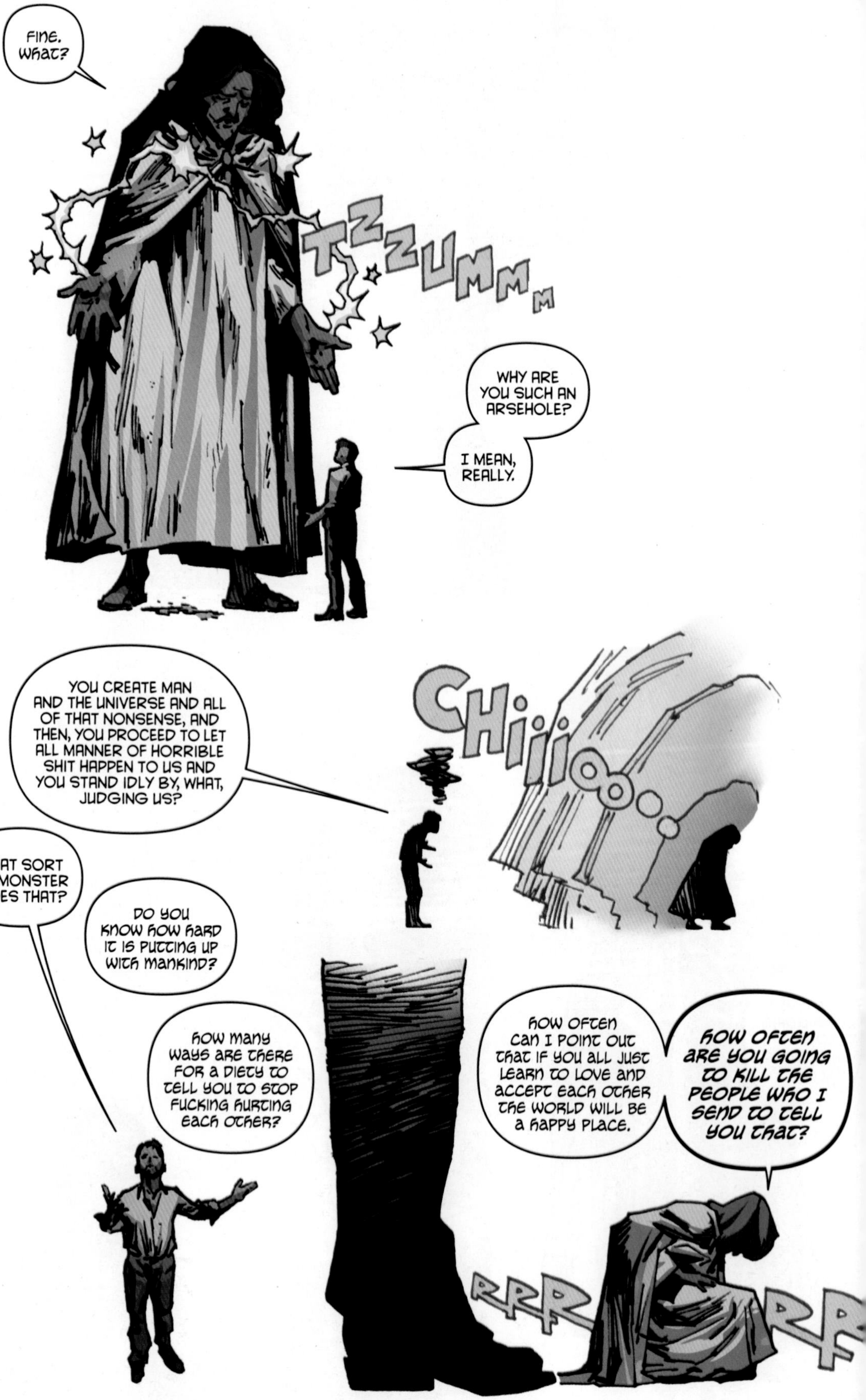
FINE. WHAT?
TZZZUMMMM
WHY ARE YOU SUCH AN ARSEHOLE?
I MEAN, REALLY.
YOU CREATE MAN AND THE UNIVERSE AND ALL OF THAT NONSENSE, AND THEN, YOU PROCEED TO LET ALL MANNER OF HORRIBLE SHIT HAPPEN TO US AND YOU STAND IDLY BY, WHAT, JUDGING US?
CHIIIOO...
WHAT SORT OF MONSTER DOES THAT?
DO YOU KNOW HOW HARD IT IS PUTTING UP WITH MANKIND?
HOW MANY WAYS ARE THERE FOR A DIETY TO TELL YOU TO STOP FUCKING HURTING EACH OTHER?
HOW OFTEN CAN I POINT OUT THAT IF YOU ALL JUST LEARN TO LOVE AND ACCEPT EACH OTHER THE WORLD WILL BE A HAPPY PLACE.
HOW OFTEN ARE YOU GOING TO KILL THE PEOPLE WHO I SEND TO TELL YOU THAT?
RRR
RR

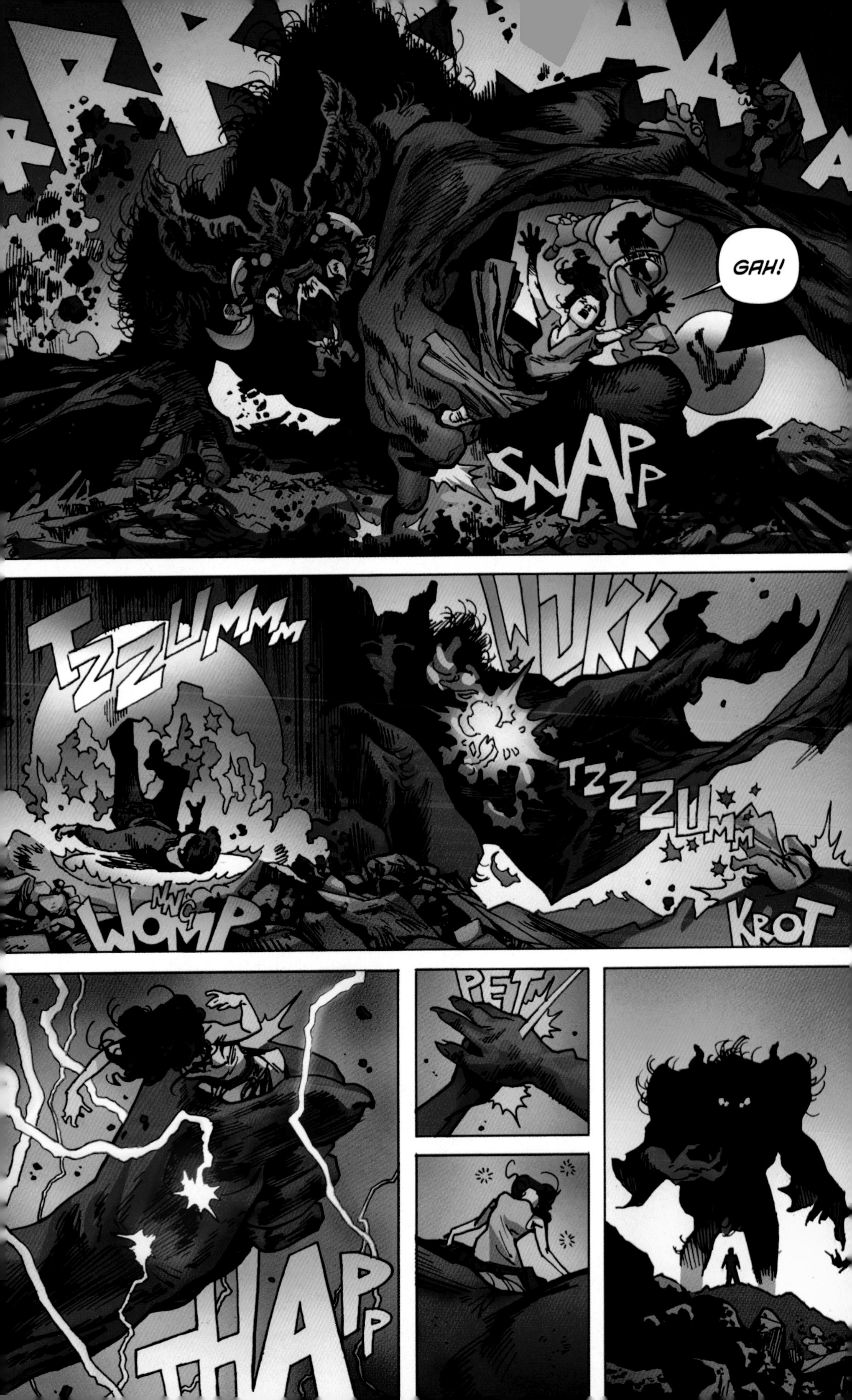
GAH!
SNAPP
TZZUMMM
WUKK
TZZZUMMM
NNG
WOMP
KROT
PET
THAPP

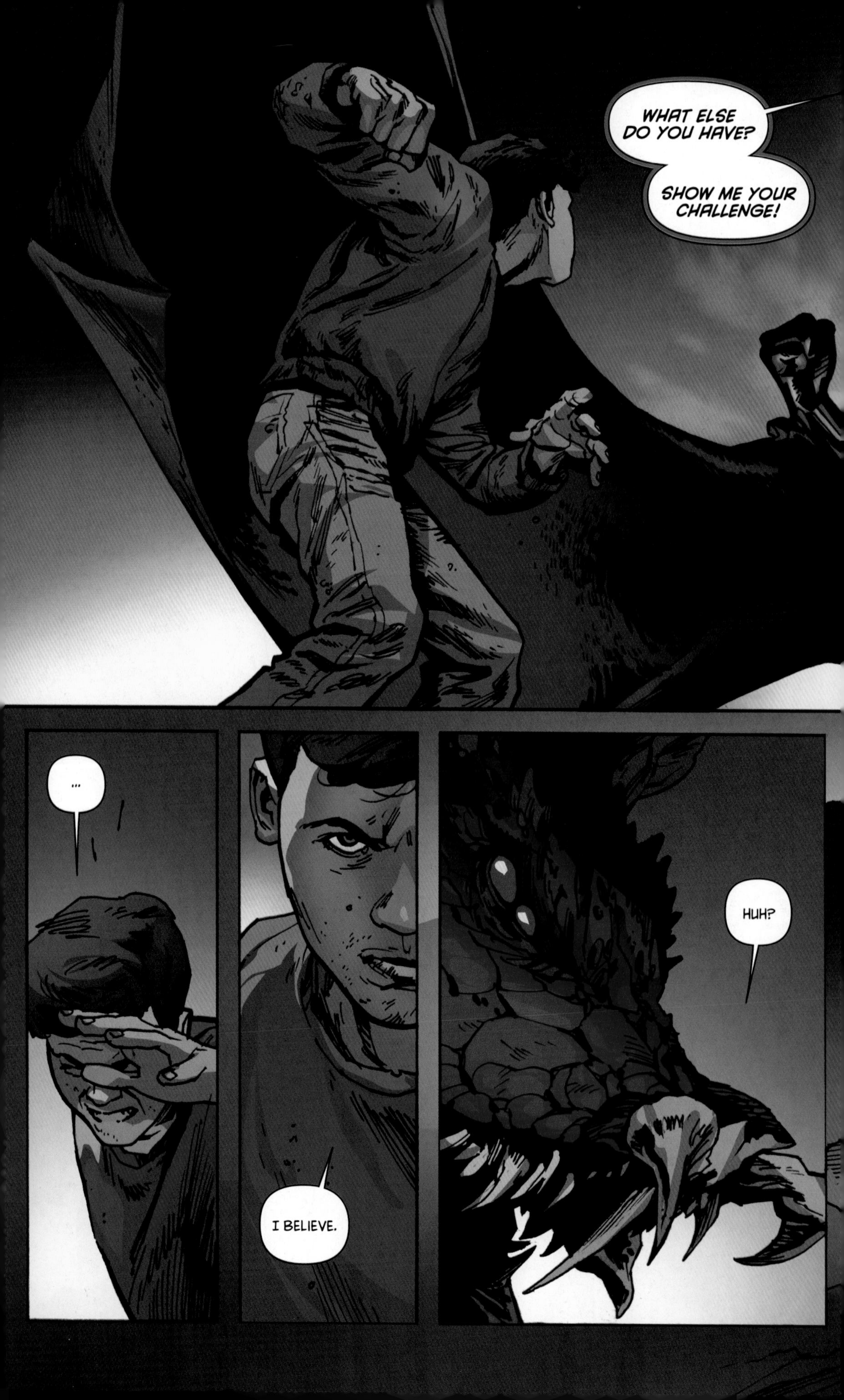
WHAT ELSE DO YOU HAVE?
SHOW ME YOUR CHALLENGE!
...
I BELIEVE.
HUH?

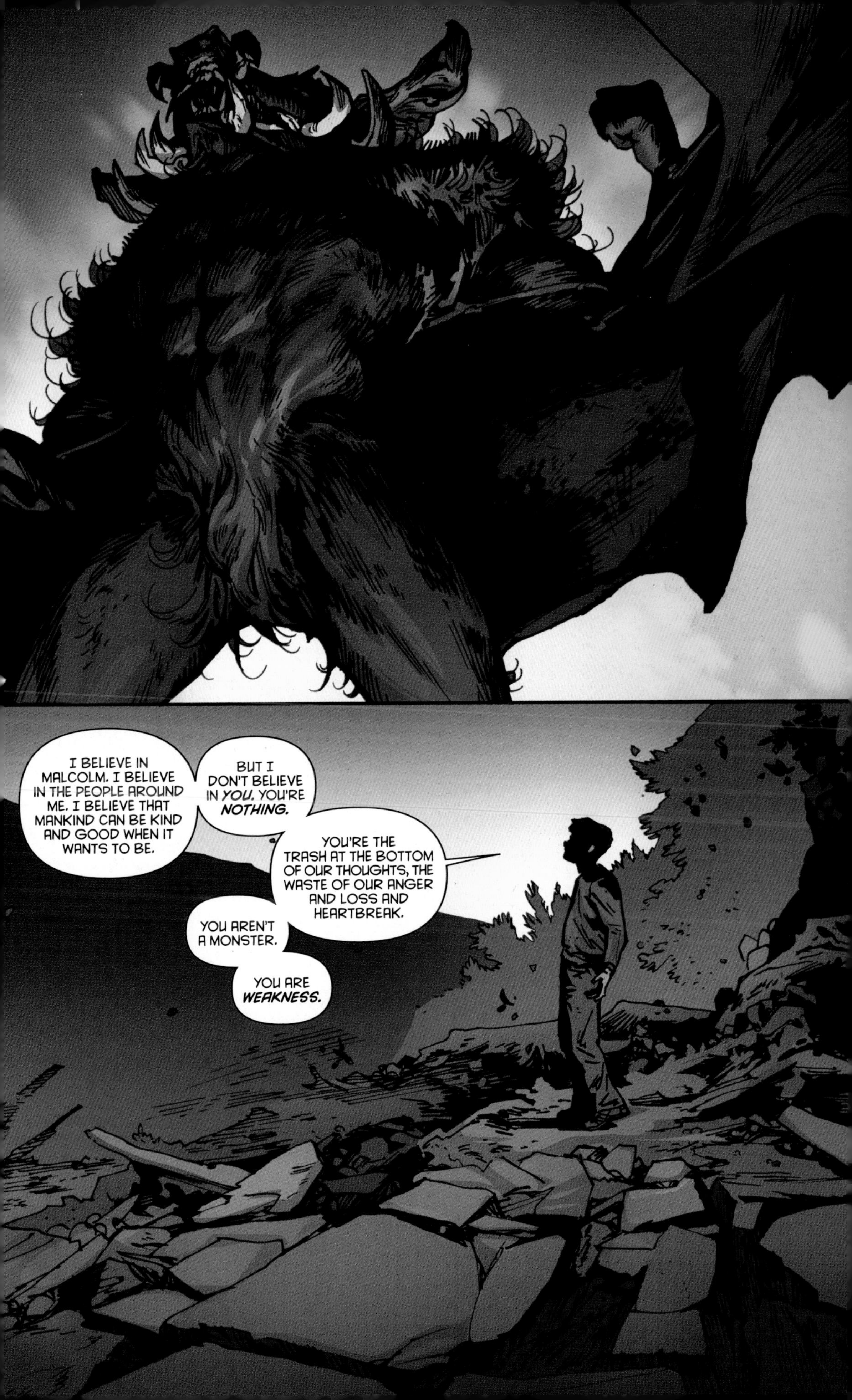
I BELIEVE IN MALCOLM. I BELIEVE IN THE PEOPLE AROUND ME. I BELIEVE THAT MANKIND CAN BE KIND AND GOOD WHEN IT WANTS TO BE.
BUT I DON'T BELIEVE IN *YOU.* YOU'RE ***NOTHING.***
YOU'RE THE TRASH AT THE BOTTOM OF OUR THOUGHTS, THE WASTE OF OUR ANGER AND LOSS AND HEARTBREAK.
YOU AREN'T A MONSTER.
YOU ARE ***WEAKNESS.***

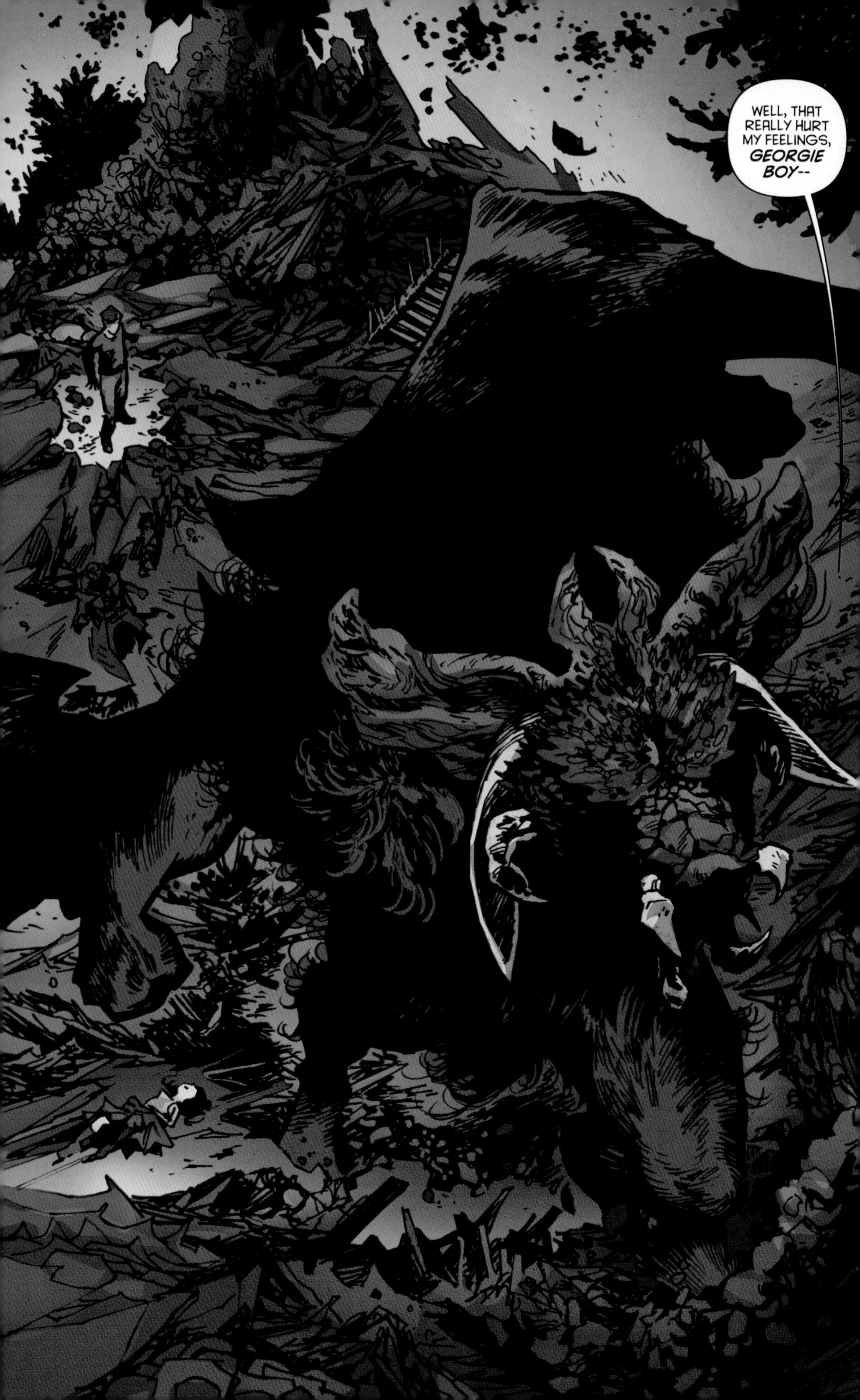
WELL, THAT REALLY HURT MY FEELINGS, *GEORGIE BOY*--

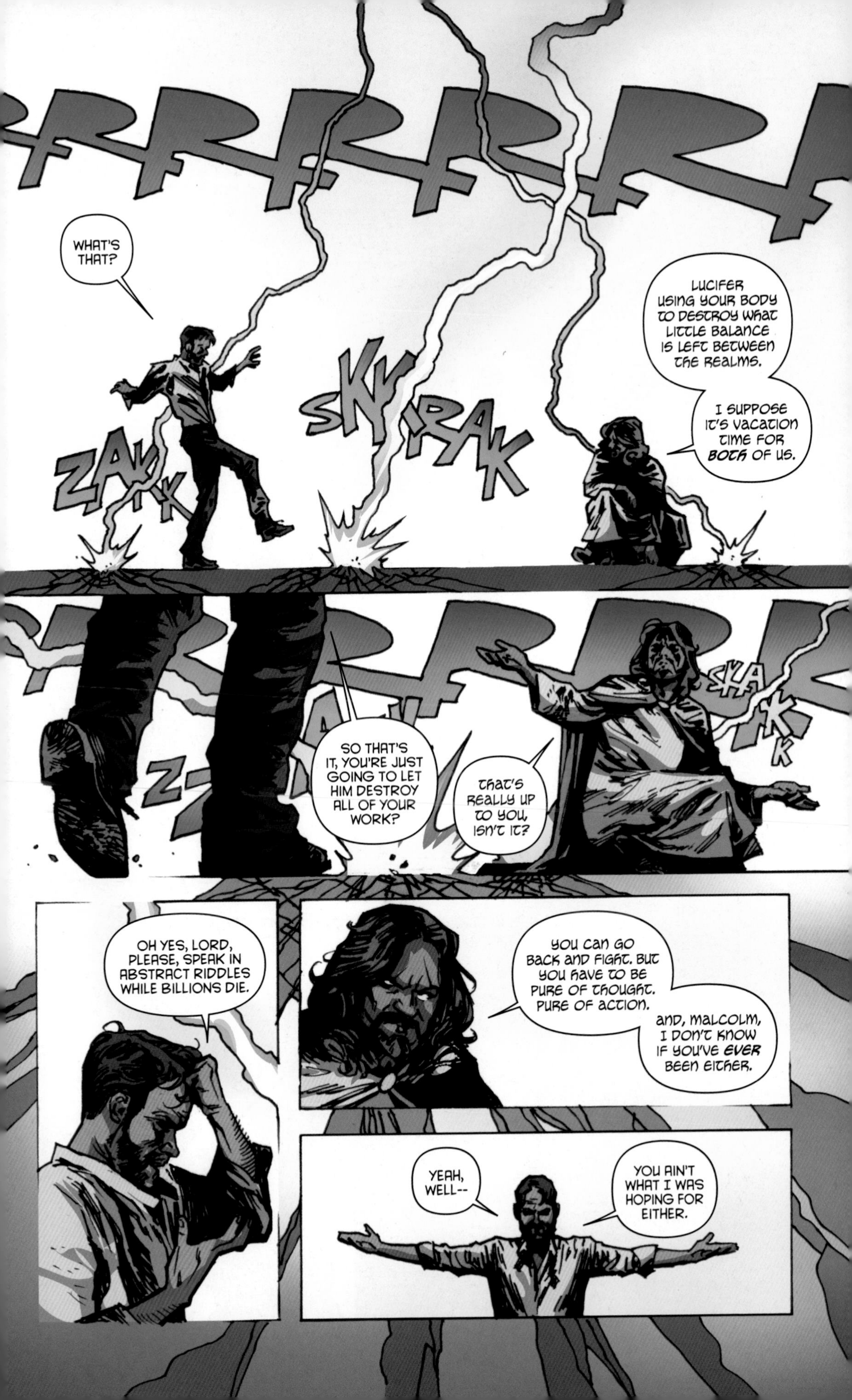
RRRRRRRR
WHAT'S THAT?
LUCIFER USING YOUR BODY TO DESTROY WHAT LITTLE BALANCE IS LEFT BETWEEN THE REALMS.
I SUPPOSE IT'S VACATION TIME FOR BOTH OF US.
ZAKKK
SKVRAK
SO THAT'S IT, YOU'RE JUST GOING TO LET HIM DESTROY ALL OF YOUR WORK?
THAT'S REALLY UP TO YOU, ISN'T IT?
SKAKK
OH YES, LORD, PLEASE, SPEAK IN ABSTRACT RIDDLES WHILE BILLIONS DIE.
YOU CAN GO BACK AND FIGHT. BUT YOU HAVE TO BE PURE OF THOUGHT. PURE OF ACTION.
AND, MALCOLM, I DON'T KNOW IF YOU'VE EVER BEEN EITHER.
YEAH, WELL--
YOU AIN'T WHAT I WAS HOPING FOR EITHER.

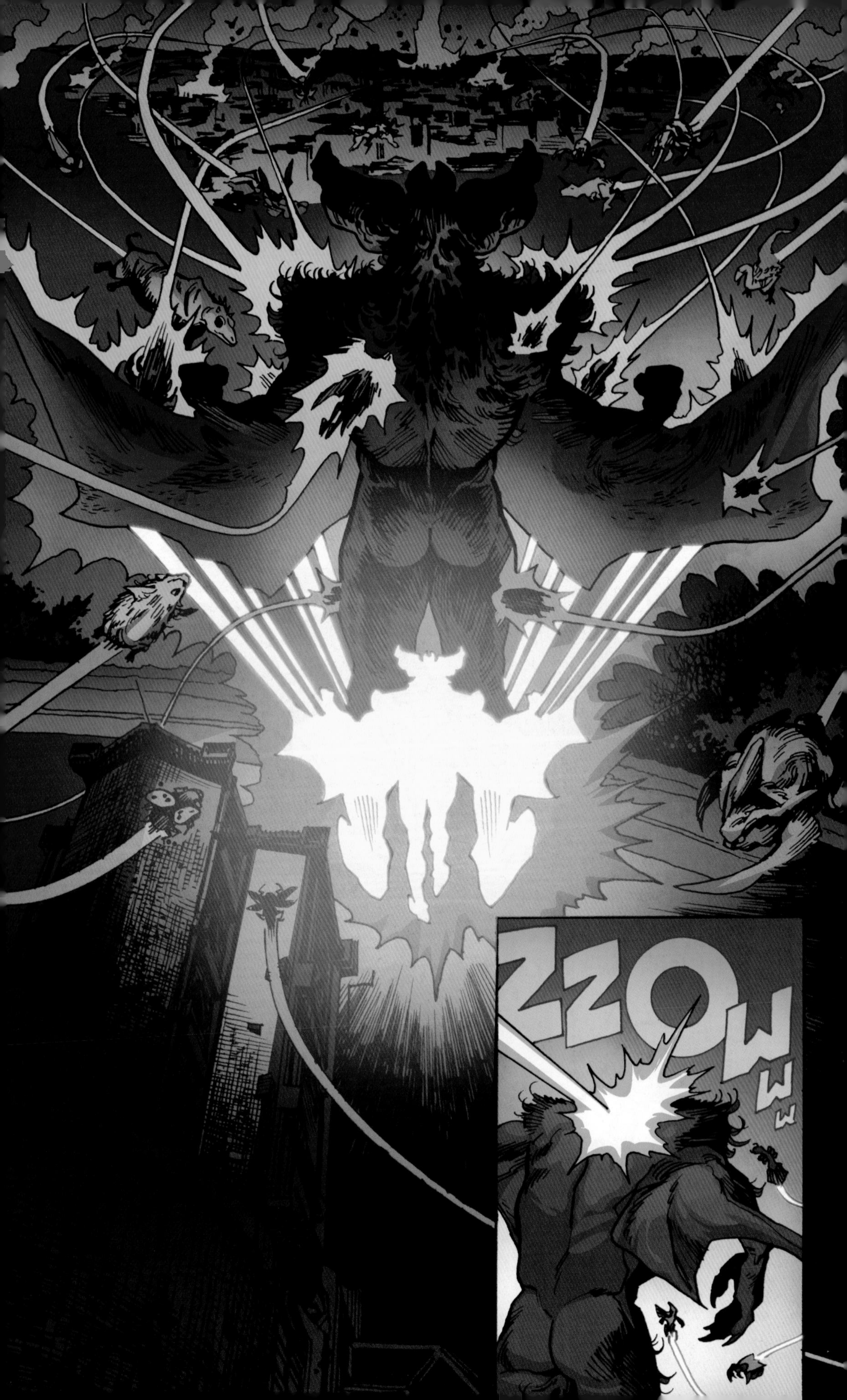
ZZOW
WW

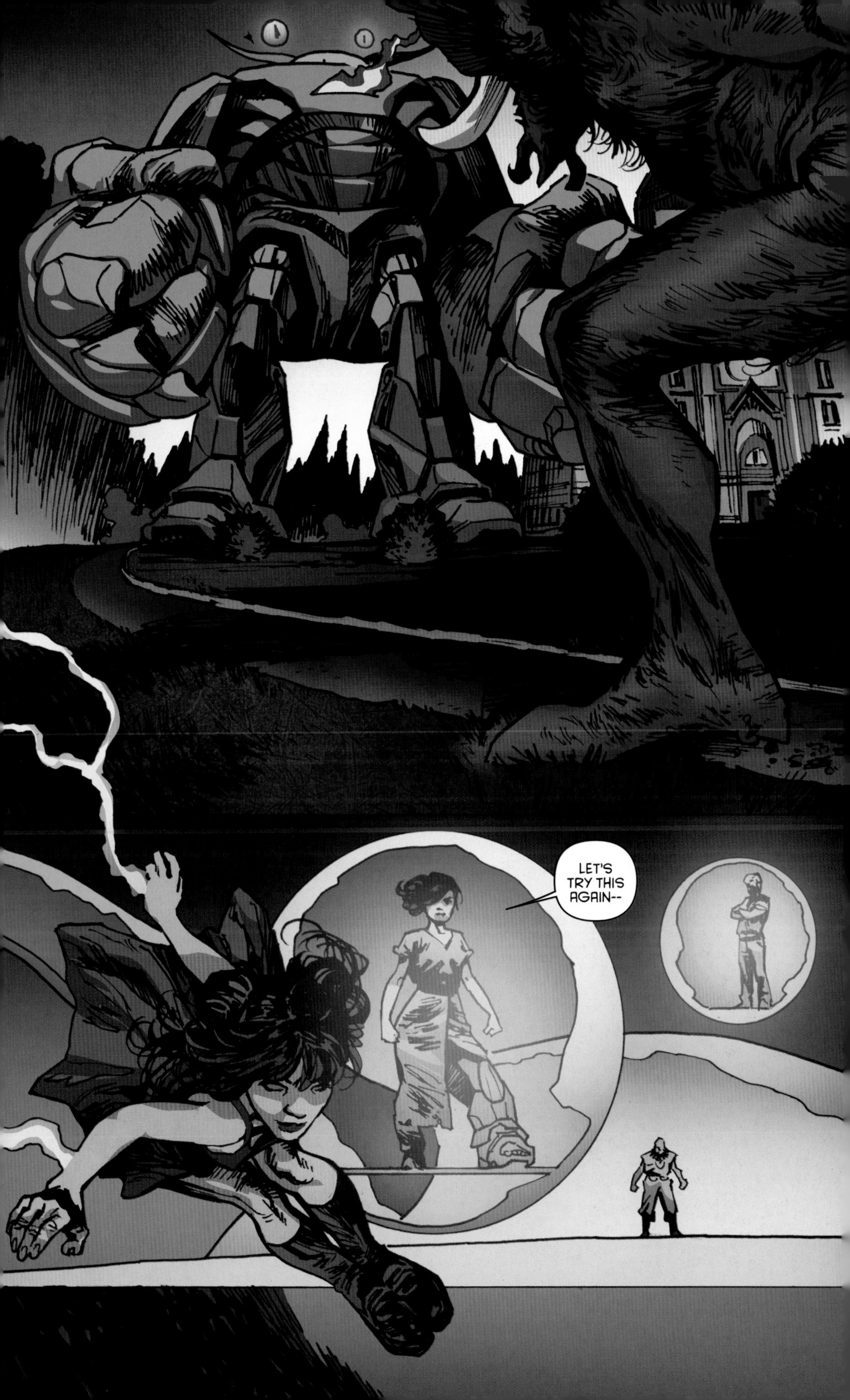
LET'S TRY THIS AGAIN--

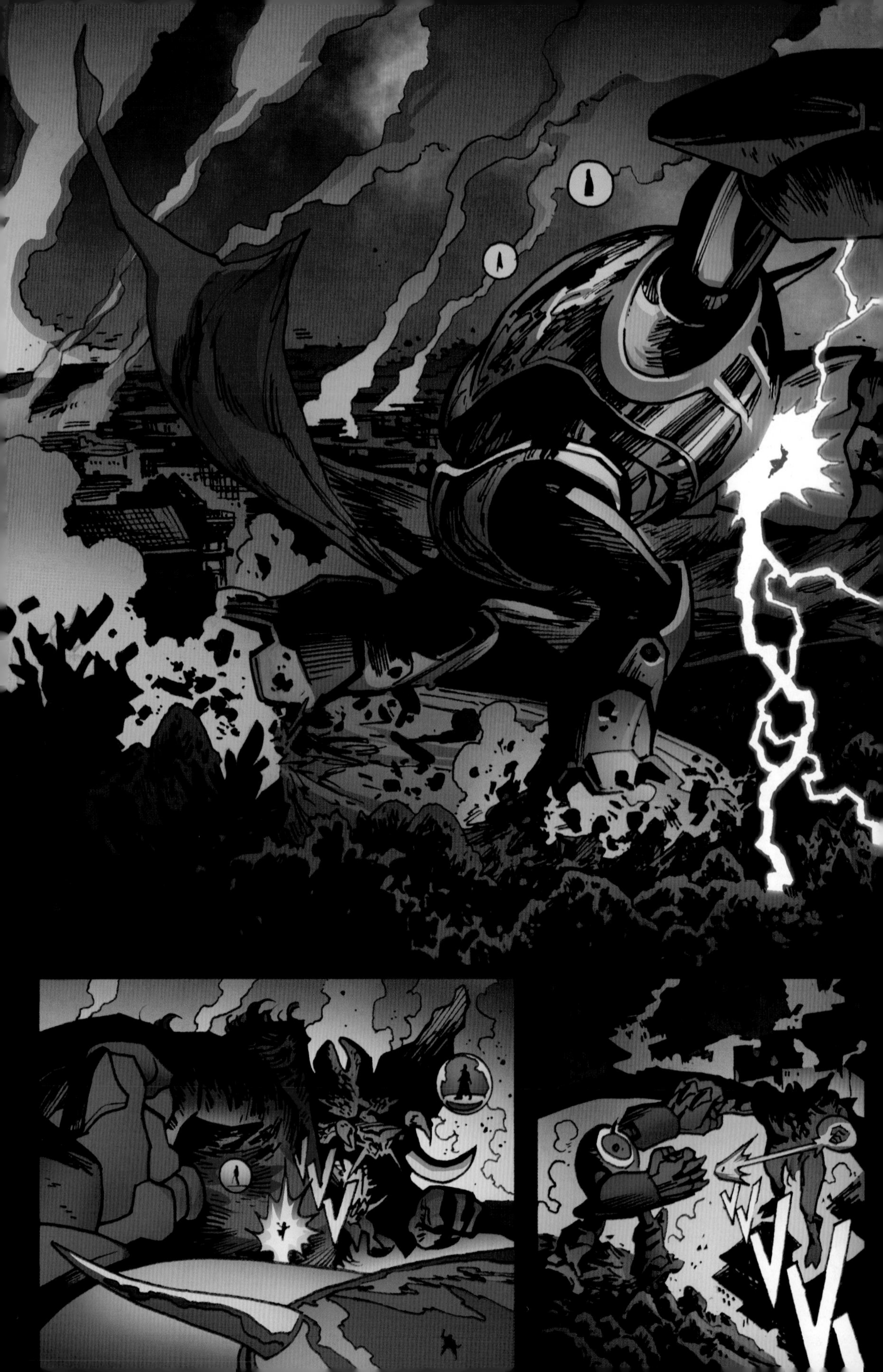

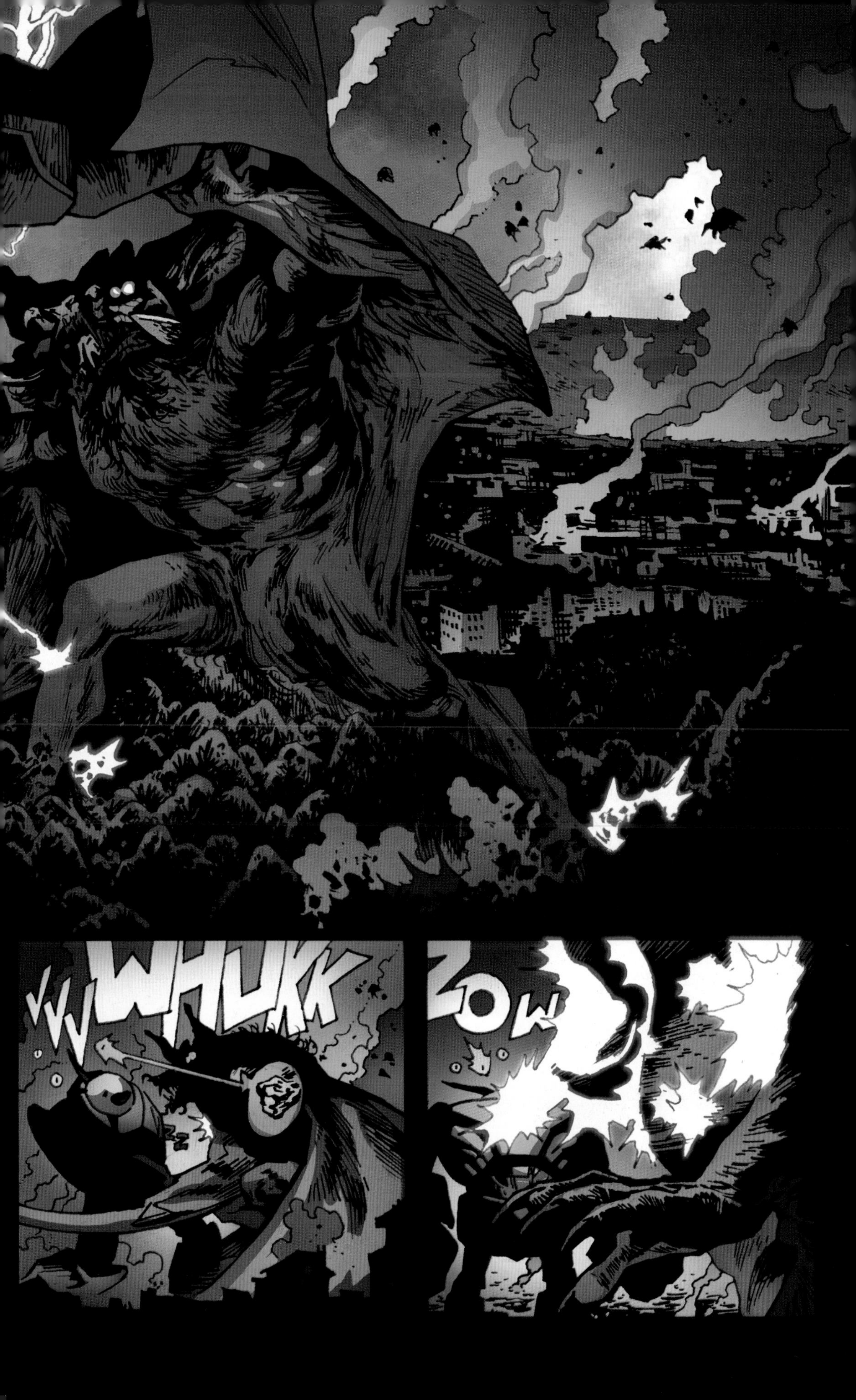
VVWHUKK
ZOW

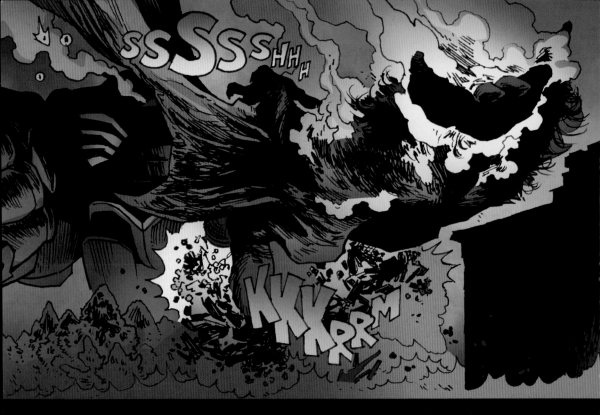

BURN YOU BASTARDS BURN!

NO...IT CAN'T...

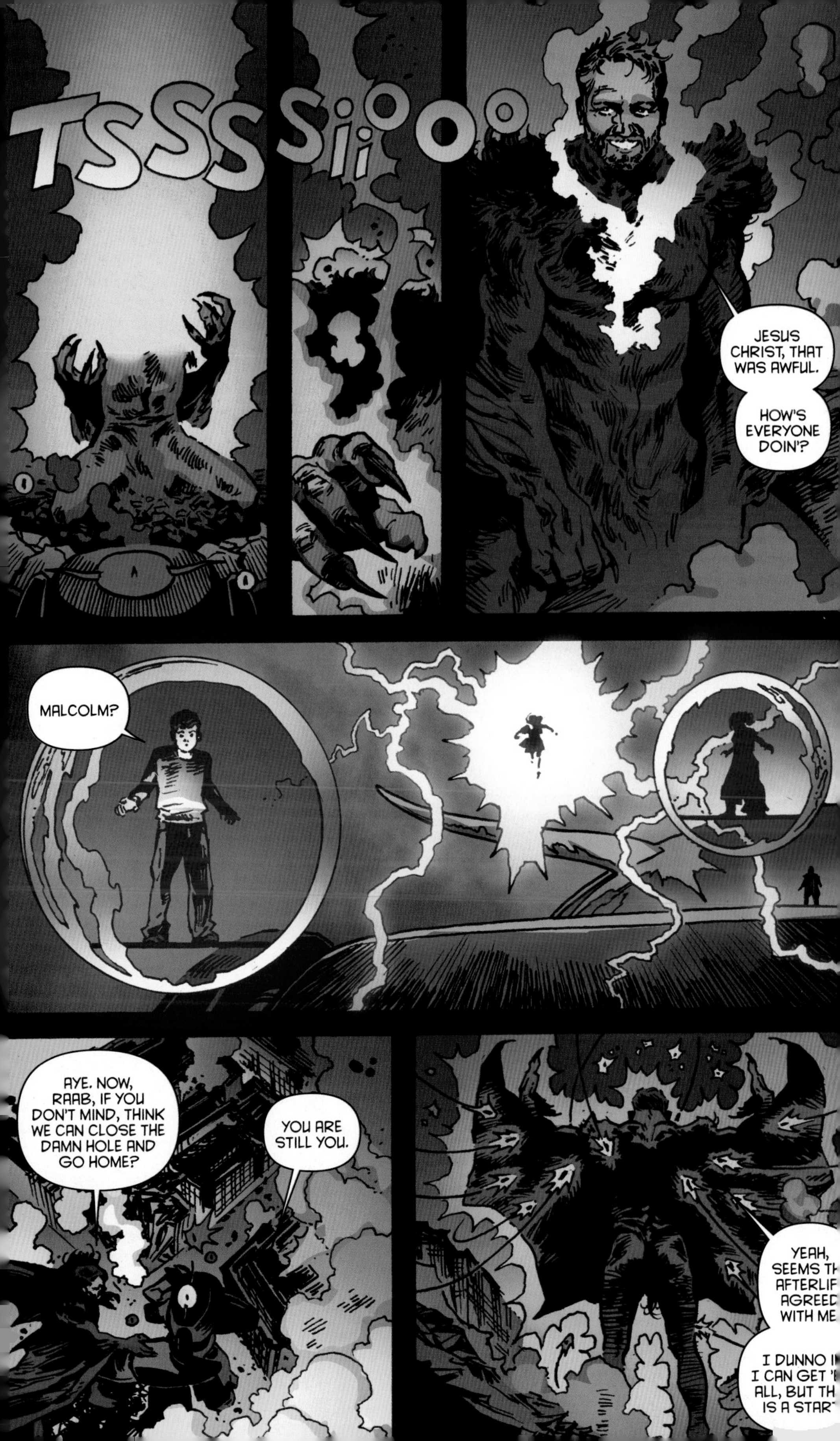
TSSSSiiOOOO
JESUS CHRIST, THAT WAS AWFUL.
HOW'S EVERYONE DOIN'?
MALCOLM?
AYE. NOW, RAAB, IF YOU DON'T MIND, THINK WE CAN CLOSE THE DAMN HOLE AND GO HOME?
YOU ARE STILL YOU.
YEAH, SEEMS TH AFTERLIF AGREED WITH ME
I DUNNO I I CAN GET ' ALL, BUT TH IS A START

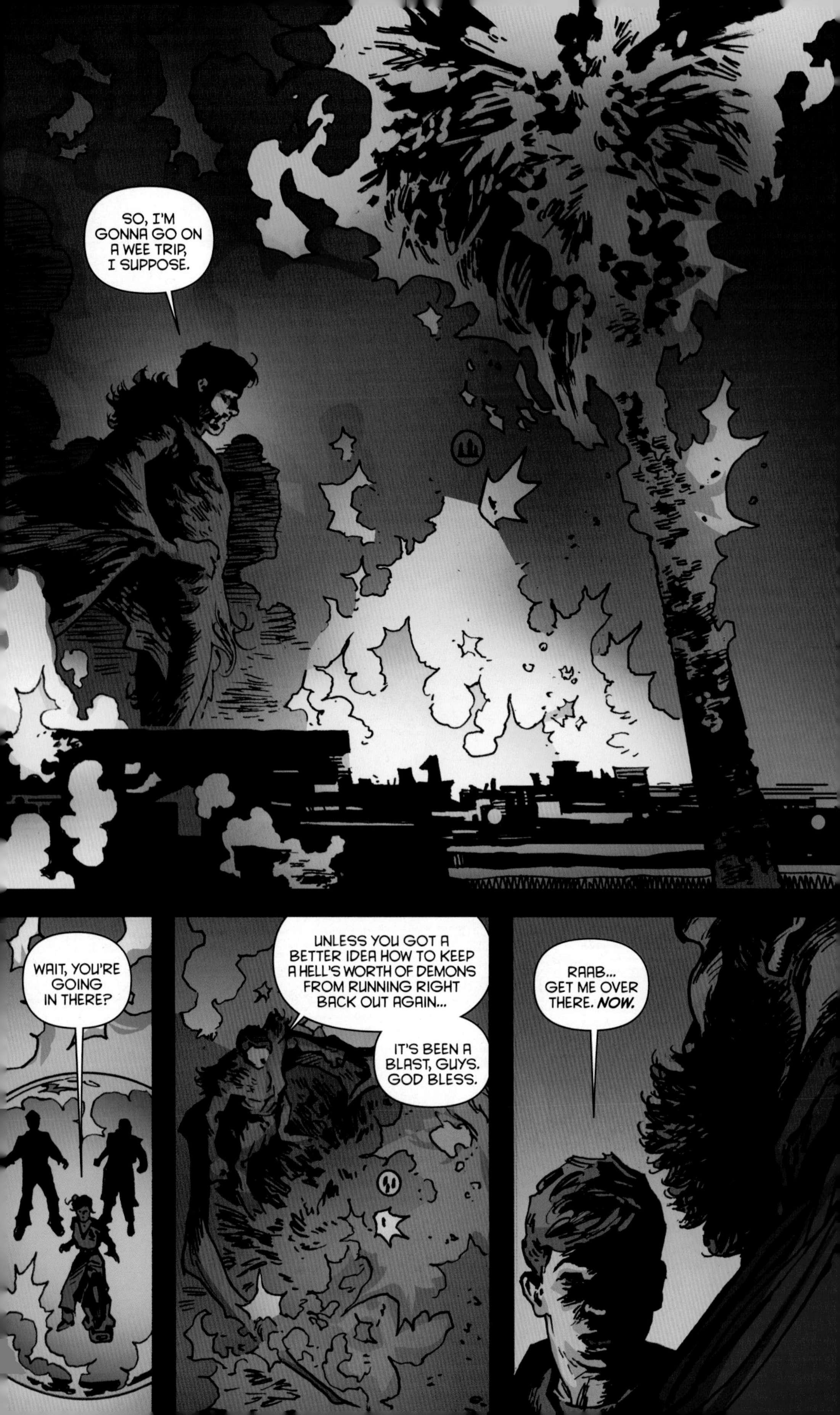
SO, I'M GONNA GO ON A WEE TRIP, I SUPPOSE.
WAIT, YOU'RE GOING IN THERE?
UNLESS YOU GOT A BETTER IDEA HOW TO KEEP A HELL'S WORTH OF DEMONS FROM RUNNING RIGHT BACK OUT AGAIN...
IT'S BEEN A BLAST, GUYS. GOD BLESS.
RAAB... GET ME OVER THERE. *NOW.*

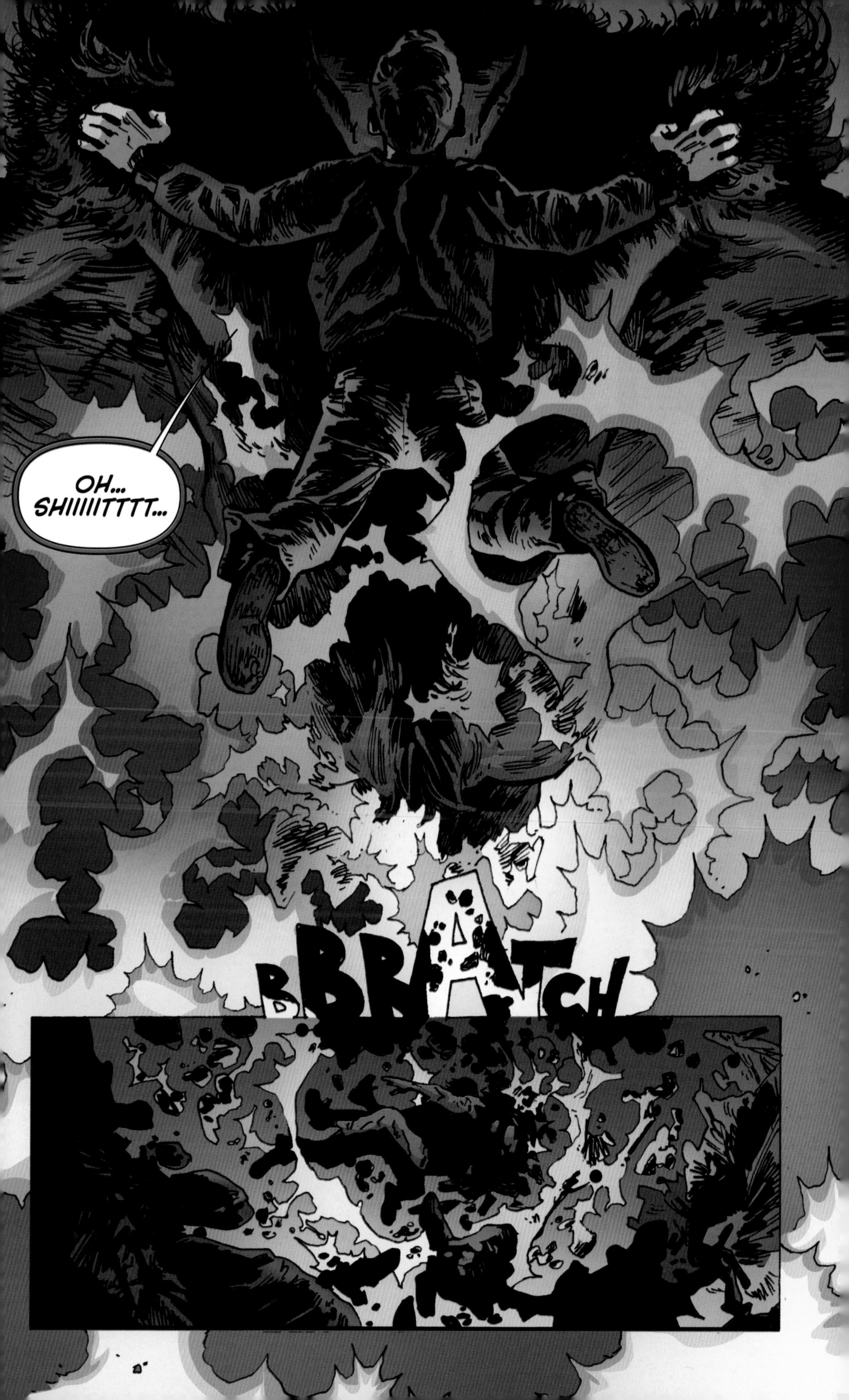
OH... SHIIIIITTTT...
BBRATCH

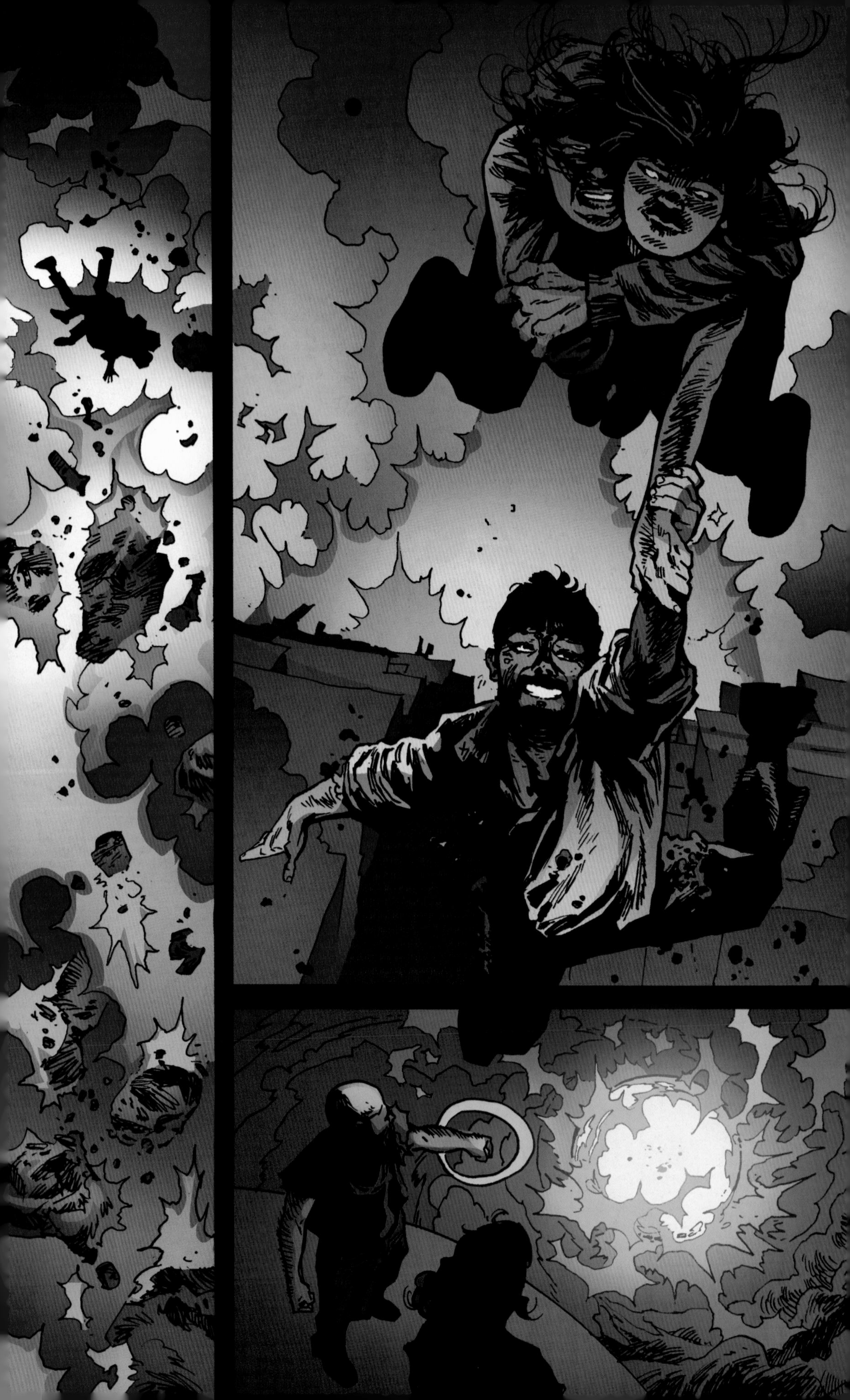

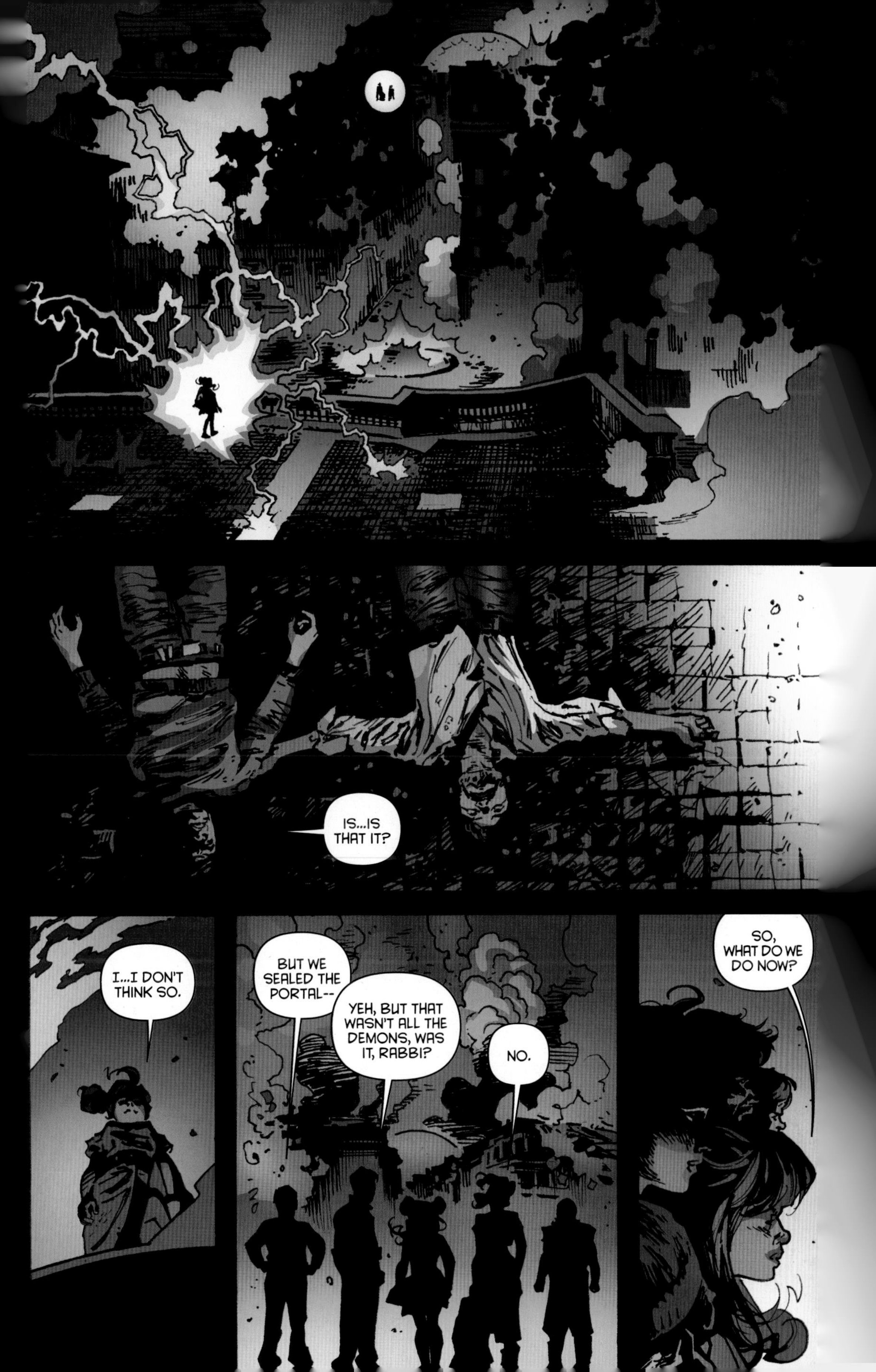
IS...IS THAT IT?
I...I DON'T THINK SO.
BUT WE SEALED THE PORTAL--
YEH, BUT THAT WASN'T ALL THE DEMONS, WAS IT, RABBI?
NO.
SO, WHAT DO WE DO NOW?

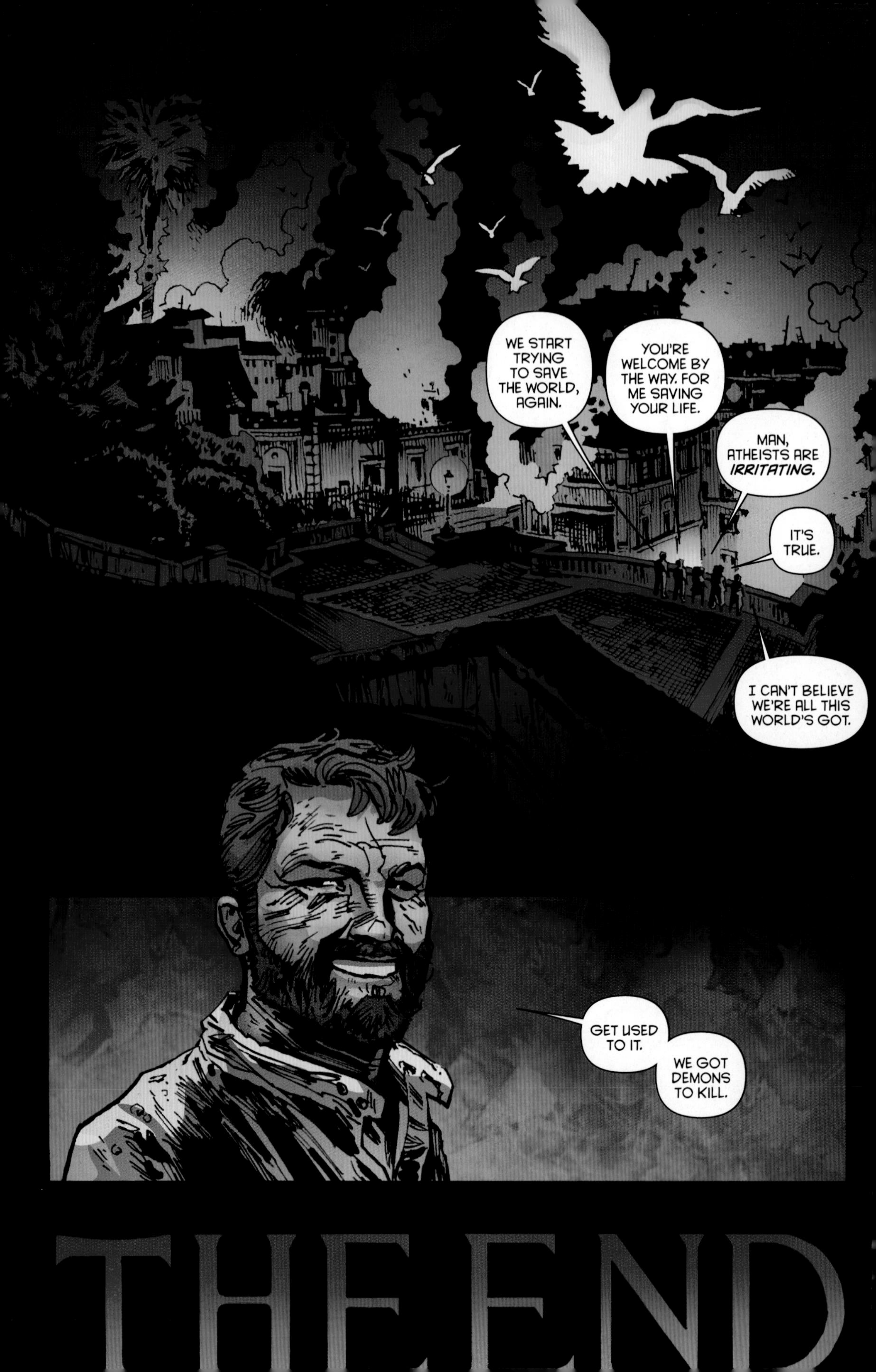
WE START TRYING TO SAVE THE WORLD, AGAIN.
YOU'RE WELCOME BY THE WAY. FOR ME SAVING YOUR LIFE.
MAN, ATHEISTS ARE *IRRITATING.*
IT'S TRUE.
I CAN'T BELIEVE WE'RE ALL THIS WORLD'S GOT.
GET USED TO IT.
WE GOT DEMONS TO KILL.
THE END

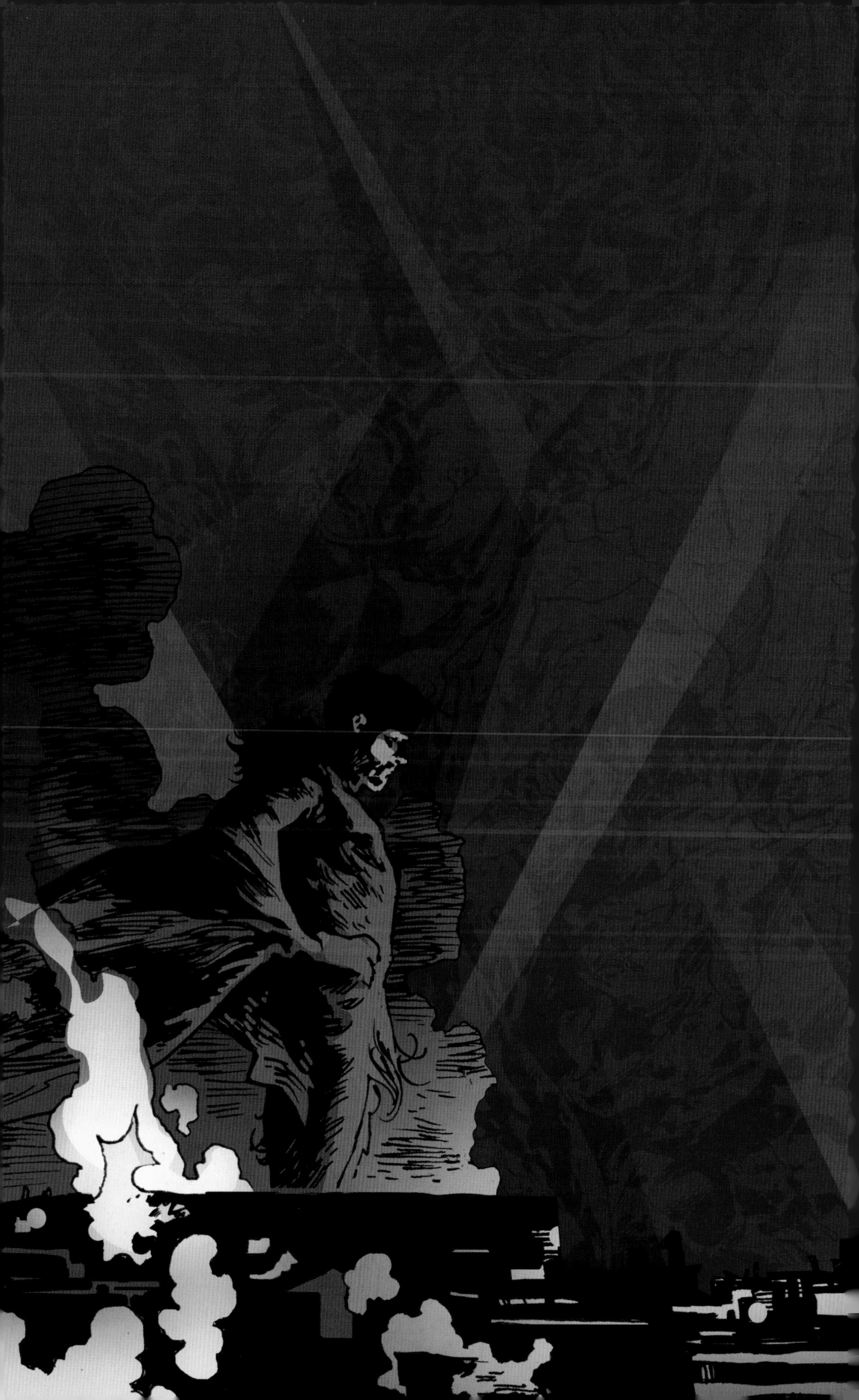

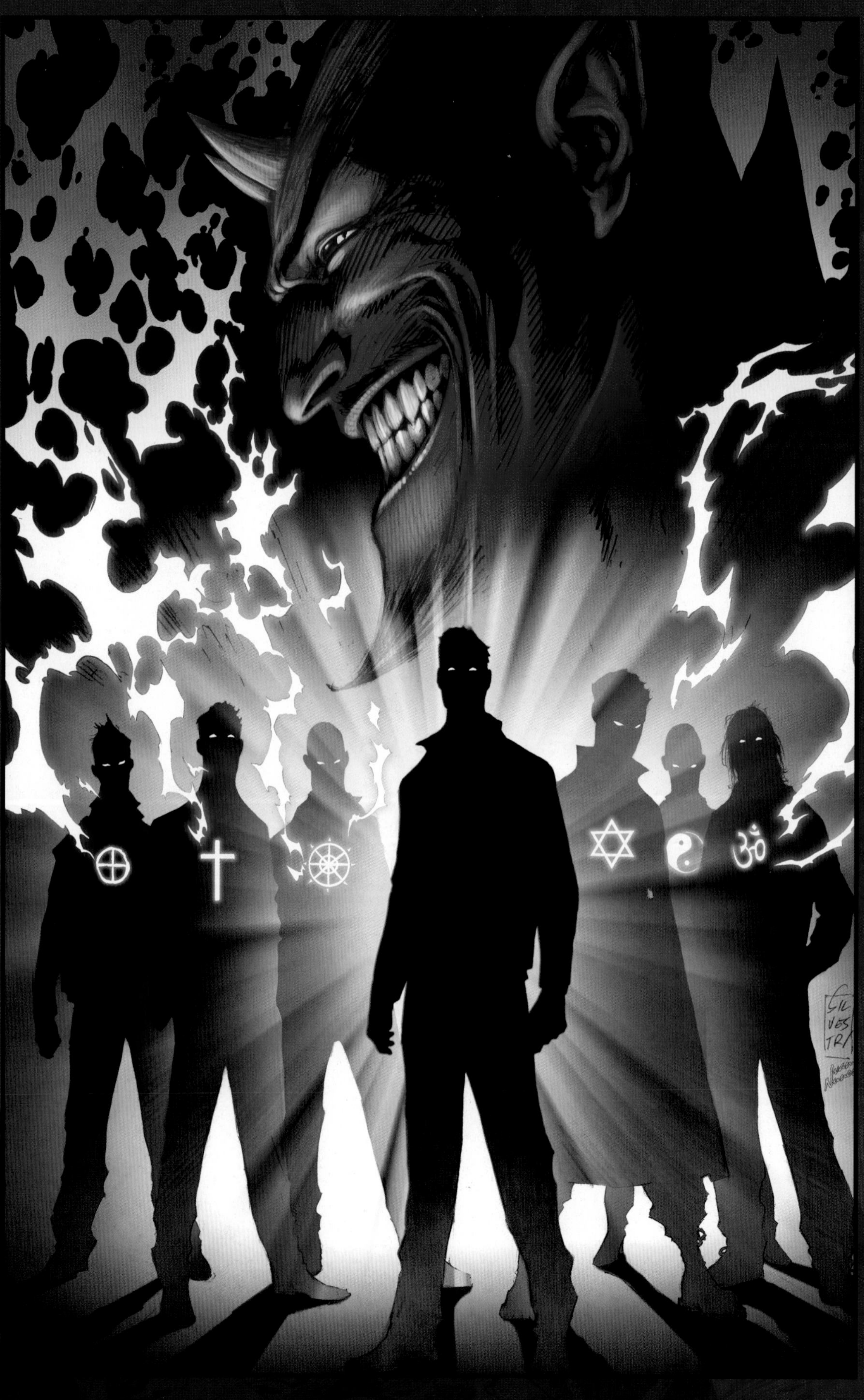

ISSUE #1 cover art by **MARC SILVESTRI** colors by IVAN NUNES

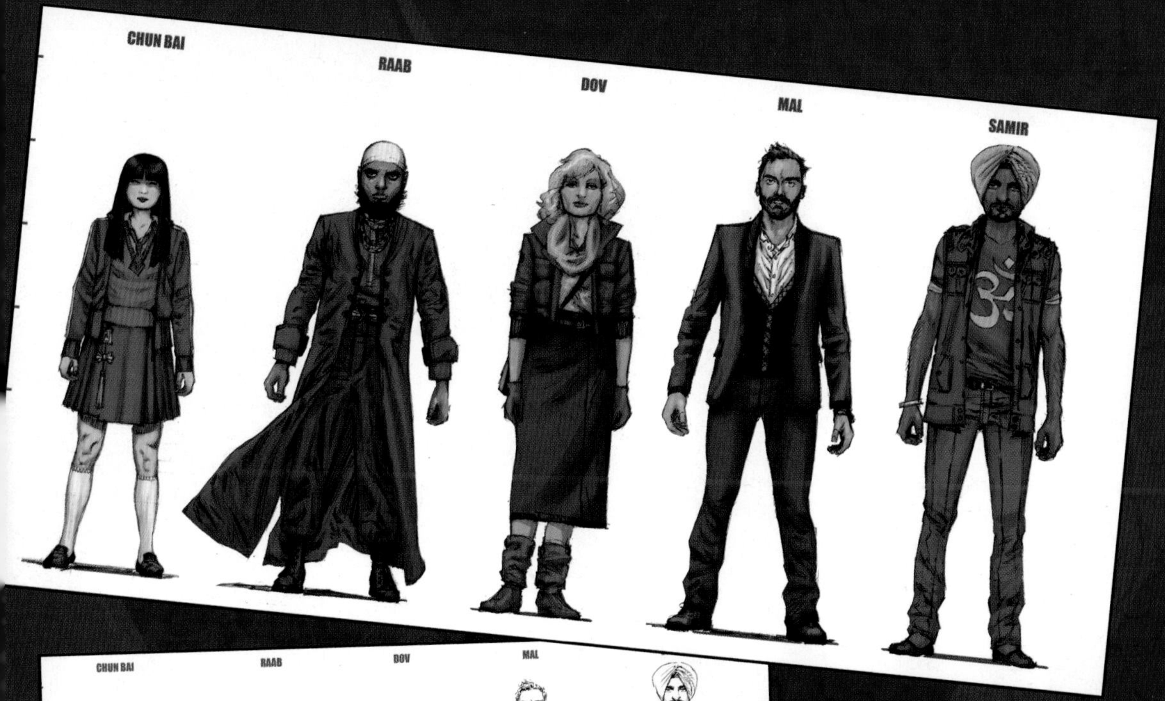
CHUN BAI
RAAB
DOV
MAL
SAMIR

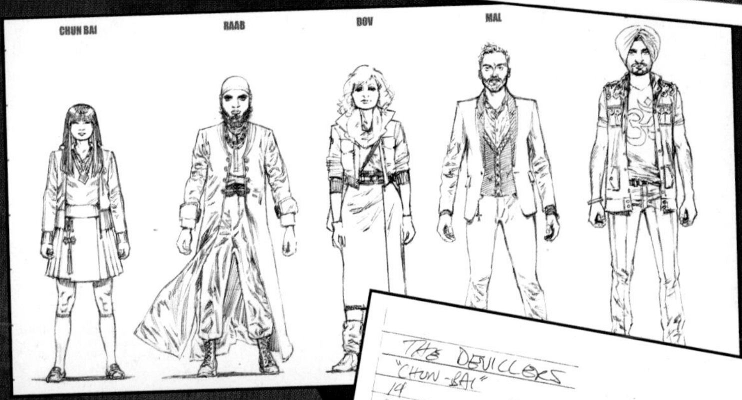
CHUN BAI
RAAB
DOV
MAL

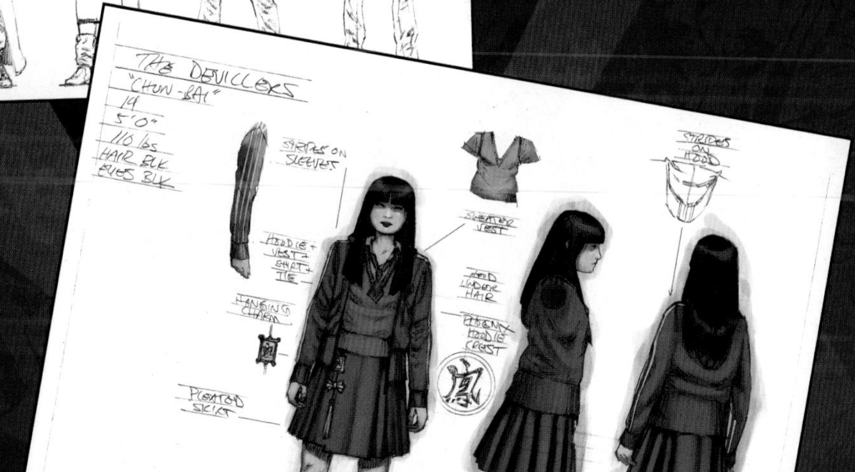
THE DEVICLEKS
"CHUN-BAI"
14
5'0"
110 lbs
HAIR BLK
EYES BLK
STRIPES ON SLEEVES
HOODIE + VEST + SHIRT + TIE
HANGING CHARM
PLEATED SKIRT
HIGH SOCKS
SWEATER VEST
HOOD UNDER HAIR
PHOENIX HOODIE CREST
STRIPES ON HOOD

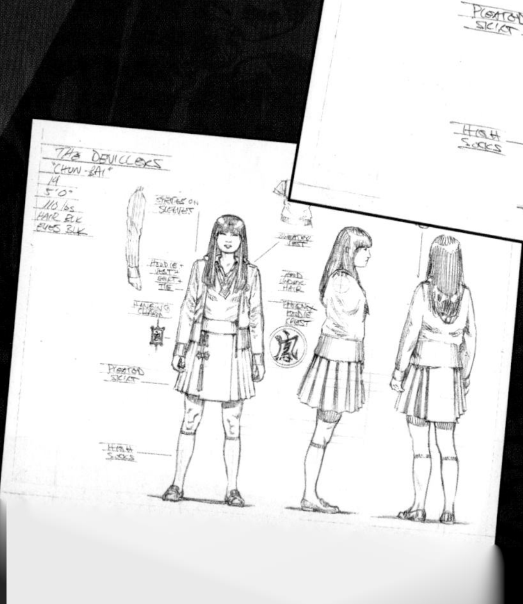
THE DEVICLEKS
"CHUN-BAI"
14
5'0"
110 lbs
HAIR BLK
EYES BLK
STRIPES ON SLEEVES
HOODIE + VEST + SHIRT + TIE
HANGING CHARM
PLEATED SKIRT
HIGH SOCKS
HOOD UNDER HAIR
PHOENIX HOODIE CREST

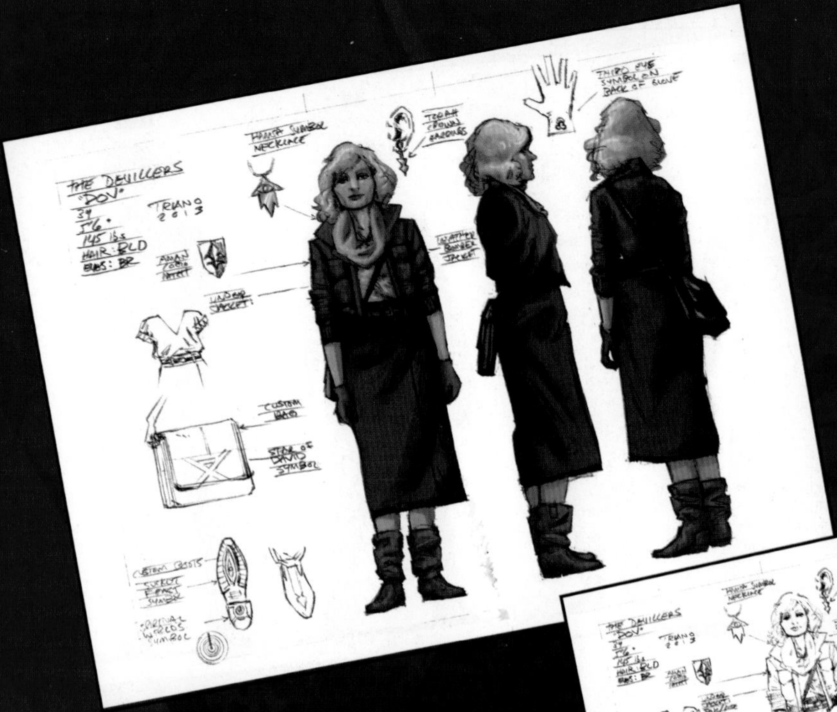
THE DEVILLERS
"DOV"
39
5'6"
145 lbs
HAIR: BLD
TRIANO 2013
HAMSA SYMBOL NECKLACE
TORAH CROWN EARRINGS
THIRD EYE SYMBOL ON BACK OF GLOVE
CUSTOM BAG
STAR OF DAVID SYMBOL
CUSTOM BOOTS

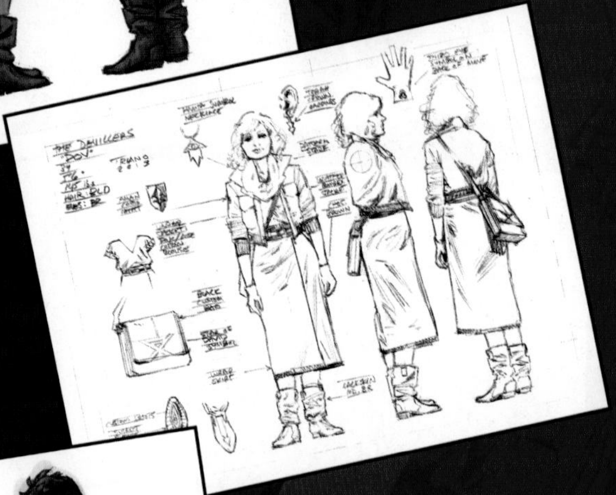
THE DEVILLERS
TRIANO 2013

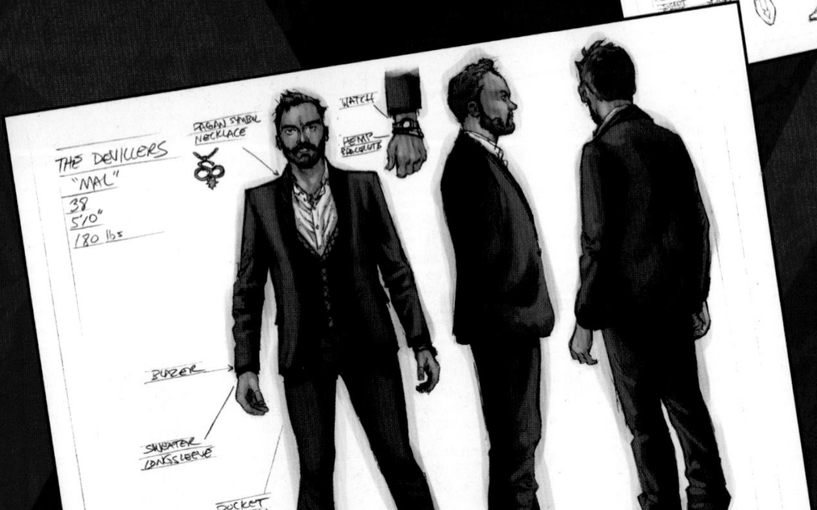
THE DEVILLERS
"MAL"
38
5'10"
180 lbs
PAGAN SYMBOL NECKLACE
WATCH
HEMP BRACELETS
BLAZER
SWEATER LONGSLEEVE
POCKET ROSARY

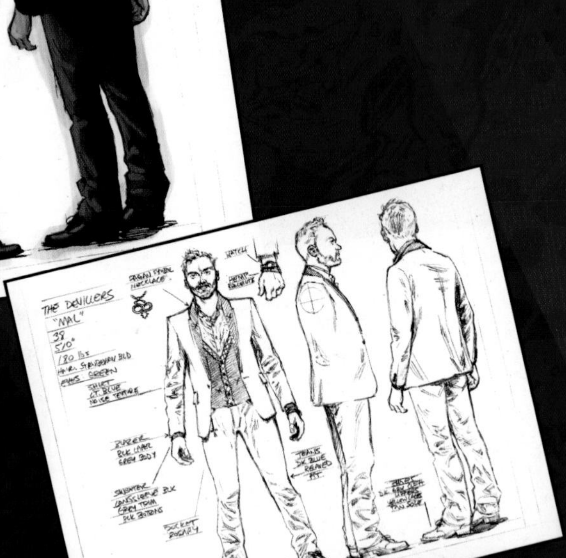
THE DEVILLERS
"MAL"
38
5'10"
180 lbs
PAGAN SYMBOL NECKLACE
WATCH
BLAZER
POCKET ROSARY

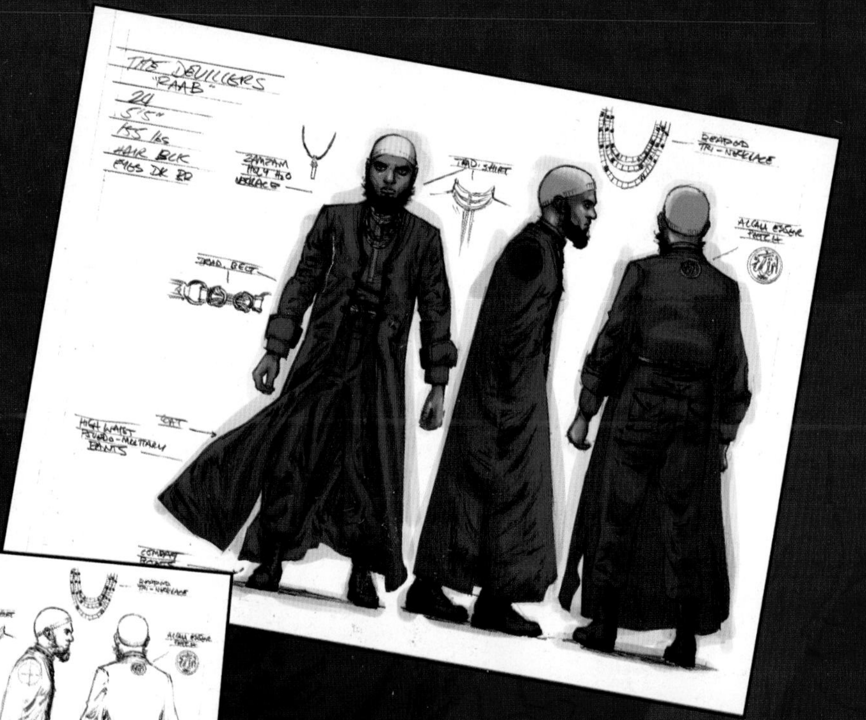
THE DEVILLERS
"RAAB"
24
5'5"
155 lbs
HAIR BLK
EYES DK BR
TRAD. SHIRT
BEADED TRI-NECKLACE
TRAD. BELT
COAT
HIGH WAIST PSEUDO-MILITARY PANTS

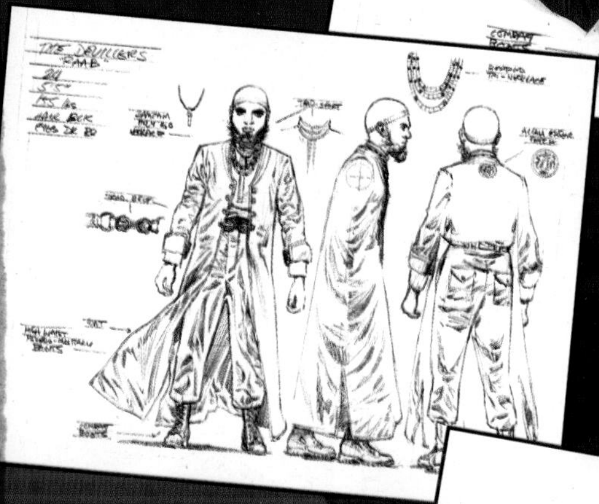

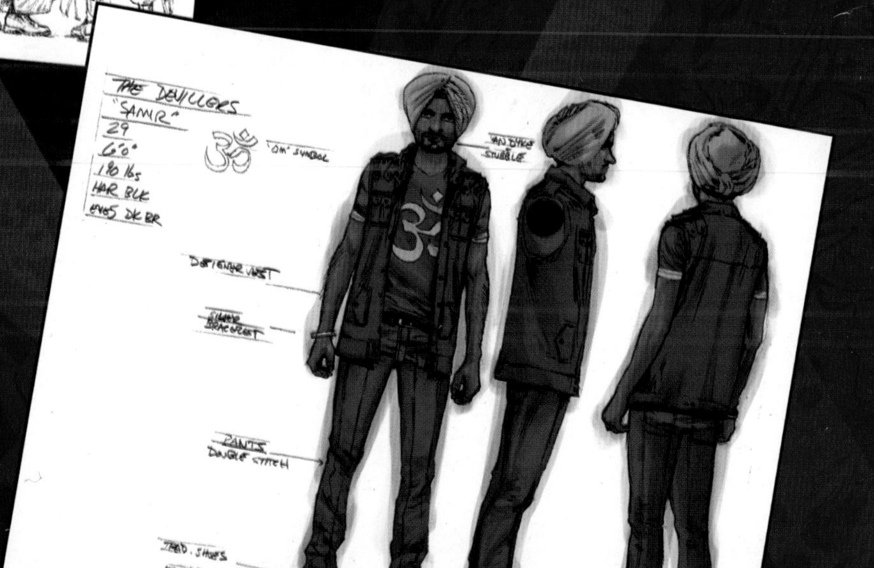
THE DEVILLERS
"SAMIR"
29
6'0"
180 lbs
HAR BLK
EYES DK BR
'OM' SYMBOL
STUBBLE
PANTS
DOUBLE STITCH
TRAD. SHOES
NO SOCKS

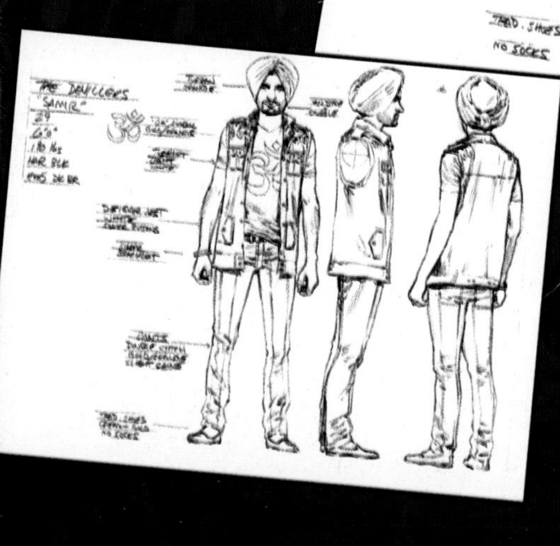

JOSHUA HALE FIALKOV • MATT TRIANO

THE DEVILERS ™